Watercolour Artist's Colour Mixing Bible

Watercolour Artist's Colour Mixing Bible

A Visual Guide to More Than 2500 Mixes and Glaze Effects

Moira Clinch

David Webb

SEARCH PRESS

A QUARTO BOOK

Published in 2006 by Search Press Ltd.
Wellwood
North Farm Road
Tunbridge Wells
Kent TN2 3DR
United Kingdom

ISBN 1-84448-139-5

QUAR.WCM

Conceived, designed and produced by
Quarto Publishing plc
The Old Brewery
6 Blundell Street
London N7 9BH

Senior editor Jo Fisher
Designer Karen Skånberg
Picture researcher Claudia Tate
Photographers Paul Forrester and Phil Wilkins
Copy editor Fiona Corbridge
Proofreader Carol Baker
Indexer Pamela Ellis

Art director Moira Clinch
Publisher Paul Carslake

Manufactured by Modern Age Repro House Ltd, Hong Kong

Printed by Midas Printing International Ltd, China

9 8 7 6 5 4 3 2 1

ACKNOWLEDGEMENTS

Key: t top, b bottom
17 Robert Tilling; 20 Diane Maxey; 21 Ruth Baderian; 23 Julian Bray; 24 Julian Bray; 25 t Alan Oliver; 25 b Jeanne Dobie; 27 Claire Schroeven Verbiest; 29 Catherine Headley; 32 Peter Kelly; 33 t Moira Clinch; 33 b Dana Brown; 34 Nick Hebditch; 35 Bryn Craig; 36 Ann Smith; 37 Roberta Carter Clark; 38 t Moira Clinch; 38 b Diane Maxey; 39 Jane Leycester Paige.

All other photographs and illustrations are the copyright of Quarto Publishing plc. While every effort has been made to credit contributors, we apologize should there have been any omissions or errors.

While every care has been taken with the printing of the colour charts, the four-colour printing process means that the publishers cannot guarantee total accuracy in every case.

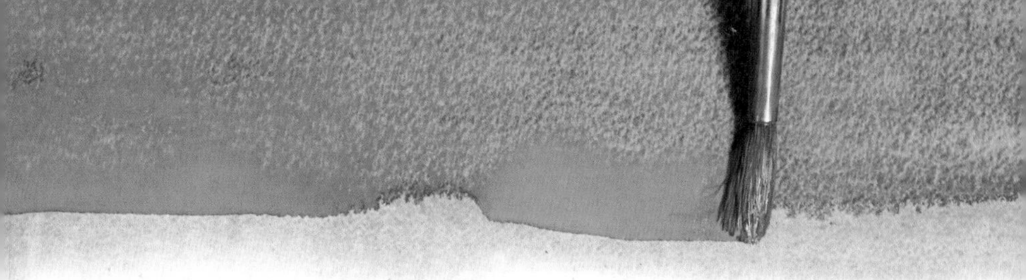

Contents

This book takes the guesswork out of choosing watercolour pigments. See at a glance how the colours perform – both alone and in hundreds of specially mixed samples.

Foreword

The modern watercolour artist has a veritable Pandora's paintbox of pigments to choose from. The amount of choice can be daunting when faced in an art supply shop with hundreds of colours from a variety of manufacturers. Should you buy cobalt turquoise or cobalt turquoise light? What would be a good alternative for aureolin yellow? Which mixes will give new depth and interest to your landscape shadow colours?

While painting the colour swatches for this book, I felt as though I was conducting several illicit love affairs. Colours I had not used for some time I rediscovered with a new passion – how could I have allowed terre verte to disappear from my paintbox? I was tempted by newly created colours with characteristics including improved brightness, greater transparency or an inclination to granulate. And of course, all the old faithfuls still deserve their place on my palette – I decided that ultramarine blue is still the best warm, rich blue, with its delightful, unpredictable granulation.

This book is here to help you select your colours. It aims not to be prescriptive, but to give the beginner both a starting point and some inspiration. Check out the mixes before you buy the (sometimes expensive) paints and decide which colours will work best for you. I hope that more experienced artists will be inspired to experiment with some of the different colours featured here; I know how easy it is to fall back on those tried-and-trusted favourites that have characteristics with which you are familiar. You might also like to discover some of the exciting new colours recently developed by manufacturers.

Think about producing your own mixing samples. They don't have to be works of art, it is fun to do, and you will learn a lot about the handling of the different pigments. Colour, texture, workability and permanence can vary between manufacturers, so it makes sense to paint some samples of a new colour before you launch into making pictures. Aside from this, the samples look great pinned to your studio wall!

When preparing the swatches, I was surprised at the beauty of some of the results. Sometimes I wanted to stop painting samples and incorporate the mix into a painting straight away. I hope you will find mixes in the directory that have the same effect on you.

My thanks are due to David Webb, who provided the core of the articles for the introduction; to the artists who provided their paintings; and to the several manufacturers who generously supplied paints and papers.

How the swatches were painted

The swatches were painted on Bockingford 300gsm NOT watercolour paper, which was chosen for its whiteness and texture.

To achieve accurate ratios of paint in the mixes, each colour was mixed from a 5ml tube of paint and 20ml (0.7 oz) of water. Using a dropper, the mixes could then be "dropped" accurately to the required 60:40 ratio. (NB For your own mixes, see page 14 for advice on paint consistency.)

The palette mixes were a straight 60:40 mix of the two colours.

For the mixes on paper, more water was added to produce the correct 60:40 ratio.

The paper, or the initial colourwash, was generally primed first (see page 15). Clean water was used for every mix.

I hope that the new possibilities explored in the directory will inspire you to try some different colours and experiment with exciting new mixes.

Materials and Equipment

Paper

There is a wide range of papers for watercolour painting. Each paper has its own individual characteristics and plays an important role in the way a finished painting will look. When choosing paper, the two main factors to consider are the surface and weight.

Surfaces

There are three main paper surfaces: smooth or hot-pressed (HP), medium or cold-pressed (NOT) and rough.

Hot-pressed paper is the smoothest of the three surfaces and is so called because it is pressed between sheets of hot metal during the manufacturing process. Of the three, it is the most suitable for pen and wash and highly detailed illustration techniques. However, for the artist who paints pure watercolour washes with a large brush, it can be a difficult surface to master.

Medium-surface paper (or cold-pressed paper) is often referred to as NOT, simply because it is not hot-pressed. It has a more textured appearance and will readily take a wash. It is probably the most popular of the three and the one most commonly available in sketch pad form.

Rough paper obviously has the most textured surface. It is ideal for techniques such as drybrushing, and its coarse surface gives a more broken edge to brushstrokes.

Weight and thickness

Watercolour paper is available in a variety of thicknesses. Its weight is measured in grammes per square metre (gsm) or pounds (lb). The thinnest papers are around 185gsm (90 lb). The heaviest and thickest are around 640gsm (300 lb). The thinnest papers are really only suitable when working on a small scale, as they are unable to take a great amount of water without cockling – a loose wash will cause the surface to ripple and buckle. Cartridge, or sketching, paper should therefore never be used with watercolour paints. Thicker papers are much more suitable for the application of washes.

WATERCOLOUR PAPERS

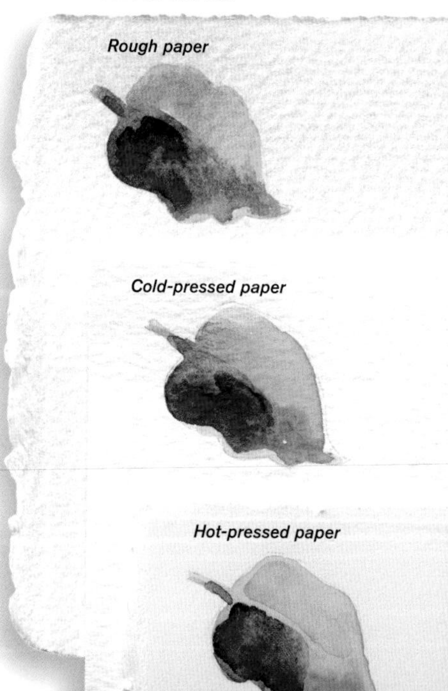

Buying paper

Paper can be bought in sheets, sketch pads or blocks. Individual sheets are usually sold in three sizes: full imperial, half imperial or quarter imperial.

Sketch pads are available in a variety of sizes, with the paper gummed down one side or spiral-bound. Blocks are like sketch pads, but are glued around all four edges. They are useful for painting outdoors, as they don't flap about in a breeze and the pages remain flat. When you've finished your painting, split the page from the rest of the block by inserting a blunt knife into the small opening on one side.

Paper colour

Some papers are whiter than others; a whiter paper will give brighter highlights and slightly brighter colours. For a more subtle effect, choose paper that is less white. Toned or coloured watercolour papers are also available, for use with body colour (see page 22).

TIP: Paper sizes

Full imperial
560mm x 760mm
22" x 30"

Half imperial
560mm x 380mm
22" x 15"

Quarter imperial
280mm x 380mm
11" x 15"

TIP: How to stretch paper

Thin paper can be stretched so that it will take a wash without cockling. You will need a board that is bigger than the paper.

- **First, soak the paper in cold water for a few minutes.**
- **Lay the paper on the board and soak off the excess water with a sponge, taking care not to damage the surface. Dab with the sponge; don't wipe.**
- **Attach the paper to the board with gummed paper tape. Stick the tape along the entire length of all four edges, with half of its width on the paper and the other half on the board. (The tape holds the paper firmly in place as it dries out and becomes taut and flat. The paper will then readily accept a wash. When the painting is finished, simply cut it from the board with a craft knife.)**

Ivory white watercolour paper

White watercolour paper

Toned watercolour paper

Paints

Watercolour paints are available in two different forms: tubes and pans. Tube paint is the consistency of toothpaste. Pans are solid cakes of colour and are usually contained in plastic shells.

The quality of both types of paint is the same. However, each has advantages and disadvantages. Tube colour can be more convenient, as it is softer and quicker to use. This can be desirable if you are painting a sunset from life and the sun is quickly dipping over the horizon. On the downside, tubes can be messy if you haven't used them before and, on occasion, the screw-top lids can roll away out of sight. Pans are more portable, but as the paint is solid, more work is required to obtain sufficient colour.

Both tubes and pans are available in two different standards: students' colour and artists' colour. The established manufacturers produce both. Students' colours, as you may have guessed, are cheaper. They are produced in a wide range and, usually, there is a single price for all colours. They are not as bright or intense as artists' colours.

Artists' colours are used by most professionals. These pigments are much more concentrated and, if you've only ever used the student variety, their intensity may take you by surprise. The difference in price may also take you by surprise! Artists' colours vary in price. They are usually produced in price-banded series: Prussian blue might be in series 1 (the cheapest series), whereas cobalt blue might be in series 4 (the most expensive series). A series 1 colour may cost around twice as much as a similar colour in the students' range, and a colour from series 4 may be up to four times the price.

So what do you choose – students' or artists' watercolours? For the beginner who may be on a tight budget, students' colours are a reliable option, provided they are produced by a well-known company. There

PAINTS *Watercolour paints are available in:*
1 *5ml tubes*
2 *10ml tubes*
3 *15ml tubes*
4 *Full pans*
5 *Half pans*
6 *Boxed sets with a good range of colours for beginners*

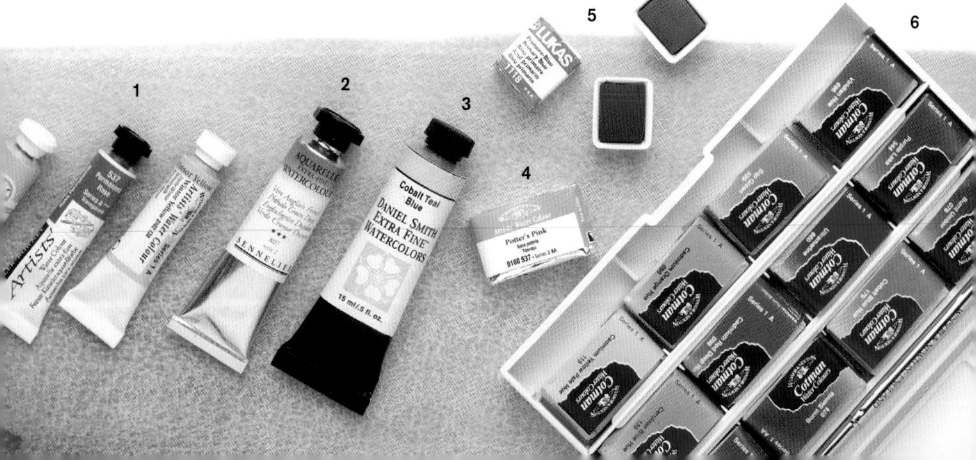

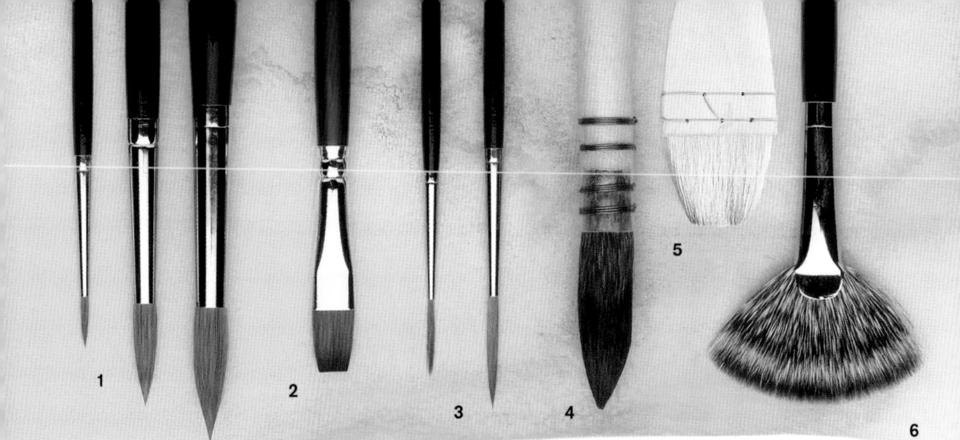

BRUSHES *A good starter kit includes:*
1 *Three round brushes (number 2 for detail, and numbers 6 and 10 for washes)*
2 *A flat brush for working lines in various thicknesses*
3 *Two rigger brushes for fine detail*
4 *A pointed mop brush and* **5** *a hake brush for large washes*
6 *A fan brush for blending*

is another argument in favour of students' colours: if you spend a fortune on a handful of tubes or pans, it can have the effect of making you hesitant when it comes to actually using them! If you want to make progress in watercolour painting, it does entail the use of quite a lot of paint. So it might be best to buy students' colours initially and then, once you've become more experienced and confident, take the next step up to artists' colours.

Brushes

The range of brushes available to the watercolourist is so vast that it can be quite confusing trying to work out which one is right for you. Brushes are made from natural hair, such as sable or squirrel, or synthetic fibres. The most expensive, and still regarded as the best by many, is the sable. A large sable brush from a reputable company can easily cost over £100. Sables are beautifully made and always return to a good point.

The water-holding capacity of a brush should be considered. If you are painting a large area, like a sky, it's important that the brush holds as much water as possible. Brushes made from natural hair hold more water than synthetic brushes. (This may change, as synthetic brushes are being improved upon all the time.) Squirrel-hair brushes have a good water-holding capacity, which makes them a favourite for painters with a loose style of working. However, these brushes can be difficult for beginners to use, as they do not readily spring back to their original shape like a sable or a synthetic brush does.

There are some very good, reasonably priced synthetic brushes on the market. They usually possess a well-defined point, are quite springy and readily return to their original shape. Brushes made of a mixture of natural and synthetic fibres are also good.

All brushes, whether natural or synthetic, are made in a variety of shapes and sizes. Brush sizes vary according to manufacturer. For instance, a size 7 from one company may be identical to a size 14 from another. Bear this in mind when purchasing from a mail-order company. There are various shapes on the market, but, for the most part, three brush shapes are quite sufficient for most purposes: the round, the flat and the rigger.

Mixing palettes

Palettes can be made from china, plastic or enamelled metal. Some have a hinged lid. Others have wells located around a central well. Stacking palettes are also available.

When choosing a palette, the main consideration is the size of the mixing wells. Look for one with four to six large wells that will be sufficient for mixing considerable amounts of colour, as opposed to one with lots of tiny, rather useless mixing wells.

Other equipment

Watercolour papers have quite a soft surface, which is easily dented. It is advisable to use a soft graphite pencil, such as a 3B or even softer, for making outlines. Erasers should be used with care too. Kneaded erasers are best; mould them into shape with your fingers.

It's best to have two water jars: use one for cleaning your brush and the other for dipping into when you want to mix colour. It means that the water in the mixing jar (which must not become too dirty) doesn't have to be changed quite as often. Keep paper towels on hand for spillages and for removing excess water from the brushes.

TIP: On location

If you are painting on location, try using collapsible jars such as these to keep your water clean. They are very light and easily portable. Carry a larger container of water to replenish the water in the jar as it becomes contaminated with pigment.

OTHER EQUIPMENT
1 *Clean water jars*
2 *Small, sealable containers for storing mixed paints*
3 *Selection of palettes*
4 *Natural sponge for large washes and lifting out. (These give much softer marks than synthetic sponges and don't scratch the paper.)*
5 *HB pencil for rough sketching. Use lightly so as not to indent the paper surface.*
6 *Paper towels for mopping and lifting*
7 *Soap. This is essential for cleaning brushes after using masking fluid.*
8 *A kneadable eraser*

For paper that is not to be stretched, keep it flat by attaching it to the board with masking tape all around the outside edge. If you have access to an electricity supply, a hair dryer is very useful for drying large washes – it can be very irritating to spend half your time watching paint dry.

Mediums

Mediums are specially formulated additives that change the characteristics of watercolours, extending its artistic potential or simply making it easier to work with. They may be used to alter the rate of drying time, increase gloss, improve flow, add texture or act as a resist (see Tip box, right).

Boards and easels

It is much easier to paint if the paper is attached to a board of some sort. Marine ply probably makes the best support. If you intend to stretch the paper, the board needs to be a little bigger than the paper – a couple of centimetres wider all around.

It helps to have the board raised at an angle. This allows washes to flow gently down the paper and also helps the paint to dry evenly. If the board is flat, the paint may dry in uneven patches. Support the board with a block of some kind, or use one of the many tabletop easels on the market.

Many people prefer to stand when painting. This allows you to step back from your work at frequent intervals in order to take in your painting as a whole and spot potential problems. Standing also allows you to use the whole of your arm, as opposed to just your wrist. This greater freedom of movement helps to prevent your work from appearing too "tight".

TIP: Mediums

A variety of mediums is available – those listed here are some of the more common ones. A medium generally refers to a liquid that is added to the watercolour mixture (refer to the manufacturer's instructions).

Gum Arabic
This increases the transparency, luminosity and gloss of the paint. It also lengthens the drying time.

Ox gall
This is a wetting agent that increases the flow of the paint.

Granulation medium
This medium imitates the attractive, speckled texture effect of granulation (see page 28).

Blending medium
Use this to slow down the drying rate. This can be particularly useful on hot days when you need more time to work and blend the colours.

Lifting preparation
If applied to the paper before starting, this medium will help in removing mistakes.

Masking medium
This acts as a resist that can be painted over and removed at a later stage. Apply it to small areas that are to be kept white or to small areas of colour that need to be retained.

Painting Techniques

The techniques discussed on the following pages reveal the distinctive characteristics of watercolour painting. Most of them deal with different methods of mixing pigments together, either on a palette or on paper, for a variety of effects. However, if you are after purity of colour, all of these techniques may also be used with colours direct from the tube or pan, and mixed only with water.

TIP: Mixing paint

Always make sure you mix enough paint before you start work. Mixing more in the middle of a painting will result in inconsistency of colour.

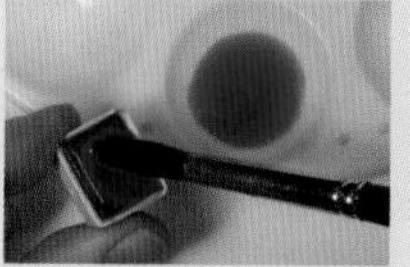

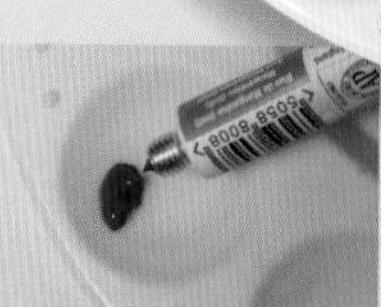

Dry paint in pans, although economical, requires a lot of preparatory mixing. Tubes are easier to use, but take care not to waste the pigment.

Colour consistency

One of the first considerations is how strong you want the colour to be. This is controlled by the amount of water you add: more water makes the colour paler and more transparent; less water makes the colour stronger. Try the experiments with the colours shown below to get a feel for the differing colour consistencies. Generally it is a good idea to first mix the paint to a milky, or middling, consistency, as it is then easy to either dilute or strengthen it. One of the key factors to remember when adding more water is that it should be clean, not polluted with previous colours.

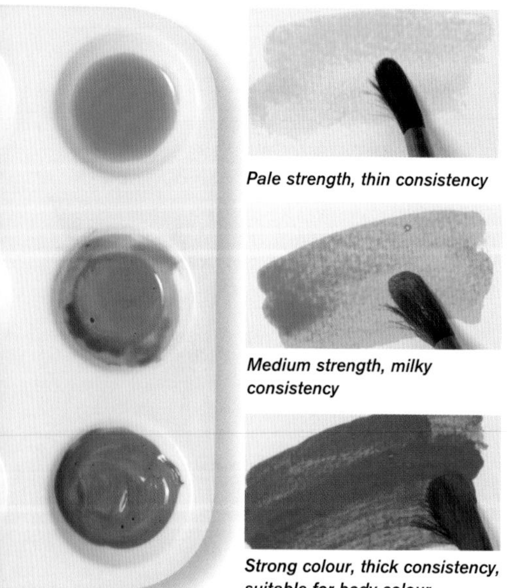

Pale strength, thin consistency

Medium strength, milky consistency

Strong colour, thick consistency, suitable for body colour

Colour mixing

All the charts in the directory section have been painted to help you select a desired colour mix. The mixed colours are shown both as they appear when mixed together on a palette before being painted onto paper and also as they appear when painted as two separate flat washes, one on top of the other. (The transparent nature of watercolour means that this creates a third colour.)

Mixing on a palette

When mixing two colours together to make a third, first put a little clean water into the

◀ **MIXING ON A PALETTE** *Put the two colours you wish to mix into two separate wells (1 and 2) and add water to each to achieve a milky consistency. Put some clean water into another well (3). Then, add the diluted lighter colour to the water and gradually add the darker colour (4, 5). Mix evenly (6).*

mixing well. Using the lighter of the two colours, lift a little on the brush and dissolve it fully in the water. Wash the brush in the water jar and then add a little of the darker colour to the well. Mix the two colours thoroughly. If you do not, an undiluted streak of pure colour may find its way onto the paper, which you will then have to try to correct.

Always put the lightest colour in the mixing well first, and then add the darker

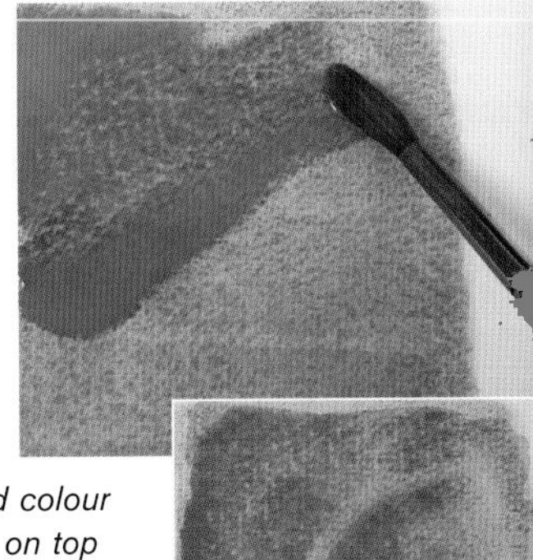

▶ **MIXING ON PAPER** *Lay the first wash and allow to dry. Add the second colour lightly so that it sits on top of the first (above right). Take care not to scrub with the brush, as this will move the first wash, resulting in unattractive blotches and a muddy colour (right).*

TIP: Prime with water

The essence of all washes is controlling the pigment while it is still suspended in water. Once it starts to dry or be absorbed by the paper, it becomes difficult to move around easily. Try "priming" the area of paper you want to paint with clean water: this creates a receptive, moist surface for you to brush the pigment onto and prevents the paper from absorbing the pigment too quickly.

The water wash needs to dry to a semi-dry state before paint is added. If it is too wet, the paint will move around too much and will take a long time to dry. However, if the water has dried too much, you lose the benefit of priming the surface. Ideally, the paper should have a slightly moist sheen.

This method can also be used when applying a second colour over an initial layer. Gently wash water over the first layer before dropping or softly brushing on the second colour.

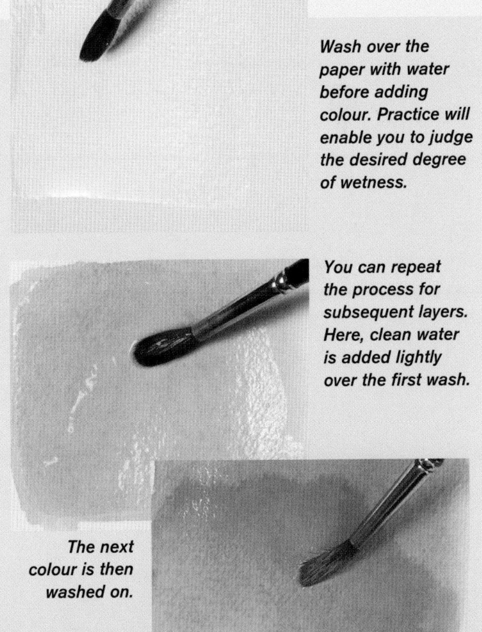

Wash over the paper with water before adding colour. Practice will enable you to judge the desired degree of wetness.

You can repeat the process for subsequent layers. Here, clean water is added lightly over the first wash.

The next colour is then washed on.

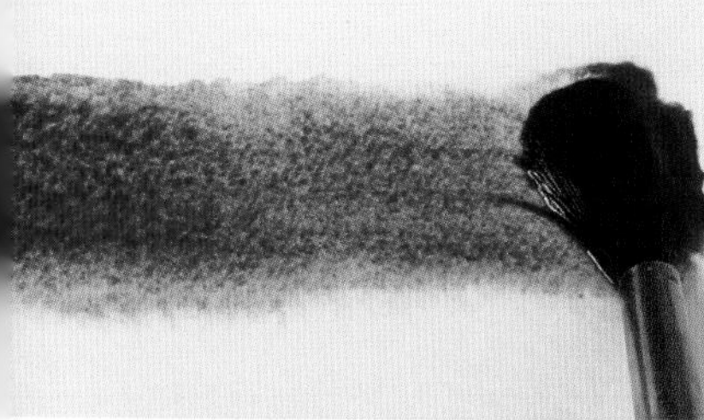

FLAT WASH *Apply a smooth, broad stroke with a large brush.*

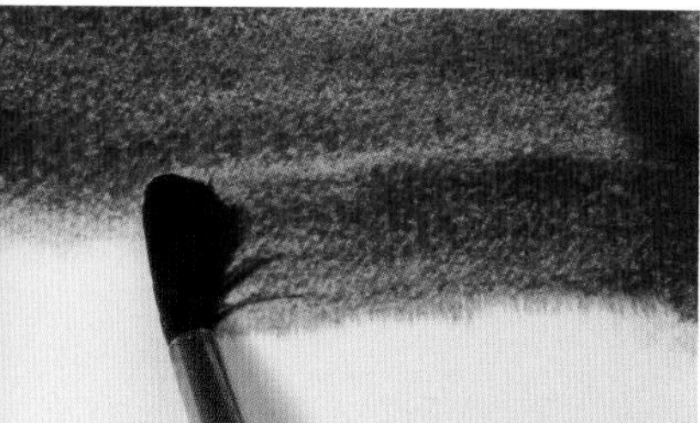

While the paint is still wet, add further strokes, each touching the one before.

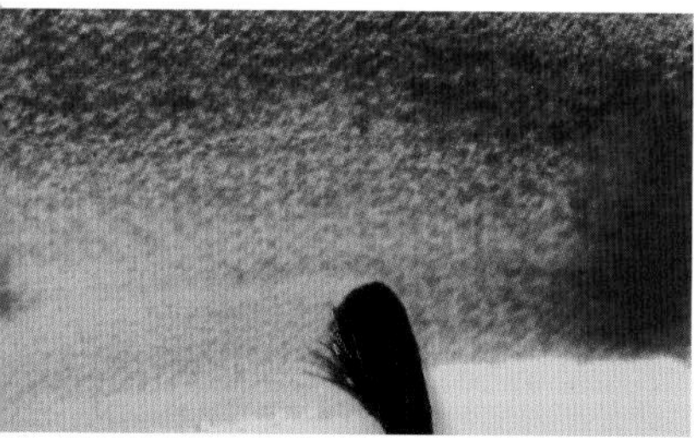

GRADED WASH *Dilute subsequent strokes with water.*

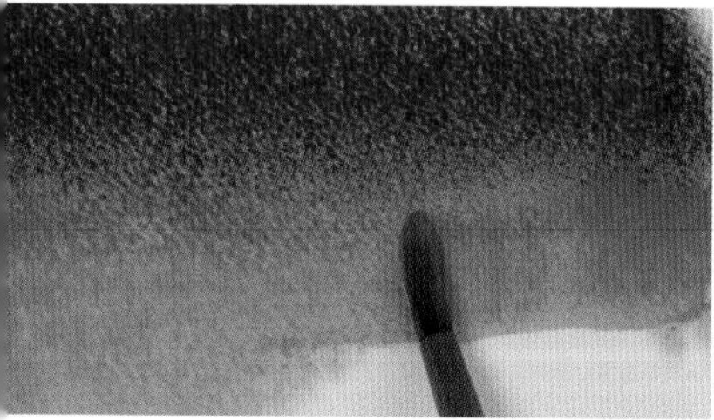

MULTICOLOURED GRADED WASH *Add different colours gradually.*

colour in small quantities until the desired colour is reached. (It's important to do it in this order; otherwise, the dark colour will overpower the light colour. A colour such as Prussian blue is extremely potent – it may surprise you just how quickly it can overpower another colour.) If you wish to make the new colour lighter, add more water.

Mixing on paper

Mix the two colours in separate palette wells, using clean water for each mix. Apply one colour to the paper as a wash and allow to dry thoroughly (unless using the wet-into-wet or backrun techniques; see pages 18–19).

Then apply the other colour as a second wash over the first. Use gentle brushstrokes in order not to disturb the first layer of colour – even though the initial layer is dry and partly absorbed by the paper, some pigment may still move if you are heavy-handed. For a really flat wash, apply water to the paper before painting (see Tip, page 15).

Flat washes

A flat wash is the most basic technique, and every watercolour artist should learn it. It has to be carried out fairly quickly, while the paint on the paper remains wet. To achieve a flat, clean wash, each brushstroke should be done only once and not reworked.

Mix the watercolour pigment with enough water to make a milky consistency (see page 14), and make up enough colour for the area you wish to paint. (It is generally a good idea to mix more paint than you think you will need: if you have to interrupt your painting to mix more, your work will dry on the paper and you will not be able to add further flat washes smoothly.)

Raise the board at an angle, to allow the paint to flow gently down the paper. Load the brush with colour. It is best to use the largest

WATERCOLOUR WASHES
This soft mix of flat and multicoloured blended washes captures the moment of sunset perfectly. The headland, painted wet-on-dry, rises ethereally out of the mist. The glow of the aqua sea has been achieved by allowing the white of the paper to shine through. The artist has used cobalt blue, ultramarine blue, cerulean blue, Payne's grey, vermilion and Naples yellow.

brush you can; both flat or round brushes are suitable.

Using slow, even pressure, paint a horizontal stroke across the paper. Reload the brush and paint a second horizontal stroke, touching the base of the first where the paint has gathered. The first stroke should flow down into the second. Repeat the process until you have covered the desired area. Lay the board flat and allow to dry. If the pigment begins to settle unevenly, with random areas of stronger pigment forming, try slanting the board at different angles.

Graded washes

Once you have mastered a flat wash, you can move on to a graded wash. This is a very useful technique for describing large expanses of sky where the colour fades towards the horizon.

Load the brush with colour and paint a couple of horizontal strokes as before. Then dip the brush in clean water to create a more diluted mix (do not agitate the brush or you will lose too much pigment). Paint another couple of bands, and repeat the diluting and painting process until you have covered the desired area.

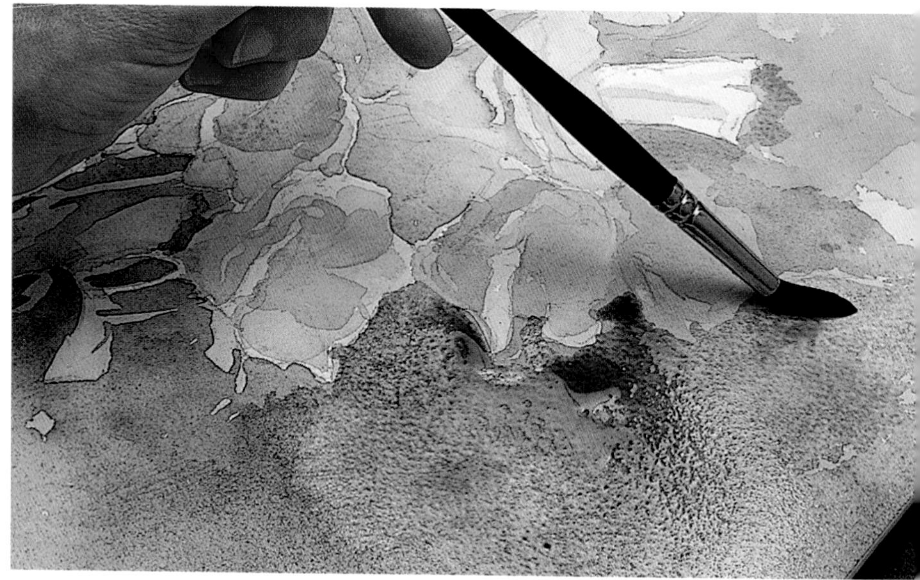

A multicoloured graded wash, where two (or more) colours are blended together, is also possible. Paint horizontal bands of each colour next to each other – these will blend and flow together naturally. No two blends will ever be the same.

WET-INTO-WET *This technique is ideal for creating lively backgrounds as a variety of colours may be dropped into the wet areas. This is a more interesting effect than the use of a single colour, while the soft, blended edges do not conflict with the detail work on the flowers.*

Wet-into-wet

Wet-into-wet is the technique of applying wet colour into another colour that is still wet. It differs from a graded wash in that the pigments are applied in a more random manner, rather than in blended bands of colour. Wet-into-wet is used to give variety to a background or surface area. There is an element of chance to this technique; however, the more you practise, the luckier you will get! If you were to paint the same scene twice using the wet-into-wet technique, you would not be able to achieve exactly the same result in each. Sometimes the most wonderful effects appear as the colours flow together.

You can increase your chances of success by taking certain steps. Have colours already mixed in your palette before you start, because you need to work quickly. If you apply a wash, the next colour must be ready to drop in straight away. If you have to waste time mixing another colour, the wash will begin to dry, and this is when disaster strikes. Placing a fully loaded brush onto colour that is starting to dry will create what is commonly known as a "cauliflower", or backrun. Some artists actively encourage the

TIP: Backruns

Backruns, or "cauliflowers", generally form where you least want them. However, if you actually want to create this effect, there are some ways to encourage its development. Apply paint to paper primed with water and allow it to dry to a semi-dry state (see Tip, page 15). Then drop in or gently brush on the second colour. If the second colour has a slightly higher water-to-pigment ratio than the first, a backrun will form.

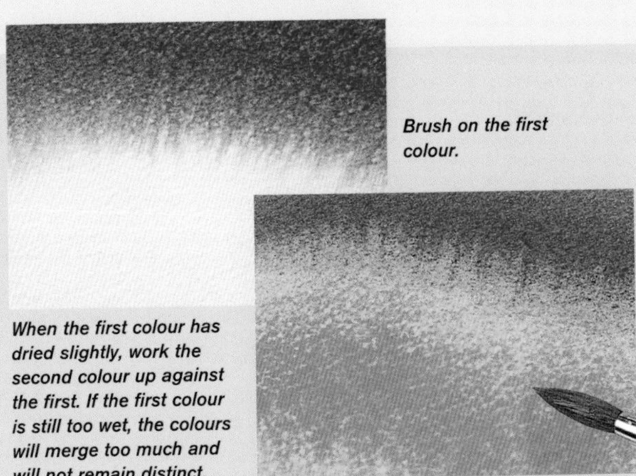

Brush on the first colour.

When the first colour has dried slightly, work the second colour up against the first. If the first colour is still too wet, the colours will merge too much and will not remain distinct.

appearance of these tidemarks, while others try to prevent them. As long as the surface to which you are adding colour remains quite wet, backruns will not form. However, once the first wash shows signs of drying, it is probably too late to apply any more colour. Of course, once it dries completely, you can glaze another colour over the top.

The wet-into-wet technique produces soft, diffused edges. It is most effective when used in conjunction with other techniques such as drybrushing and wet-on-dry, which give harder edges.

Wet-on-dry

Watercolour paintings are created using a number of techniques. The act of painting a wash on a dry sheet of watercolour paper is called "wet-on-dry". When you glaze a wash of colour over a dried wash, you are also working wet-on-dry.

WET-ON-DRY *The detail on the petals has been achieved by gradually building up layers of colour. The key is that the previous layer must be dry so that crisp edges can form, helping to describe the shape of the flower.*

HIGHLIGHTS

The background colour and the white highlights on the irises have been achieved by leaving areas of the paper unpainted. Leaving reserved areas white is a classic watercolour technique – but, with complex shapes such as these, it takes much patience and practice.

Preserving highlights

There are times when you will want certain parts of your painting to retain the original white of the paper (for highlights, for example). Therefore, the parts of the paper that are to remain untouched by paint must be preserved. The classic way of doing this is to plan the untouched areas, draw them out and then paint around them. This is not always easy. If the area to be preserved is a complicated shape or contains many small shapes, it may be difficult to paint around without parts of the wash drying unevenly.

Masking fluid

Masking fluid can be used to block off an area of paper and preserve its original state. The liquid latex solution is brushed onto the area to be masked. It dries quickly once exposed to the air, and you can then paint over the top of it. Once the paint is dry, you peel off the dried masking fluid to reveal the untouched paper beneath. Take care when removing it, because it is easy to damage the soft surface of the watercolour paper. Some papers are better suited to this treatment than others. Try it out on a small sample of paper beforehand.

MASKING FLUID

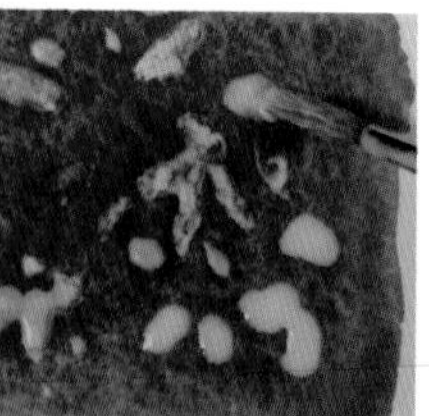

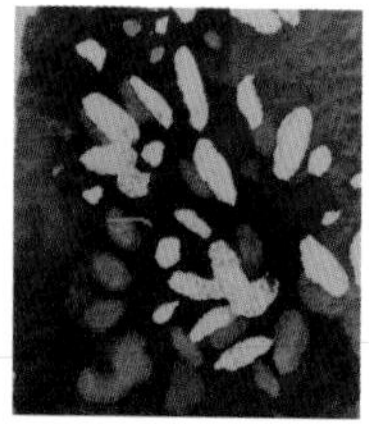

Apply masking fluid to the details you wish to keep white before painting freely over the area. Once the paint is dry, rub off the mask.

LIFTING OFF WITH A TISSUE

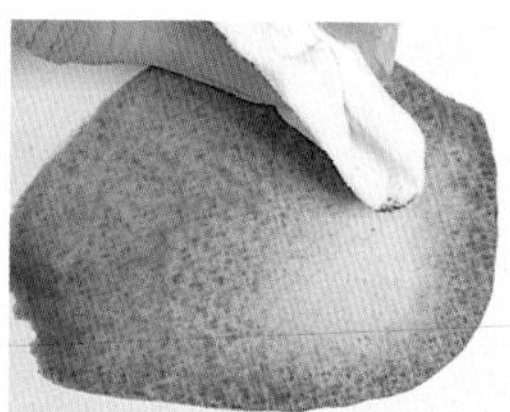

While the paint is wet, use an absorbent tissue or sponge to soak up the pigment, leaving a soft colour.

LIFTING OFF WITH A BRUSH

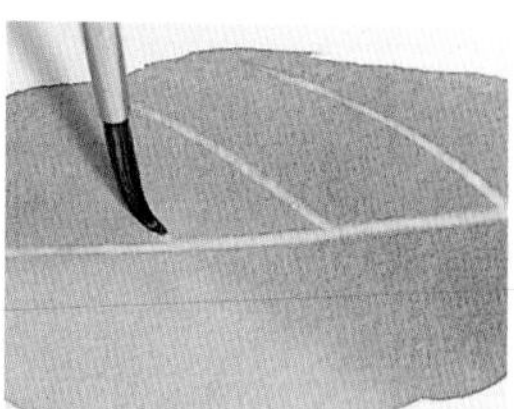

Use a clean, damp brush and stroke repeatedly over dried paint to lift most of the pigment. Blot dry.

Another point worth noting is that masking fluid will ruin brushes, so make sure that you don't apply it with your best sable! Use a matchstick or an old brush. There are also some companies that now produce masking fluid with a penlike applicator.

Lifting off

It is also possible to remove colour by a technique called "lifting off". A clean sponge, a piece of paper towel or a damp brush is used to literally lift off colour. This technique can be employed to remove areas from a still-wet sky to suggest clouds, for example.

It is also possible to lift off colour from areas that have already dried by stroking a clean, damp brush across them. If you rinse the brush and repeat the action you should be able to remove most of the colour. Small areas are the easiest to do. Some papers are much more absorbent than others, which makes lifting off more difficult. Certain colours will stain the paper, and these are hard to remove – it is seldom possible to get right back to the pure white of the original paper, but the technique is effective up to a point.

DRYBRUSH WORK *This rough stonework has been captured using the drybrushing technique. Both transparent and opaque watercolours have been used to give a rich and varied texture. The main colours are brown madder, raw sienna, new gamboge, cadmium red and viridian.*

Drybrushing

This is a useful technique for suggesting sunlight on water or creating the texture of bark on a tree. If used sparingly, it can be very effective. Drybrushing requires some practice, so hoard scraps of watercolour paper to try it out on. Rather than creating a smooth-looking brushstroke, drybrushing gives a broken effect. It is easiest to achieve on papers with a "tooth", or rough surface. The smooth surface of hot-pressed paper is too regular for this technique.

Get some colour on your brush, but not too much water. Quickly and lightly skim the brush across the surface of the paper. The paint tends to adhere to the raised areas but will not settle into the depressions in the paper (as long as the brush is not too wet).

Glazing

You have already seen how to physically mix two colours together to get a third, both on a palette and on paper (see pages 14–15). Mixing on paper is called "glazing", and the varying transparent or opaque properties of each watercolour pigment produce a different result in each mix. The beauty of glazing (especially with the more transparent colours) is that the two original colours are still visible as layers, even while mixing to create a third colour. For example, a wash of cobalt blue under a wash of transparent yellow will appear green in the areas where the two colours overlap. The underlying wash must be completely dry before the second wash is applied; otherwise, the original wash will be lifted off by the second. If you are at all uncertain about applying a particular colour over another, it is wise to test it out on some scrap paper first.

Body colour

The principal property of watercolour is its translucency; this allows the white of the paper to glow through the painted layers. Body colour is the term used for water-based paints that are opaque in nature. Generally this refers to Chinese or zinc white mixed either with water or with other watercolour pigments. Although opaque if used thickly, these mixtures can be thinned with water to create a milky, semi-transparent veil over an underlying wash. This has an attractive chalky effect and can be used to contrast

▲ **GLAZING** *With transparent colours, the underlying colours shine through, creating subtle veils of colour. In the painting above, the leaves clearly appear as leaves, but the red of the fruit mysteriously shows through.*

◀ **AT-A-GLANCE** *Seen as two bands of colour in the first sample, the lemon yellow painted over cobalt blue creates a characterful green. Seeing the green in isolation (below), it is hard to believe it is the centre of the first sample.*

▶ **GLAZING WITH OPAQUE AND TRANSPARENT COLOURS**
The building in the painting opposite has been built up with a succession of transparent glazes. Light red and dioxazine violet have been glazed over the previously painted brickwork to create areas of shadow. The sky has been underpainted with yellow-orange, and then glazed over with opaque body colour and a variety of blues for a lively, scudding cloud effect.

with transparent areas of a painting.

Care must be taken with body colour, as you can easily lose the transparency of a watercolour painting by using too much. Always plan a painting and decide in advance how much body colour you are going to use; don't just slap it on as a last resort.

Body colour can also be used to create highlights. Highlights in watercolour painting are usually formed from the unpainted white of the paper, as this will always be whiter than any paint. However, highlights formed from body colour can be very successful, as seen in the examples shown on these pages.

▶ **BODY COLOUR FOR DETAIL** *Washes of ultramarine blue and cobalt blue for the sky and yellow ochre for the sand provide the basis for this painting. These are then mixed with cadmium red or process yellow to create the colours in the scene. The details and highlights have been added with opaque white used raw or mixed with the other colours to create a variety of body colours.*

▲ **STRENGTH OF COLOUR** *The opacity of titanium white and lemon yellow is used here to create the effect of vibrant sunlight. The colour is further enhanced by dramatically contrasting it with cobalt and ultramarine blues.*

▶ **WHITE DETAIL** *Soft glazed washes of reds and yellows are mixed with cobalt blue and viridian to create a misty backdrop that contrasts with the fine linear detail on the chairs. These complex patterns form the focal point of the composition.*

The Properties of Pigments

Organic pigments

Organic pigments are those containing carbon atoms; that is, they have been produced from living matter or matter that was once part of living things. Historically, these included colours such as rose madder, carmine and Indian yellow. Today, most of these pigments have been replaced by synthetic versions, though all still have a carbon base. These modern organic pigments are known for their clarity and translucency.

Dye/staining colours

Dye, or staining, colours are part of the synthetic organic group. These colours differ from pigments in that they are completely dissolved, as opposed to being suspended in a liquid. Pigments tend to form a layer on the surface of the paper, whereas dyes will actually stain the paper. In practice, this property makes dye colours difficult to correct and lift off with a damp brush.

Inorganic pigments

These pigments do not contain carbon and are obtained from substances that were never part of living matter. Inorganic colours include pigments containing insoluble compounds composed of metallic oxides and salts. Natural inorganic pigments constitute the earth colours: the umbers, ochres, siennas, chromes, cobalts, titaniums, ultramarine blue, viridian, lamp black and the whites. As with organic pigments, many of these natural earth colours are now produced synthetically. Other synthetic inorganics include cadmiums, cobalts, iron and other metal oxides.

ORGANIC COLOUR SAMPLES

Carmine

Quinacridone violet

Indanthrene blue

DYE COLOUR SAMPLES

Aureolin yellow

Indigo

Permanent rose

INORGANIC COLOUR SAMPLES

Raw umber

Cobalt blue

Titanium buff

Transparency and opacity

Transparency is the key characteristic of watercolour. Because the whiteness of the paper plays an important role in watercolour painting and is required to remain visible after washes have been built up on it, knowledge of the transparency and opacity of colours is crucial. Watercolour pigments vary in their relative levels of transparency, and some are more opaque than others. The more transparent pigments make cleaner washes and colour mixes as they refract light in the same way as a stained glass window. The more opaque colours tend to give flatter washes and are more robust in covering

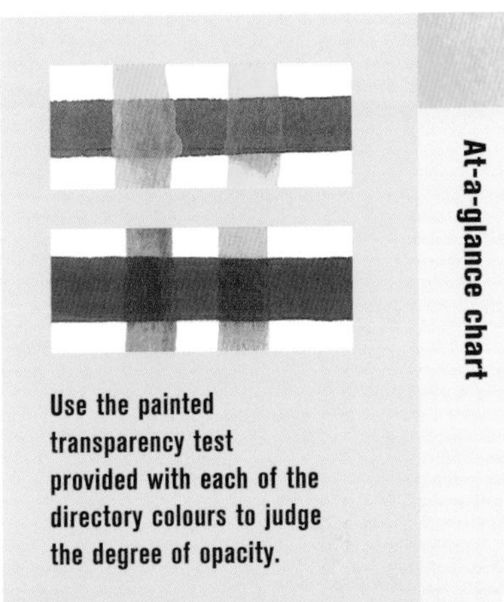

At-a-glance chart

Use the painted transparency test provided with each of the directory colours to judge the degree of opacity.

TRANSPARENCY AND OPACITY *These two properties have been used very effectively here. While opaque dark brown mixes act as a dense background, the white of the paper glows like sunlight through the transparent mixes used for the flowers and foliage: aureolin yellow, permanent rose, brilliant orange, phthalo crimson, phthalo green and cobalt blue.*

underlying washes. Their matte quality makes them useful in toning down colour mixes. Opaque pigments can be made more transparent with the addition of extra water. Pigments are usually labelled as transparent, semi-transparent and semi-opaque.

Granulation

Certain pigments (such as ultramarine blue) share a characteristic that leads them to settle into groups or clump together. This can be further enhanced by the texture of the paper. When a wash containing a pigment of this type is applied to paper, the granules clump together and settle into the depressions on the surface of the paper. This is known as granulation. The rougher the surface of the paper, the more pronounced the effect. It is still noticeable on smoother papers as the textured effect results more from the clumping together (or flocculation) of the pigment than the surface of the paper. It is also noticeable if the granulating colour

BLENDING *A granulating colour such as manganese blue can be blended with a non-granulating one such as alizarin crimson.*

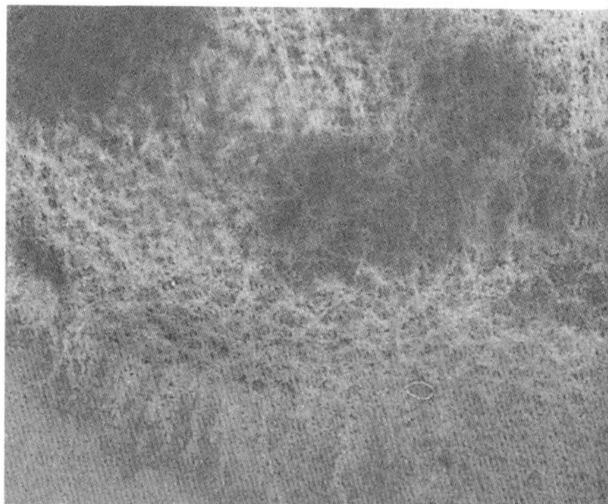

Granulation will appear in the area of the blend.

TIP: Granulating medium

A special medium is available that can be mixed with all colours to make them granulate. This exaggerates the effect of those colours that granulate naturally and also makes it possible for the phthalocyanine and quinacridone colour families to granulate. For maximum effect, use the medium and pigment undiluted with water.

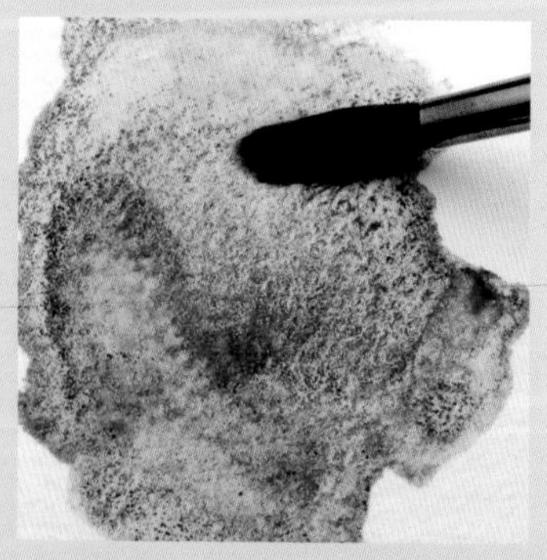

is mixed with a non-granulating colour. Ultramarine blue mixed with burnt sienna produces a pleasing grey, which is useful for portraying cloud shadows. The burnt sienna is quite clear, but the granulation of the ultramarine blue is still apparent. This interesting effect can be put to good use in areas of drama, for example. However, if you are aiming for a smoother effect, it is advisable to choose colours that don't granulate. The use of distilled water can reduce the inclination of colours to granulate.

GRANULATION FOR ATMOSPHERE

Mixes of yellow ochre, alizarin crimson, cerulean blue, burnt sienna and French ultramarine blue have created the hazy light in the picture above. The haze is enhanced by the texture of granulation.

At-a-glance chart

Use the painted header strip and texture swatch provided with each of the directory colours to judge the degree to which each colour will granulate.

The Colour Wheel

Much has been written about the theory of the colour wheel, and few art books would be complete without some version of it. At its simplest, it is a tool to help you organize and understand aspects of each colour in the spectrum. The wheel at its most basic consists of the three primary colours, so the wheel featured in this book appears in a triangular form.

Primary colours

The colours red, yellow and blue cannot be mixed from any other colours and are therefore known as primary colours. There are, however, many variations of each – some are cool, while others are warm. For example, the colour red includes cadmium red, bright red, crimson, brilliant red, flame red and carmine.

Warm and cool colours

The colour wheel contains warm colours such as yellows, oranges and reds, and cool colours such as violets, blues and greens. However, there are warm and cool versions of every colour, no matter where it appears on the wheel. Blue is a cool colour, but within its colour range, some blues are warm (such as ultramarine blue) and some are cool (such as cerulean blue). Similarly, lemon yellow is cool, whereas cadmium yellow is warm.

Secondary colours

If any two primary colours are mixed together, the result is a secondary colour. Yellow and red produce orange, yellow and blue combine into green, and blue and red

VARIATIONS OF A PRIMARY COLOUR

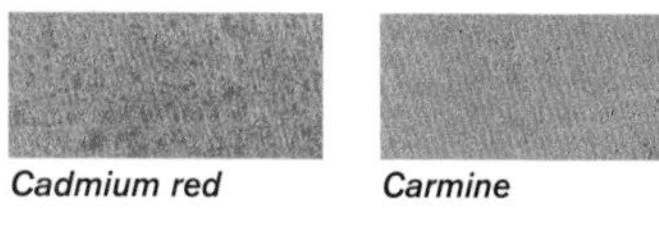

Cadmium red *Carmine*

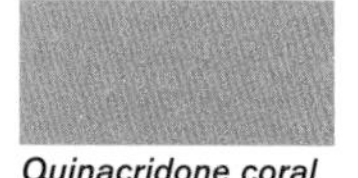

Quinacridone coral

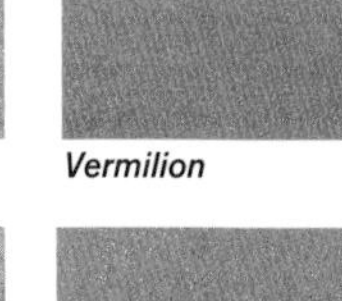

Vermilion

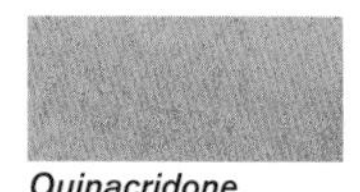

Quinacridone magenta

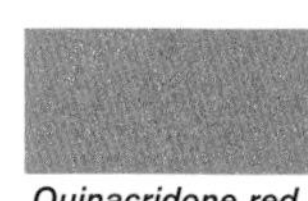

Quinacridone red

WARM COLOURS **COOL COLOURS**

Cadmium yellow *Lemon yellow*

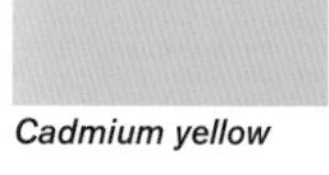

Ultramarine blue *Cerulean blue*

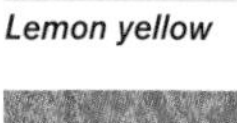

Cadmium red *Quinacridone red*

SECONDARY COLOURS

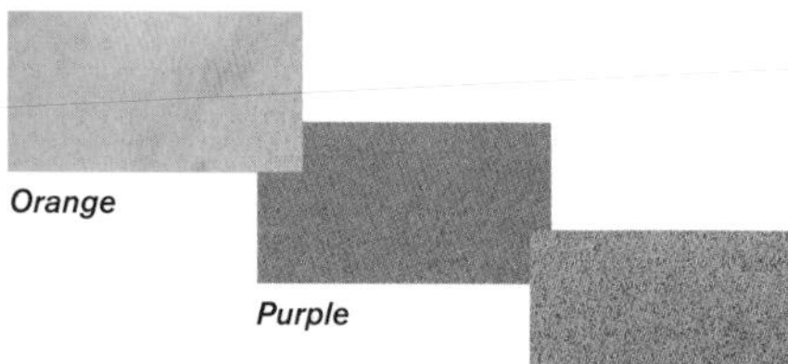

Orange

Purple

Green

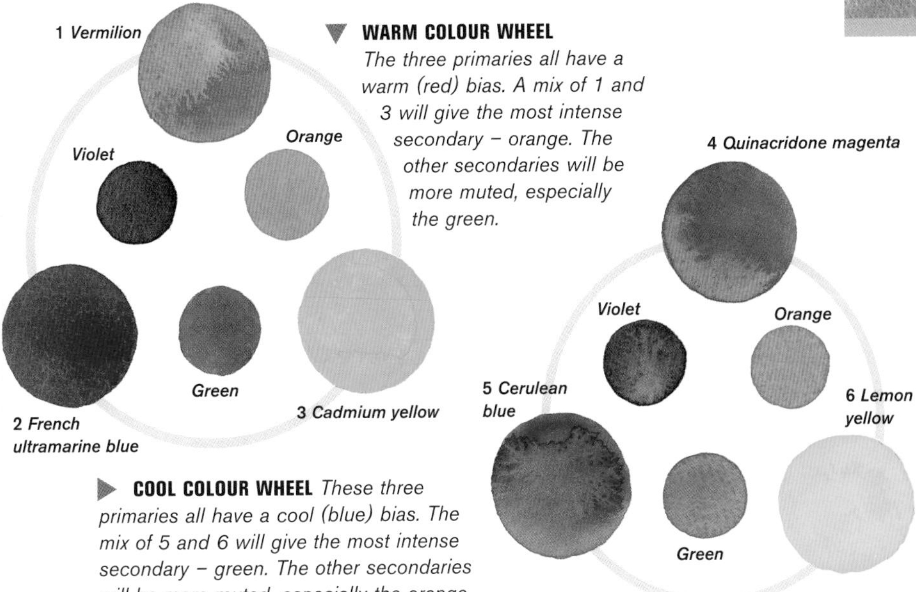

▼ **WARM COLOUR WHEEL** *The three primaries all have a warm (red) bias. A mix of 1 and 3 will give the most intense secondary – orange. The other secondaries will be more muted, especially the green.*

▶ **COOL COLOUR WHEEL** *These three primaries all have a cool (blue) bias. The mix of 5 and 6 will give the most intense secondary – green. The other secondaries will be more muted, especially the orange.*

make purple. The primary colours you choose have a distinct effect on the secondary colours that you are able to mix from them. (The red, for example, might be alizarin crimson or cadmium red, both of which make a different orange when mixed with yellow.)

Intense secondaries

For intense secondary colours, use primaries that contain a similar warm or cool bias.

To make an intense orange, mix cadmium red (a warm red, containing a lot of yellow) with a warm yellow such as cadmium yellow, rather than a cool yellow such as lemon yellow. To make an intense green, mix cool lemon yellow with a cool cerulean blue. To make an intense purple, mix alizarin crimson (a cool red with a blue bias) with ultramarine blue (a warm blue with a red bias).

Neutral secondaries

If you want more muted secondary colours, choose primaries that are further away from each other on the colour wheel – for example, orange made from alizarin crimson and lemon yellow, green from cadmium yellow and ultramarine blue, and purple from cadmium red and Prussian blue.

It is best to have two or more of each primary colour in your paintbox, some on the cool side and some on the warm side.

TIP: Making a colour wheel

By painting your own versions of the two primary colour wheels shown above, it becomes easier to understand the relationships and colour mixing potential of the primary colours.

You can also experiment with other primary colours from your paintbox to see the effect that the warm or cool bias inherent in each colour has on the secondary mix.

Tertiary colours

Tertiary colours appear between a primary and its secondary on the colour wheel. For instance, yellow–green is the result of mixing yellow (primary colour) with green (secondary colour).

Complementary colours

The complementary colours are those that lie opposite each other on the colour wheel. Red and green are complementary, as are yellow and purple, and blue and orange. If you place complementary colours next to each other in a painting, it has the effect of making each one appear more intense.

▲ **TERTIARY MIXES** *The lazy calm of the river is captured by a subtle palette of Naples yellow, cadmium orange, cobalt blue and raw umber. Neutral tertiary mixes made from these colours unify the scene. The artist defines the water and buildings by adding touches of different colours to the mixes.*

▶ **COMPLEMENTARY CONTRASTS** *This complementary colour scheme of blue and orange makes both colours "sing". It is achieved using a fairly limited palette of aureolin yellow, ultramarine blue and Winsor red, with the odd touch of cerulean blue. Up to 30 layers of glazing have resulted in the richness of the effect.*

COMPLEMENTARY FOCAL POINT

The artist spotted the perfect complementary juxtaposition of these flowers and foliage. Quinacridone magenta stands out in bright contrast against the surrounding mixes of lemon yellow and phthalo green.

Using Colour

The way you juxtapose colours will help describe the form of the subject or your initial response to it.

Warm and cool colours

We have already seen how each colour has a warm or cool bias in its position on the colour wheel. The interplay between the warm/cool contrast can be used in your compositions to create depth or a focal point, as warm colours generally advance from the picture surface while cool colours recede.

Colour and tone

Tone is a word used to describe a colour's lightness or darkness. To judge the tone of a colour, try to imagine where it would appear o a scale of black to white. For example, lemon yellow is much lighter in tone than ultramarine blue, when compared at the same strength. However, ultramarine blue, like any colour, car be lightened by diluting it with water. If enoug water is added, it is possible to make a blue that is similar in tone to, or lighter in tone than, lemon yellow. It is desirable to use a full tonal range in your paintings, with light tones for the highlights or focal points and dark tones for depth.

Colours may also be made to appear lighter by placing them next to darker colours, for contrast. A

WARM/COOL CONTRASTS *A simple palette of three main colours (warm reds, cool blues and stone) exaggerates the patterned effect of the building's design. The brickwork (cadmium red and light red) contrasts well with the recessive cobalt blue and ultramarine blue window reflections.*

Ultramarine blue at full strength and matched to its equivalent black tone.

Lemon yellow at full strength and diluted ultramarine blue matched to their equivalent black tones.

TONES AND SHADOWS
Paint has been used both straight from the tube and mixed to create the shades and neutral colours seen here. A fairly limited palette of alizarin crimson, cadmium yellow, Prussian blue, viridian, lamp black and yellow-green is very effective in the complex shadow patterning. On the ground, the patch of orange sunlight has been overlaid with a violet mix for some particularly vibrant shadows.

strong colour will contrast with diluted versions of the same colour. Of course, a light colour such as lemon yellow will contrast sharply with a dark colour like indigo.

Shades

A shade is a colour that has been darkened by adding another colour to it. As an example, if you were to add a little green to a red (green is complementary to red), the red would become darker.

Tints

Another way to make colours lighter (as well as by diluting them) is to mix them with white (see pages 240–243). White paint is opaque, and when another colour is mixed with it, it creates a tint. However, once you have added white to a colour, the transparency is lost.

Watercolour paper is available in various tints as well as white. Bear in mind the fact that all the washes you apply to the paper

ANN
SMITH
SWS

▶ **COLOUR JUXTAPOSITION**
Contrasts using warm, cool and complementary colours are used here to make the flowers stand out from the background. To give unity, touches of warm scarlet lake have been added to the cool blue/violet shadows.

◀ **COMBINING CONTRASTS**
The artist has used three types of contrast to make the flower a focal point: tonal, complementary and the warm/cool contrast. The flowers (painted in cadmium yellow and Winsor red) are much lighter, brighter and warmer than the cool, recessive violet and blue background mixes.

will be influenced by its base colour. If you want whites in a painting on tinted paper, you will have to use opaque white paint.

Making colours look brighter

It is possible to make a colour appear brighter by placing certain colours next to it. As already mentioned, if complementary colours appear close to each other in a painting, they make each other look more intense.

A neutral colour, or shade, can also make another colour appear brighter. Adding a little of a colour's complement to it will create a more muted version of the original. This will have the effect of lifting the original when the resulting mixture is placed next to it.

In addition, the warm/cool contrast can be employed to brighten colours: place a warm colour next to a cool colour to immediately intensify both colours.

▲ **HARMONY** *A palette of harmonious colours has been used here to produce this serene autumnal scene. The colours used (lime, yellow, orange and red) are adjacent to one another on the colour wheel.*

▼ **VARIETY** *This scheme is both complementary and harmonious. While the harmonious range of pinks and reds dominate the piece, the use of red's complementary colour, green, provides variety. However, the green is used very simply a a pale wash to maintain the harmonious palette.*

Colour harmony

It is important that the colours you choose for your palette, or a particular painting, harmonize with one another and do not clash (unless that's the effect you want). The colours should have some kind of unity throughout the painting. One method of ensuring this is to use, as the predominant colours in your painting, colours close to one another on the colour wheel. For example, create compositions of mainly yellow, green and orange, or varying shades of cool red and violet. Another way to create this harmony is to use a limited palette. A palette of six colours, comprising a warm and a cool version of each primary, will provide many combinations. However, even a three-colour palette will give you a wide variety of mixes. A palette consisting of alizarin crimson, raw sienna and ultramarine blue will produce a wide range of harmonious colours.

RECOMMENDED LIMITED PALETTE

WARM COLOURS

Ultramarine blue

Vermilion

Cadmium yellow

COOL COLOURS

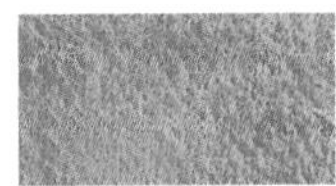

Cerulean blue

Quinacridone red

Lemon yellow

CLEVER COLOUR MIXING

A limited palette of permanent rose, cobalt blue and aureolin yellow ensures the cohesiveness of this painting. This trio of pigments has been mixed to produce a variety of colours, displaying the artist's superior colour mixing experience. Tiny touches of dioxazine violet were used on some of the flowers.

aureolin yellow
PY40
page 44

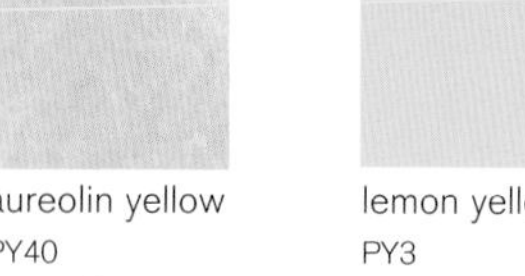

lemon yellow
PY3
page 48

transparent
yellow PY150
page 52

cadmium yellow
medium PY35
page 56

Indian yellow
PY153
page 60

permanent carmine
(quinacridone pyrrolidone)
page 84

quinacridone red
PV19
page 88

permanent rose
PV19
page 92

quinacridone
magenta PR122
page 96

quinacridone violet
PV19
page 100

the colour mixing

cobalt blue
PB28
page 124

phthalo blue
PB15:3
page 128

cerulean blue
PB35
page 132

manganese blue
PB15
page 136

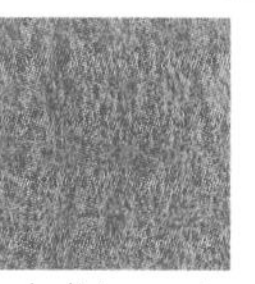
cobalt turquoise
light PG50
page 140

phthalo yellow-green
PG7+PY3+arylide yel10G
page 164

sap green
PG7+PY153+PR101
page 168

green-gold
PY129
page 172

titanium buff
PW6.1
page 176

raw umber
PBr7
page 180

potter's pink
PR233
page 204

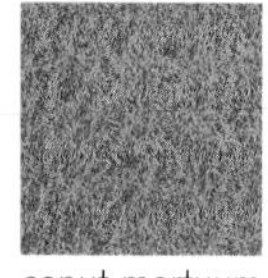
caput mortuum
violet PR101
page 208

purpurite genuine
C.I. name n/a
page 212

burnt umber
PBr7
page 216

sepia
PBk6+PR101
page 220

For an explanation of the pigment codes (C.I. name), see page 250

Naples yellow
PY35+PR101+PW4
page 64

cadmium orange
PO20
page 68

vermilion
PR242
page 72

cadmium red medium PR108
page 76

quinacridone coral
PR209
page 80

cobalt violet
PV14
page 104

dioxazine violet
PV23
page 108

indanthrene blue
PB60
page 112

ultramarine blue
PB29
page 116

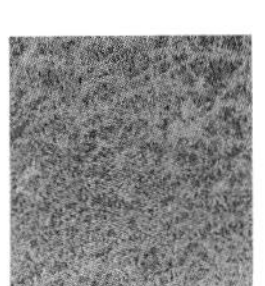
lapis lazuli genuine
C.I. name n/a
page 120

directory

The colour mixing directory mixes each of the 50 colours shown here with a palette of 18 colours in controlled tests.

cobalt turquoise
PB36
page 144

phthalo green
PG7
page 148

viridian
PG18
page 152

terre verte
PG18+PG23+PB28
page 156

Hooker's green medium PG36+PY110
page 160

yellow ochre
PY43
page 184

quinacridone gold
PO49
page 188

raw sienna
PBr7
page192

transparent red-brown PR206
page 196

Indian red
PR101
page 200

indigo
PBk6+PV19+PB15
page 224

perylene green
PBk31
page 228

Davy's grey PG17+PBk6+PW4+PBk19
page 232

ivory black
PBk9
page 236

Chinese & titianium white PW4/PW6
page 240

50 colours, each arranged over four pages, are mixed in different ways with a control palette of 18 colours to give more than 2500 possibilties.

using the colour

Name of ***colour.*** *Each colour is split into two sections, over four pages.*

Description of the colour.

List of the ***palette colours*** *with which the colours are mixed. There are 18 palette colours in total; each section features nine.*

The left-hand page of each colour displays the results when the ***colour*** *is mixed with each of the* ***palette colours*** *on a mixing palette, before being applied to paper. The colours are mixed in a 60:40 ratio (colour: palette colour).*

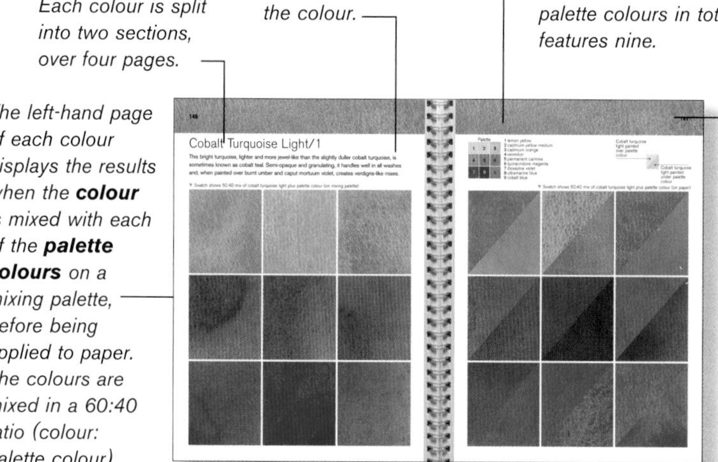

The right-hand page of each section displays the results when the mix is made on paper, by glazing a layer of the ***colour*** *either above or beneath each of the* ***palette colours****. The colours are also mixed in a 60:40 ratio (see page 7).*

▶ *The palette colours and their colour index (C.I.) names. If you find it difficult to obtain any of the colours, use the comparison charts (page 250) to find the closest match.*

1	2	3
4	5	6
7	8	9

1 Lemon yellow PY3

2 Cadmium yellow medium PY35

3 Cadmium orange PO20

4 Vermilion PR242

5 Permanent carmine C.I. N/A

6 Quinacridone magenta PR122

7 Dioxazine violet PV23

8 Ultramarine blue PB29

9 Cobalt blue PB28

Transparency
1 (opaque)
4 (transparent)

Staining
0 (weak staining power)
3 (strong staining power)

Granulation
as single colour
0 (non-granulating)
3 (strongly granulating)
in mixes
0 (non-granulating)
3 (strongly granulating)

Permanence
1 (least permanent)
3 (excellent)
N/A (information as to this colour's permanence is not yet available)

See page 255 for information on how lightfast ratings were produced.

mixing directory

The properties of the pigment are demonstrated visually, using two different strengths of paint.

The panel at the head of each page shows the pigment in a medium strength wash with some variegation, to display the full character of the colour.

This list describes the properties of the pigment.

The swatches were painted to show variegation where appropriate.

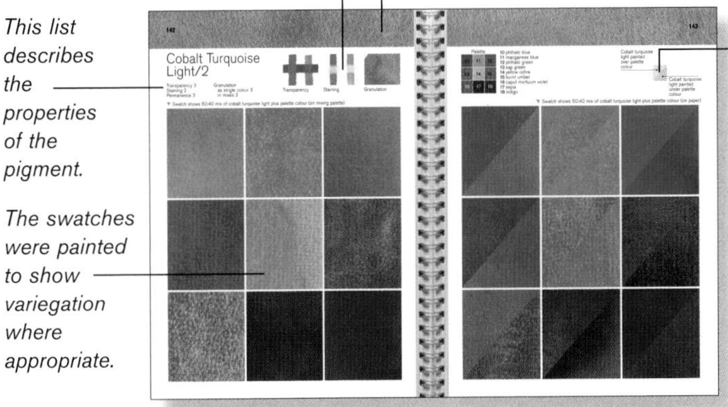

Each of the swatches on the right-hand page is divided diagonally into two. This diagram illustrates which half of the swatch shows the colour painted above the palette colour, and which half shows it painted beneath.

11 Manganese blue PB15

10 Phthalo blue PB15:3

12 Phthalo green PG7

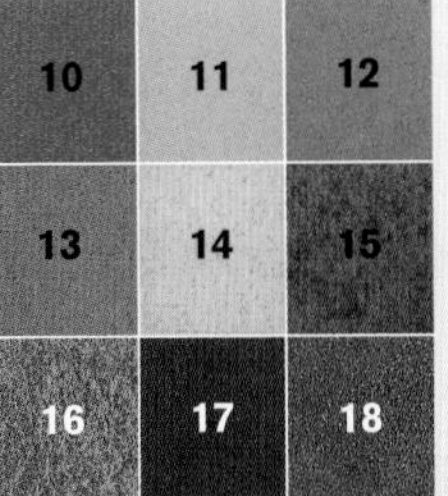

13 Sap green PG7+PY153+PR101

14 Yellow ochre PY43

15 Burnt umber PBr7

16 Caput mortuum violet PR101
Also known as Mars violet.

18 Indigo PBk6+PV19+PB15

17 Sepia PBk6+PR101

Aureolin Yellow/1

A cool, transparent yellow, good for glazing and mixing with blues to make bright acid greens. Easy to work with for flat washes. The pigment may vary between suppliers – some versions have a green bias. It is the least permanent of the yellows featured in this book.

▼ Swatch shows 60:40 mix of aureolin yellow plus palette colour (on mixing palette)

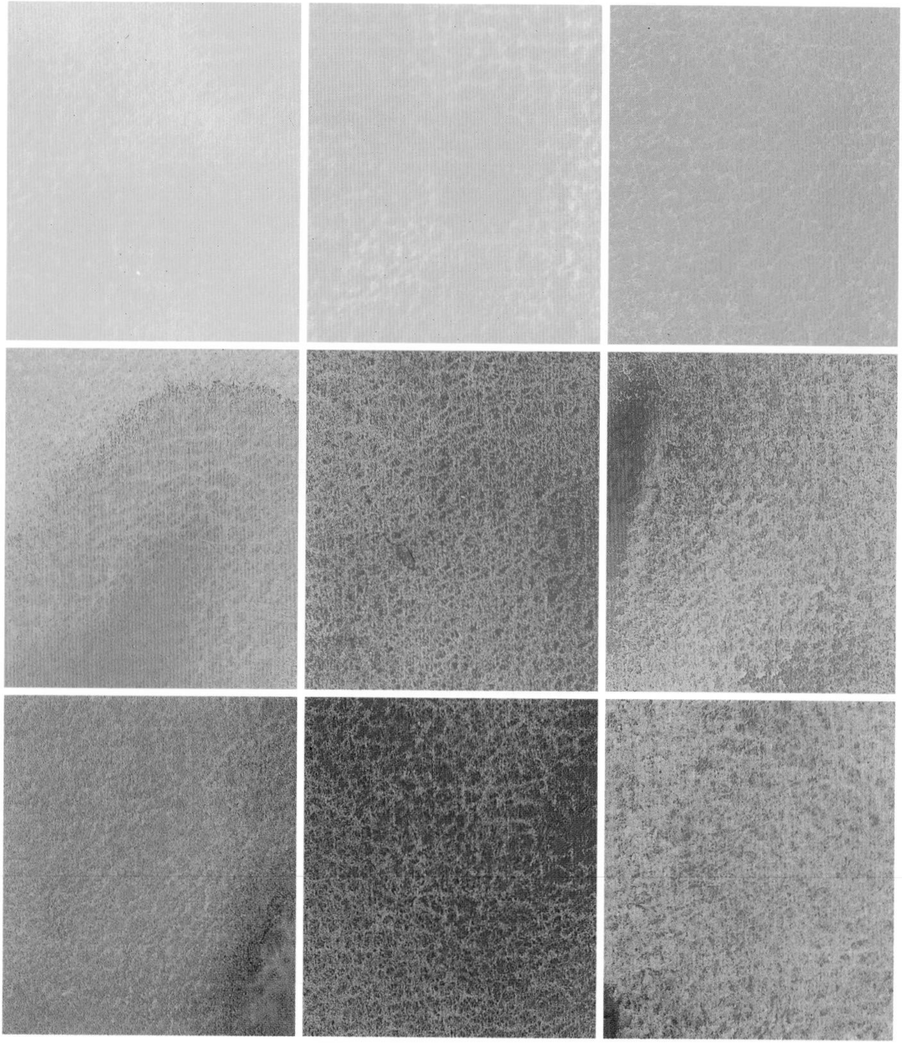

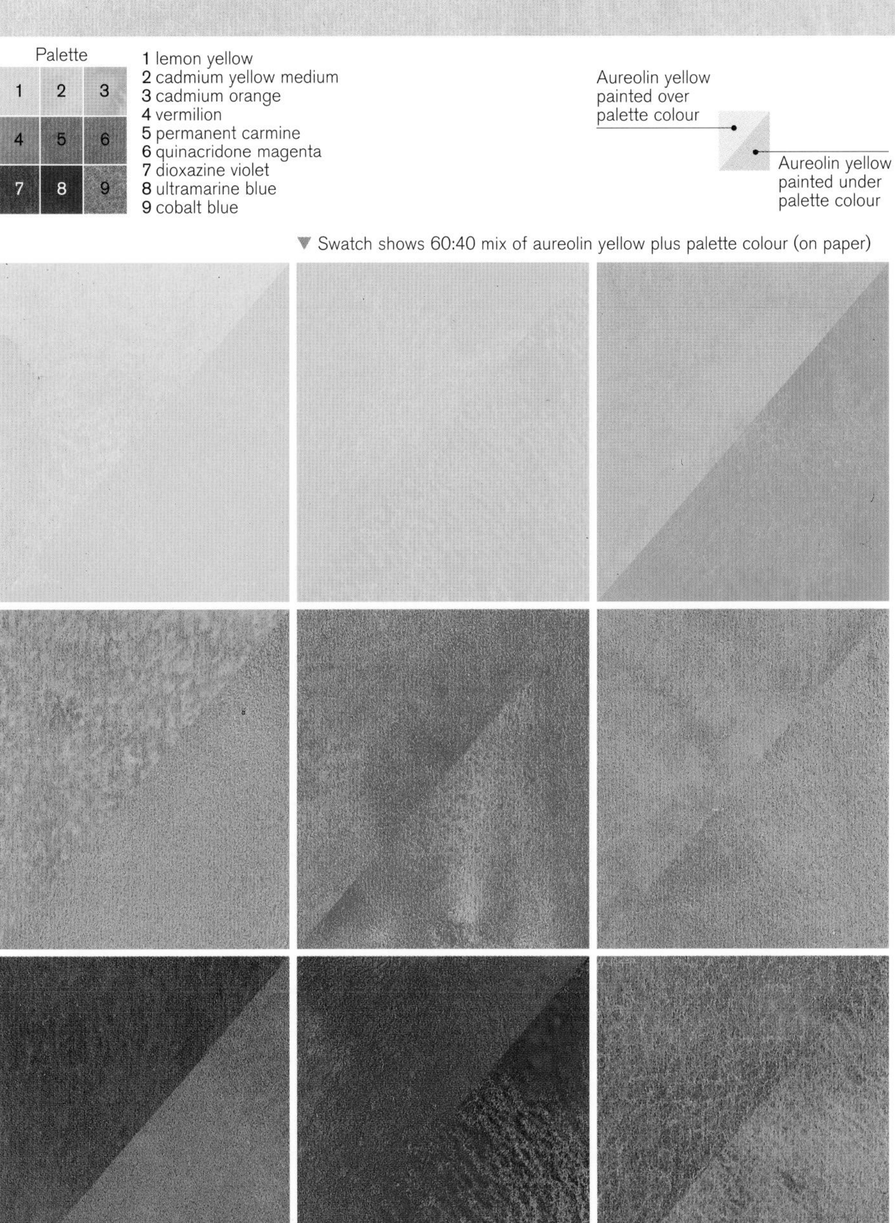

▼ Swatch shows 60:40 mix of aureolin yellow plus palette colour (on paper)

Aureolin Yellow/2

Transparency 4
Staining 2
Permanence 1

Granulation
as single colour 0
in mixes 1

Transparency

Staining

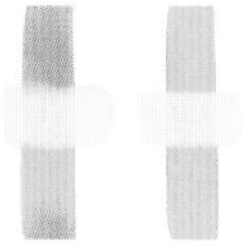

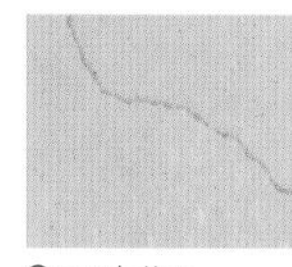
Granulation

▼ Swatch shows 60:40 mix of aureolin yellow plus palette colour (on mixing palette)

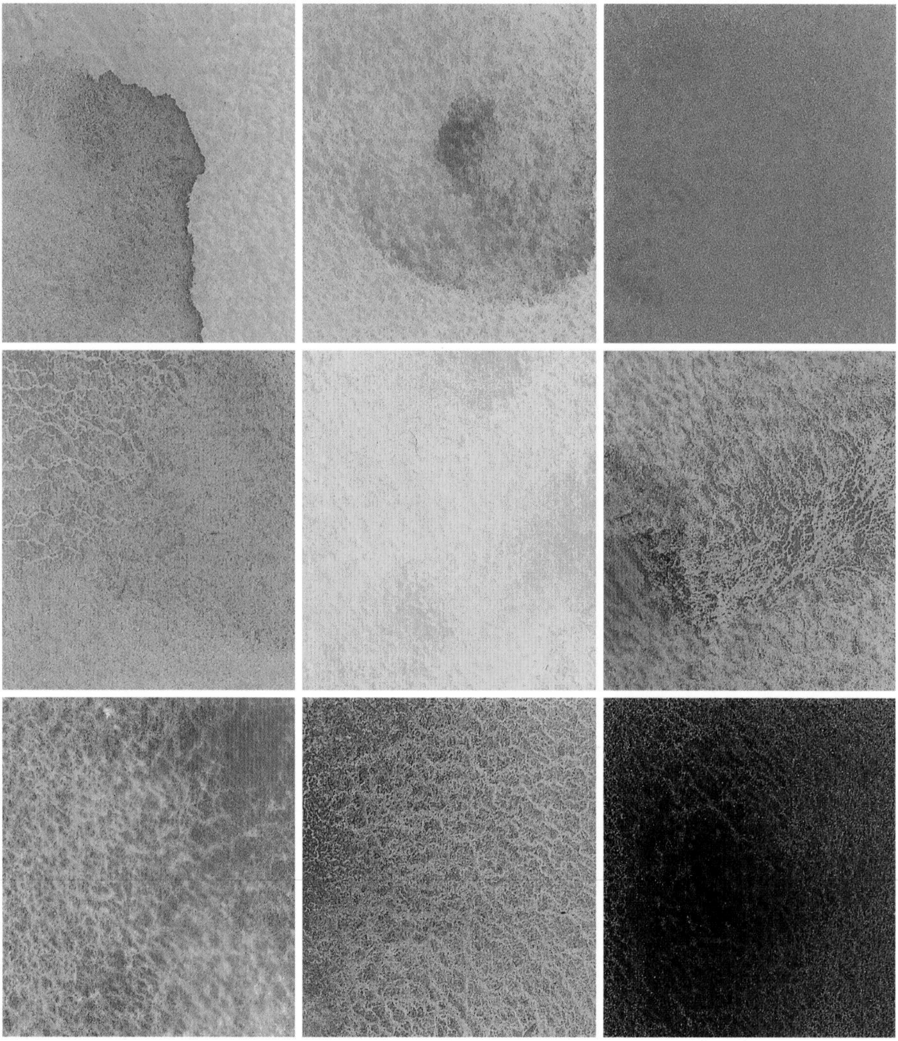

Palette

10	11	12
13	14	15
16	17	18

10 phthalo blue
11 manganese blue
12 phthalo green
13 sap green
14 yellow ochre
15 burnt umber
16 caput mortuum violet
17 sepia
18 indigo

Aureolin yellow painted over palette colour

Aureolin yellow painted under palette colour

▼ Swatch shows 60:40 mix of aureolin yellow plus palette colour (on paper)

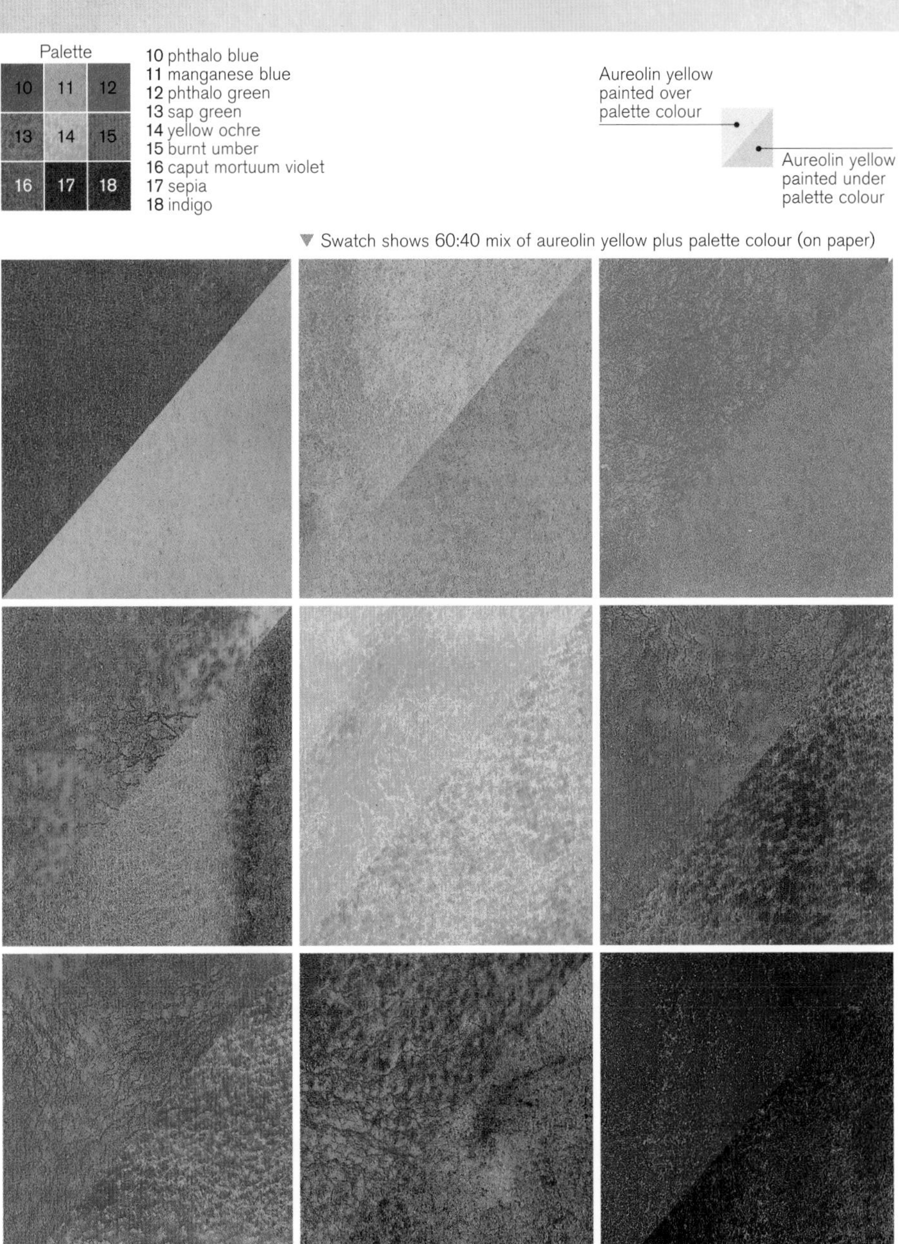

Lemon Yellow/1

A cool, opaque yellow. Its slight chalkiness creates softer greens than aureolin yellow. For flat washes, use it alone or mix it with other colours on a palette. It can become mottled if applied straight to paper, so prime paper first (see page 15).

▼ Swatch shows 60:40 mix of lemon yellow plus palette colour (on mixing palette)

Palette

1	2	3
4	5	6
7	8	9

1 lemon yellow
2 cadmium yellow medium
3 cadmium orange
4 vermilion
5 permanent carmine
6 quinacridone magenta
7 dioxazine violet
8 ultramarine blue
9 cobalt blue

Instead of overpainting the palette colour with itself in the mixes on paper, the upper triangle shows a single wash and the lower, a double wash.

Lemon yellow painted over palette colour

Lemon yellow painted under palette colour

▼ Swatch shows 60:40 mix of lemon yellow plus palette colour (on paper)

Lemon Yellow/2

Transparency 1
Staining 1
Permanence 2

Granulation
as single colour 0
in mixes 1

Transparency

Staining

Granulation

▼ Swatch shows 60:40 mix of lemon yellow plus palette colour (on mixing palette)

Palette

10	11	12
13	14	15
16	17	18

10 phthalo blue
11 manganese blue
12 phthalo green
13 sap green
14 yellow ochre
15 burnt umber
16 caput mortuum violet
17 sepia
18 indigo

Lemon yellow painted over palette colour

Lemon yellow painted under palette colour

▼ Swatch shows 60:40 mix of lemon yellow plus palette colour (on paper)

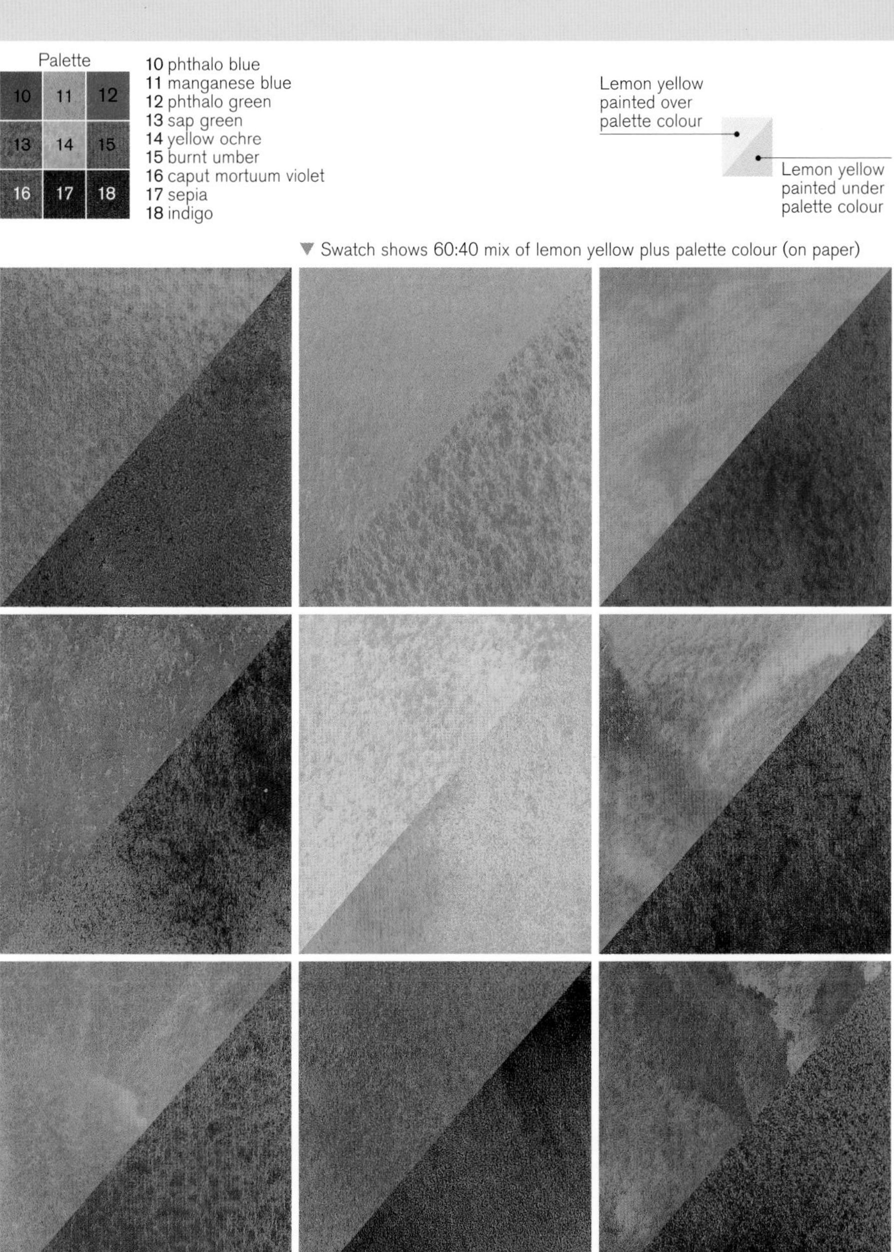

Transparent Yellow/1

Poised between cool aureolin and lemon yellows and the warmth of cadmium yellow, this colour is useful in a limited primary colour palette. The varied strengths in the wash above demonstrate its versatility: clean and acid when pale, rich and verging on ochre when strong.

▼ Swatch shows 60:40 mix of transparent yellow plus palette colour (on mixing palette)

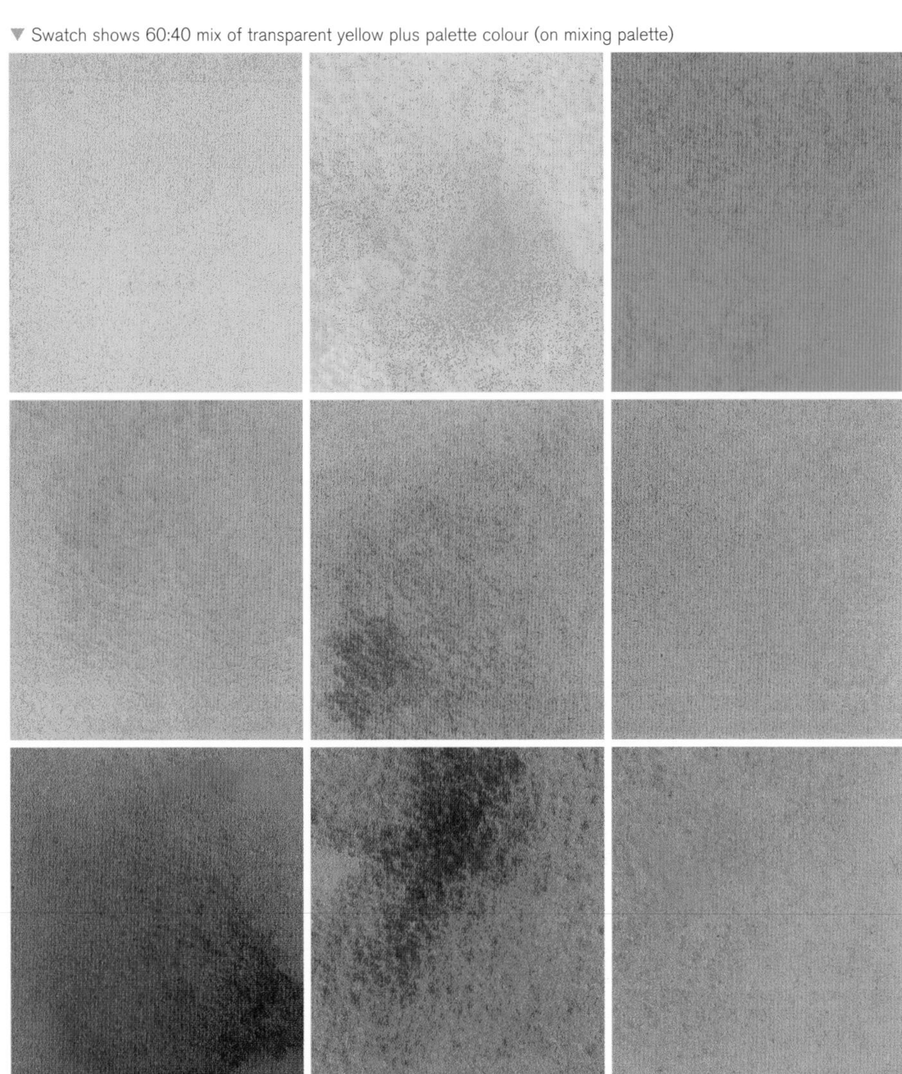

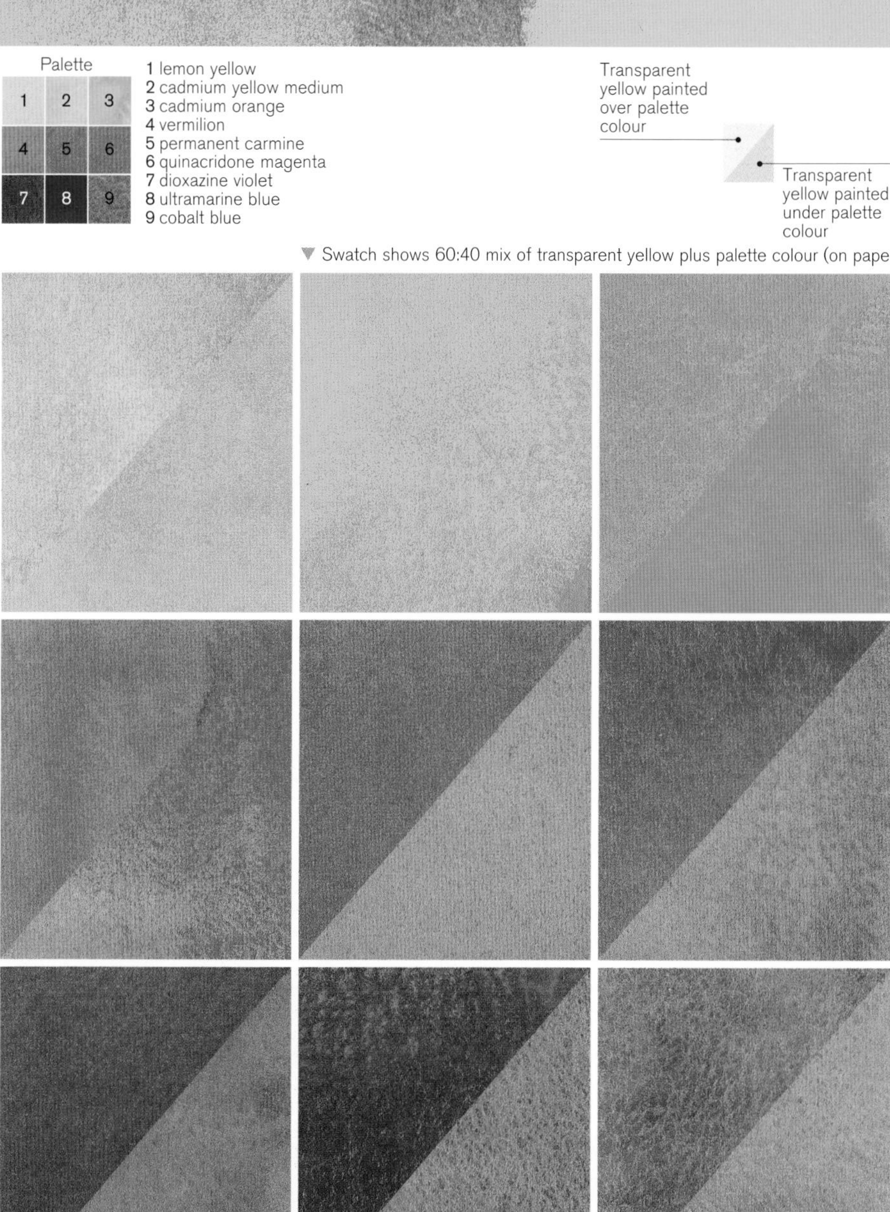

▼ Swatch shows 60:40 mix of transparent yellow plus palette colour (on paper)

Transparent Yellow/2

Transparency 4
Staining 2
Permanence 2

Granulation
as single colour 0
in mixes 0

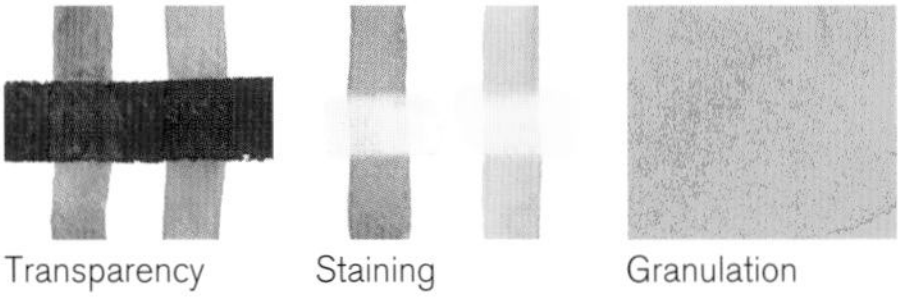

Transparency

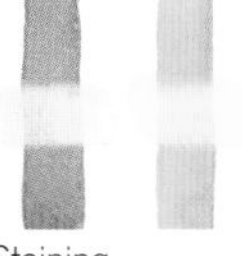

Staining

Granulation

▼ Swatch shows 60:40 mix of transparent yellow plus palette colour (on mixing palette)

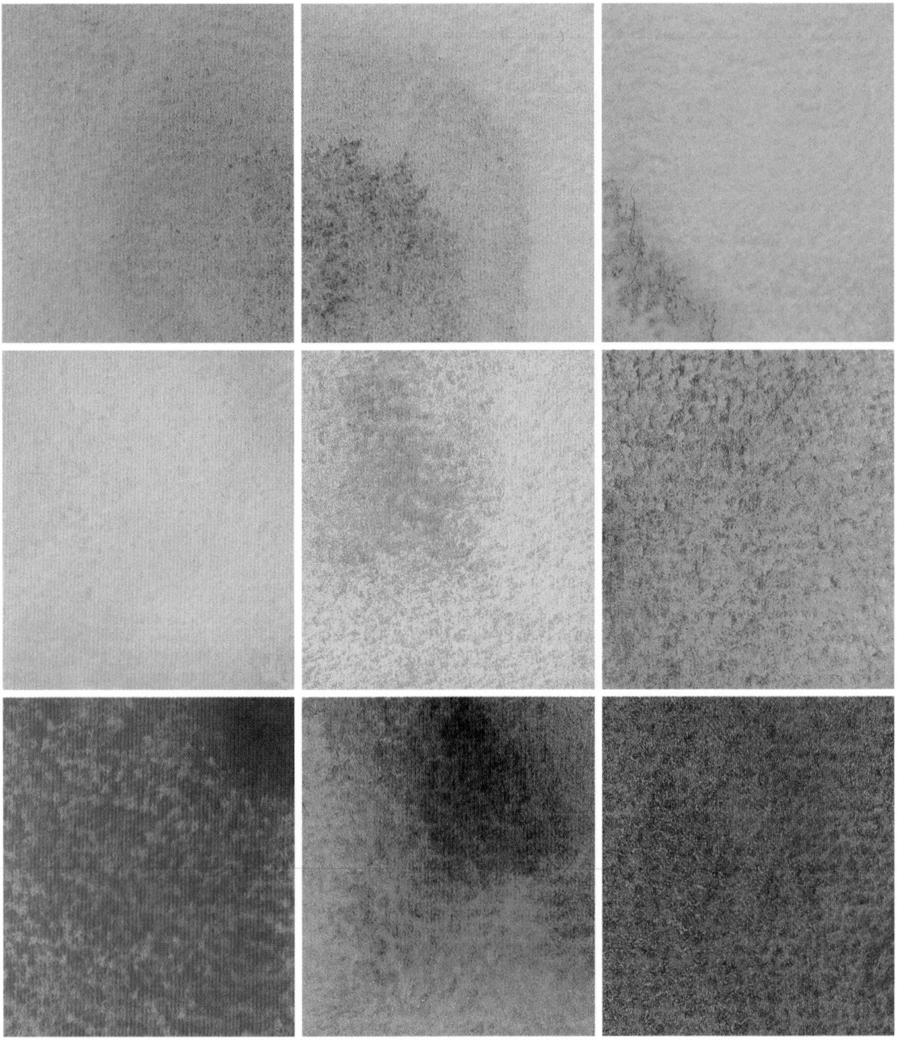

Palette

10	11	12
13	14	15
16	17	18

10 phthalo blue
11 manganese blue
12 phthalo green
13 sap green
14 yellow ochre
15 burnt umber
16 caput mortuum violet
17 sepia
18 indigo

Transparent yellow painted over palette colour

Transparent yellow painted under palette colour

▼ Swatch shows 60:40 mix of transparent yellow plus palette colour (on paper)

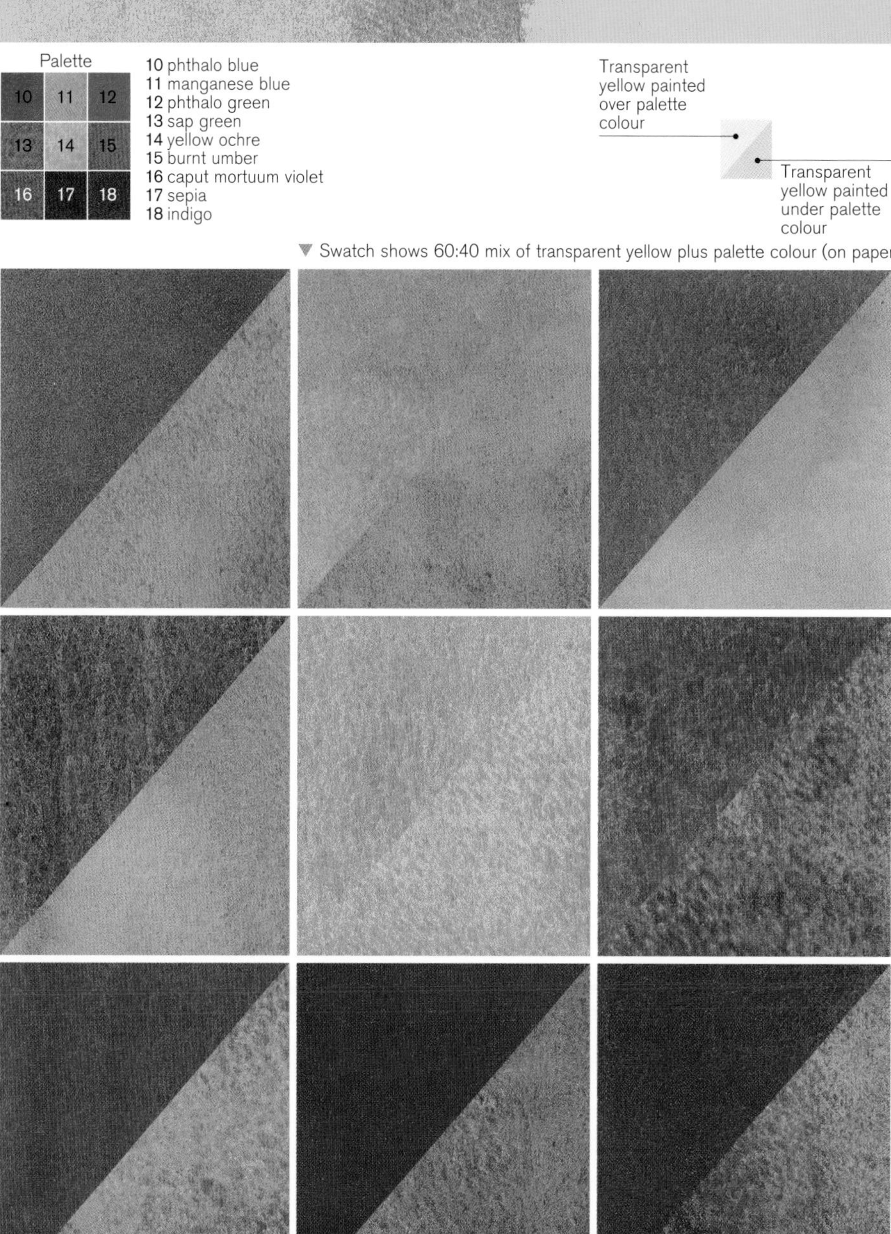

Cadmium Yellow Medium/1

An opaque yellow pigment with a warm edge, great for mixing orange hues and mossy greens. It mixes well both on a palette and in glazed layers on paper.

▼ Swatch shows 60:40 mix of cadmium yellow medium plus palette colour (on mixing palette)

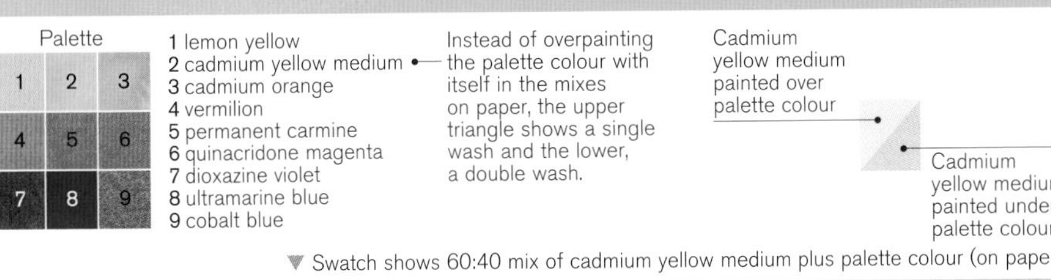

▼ Swatch shows 60:40 mix of cadmium yellow medium plus palette colour (on paper)

Cadmium Yellow Medium/2

Transparency 1
Staining 2
Permanence 2

Granulation
as single colour 0
in mixes 1

Transparency

Staining

Granulation

▼ Swatch shows 60:40 mix of cadmium yellow medium plus palette colour (on mixing palette)

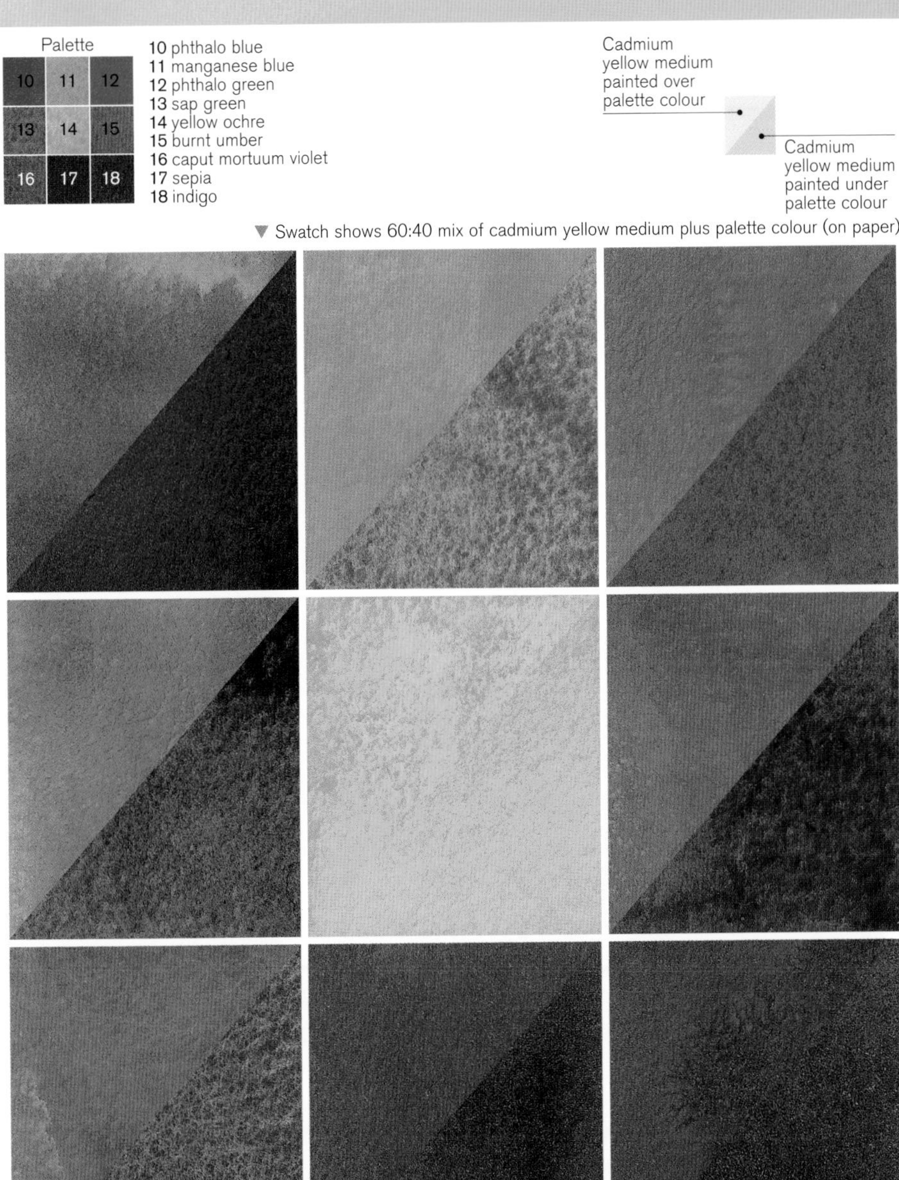

10 phthalo blue
11 manganese blue
12 phthalo green
13 sap green
14 yellow ochre
15 burnt umber
16 caput mortuum violet
17 sepia
18 indigo

▼ Swatch shows 60:40 mix of cadmium yellow medium plus palette colour (on paper)

Indian Yellow/1

A vibrant, warm, transparent yellow with a slight bias towards brown/orange when densely applied. For flat washes, use it alone or mix it with other colours on a palette. Applied directly to paper, it can become mottled, so prime paper first (see page 15).

▼ Swatch shows 60:40 mix of Indian yellow plus palette colour (on mixing palette)

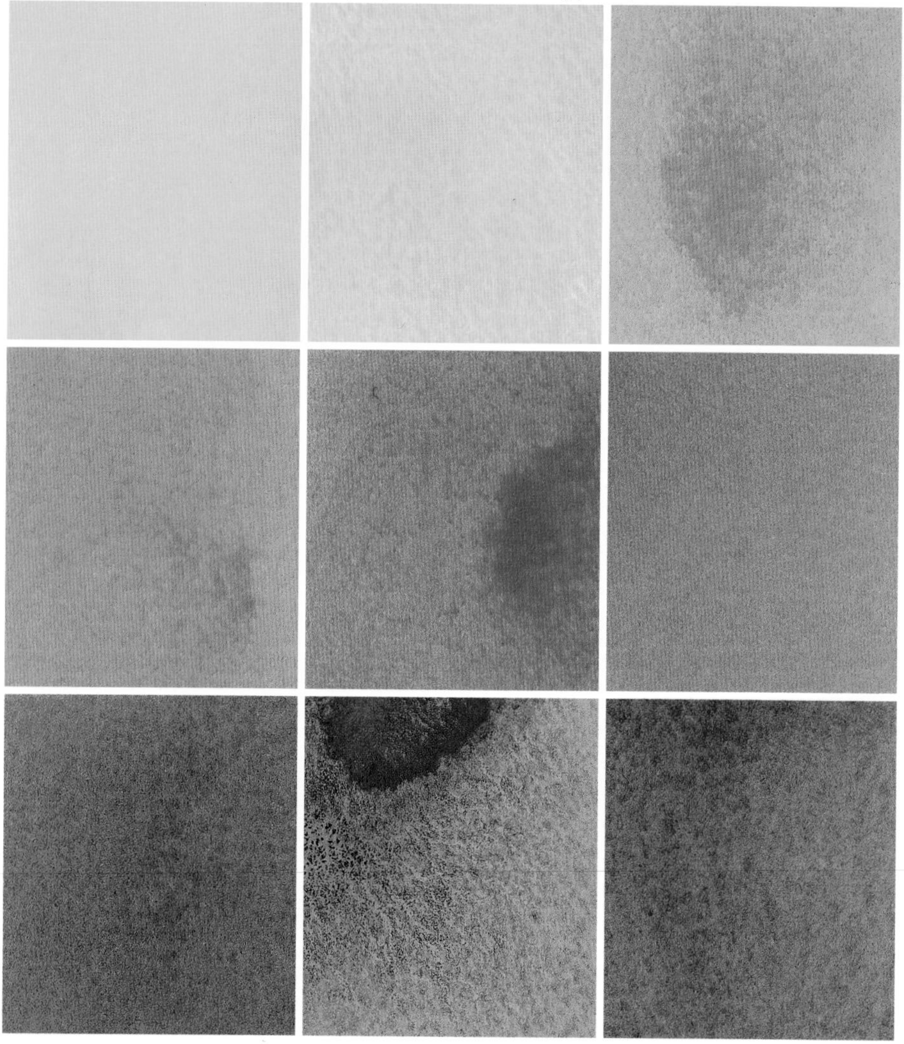

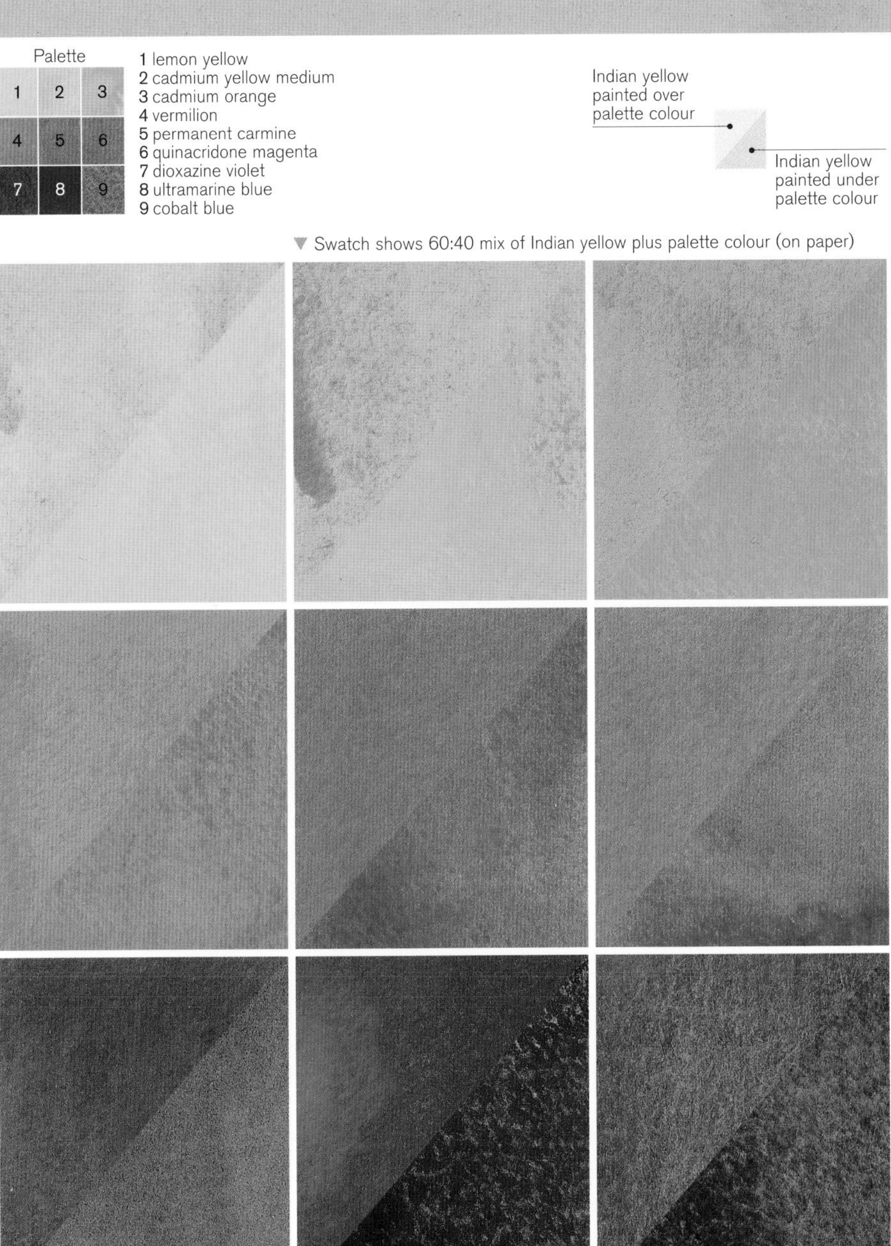

▼ Swatch shows 60:40 mix of Indian yellow plus palette colour (on paper)

Indian Yellow/2

Transparency 3/4
Staining 1
Permanence 2

Granulation
as single colour 0
in mixes 1

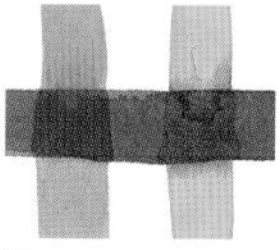
Transparency

Staining

Granulation

▼ Swatch shows 60:40 mix of Indian yellow plus palette colour (on mixing palette)

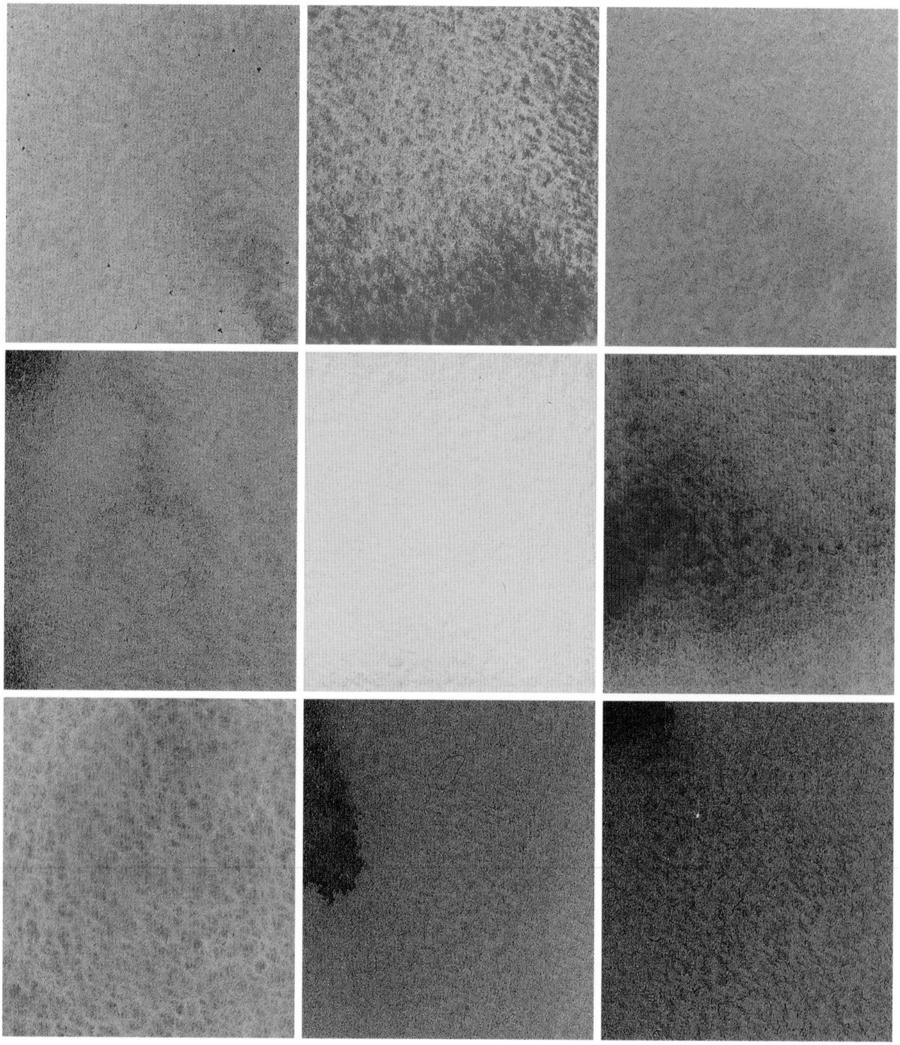

Palette

10 phthalo blue
11 manganese blue
12 phthalo green
13 sap green
14 yellow ochre
15 burnt umber
16 caput mortuum violet
17 sepia
18 indigo

Indian yellow painted over palette colour

Indian yellow painted under palette colour

▼ Swatch shows 60:40 mix of Indian yellow plus palette colour (on paper)

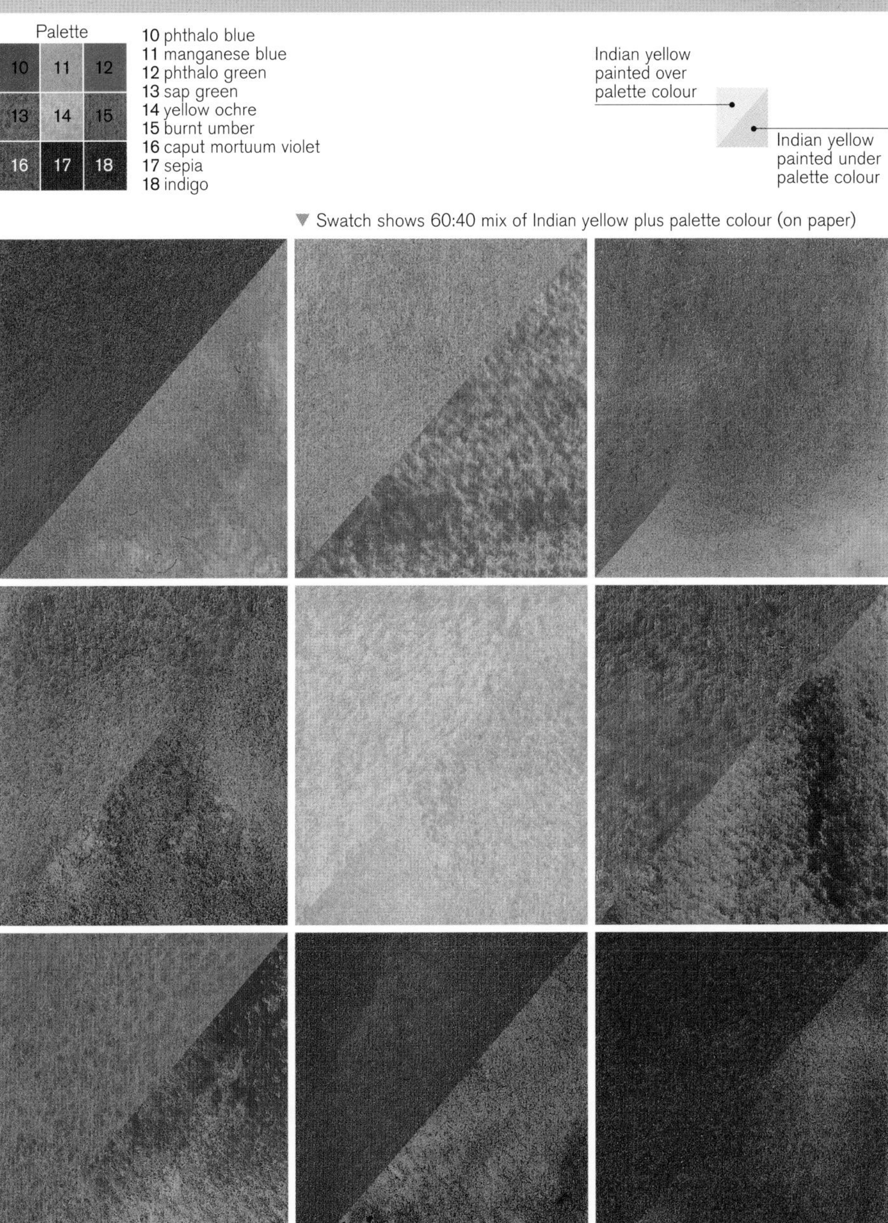

Naples Yellow/1

A soft, warm, opaque yellow/orange with a hint of white. It combines with other colours to make some beautiful muted hues. Note that it can be slightly blotchy when used in wet-on-dry mixes on paper.

▼ Swatch shows 60:40 mix of Naples yellow plus palette colour (on mixing palette)

Palette

1	2	3
4	5	6
7	8	9

1 lemon yellow
2 cadmium yellow medium
3 cadmium orange
4 vermilion
5 permanent carmine
6 quinacridone magenta
7 dioxazine violet
8 ultramarine blue
9 cobalt blue

Naples yellow painted over palette colour

Naples yellow painted under palette colour

▼ Swatch shows 60:40 mix of Naples yellow plus palette colour (on paper)

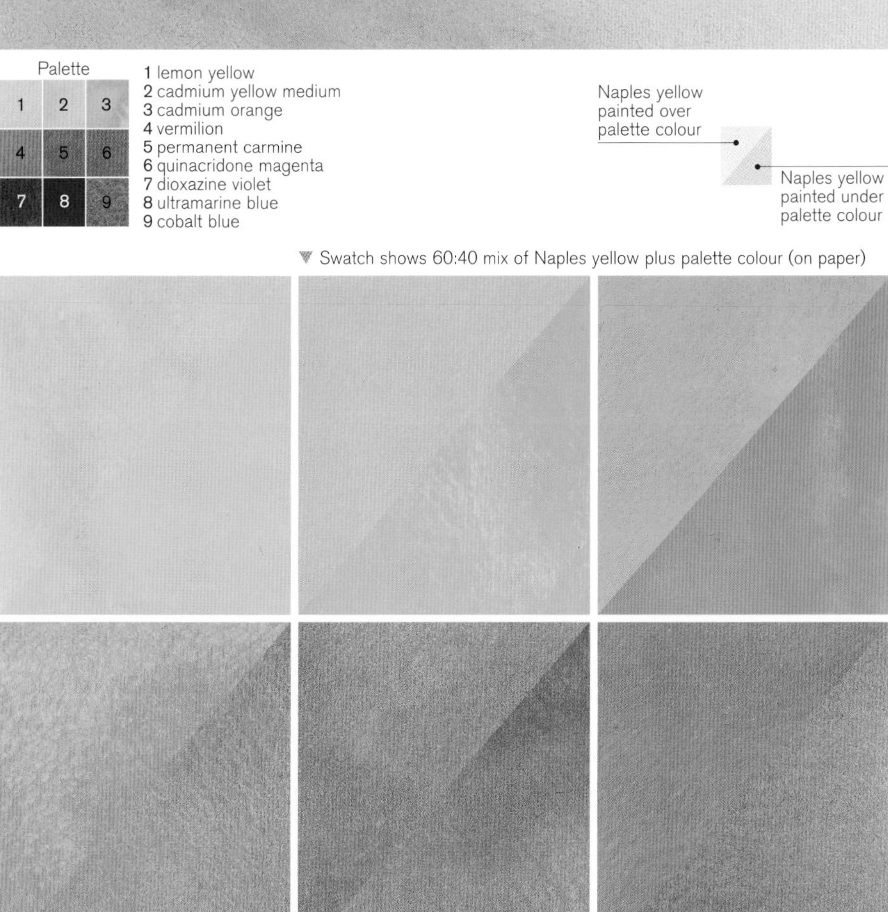

Naples Yellow/2

Transparency 1
Staining 0
Permanence 3

Granulation
as single colour 0
in mixes 1

Transparency

Staining

Granulation

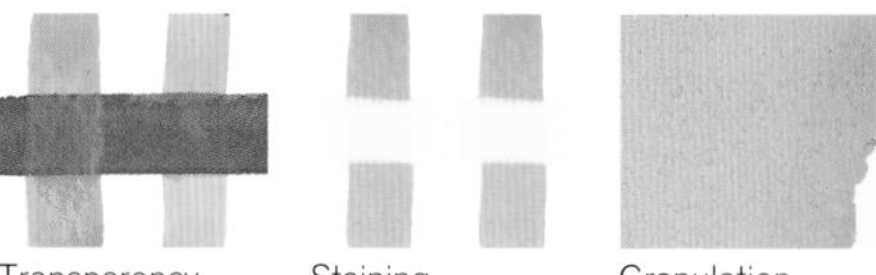

▼ Swatch shows 60:40 mix of Naples yellow plus palette colour (on mixing palette)

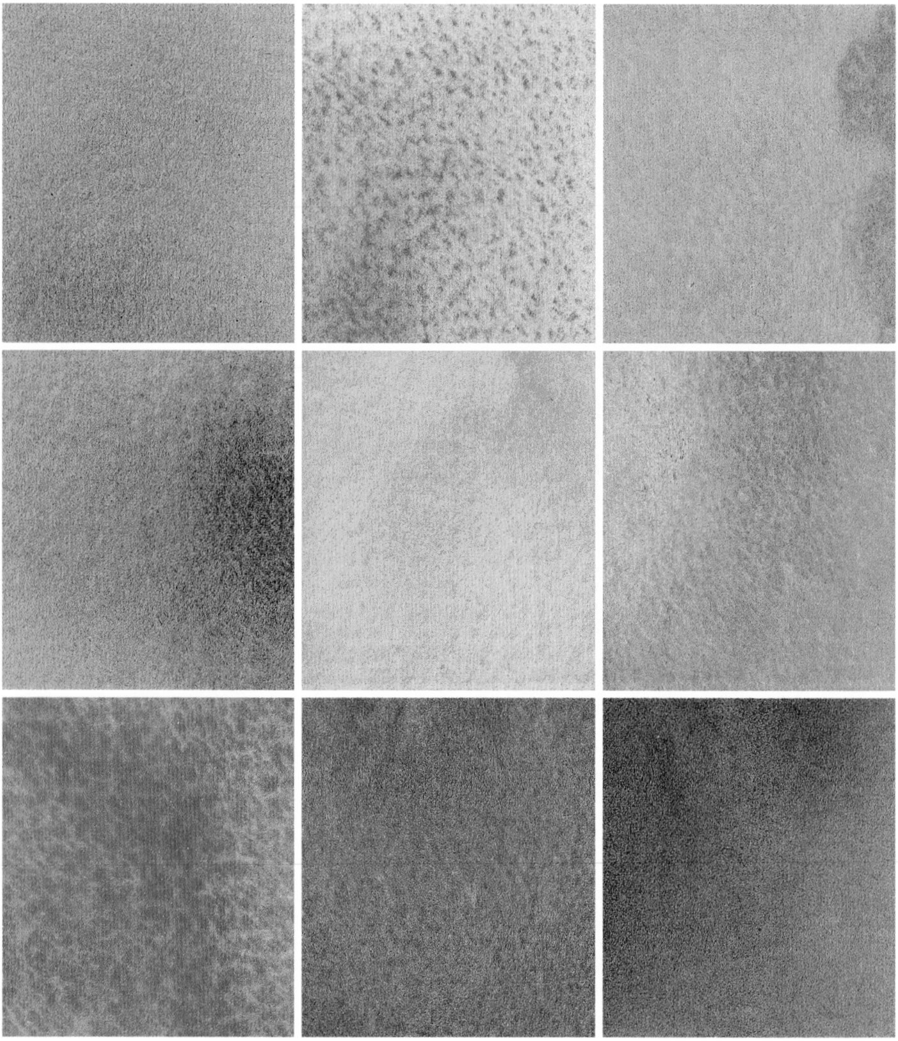

Palette

10	11	12
13	14	15
16	17	18

10 phthalo blue
11 manganese blue
12 phthalo green
13 sap green
14 yellow ochre
15 burnt umber
16 caput mortuum violet
17 sepia
18 indigo

Naples yellow painted over palette colour

Naples yellow painted under palette colour

▼ Swatch shows 60:40 mix of Naples yellow plus palette colour (on paper)

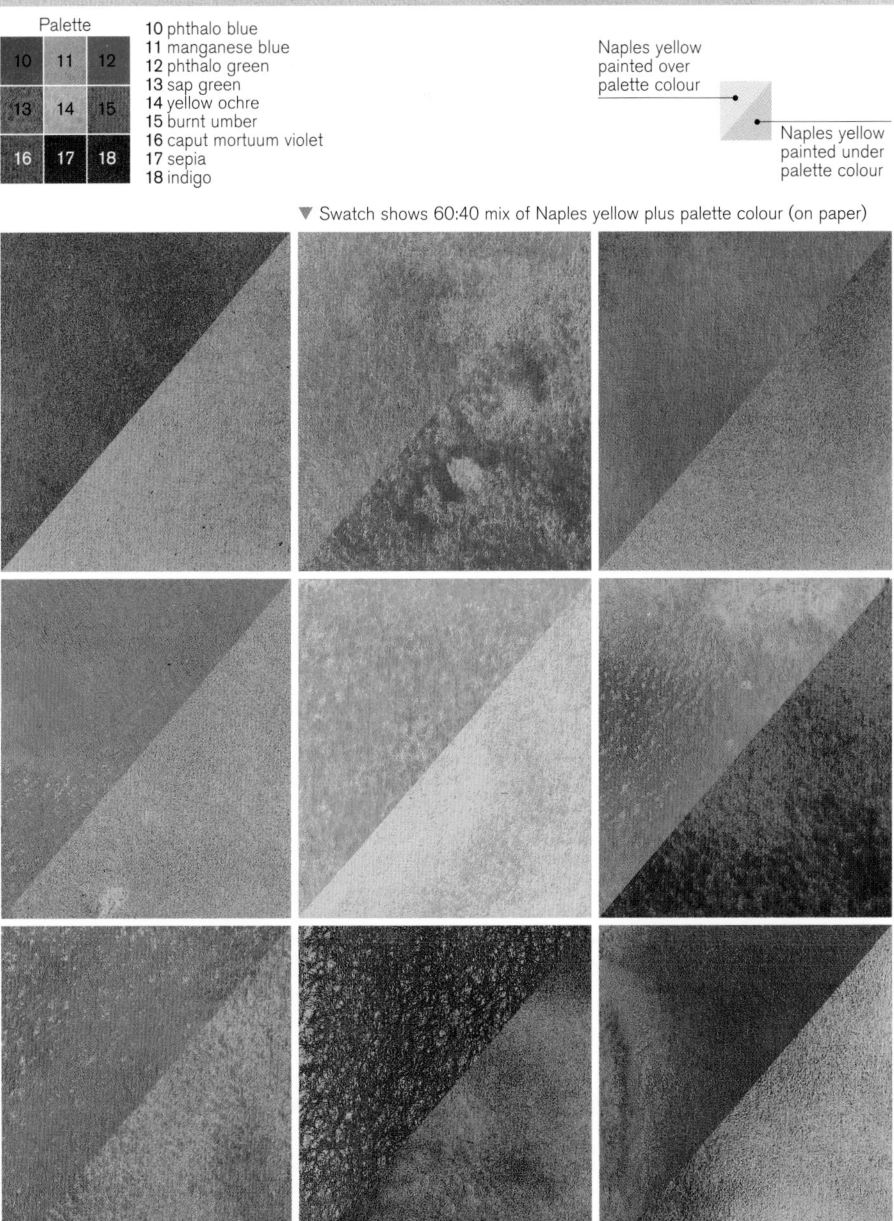

Cadmium Orange/1

An opaque orange that dominates other colours when mixed on a palette. Applied in layers, it creates some beautiful textures and depth (see the mix with manganese blue on page 71).

▼ Swatch shows 60:40 mix of cadmium orange plus palette colour (on mixing palette)

Palette

1 lemon yellow
2 cadmium yellow medium
3 cadmium orange
4 vermilion
5 permanent carmine
6 quinacridone magenta
7 dioxazine violet
8 ultramarine blue
9 cobalt blue

Instead of overpainting the palette colour with itself in the mixes on paper, the upper triangle shows a single wash and the lower, a double wash.

Cadmium orange painted over palette colour

Cadmium orange painted under palette colour

▼ Swatch shows 60:40 mix of cadmium orange plus palette colour (on paper)

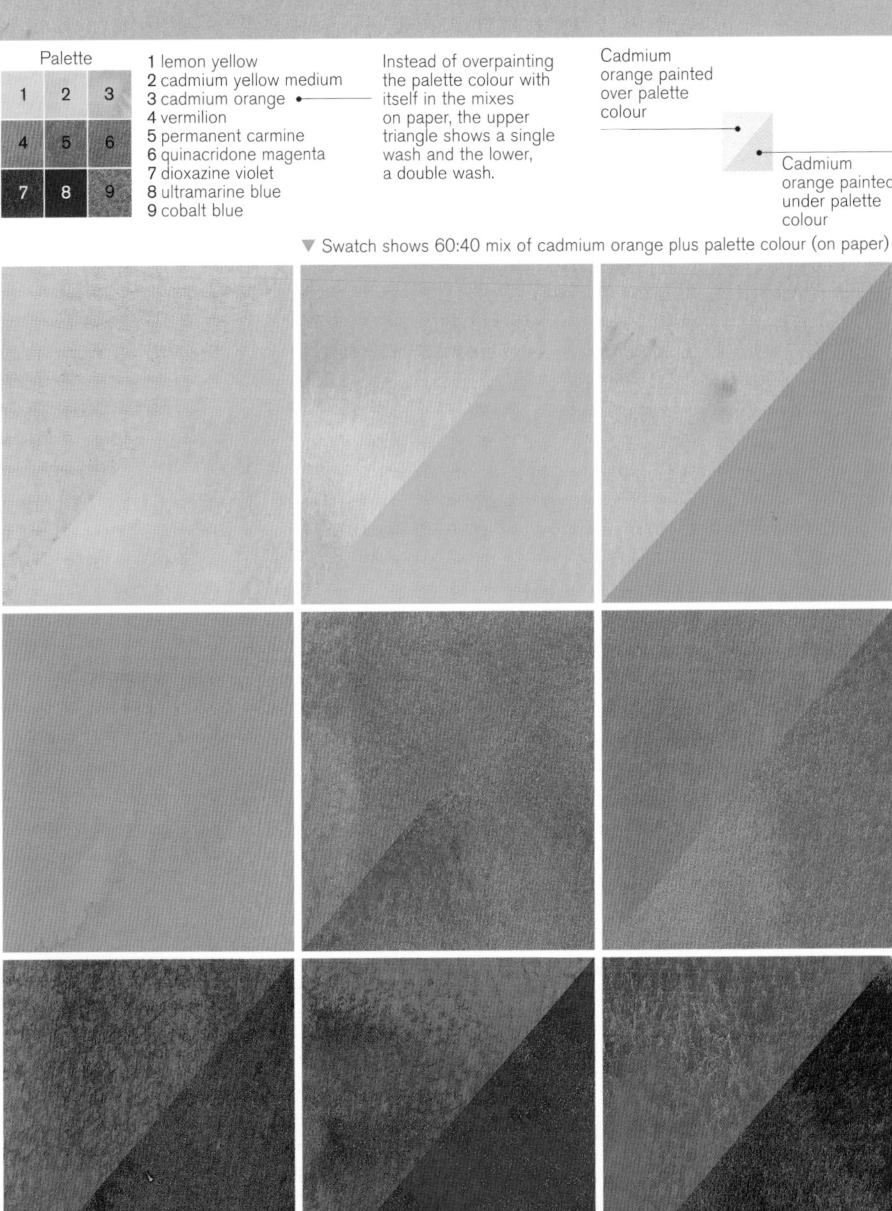

Cadmium Orange/2

Transparency 1
Staining 1
Permanence 2

Granulation
as single colour 0
in mixes 1

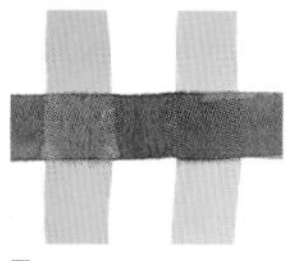
Transparency

Staining

Granulation

▼ Swatch shows 60:40 mix of cadmium orange plus palette colour (on mixing palette)

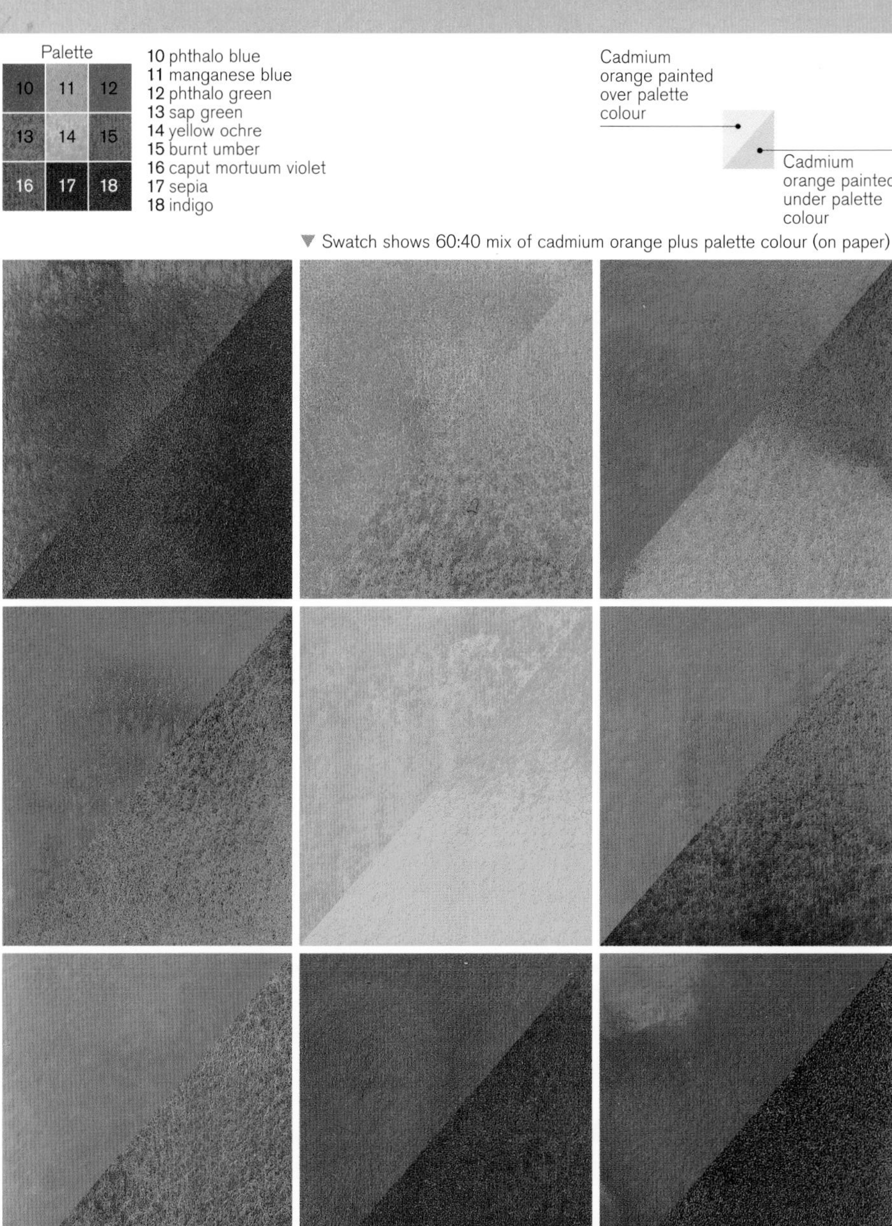

10 phthalo blue
11 manganese blue
12 phthalo green
13 sap green
14 yellow ochre
15 burnt umber
16 caput mortuum violet
17 sepia
18 indigo

▼ Swatch shows 60:40 mix of cadmium orange plus palette colour (on paper)

Vermilion/1

A red with a touch of yellow, vermilion is similar to cadmium red, but slightly less opaque. It creates flatter, non-granulating washes. When mixed with different blues, this pigment makes warm, neutral mixes and is useful for lively shadow colours.

▼ Swatch shows 60:40 mix of vermilion plus palette colour (on mixing palette)

Palette

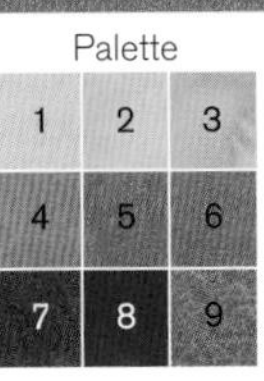

1 lemon yellow
2 cadmium yellow medium
3 cadmium orange
4 vermilion
5 permanent carmine
6 quinacridone magenta
7 dioxazine violet
8 ultramarine blue
9 cobalt blue

Instead of overpainting the palette colour with itself in the mixes on paper, the upper triangle shows a single wash and the lower, a double wash.

Vermilion painted over palette colour

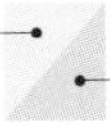

Vermilion painted under palette colour

▼ Swatch shows 60:40 mix of vermilion plus palette colour (on paper)

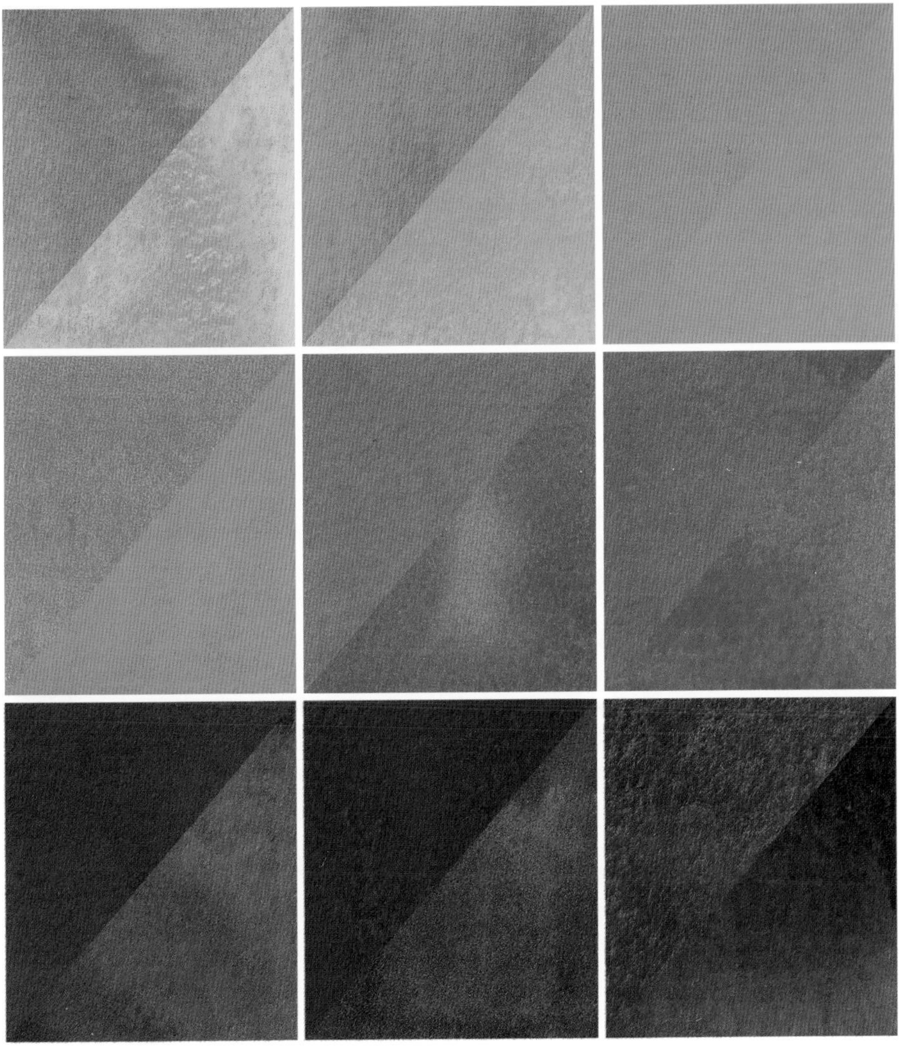

Vermilion/2

Transparency 4
Staining 3
Permanence 3

Granulation
as single colour 0
in mixes 0

Transparency

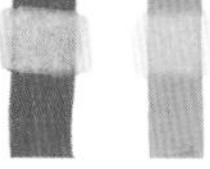
Staining

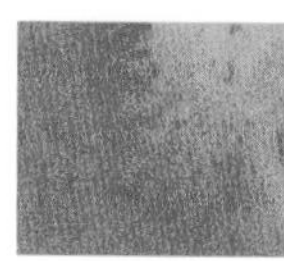
Granulation

▼ Swatch shows 60:40 mix of vermilion plus palette colour (on mixing palette)

Palette

10	11	12
13	14	15
16	17	18

10 phthalo blue
11 manganese blue
12 phthalo green
13 sap green
14 yellow ochre
15 burnt umber
16 caput mortuum violet
17 sepia
18 indigo

Vermilion painted over palette colour

Vermilion painted under palette colour

▼ Swatch shows 60:40 mix of vermilion plus palette colour (on paper)

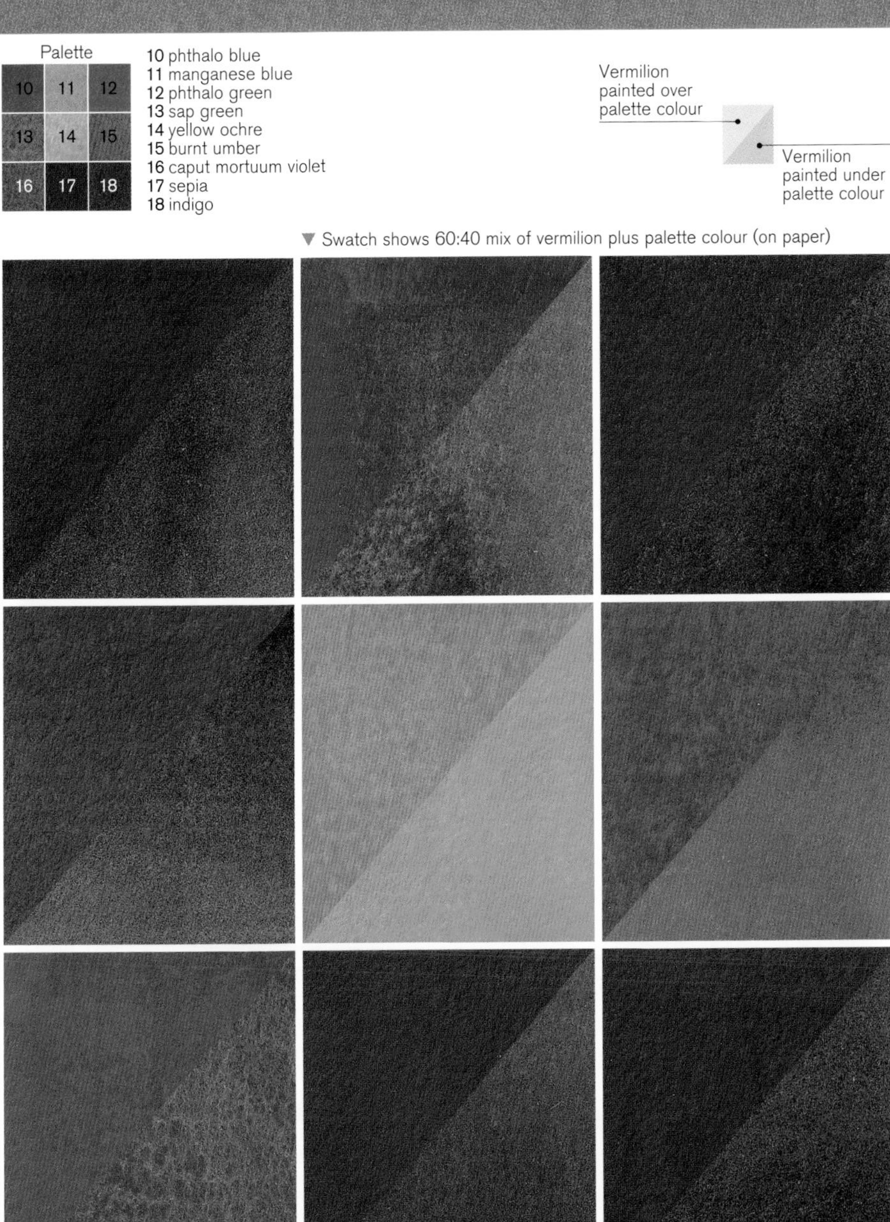

Cadmium Red Medium/1

An opaque red with a touch of yellow, this is slightly darker than vermilion and will granulate both in palette mixes and in glazed layers. Dark, medium and light versions are available.

▼ Swatch shows 60:40 mix of cadmium red medium plus palette colour (on mixing palette)

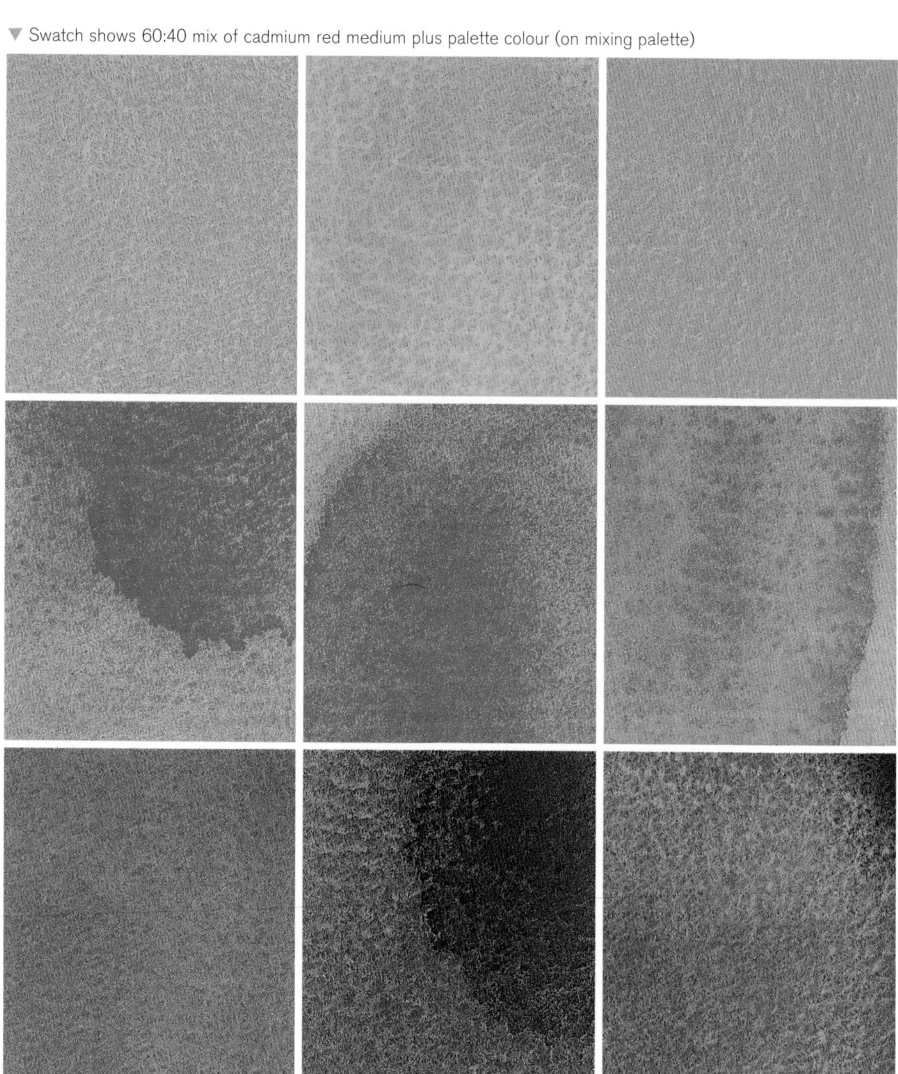

Palette

1	2	3
4	5	6
7	8	9

1 lemon yellow
2 cadmium yellow medium
3 cadmium orange
4 vermilion
5 permanent carmine
6 quinacridone magenta
7 dioxazine violet
8 ultramarine blue
9 cobalt blue

Cadmium red medium painted over palette colour

Cadmium red medium painted under palette colour

▼ Swatch shows 60:40 mix of cadmium red medium plus palette colour (on paper)

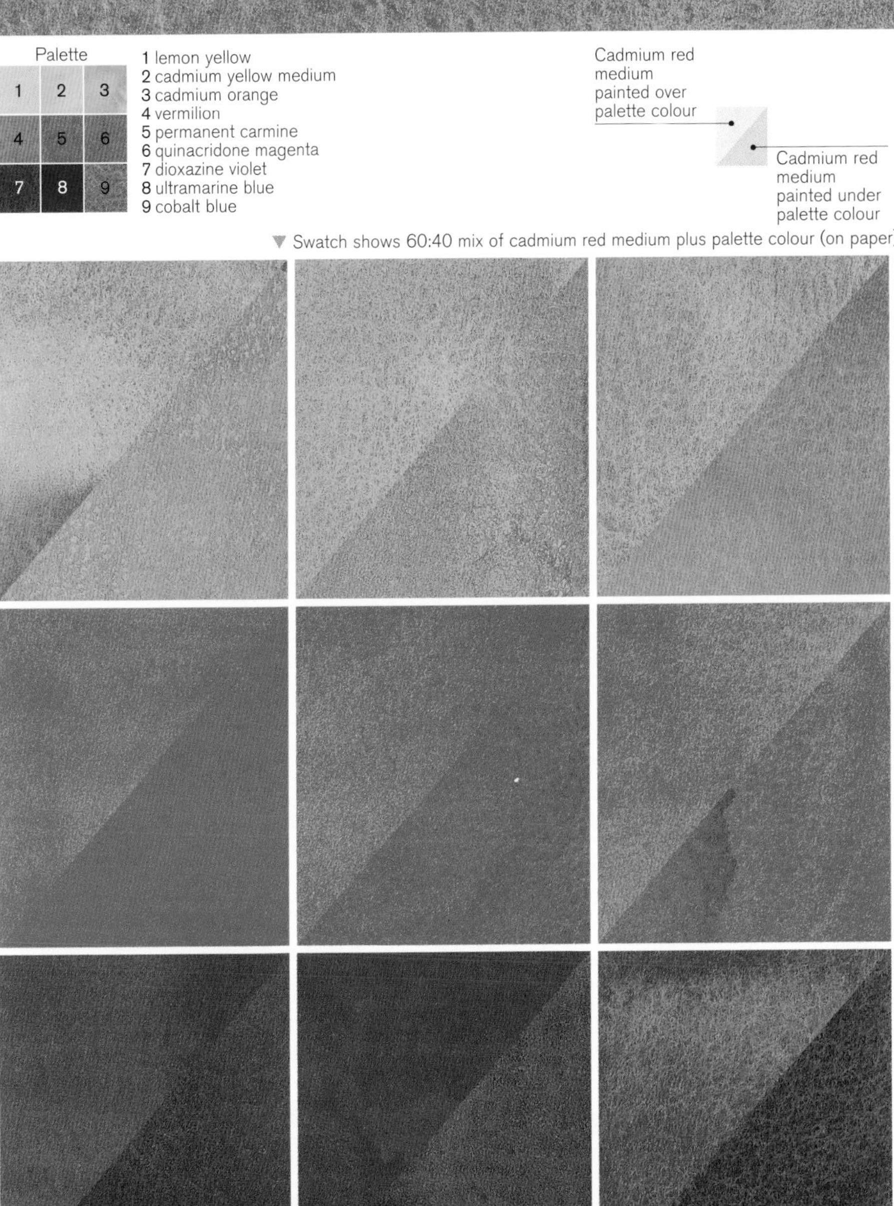

Cadmium Red Medium/2

Transparency 1
Staining 3
Permanence 2

Granulation
as single colour 3
in mixes 3

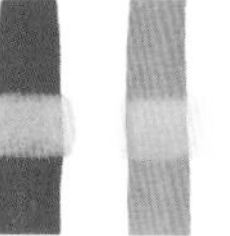
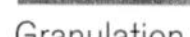

Transparency Staining Granulation

▼ Swatch shows 60:40 mix of cadmium red medium plus palette colour (on mixing palette)

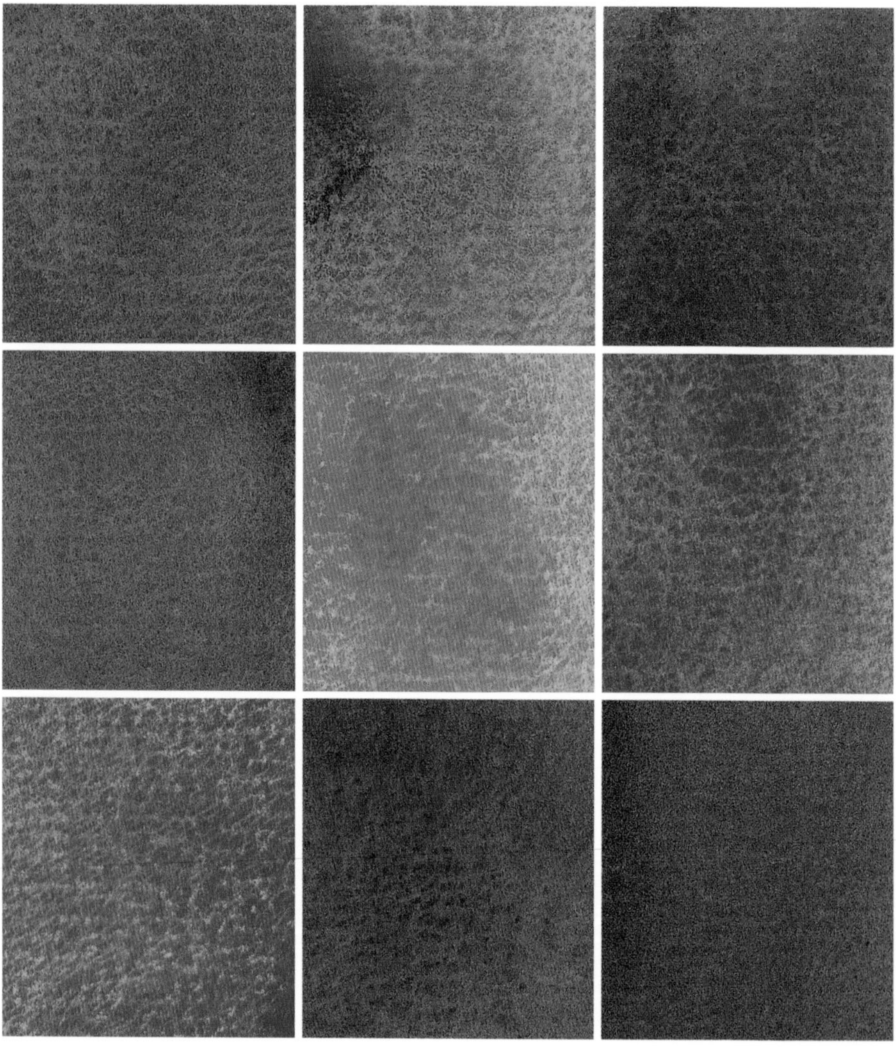

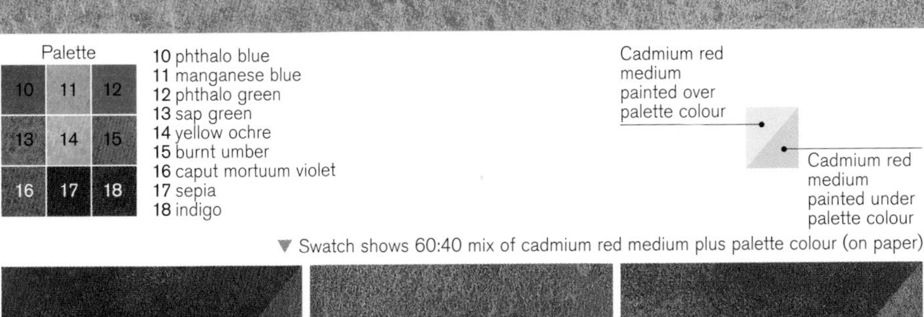

10 phthalo blue
11 manganese blue
12 phthalo green
13 sap green
14 yellow ochre
15 burnt umber
16 caput mortuum violet
17 sepia
18 indigo

Cadmium red medium painted over palette colour

Cadmium red medium painted under palette colour

▼ Swatch shows 60:40 mix of cadmium red medium plus palette colour (on paper)

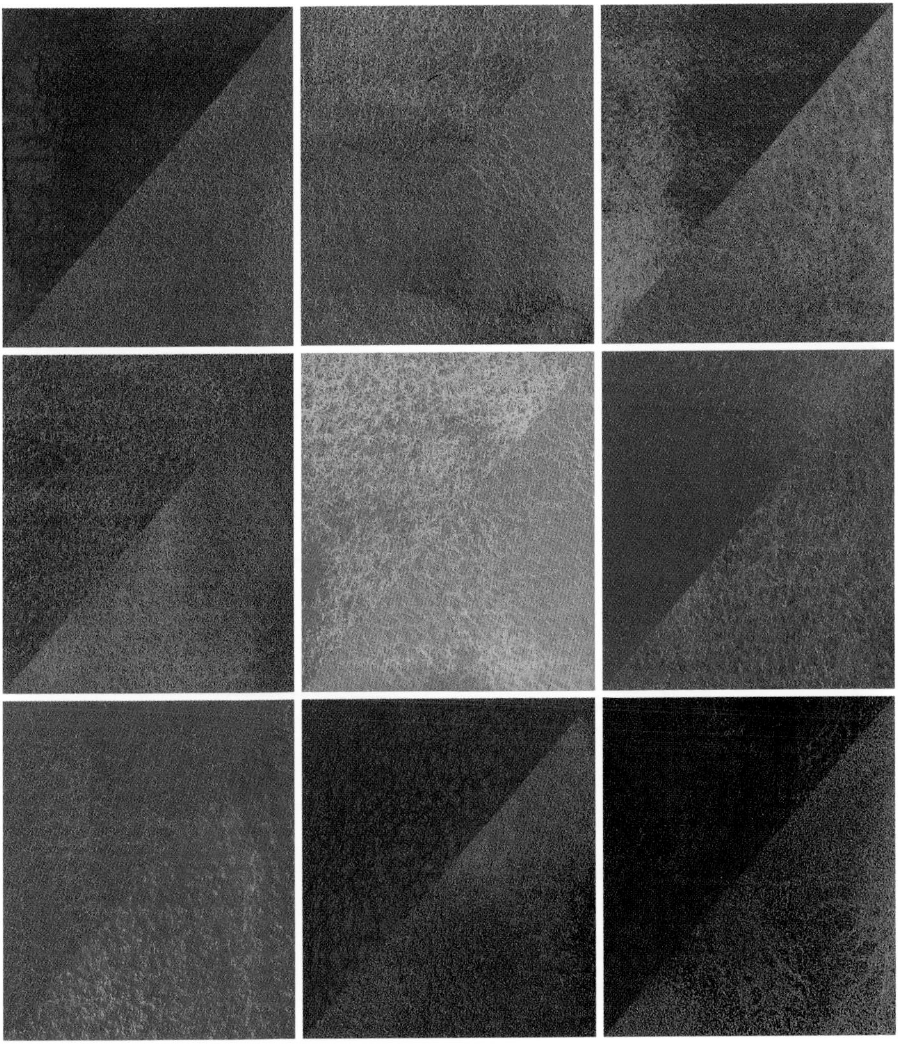

Quinacridone Coral/1

A very transparent staining red with a cool tinge in pale washes and a warmer hue in stronger washes (as seen in the strip above). This duality means it mixes well with both yellows and blues to make bright oranges and purples respectively.

▼ Swatch shows 60:40 mix of quinacridone coral plus palette colour (on mixing palette)

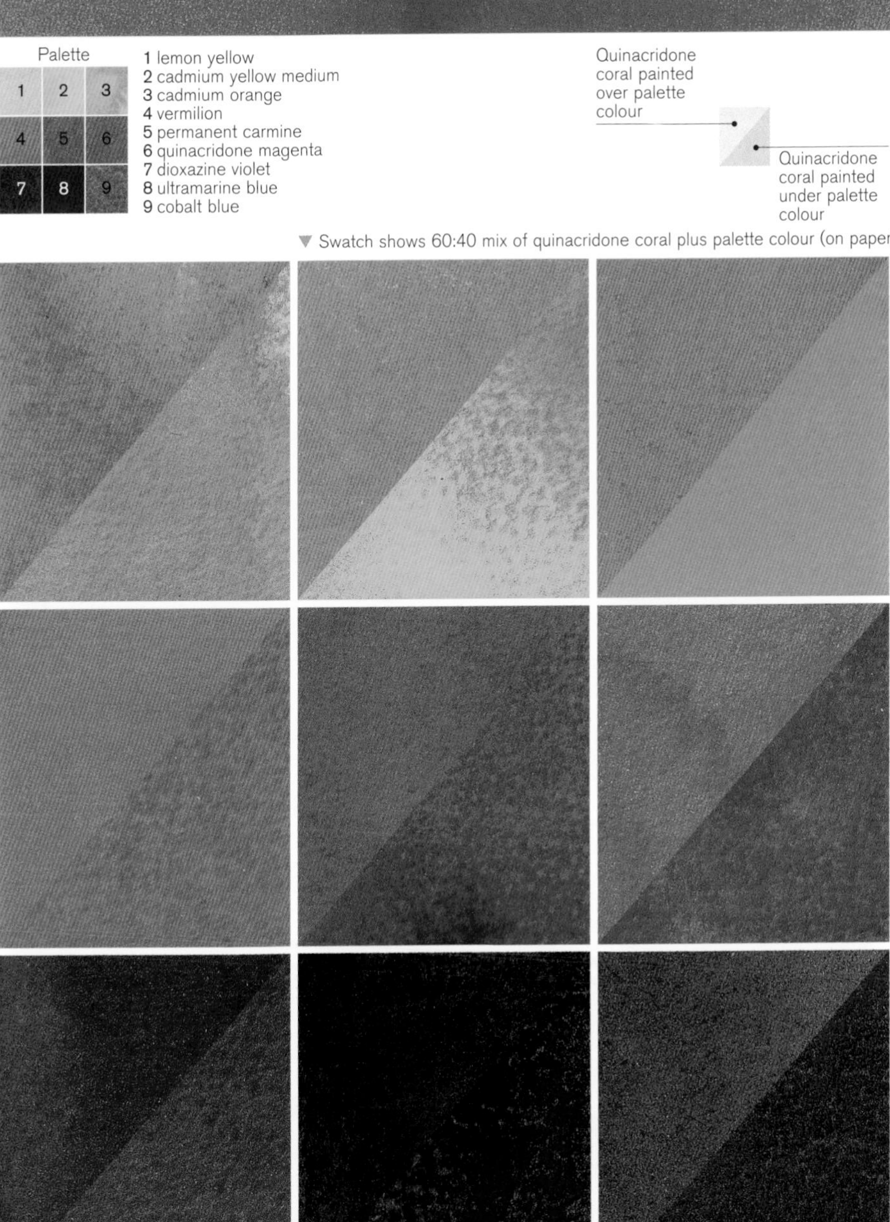
Palette
1
2
3
4
5
6
7
8
9
1 lemon yellow
2 cadmium yellow medium
3 cadmium orange
4 vermilion
5 permanent carmine
6 quinacridone magenta
7 dioxazine violet
8 ultramarine blue
9 cobalt blue
Quinacridone coral painted over palette colour
Quinacridone coral painted under palette colour
▼ Swatch shows 60:40 mix of quinacridone coral plus palette colour (on paper)

Quinacridone Coral/2

Transparency 4
Staining 3
Permanence 3

Granulation
as single colour 0
in mixes 1

Transparency

Staining

Granulation

▼ Swatch shows 60:40 mix of quinacridone coral plus palette colour (on mixing palette)

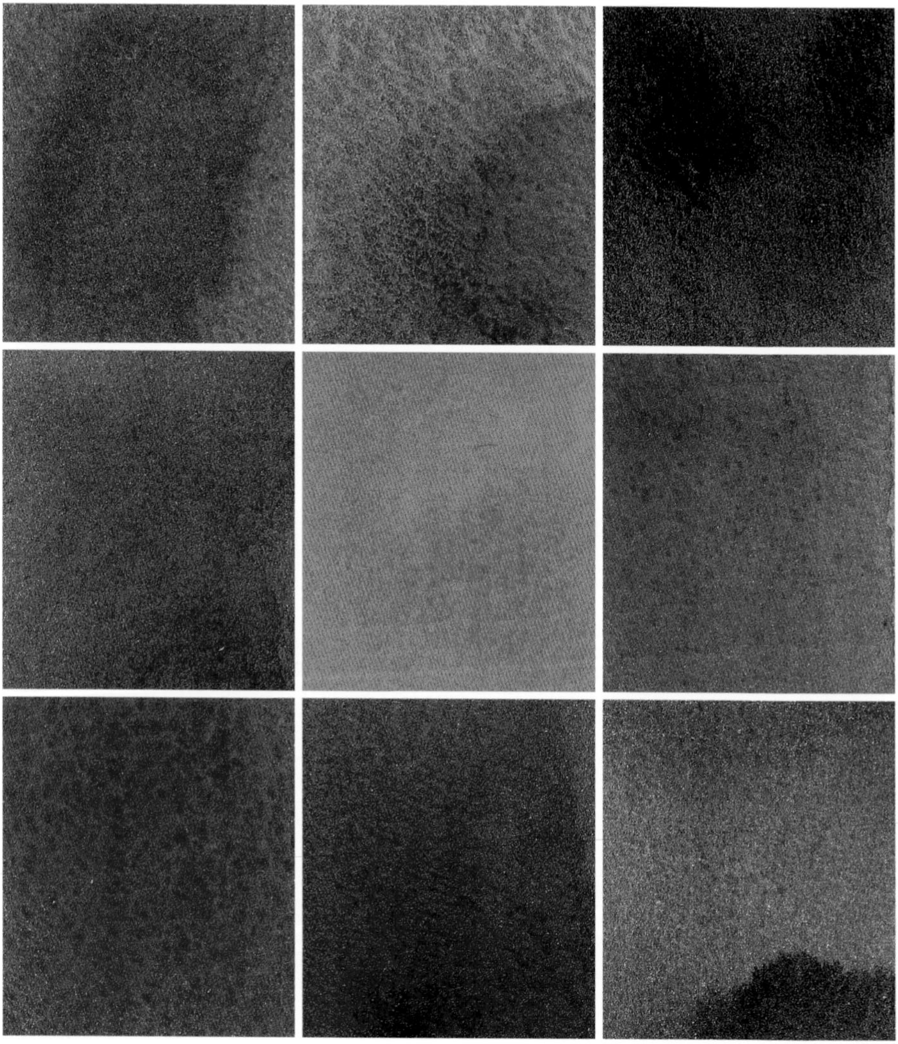

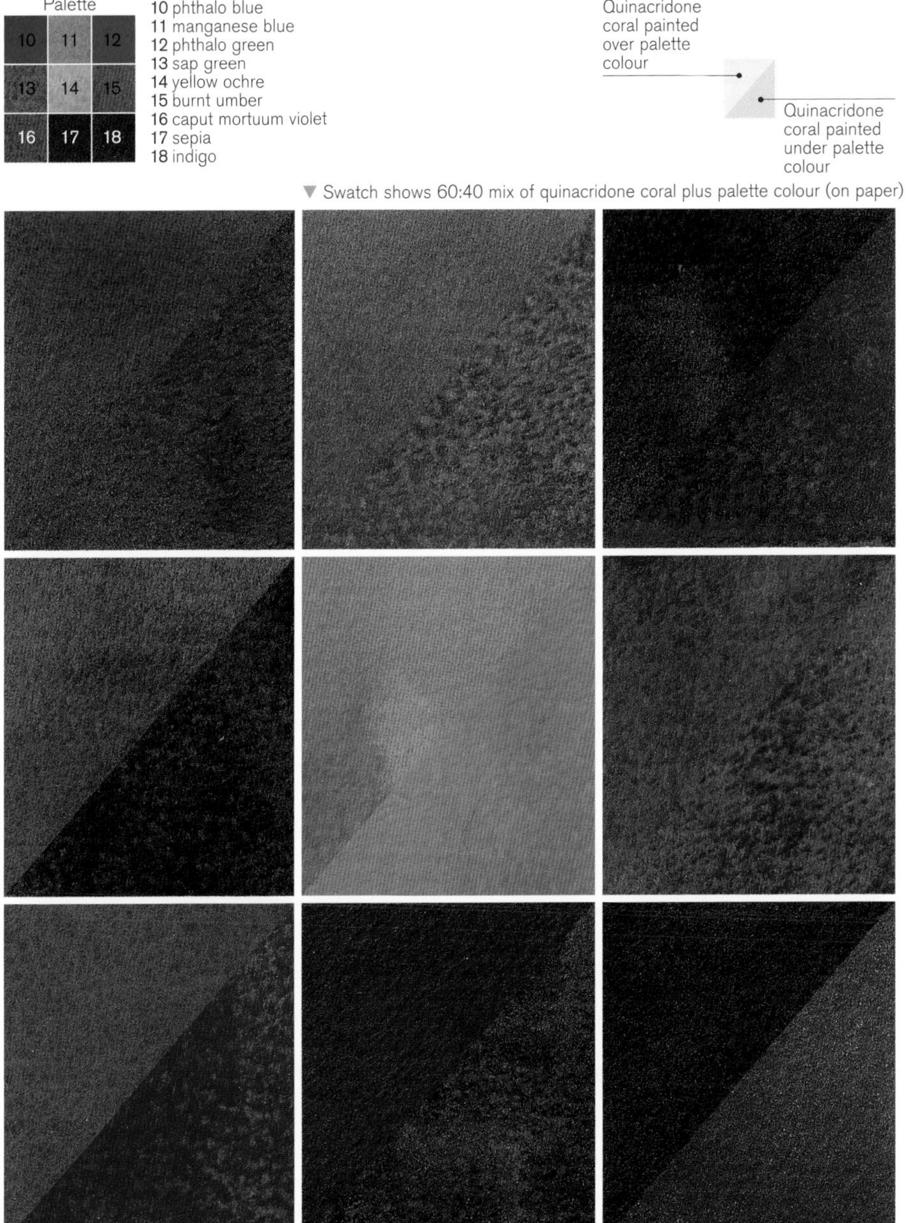

10 phthalo blue
11 manganese blue
12 phthalo green
13 sap green
14 yellow ochre
15 burnt umber
16 caput mortuum violet
17 sepia
18 indigo

Quinacridone coral painted over palette colour

Quinacridone coral painted under palette colour

▼ Swatch shows 60:40 mix of quinacridone coral plus palette colour (on paper)

Permanent Carmine/1

A semi-transparent red with a touch of blue, this pigment mixes well both on a palette and on paper. The blue bias facilitates good violet colours when mixed with cobalt or ultramarine blue.

▼ Swatch shows 60:40 mix of permanent carmine plus palette colour (on mixing palette)

Palette

1	2	3
4	5	6
7	8	9

1 lemon yellow
2 cadmium yellow medium
3 cadmium orange
4 vermilion
5 permanent carmine
6 quinacridone magenta
7 dioxazine violet
8 ultramarine blue
9 cobalt blue

Instead of overpainting the palette colour with itself in the mixes on paper, the upper triangle shows a single wash and the lower, a double wash.

Permanent carmine painted over palette colour

Permanent carmine painted under palette colour

▼ Swatch shows 60:40 mix of permanent carmine plus palette colour (on paper)

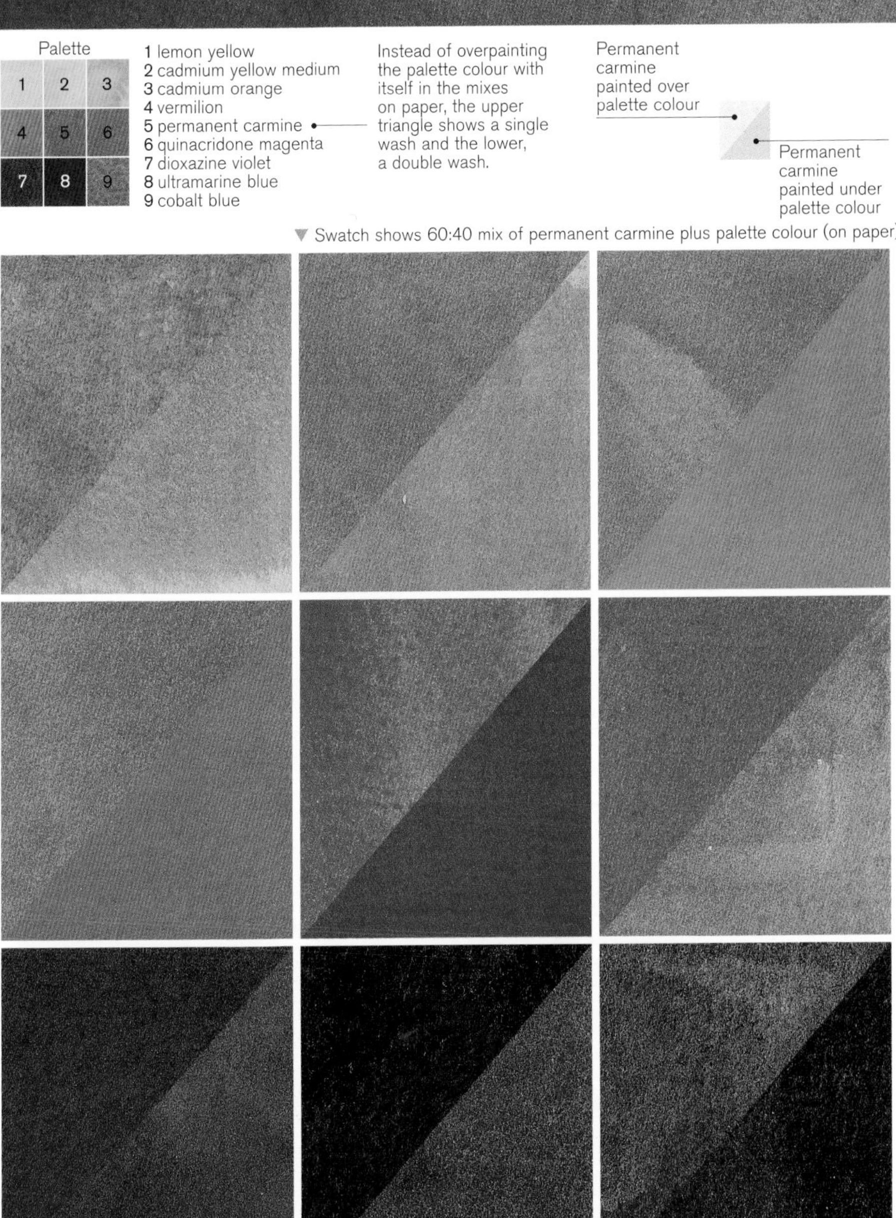

Permanent Carmine/2

Transparency 3
Staining 3
Permanence 2

Granulation
as single colour 0
in mixes 1

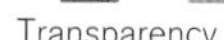

Transparency Staining Granulation

▼ Swatch shows 60:40 mix of permanent carmine plus palette colour (on mixing palette)

Palette

10	11	12
13	14	15
16	17	18

10 phthalo blue
11 manganese blue
12 phthalo green
13 sap green
14 yellow ochre
15 burnt umber
16 caput mortuum violet
17 sepia
18 indigo

Permanent carmine painted over palette colour

Permanent carmine painted under palette colour

▼ Swatch shows 60:40 mix of permanent carmine plus palette colour (on paper)

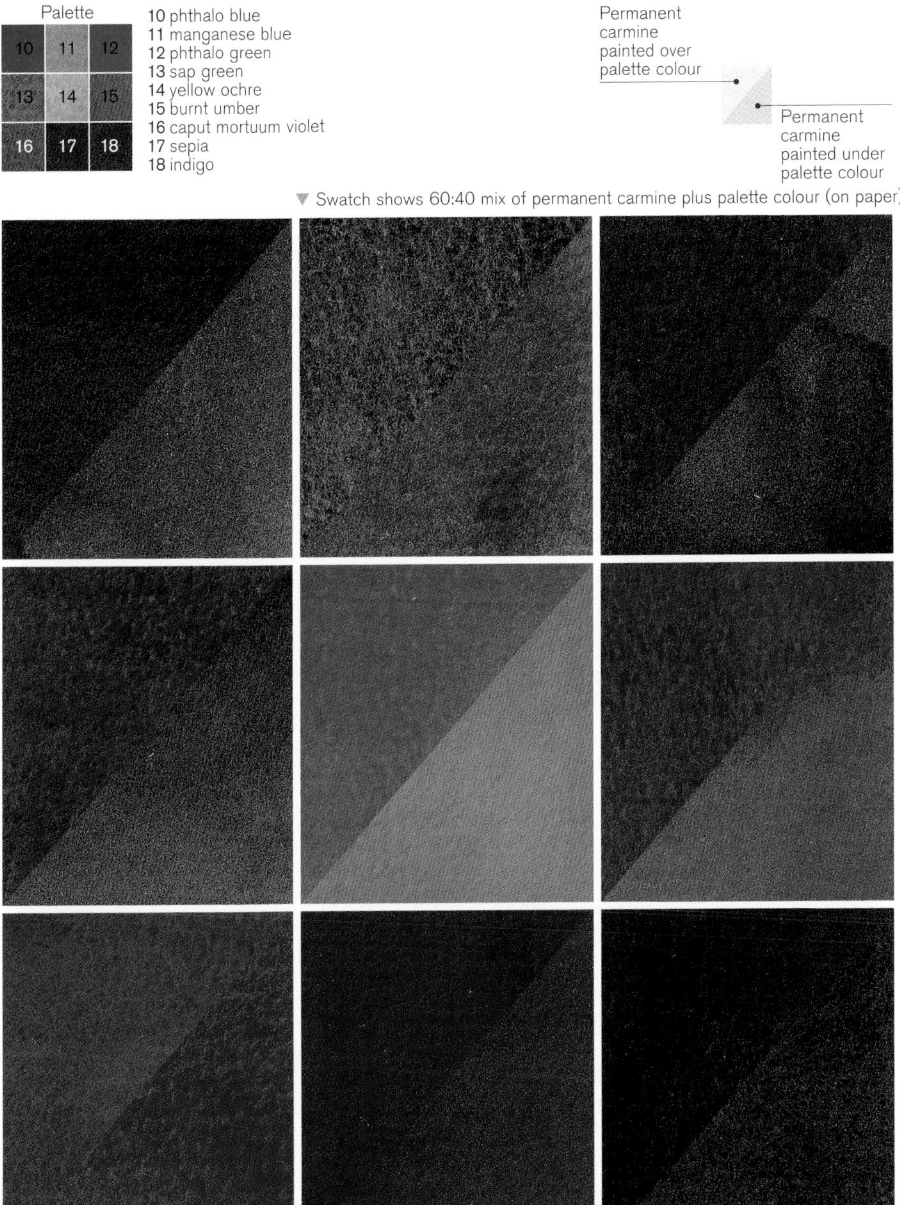

Quinacridone Red/1

A strong transparent red with a cool bias, this is a good alternative to the less permanent but popular alizarin crimson. (The quinacridone pigment is used by some manufacturers in the production of permanent alizarin crimson.)

▼ Swatch shows 60:40 mix of quinacridone red plus palette colour (on mixing palette)

Palette

1	2	3
4	5	6
7	8	9

1 lemon yellow
2 cadmium yellow medium
3 cadmium orange
4 vermilion
5 permanent carmine
6 quinacridone magenta
7 dioxazine violet
8 ultramarine blue
9 cobalt blue

Quinacridone red painted over palette colour

Quinacridone red painted under palette colour

▼ Swatch shows 60:40 mix of quinacridone red plus palette colour (on paper)

Quinacridone Red/2

Transparency 4
Staining 3
Permanence 3

Granulation
as single colour 0
in mixes 1

Transparency

Staining

Granulation

▼ Swatch shows 60:40 mix of quinacridone red plus palette colour (on mixing palette)

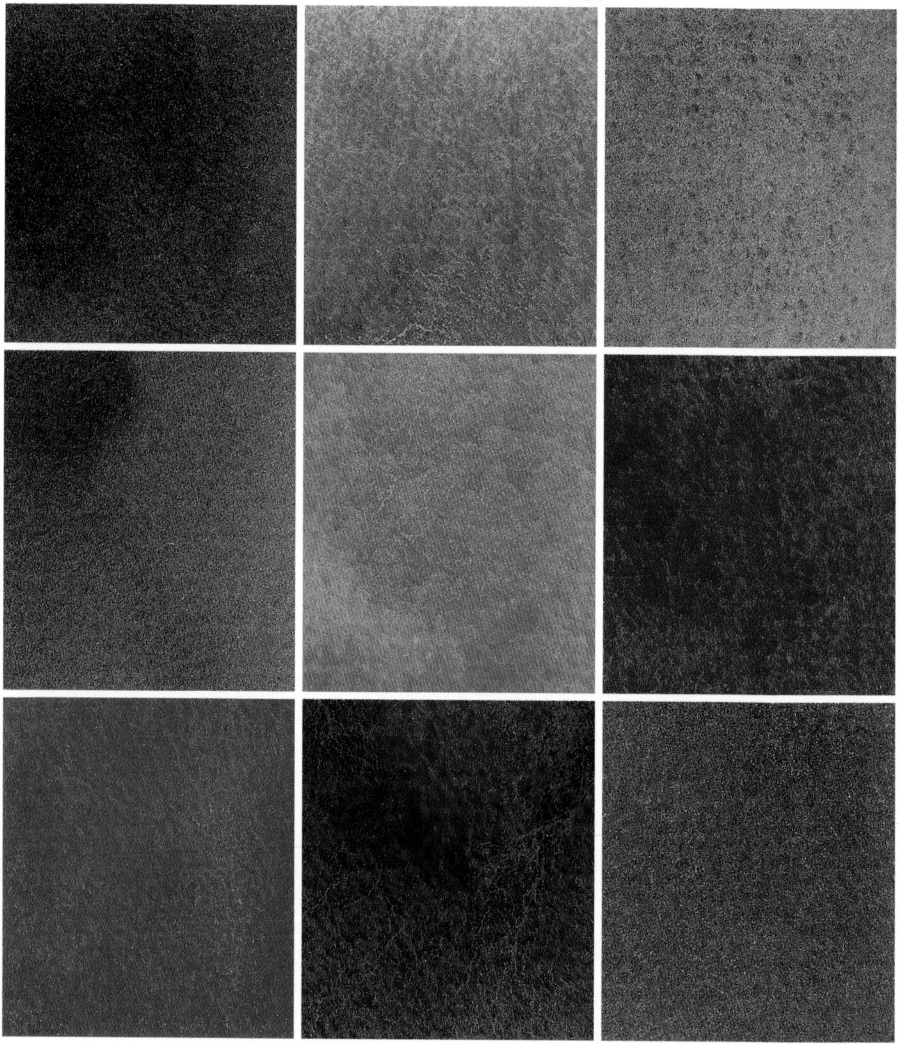

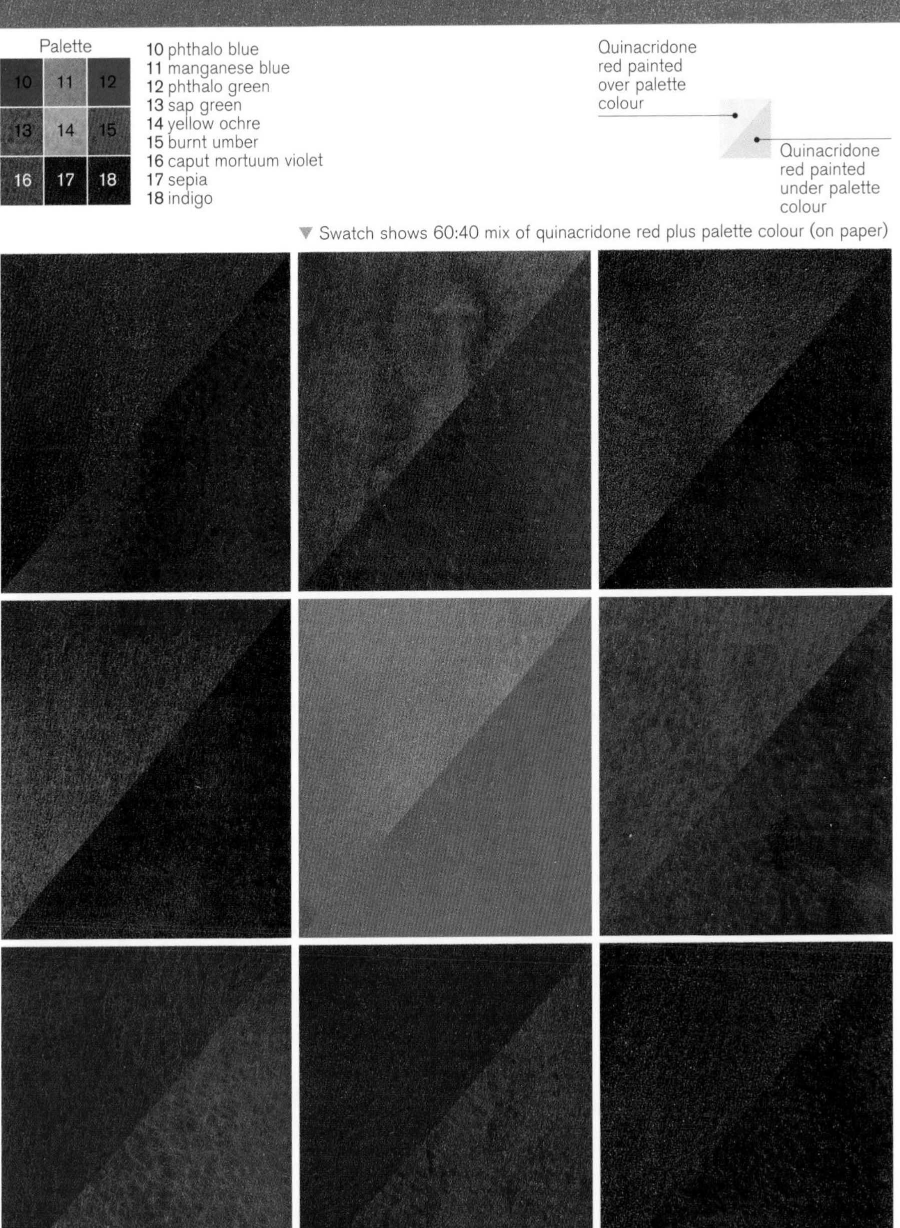

▼ Swatch shows 60:40 mix of quinacridone red plus palette colour (on paper)

Permanent Rose/1

A saturated, transparent, warm rose/red, this colour has violet undertones that also make it useful as a "cool red". This warm–cool duality means it is invaluable as the red pigment in a limited palette of transparent colours. It is essential in any floral artist's palette.

▼ Swatch shows 60:40 mix of permanent rose plus palette colour (on mixing palette)

Palette

1	2	3
4	5	6
7	8	9

1 lemon yellow
2 cadmium yellow medium
3 cadmium orange
4 vermilion
5 permanent carmine
6 quinacridone magenta
7 dioxazine violet
8 ultramarine blue
9 cobalt blue

Permanent rose painted over palette colour

Permanent rose painted under palette colour

▼ Swatch shows 60:40 mix of permanent rose plus palette colour (on paper)

Permanent Rose/2

Transparency 4
Staining 3
Permanence 2

Granulation
as single colour 0
in mixes 1

Transparency

Staining

Granulation

▼ Swatch shows 60:40 mix of permanent rose plus palette colour (on mixing palette)

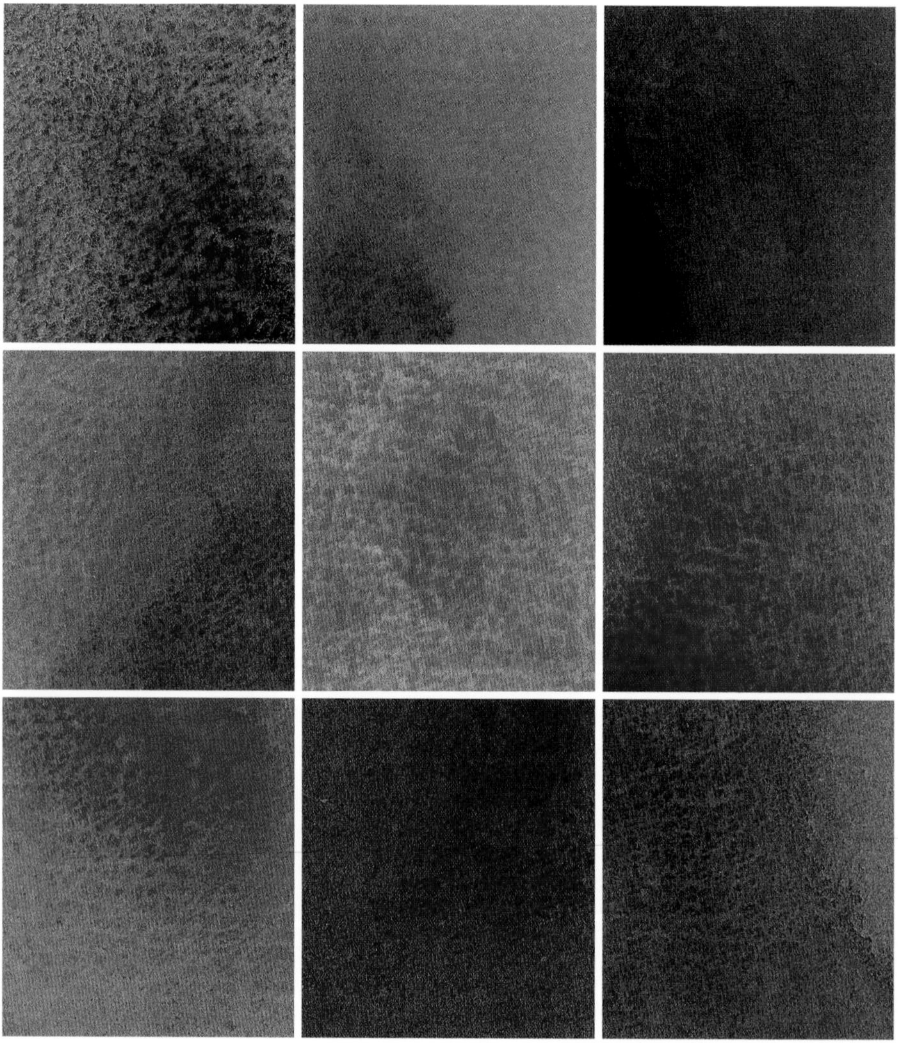

Palette

10 phthalo blue
11 manganese blue
12 phthalo green
13 sap green
14 yellow ochre
15 burnt umber
16 caput mortuum violet
17 sepia
18 indigo

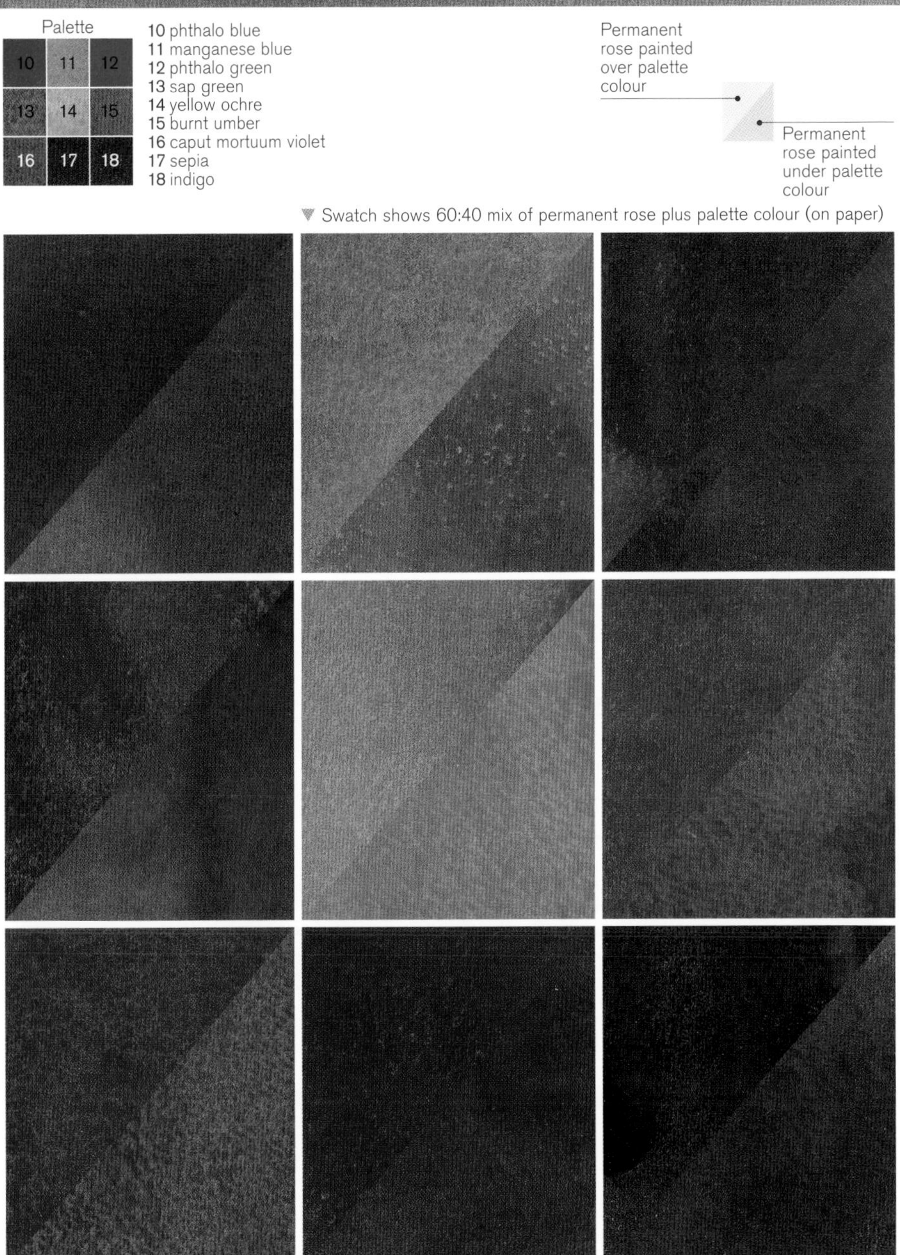

▼ Swatch shows 60:40 mix of permanent rose plus palette colour (on paper)

Quinacridone Magenta/1

Named after the bloody Battle of Magenta, Italy, in 1859, this is a strong, transparent violet/red. It mixes well in all washes. When mixed with yellows, its cool bias produces muted oranges; when mixed with blues, bright violets result.

▼ Swatch shows 60:40 mix of quinacridone magenta plus palette colour (on mixing palette)

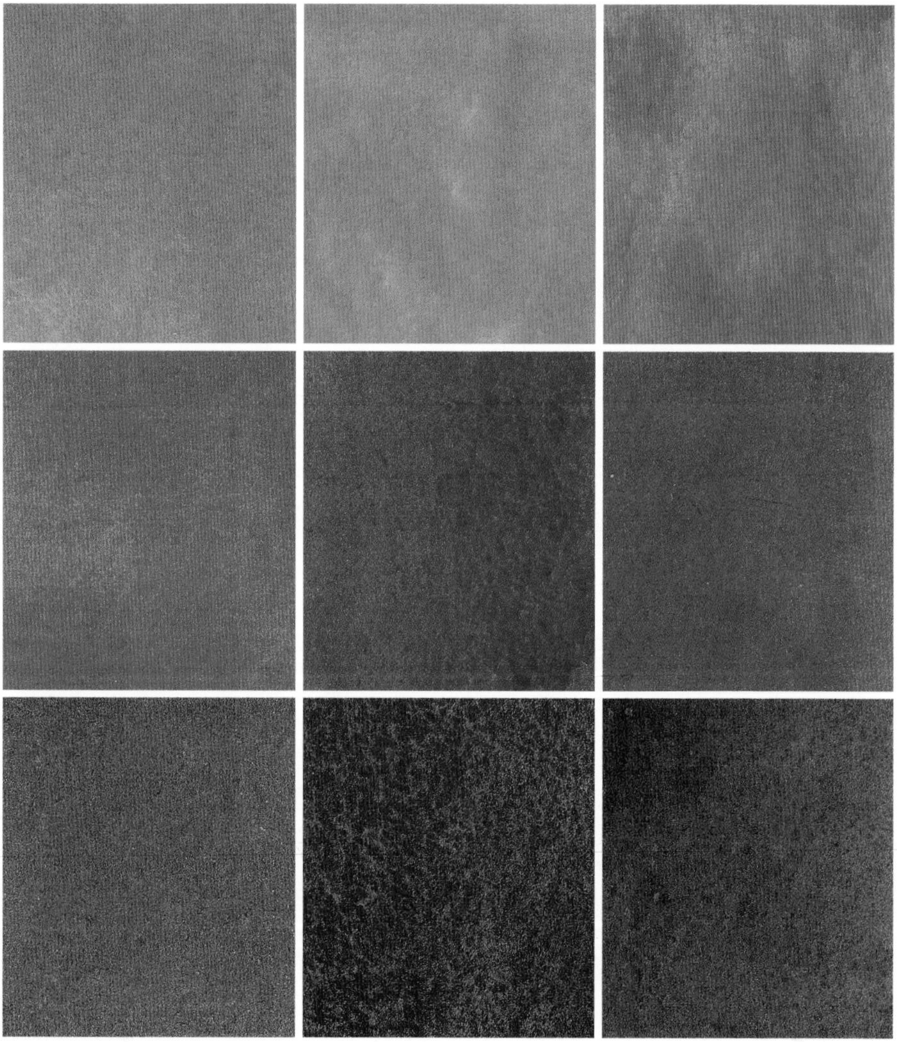

Palette

1 lemon yellow
2 cadmium yellow medium
3 cadmium orange
4 vermilion
5 permanent carmine
6 quinacridone magenta
7 dioxazine violet
8 ultramarine blue
9 cobalt blue

Instead of overpainting the palette colour with itself in the mixes on paper, the upper triangle shows a single wash and the lower, a double wash.

Quinacridone magenta painted over palette colour

Quinacridone magenta painted under palette colour

▼ Swatch shows 60:40 mix of quinacridone magenta plus palette colour (on paper)

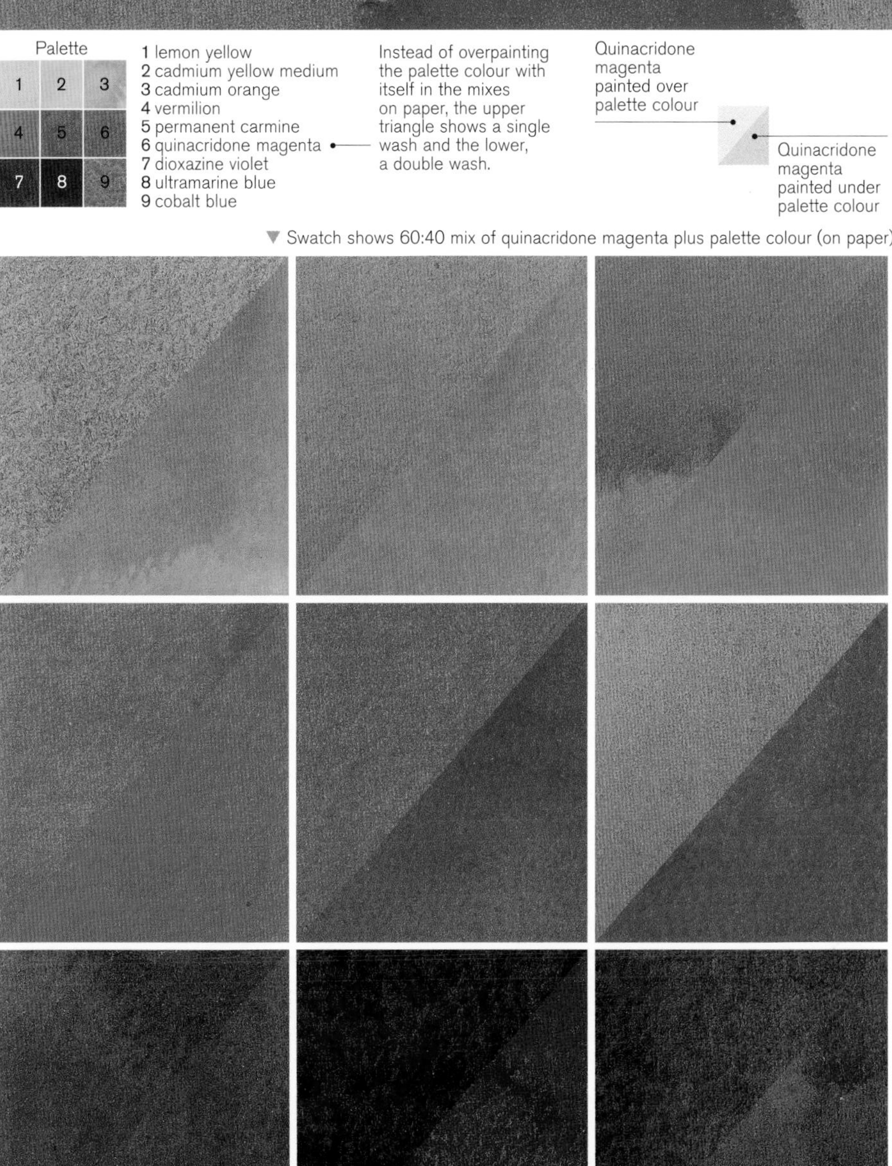

Quinacridone Magenta/2

Transparency 4
Staining 2
Permanence 2

Granulation
as single colour 0
in mixes 1

Transparency

Staining

Granulation

▼ Swatch shows 60:40 mix of quinacridone magenta plus palette colour (on mixing palette)

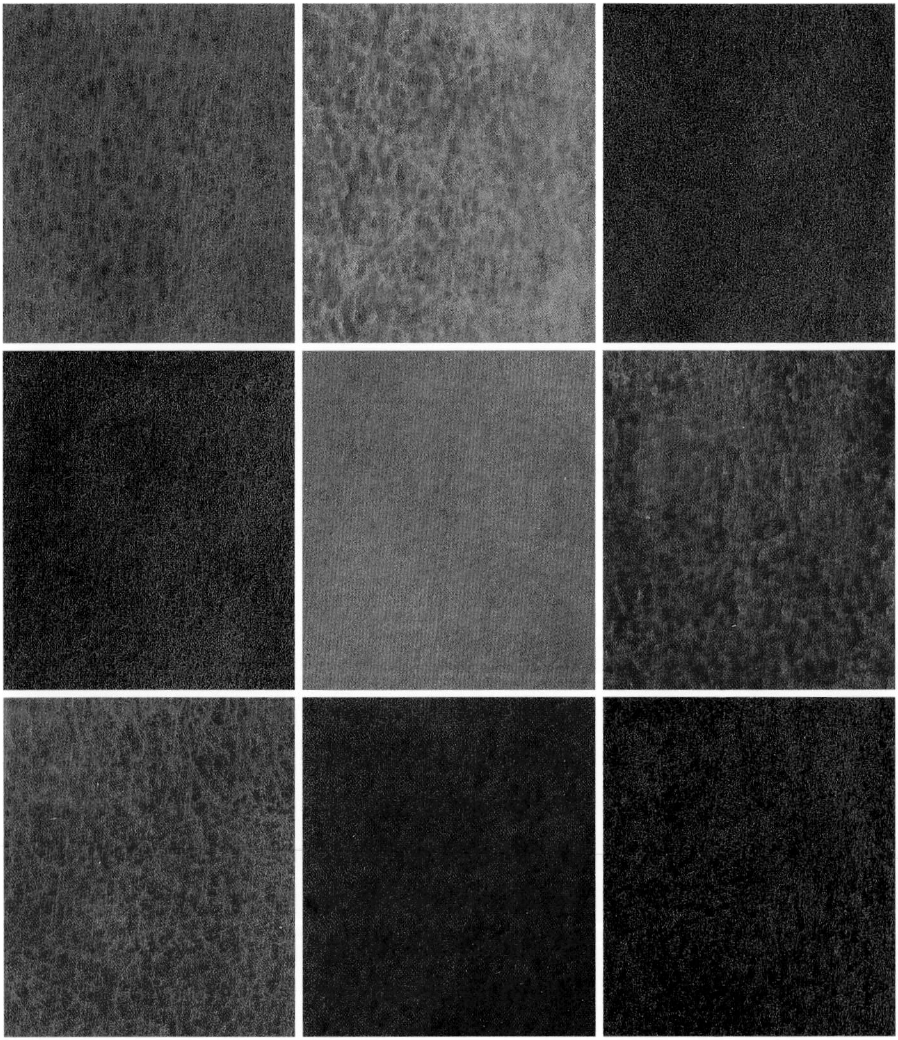

Palette

10	11	12
13	14	15
16	17	18

10 phthalo blue
11 manganese blue
12 phthalo green
13 sap green
14 yellow ochre
15 burnt umber
16 caput mortuum violet
17 sepia
18 indigo

Quinacridone magenta painted over palette colour

Quinacridone magenta painted under palette colour

▼ Swatch shows 60:40 mix of quinacridone magenta plus palette colour (on paper)

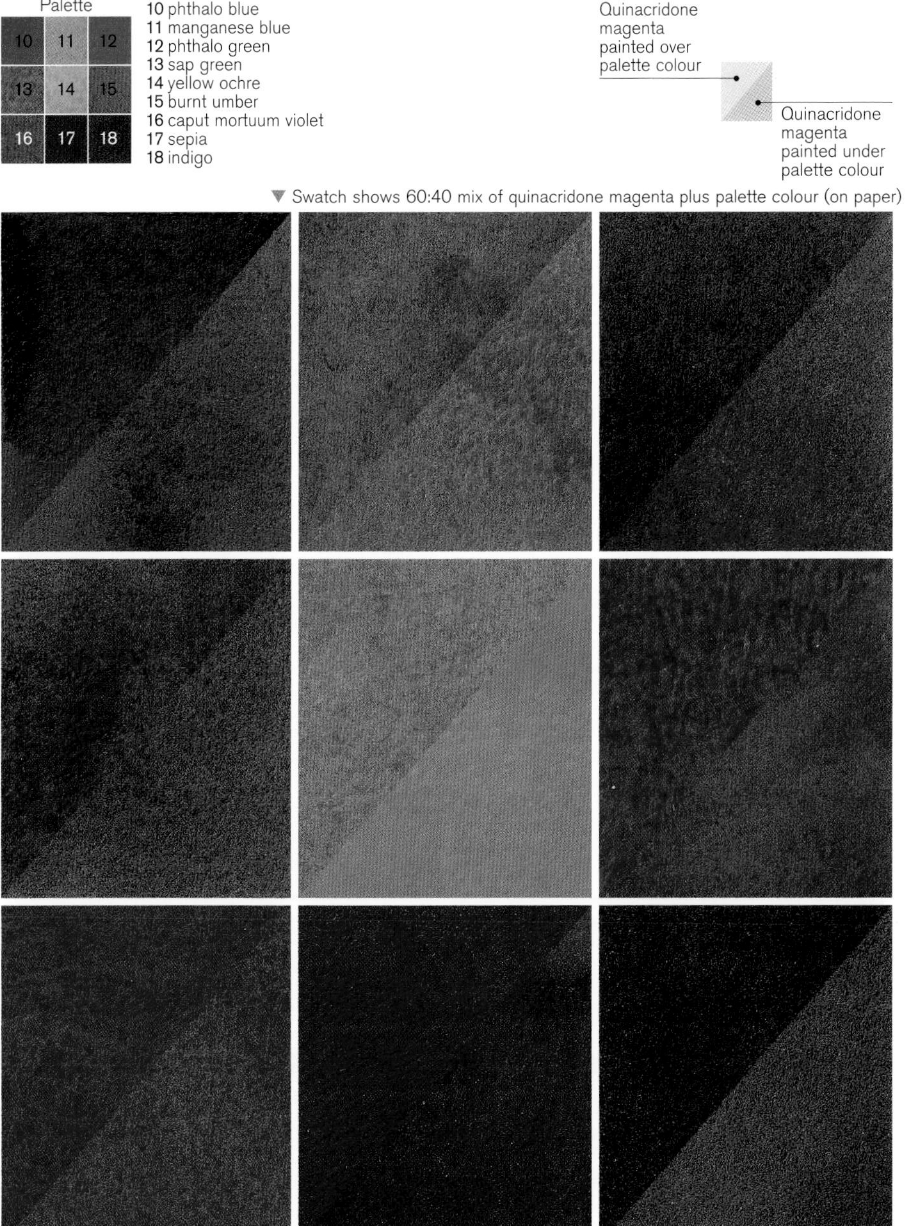

Quinacridone Violet/1

A strong, dark, transparent red/violet colour. For flat washes, use it alone or mix it with other colours on a palette. When applied as a layer under opaque colours such as lemon yellow, its dark tone accentuates the texture of the opaque colour.

▼ Swatch shows 60:40 mix of quinacridone violet plus palette colour (on mixing palette)

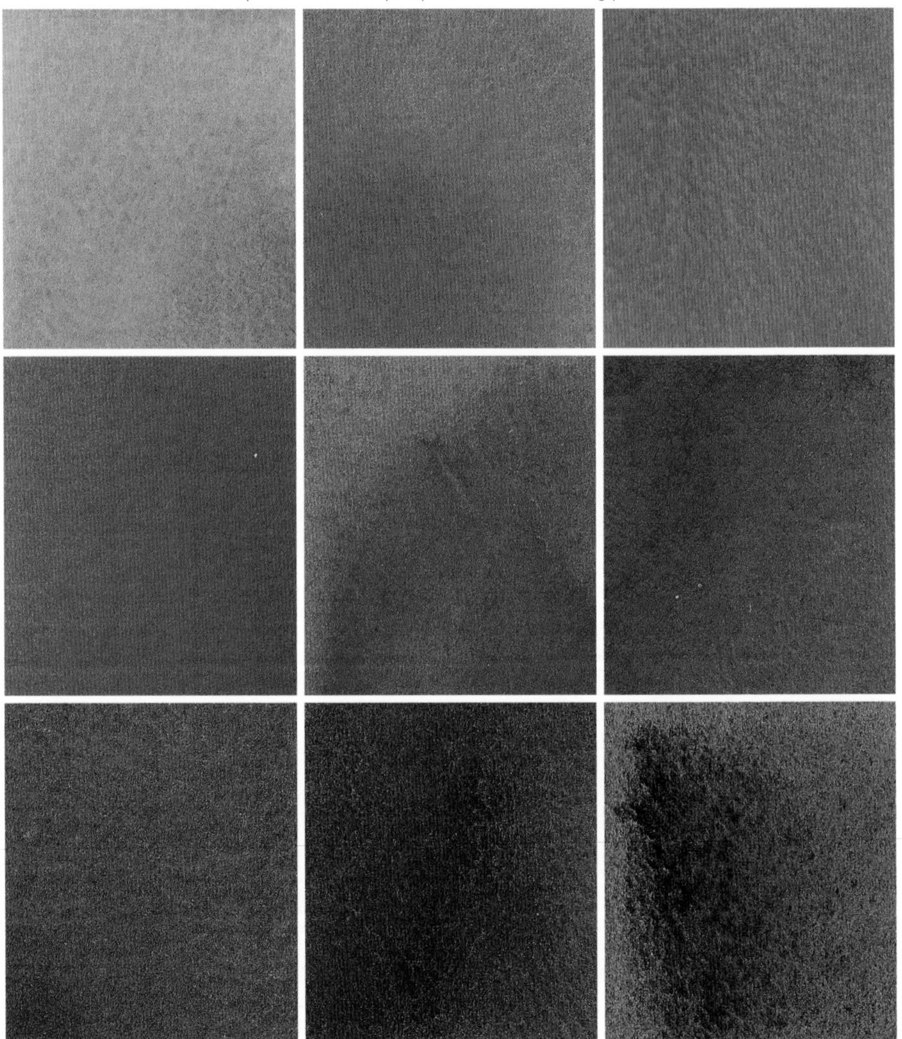

Palette		
1	2	3
4	5	6
7	8	9

1 lemon yellow
2 cadmium yellow medium
3 cadmium orange
4 vermilion
5 permanent carmine
6 quinacridone magenta
7 dioxazine violet
8 ultramarine blue
9 cobalt blue

Quinacridone violet painted over palette colour

Quinacridone violet painted under palette colour

▼ Swatch shows 60:40 mix of quinacridone violet plus palette colour (on paper)

Quinacridone Violet/2

Transparency 2/3
Staining 3
Permanence 3

Granulation
as single colour 0
in mixes 1

Transparency

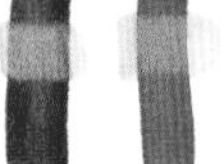
Staining

Granulation

▼ Swatch shows 60:40 mix of quinacridone violet plus palette colour (on mixing palette)

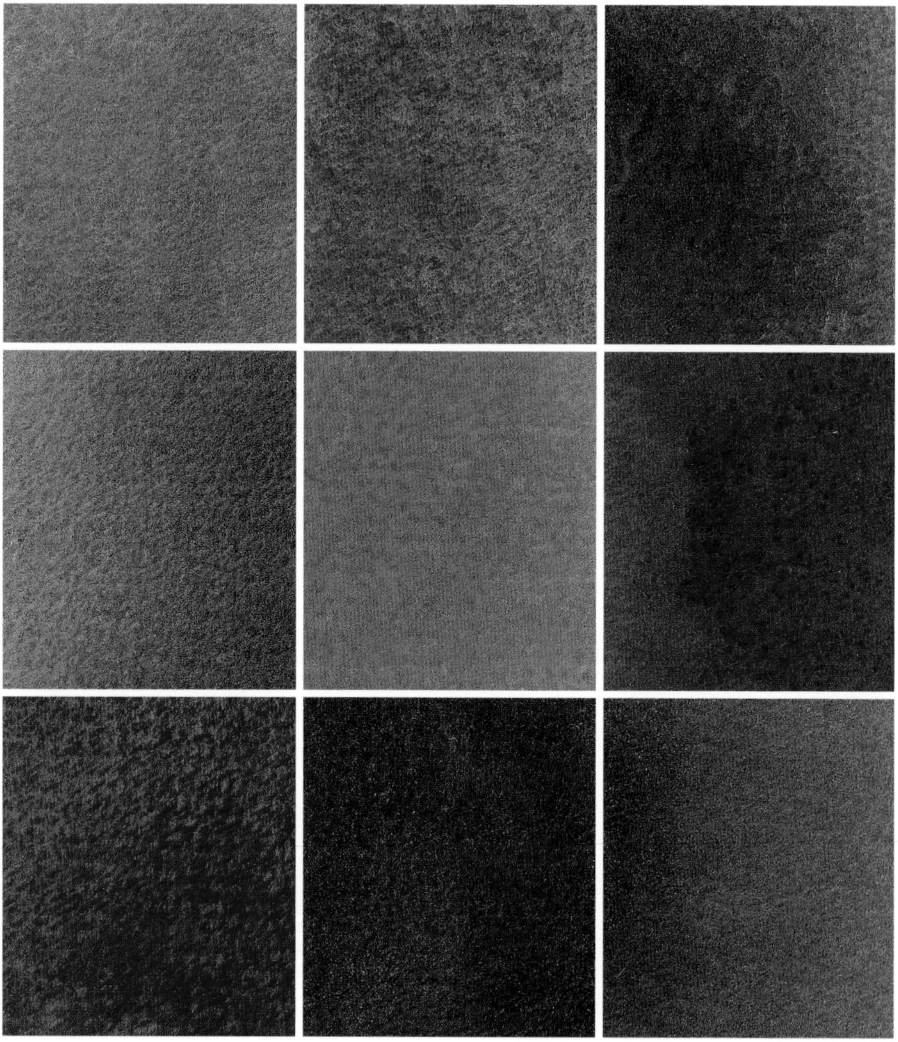

Palette

10	11	12
13	14	15
16	17	18

10 phthalo blue
11 manganese blue
12 phthalo green
13 sap green
14 yellow ochre
15 burnt umber
16 caput mortuum violet
17 sepia
18 indigo

Quinacridone violet painted over palette colour

Quinacridone violet painted under palette colour

▼ Swatch shows 60:40 mix of quinacridone violet plus palette colour (on paper)

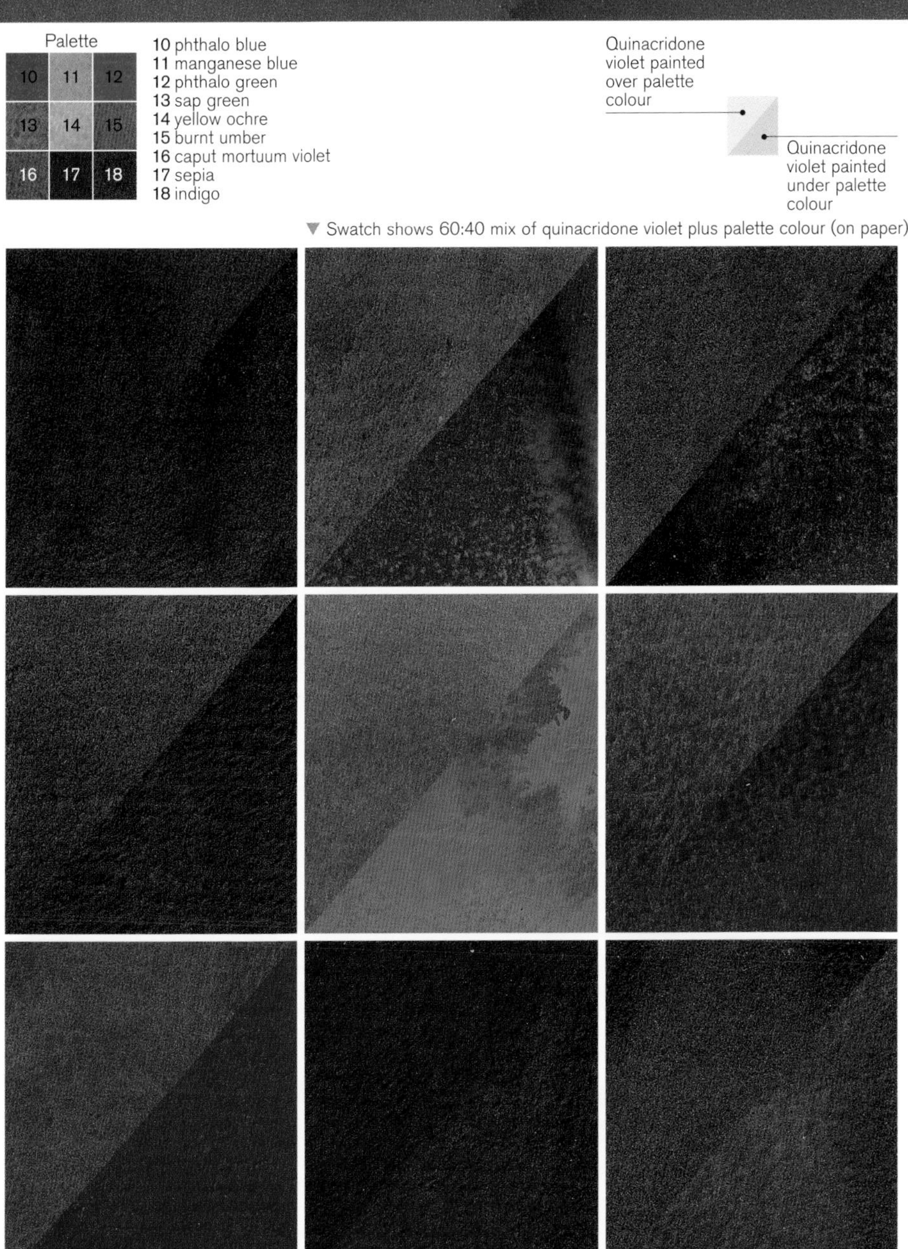

Cobalt Violet/1

A semi-opaque, warm violet pigment. This colour always granulates, which can make it difficult to handle when it is the first layer of colour. However, in palette mixes or as the second layer, it works beautifully. Its warmth and mixing texture varies according to manufacturer.

▼ Swatch shows 60:40 mix of cobalt violet plus palette colour (on mixing palette)

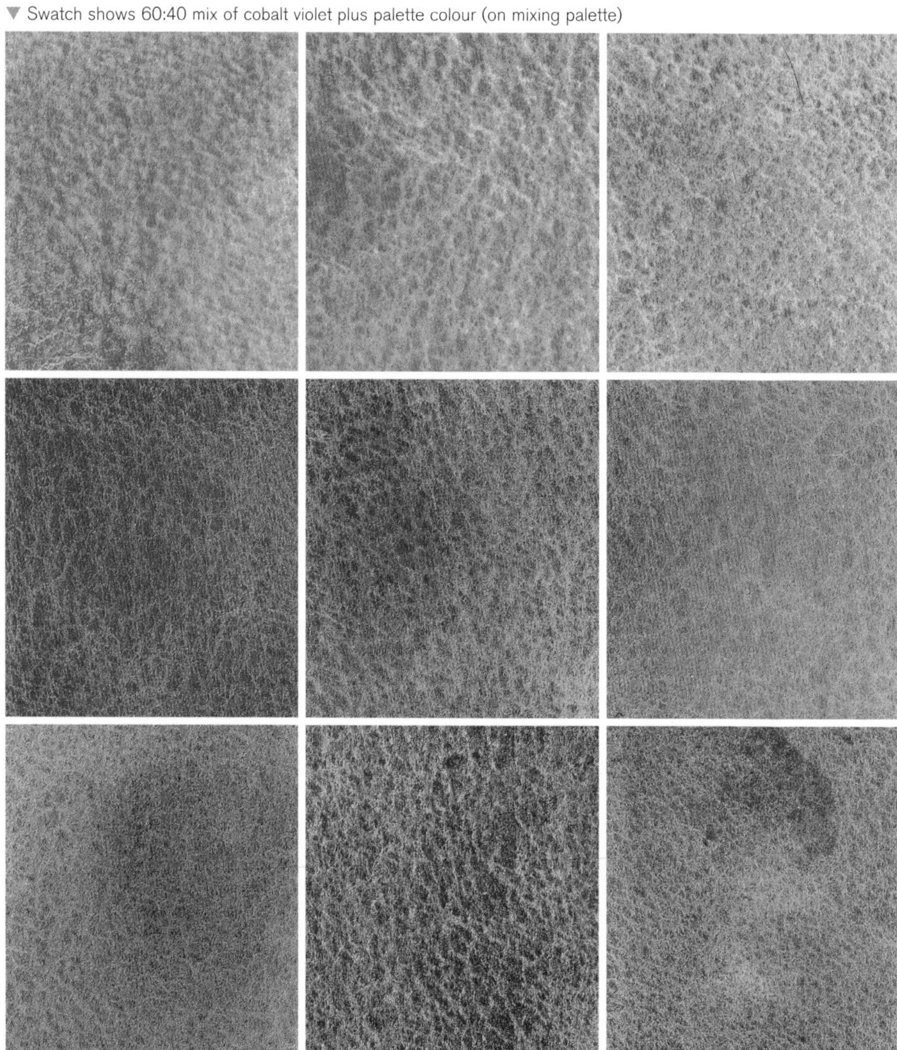

Palette

1	2	3
4	5	6
7	8	9

1 lemon yellow
2 cadmium yellow medium
3 cadmium orange
4 vermilion
5 permanent carmine
6 quinacridone magenta
7 dioxazine violet
8 ultramarine blue
9 cobalt blue

Cobalt violet painted over palette colour

Cobalt violet painted under palette colour

▼ Swatch shows 60:40 mix of cobalt violet plus palette colour (on paper)

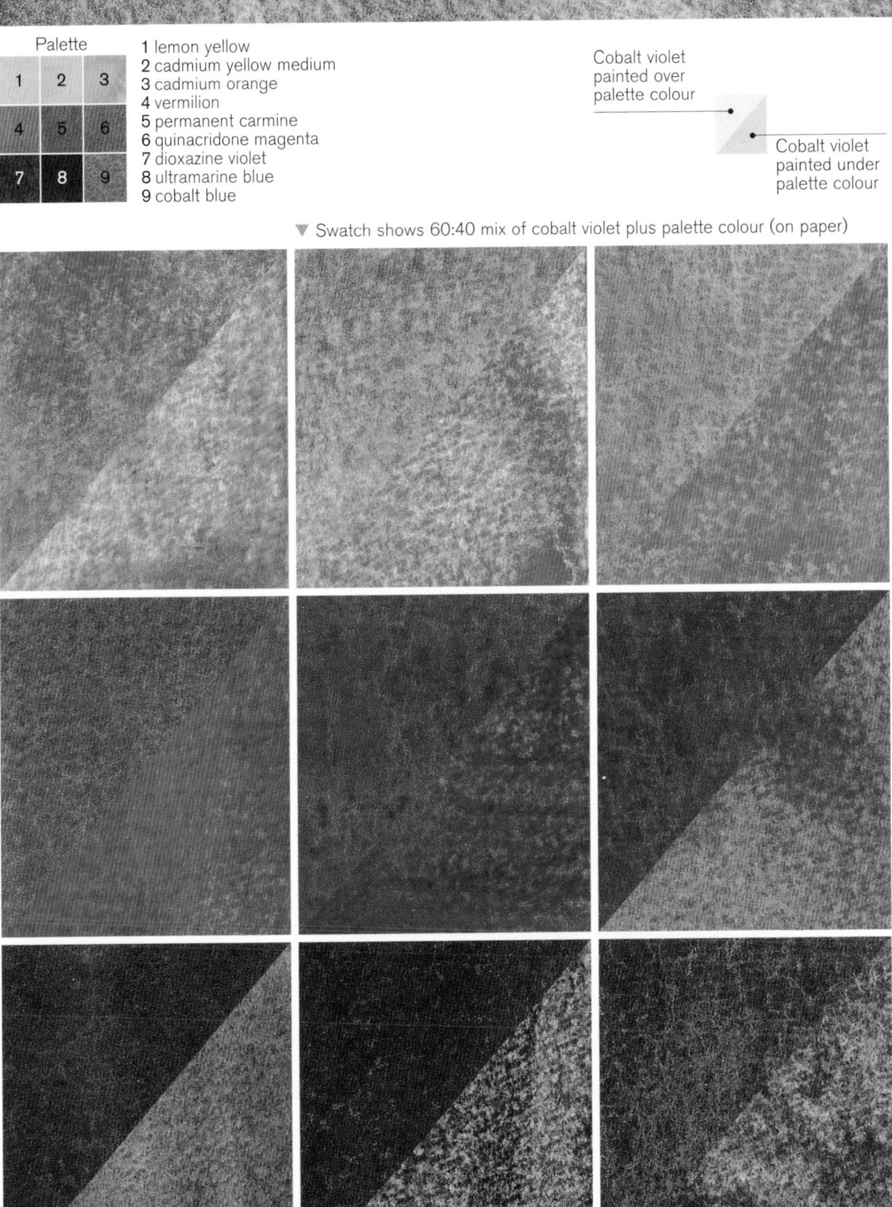

Cobalt Violet/2

Transparency 2/3
Staining 0
Permanence 3

Granulation
as single colour 3
in mixes 3

Transparency

Staining

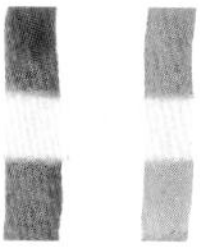

Granulation

▼ Swatch shows 60:40 mix of cobalt violet plus palette colour (on mixing palette)

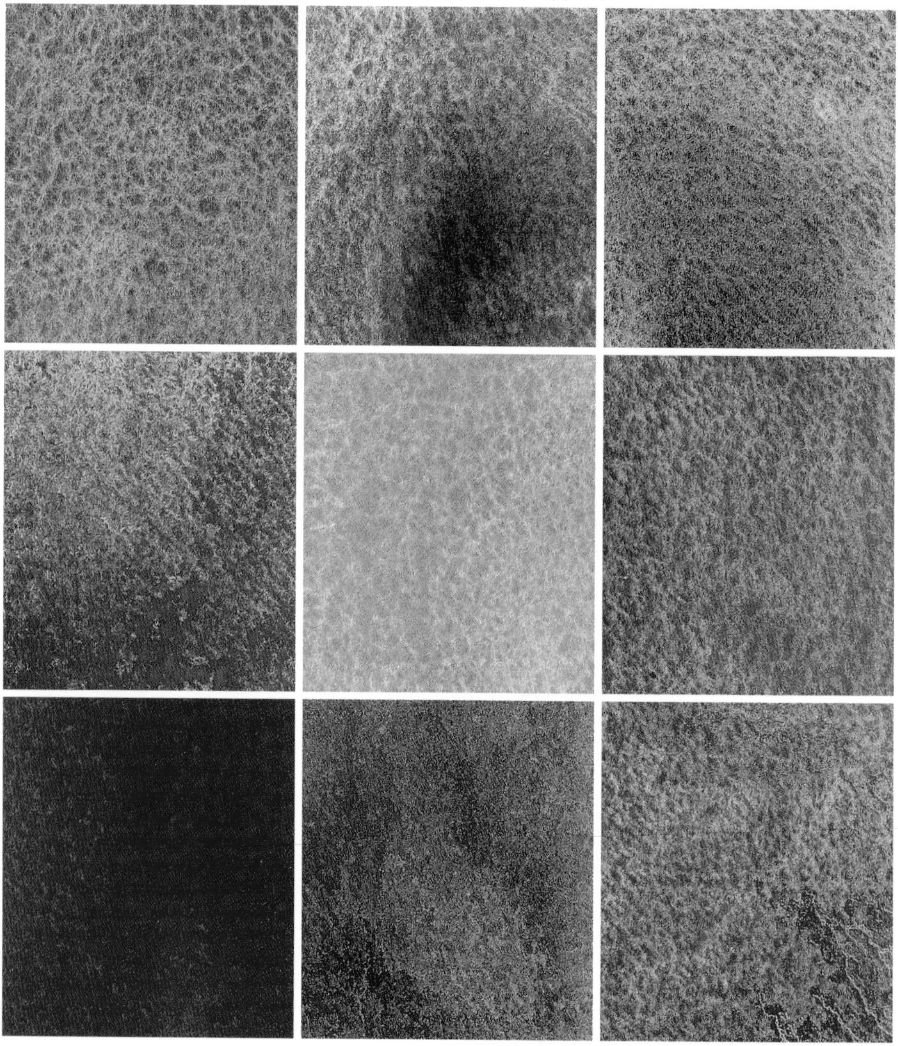

Palette

10	11	12
13	14	15
16	17	18

10 phthalo blue
11 manganese blue
12 phthalo green
13 sap green
14 yellow ochre
15 burnt umber
16 caput mortuum violet
17 sepia
18 indigo

Cobalt violet painted over palette colour

Cobalt violet painted under palette colour

▼ Swatch shows 60:40 mix of cobalt violet plus palette colour (on paper)

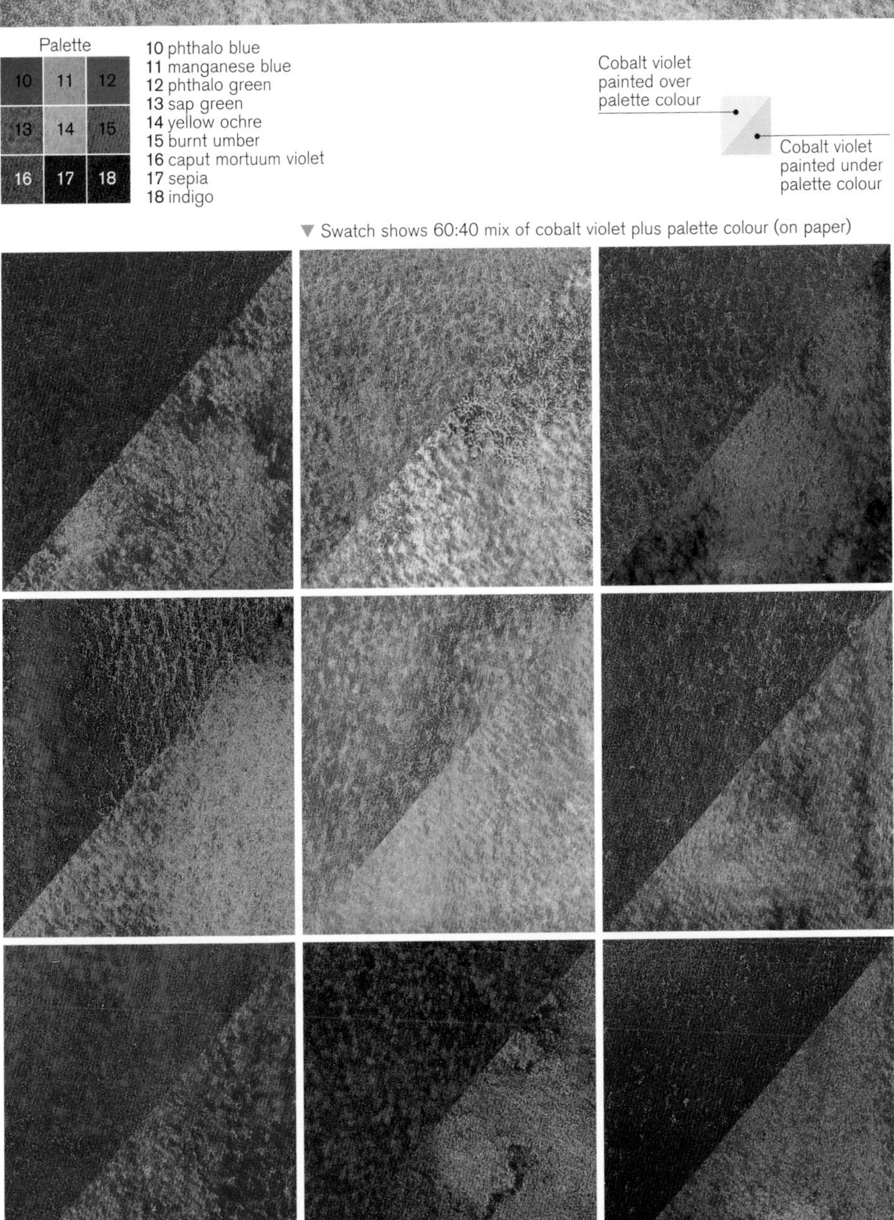

Dioxazine Violet/1

A strong, semi-transparent violet that dries to a lighter shade than expected. It has the ability to prevent colours that normally granulate from granulating. Its warmth varies according to manufacturer. This is a great colour for rich shadow mixes.

▼ Swatch shows 60:40 mix of dioxazine violet plus palette colour (on mixing palette)

Palette

1	2	3
4	5	6
7	8	9

1 lemon yellow
2 cadmium yellow medium
3 cadmium orange
4 vermilion
5 permanent carmine
6 quinacridone magenta
7 dioxazine violet
8 ultramarine blue
9 cobalt blue

Instead of overpainting the palette colour with itself in the mixes on paper, the upper triangle shows a single wash and the lower, a double wash.

Dioxazine violet painted over palette colour

Dioxazine violet painted under palette colour

▼ Swatch shows 60:40 mix of dioxazine violet plus palette colour (on paper)

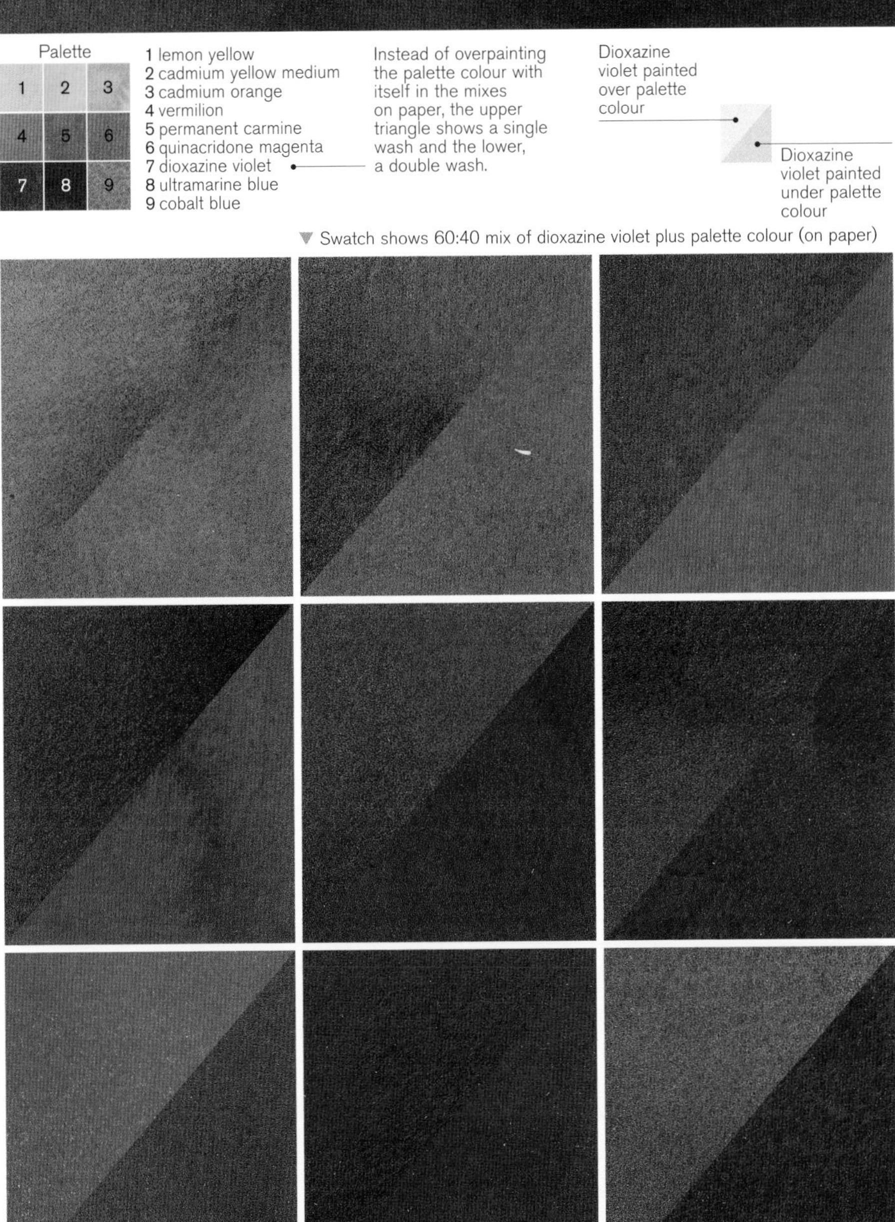

Dioxazine Violet/2

Transparency 2/3
Staining 1
Permanence 1

Granulation
as single colour 0
in mixes 0

Transparency Staining Granulation

▼ Swatch shows 60:40 mix of dioxazine violet plus palette colour (on mixing palette)

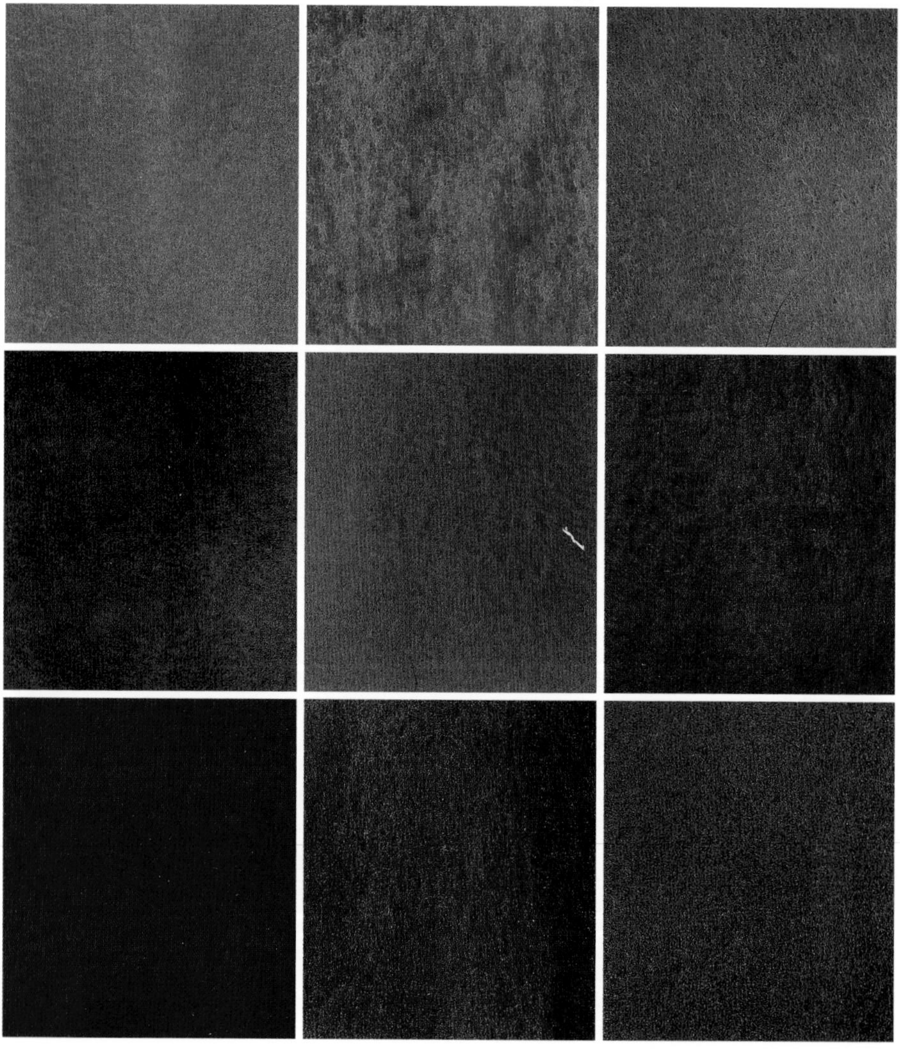

Palette

10 phthalo blue
11 manganese blue
12 phthalo green
13 sap green
14 yellow ochre
15 burnt umber
16 caput mortuum violet
17 sepia
18 indigo

Dioxazine violet painted over palette colour

Dioxazine violet painted under palette colour

▼ Swatch shows 60:40 mix of dioxazine violet plus palette colour (on paper)

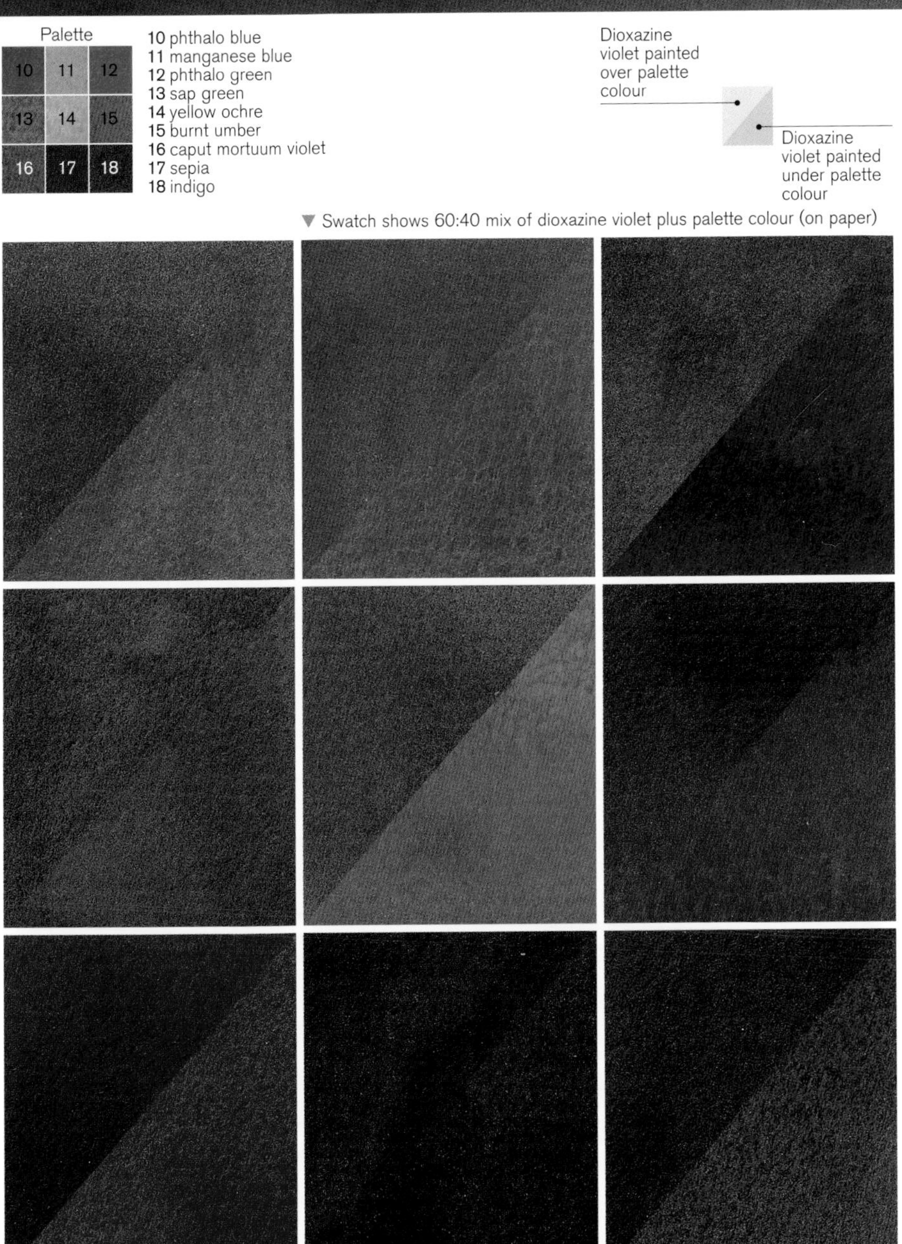

Indanthrene Blue/1

A semi-opaque, dark blue with a warm bias and a high tinting strength, this colour is much lighter when dry. It mixes well on a palette or as the first layer when mixing on paper, but as a second layer over lighter opaque colours, it can be difficult to handle as a flat wash.

▼ Swatch shows 60:40 mix of indanthrene blue plus palette colour (on mixing palette)

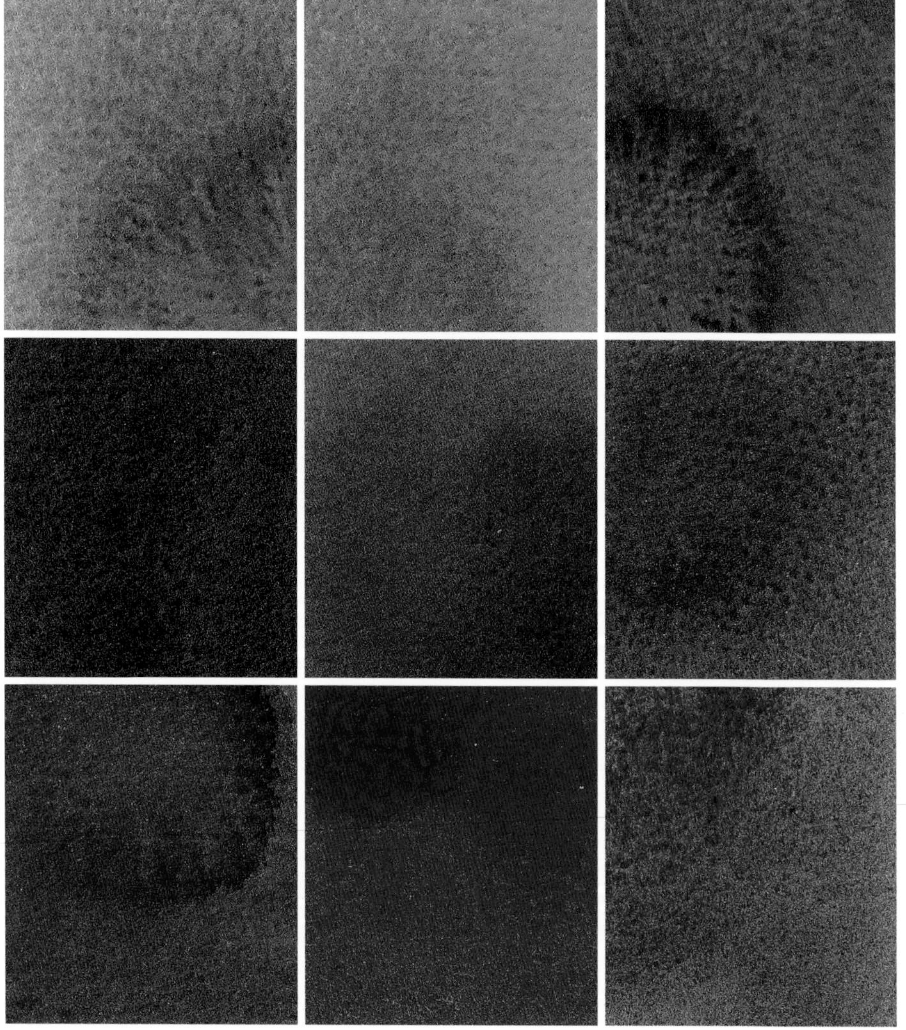

Palette

1	2	3
4	5	6
7	8	9

1 lemon yellow
2 cadmium yellow medium
3 cadmium orange
4 vermilion
5 permanent carmine
6 quinacridone magenta
7 dioxazine violet
8 ultramarine blue
9 cobalt blue

Indanthrene blue painted over palette colour

Indanthrene blue painted under palette colour

▼ Swatch shows 60:40 mix of indanthrene blue plus palette colour (on paper)

Indanthrene Blue/2

Transparency 2
Staining 3
Permanence 2

Granulation
as single colour 0
in mixes 1

Transparency

Staining

Granulation

▼ Swatch shows 60:40 mix of indanthrene blue plus palette colour (on mixing palette)

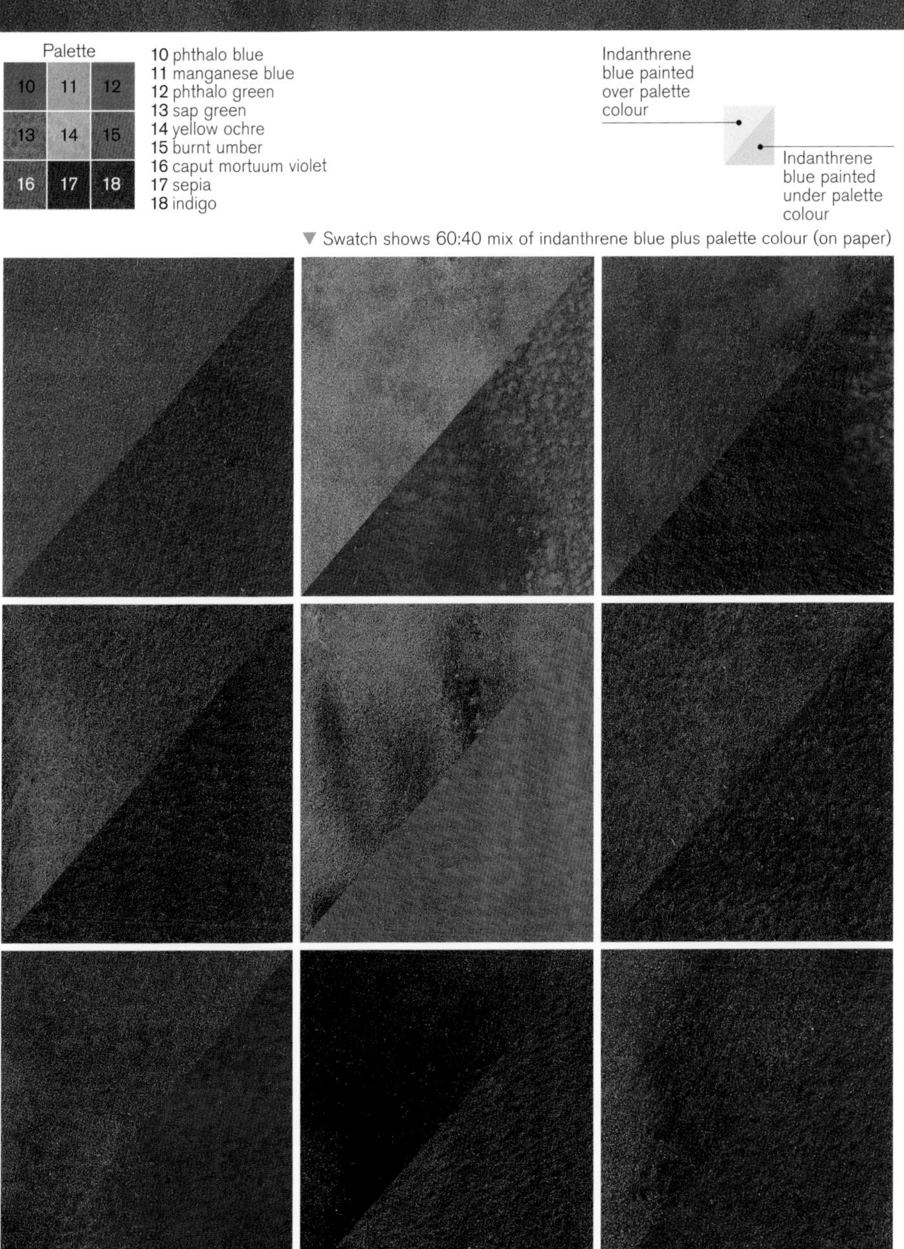

▼ Swatch shows 60:40 mix of indanthrene blue plus palette colour (on paper)

Ultramarine Blue/1

An intense dark blue with a warm bias, this colour is semi-transparent with a reliable tendency to granulate. (Brands are available that are non-granulating.) When used over oranges or reds, it creates glowing shadows. It mixes and handles well, and is invaluable in a basic palette.

▼ Swatch shows 60:40 mix of ultramarine blue plus palette colour (on mixing palette)

Palette

1	2	3
4	5	6
7	8	9

1 lemon yellow
2 cadmium yellow medium
3 cadmium orange
4 vermilion
5 permanent carmine
6 quinacridone magenta
7 dioxazine violet
8 ultramarine blue
9 cobalt blue

Instead of overpainting the palette colour with itself in the mixes on paper, the upper triangle shows a single wash and the lower, a double wash.

Ultramarine blue painted over palette colour

Ultramarine blue painted under palette colour

▼ Swatch shows 60:40 mix of ultramarine blue plus palette colour (on paper)

Ultramarine Blue/2

Transparency 2/3
Staining 1/2
Permanence 1

Granulation
as single colour 1
in mixes 3

Transparency

Staining

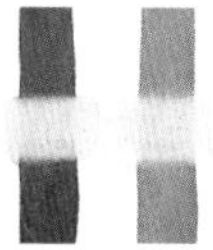

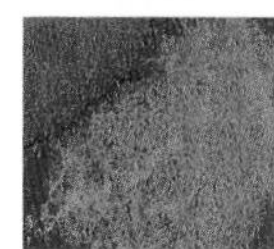
Granulation

▼ Swatch shows 60:40 mix of ultramarine blue plus palette colour (on mixing palette)

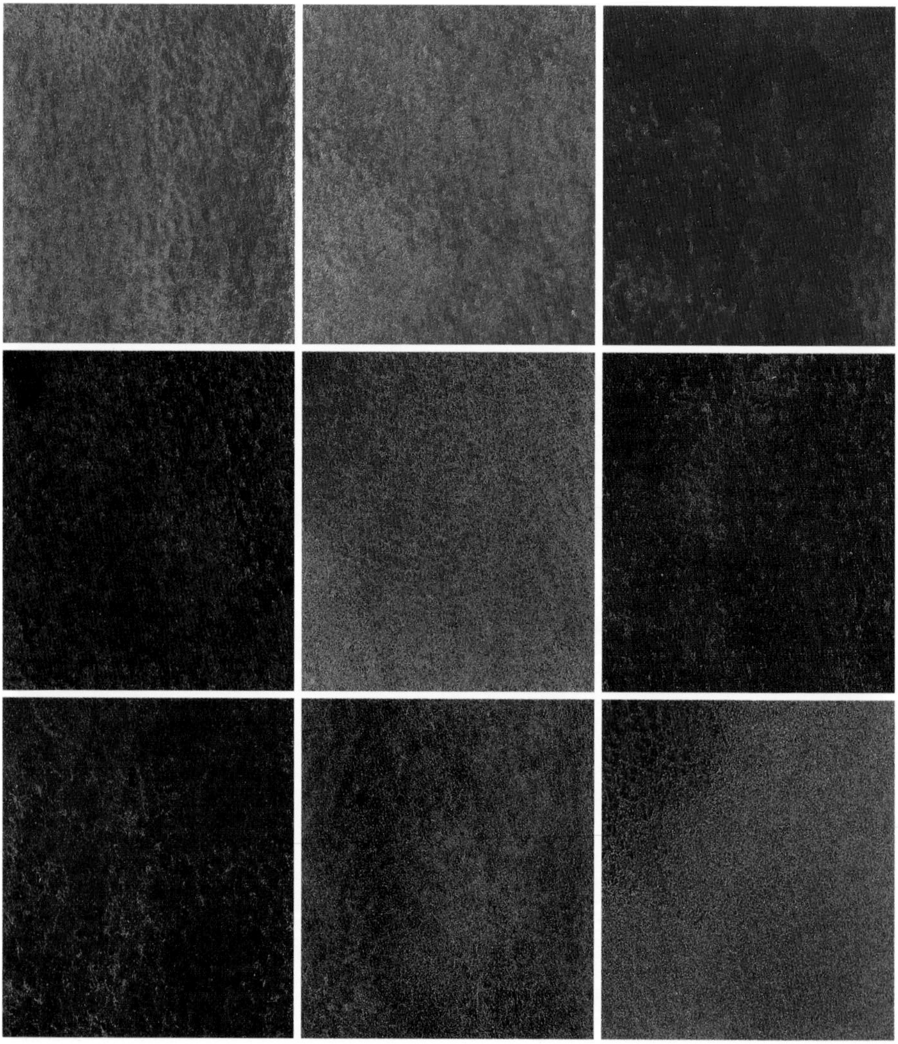

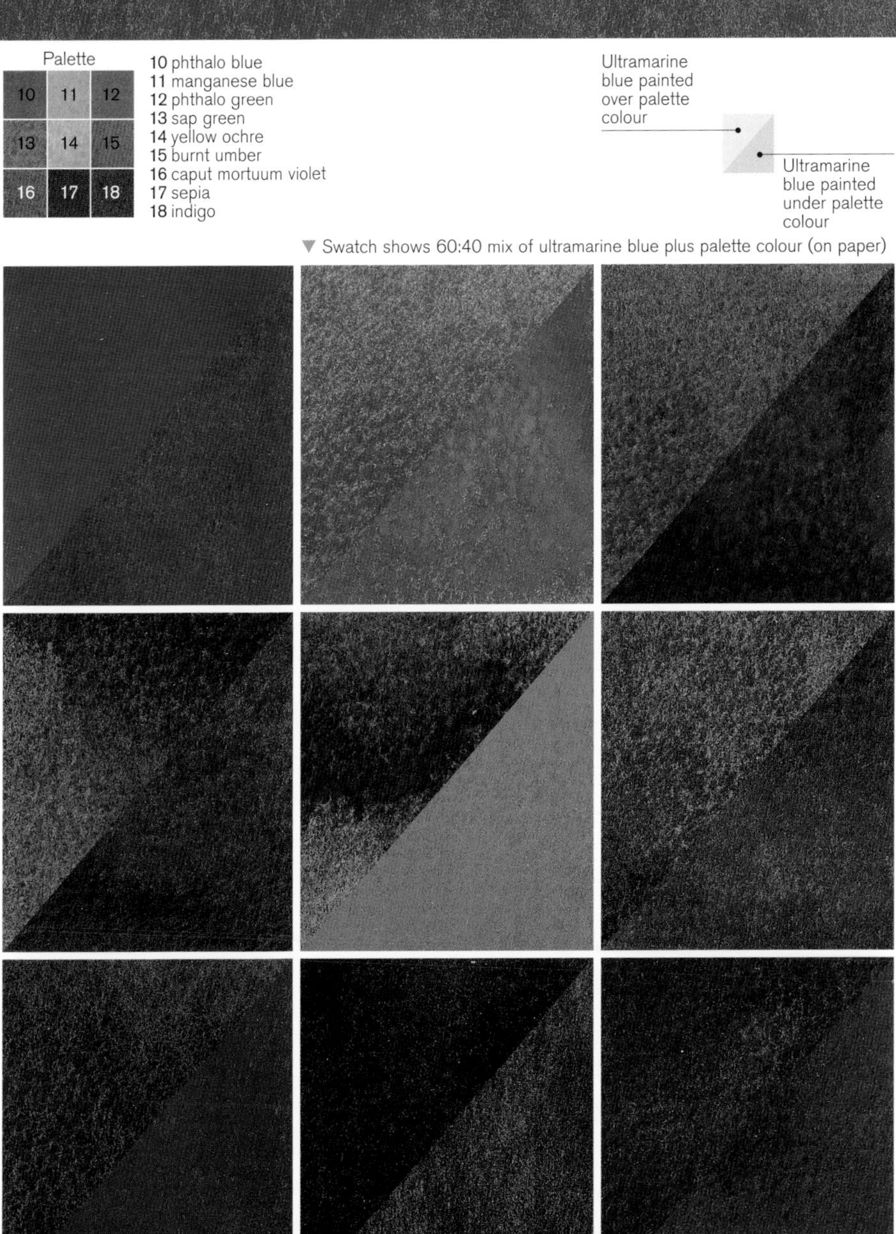

▼ Swatch shows 60:40 mix of ultramarine blue plus palette colour (on paper)

Lapis Lazuli Genuine/1

A unique colour made from authentic mineral pigments. Lapis lazuli (processed differently from this colour) was the original medieval source for ultramarine blue. This rich blue pigment has a soft grey edge and granulates beautifully in all washes.

▼ Swatch shows 60:40 mix of lapis lazuli genuine plus palette colour (on mixing palette)

Palette

1 lemon yellow
2 cadmium yellow medium
3 cadmium orange
4 vermilion
5 permanent carmine
6 quinacridone magenta
7 dioxazine violet
8 ultramarine blue
9 cobalt blue

Lapis lazuli genuine painted over palette colour

Lapis lazuli genuine painted under palette colour

▼ Swatch shows 60:40 mix of lapis lazuli genuine plus palette colour (on paper)

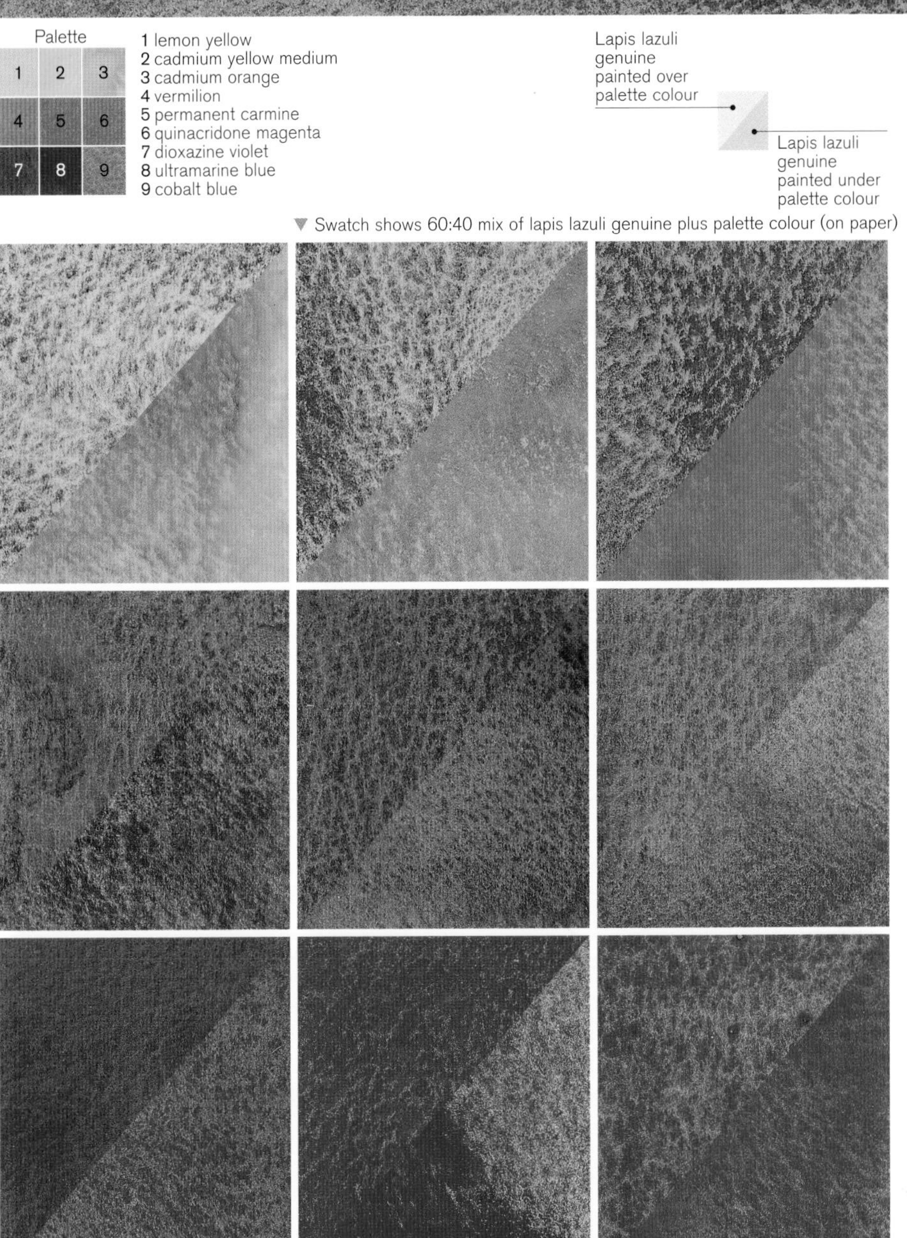

Lapis Lazuli Genuine/2

Transparency 3
Staining 0
Permanence N/A

Granulation
as single colour 3
in mixes 3

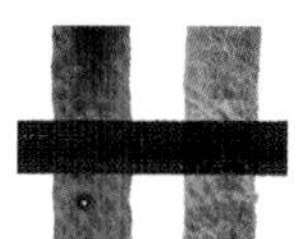

Transparency

Staining

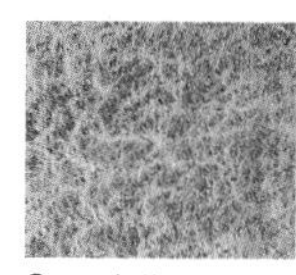

Granulation

▼ Swatch shows 60:40 mix of lapis lazuli genuine plus palette colour (on mixing palette)

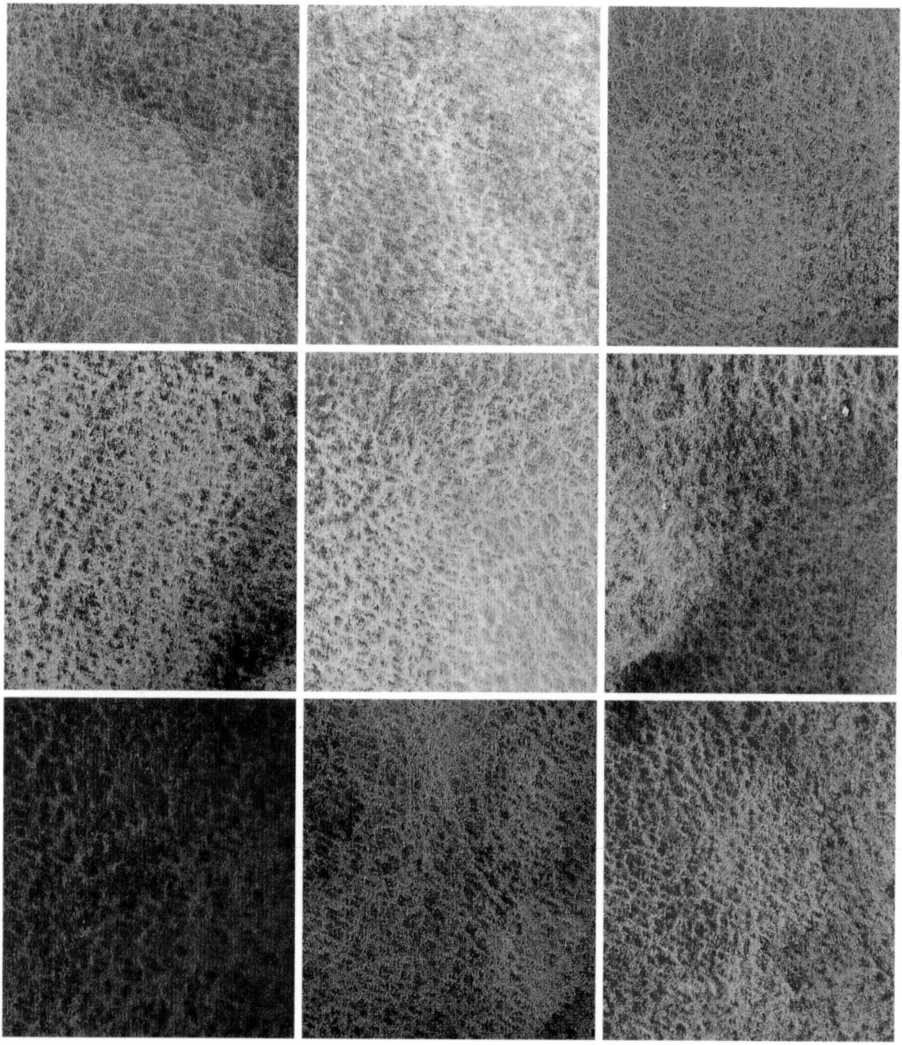

Palette

10	11	12
13	14	15
16	17	18

10 phthalo blue
11 manganese blue
12 phthalo green
13 sap green
14 yellow ochre
15 burnt umber
16 caput mortuum violet
17 sepia
18 indigo

Lapis lazuli genuine painted over palette colour

Lapis lazuli genuine painted under palette colour

▼ Swatch shows 60:40 mix of lapis lazuli genuine plus palette colour (on paper)

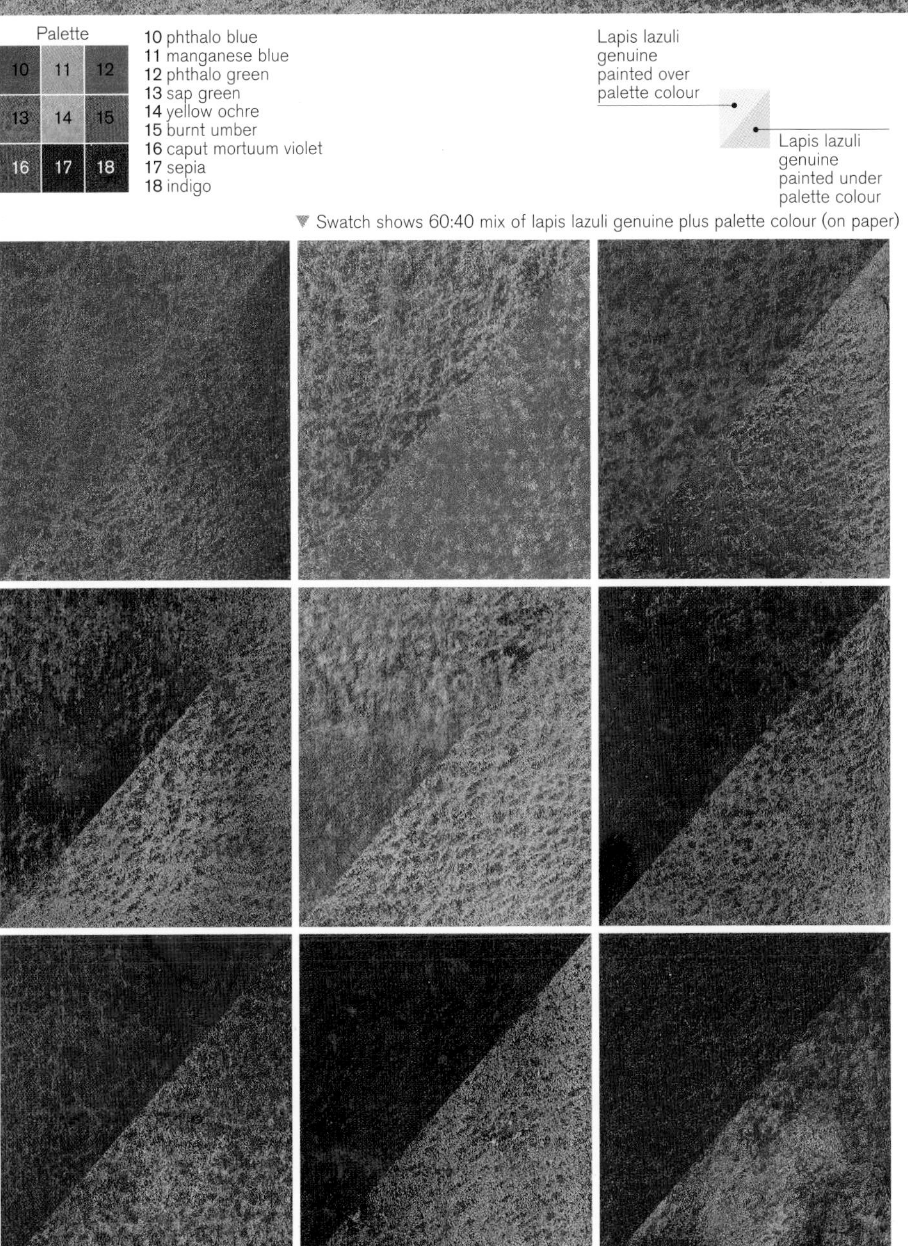

Cobalt Blue/1

Named after a medieval goblin in a German mine called Kobalt, this is a mid-toned, warm blue. It handles well in all washes and creates lovely mixes without exception. It is semi-transparent, but can be opaque if used in a strong wash, and granulates to create interesting textures.

▼ Swatch shows 60:40 mix of cobalt blue plus palette colour (on mixing palette)

Palette

1	2	3
4	5	6
7	8	9

1 lemon yellow
2 cadmium yellow medium
3 cadmium orange
4 vermilion
5 permanent carmine
6 quinacridone magenta
7 dioxazine violet
8 ultramarine blue
9 cobalt blue

Instead of overpainting the palette colour with itself in the mixes on paper, the upper triangle shows a single wash and the lower, a double wash.

Cobalt blue painted over palette colour

Cobalt blue painted under palette colour

▼ Swatch shows 60:40 mix of cobalt blue plus palette colour (on paper)

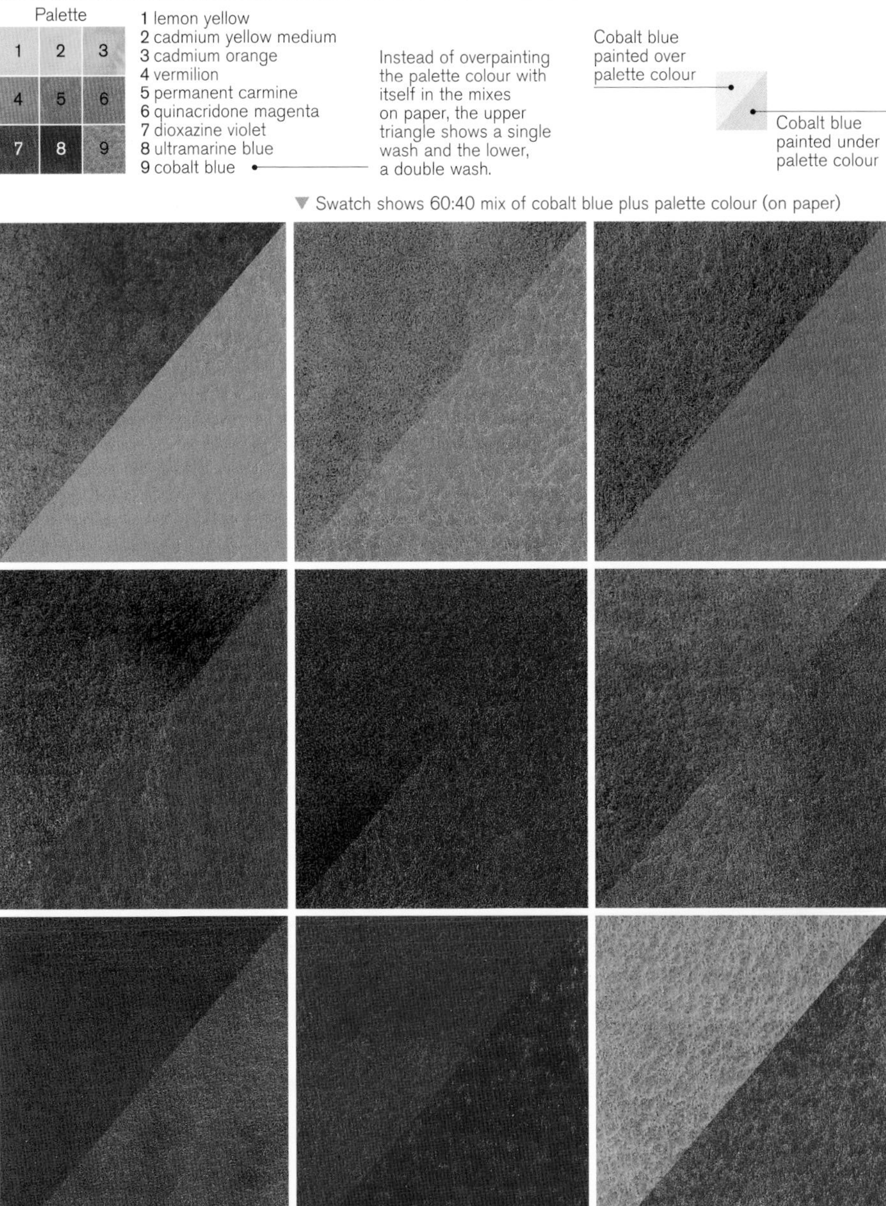

Cobalt Blue/2

Transparency 3
Staining 1
Permanence 3

Granulation
as single colour 2
in mixes 2

Transparency

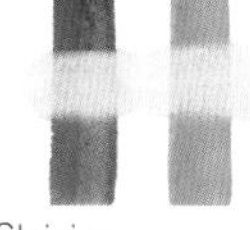
Staining

Granulation

▼ Swatch shows 60:40 mix of cobalt blue plus palette colour (on mixing palette)

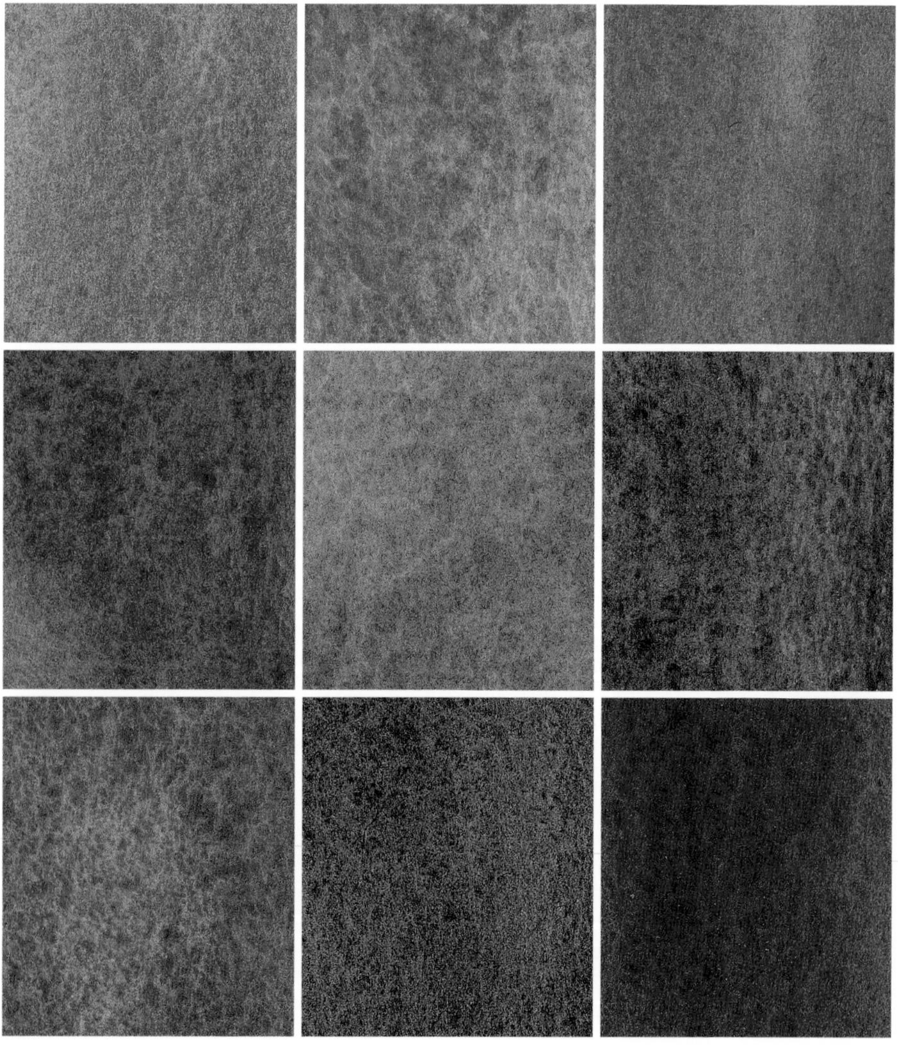

Palette

10	11	12
13	14	15
16	17	18

10 phthalo blue
11 manganese blue
12 phthalo green
13 sap green
14 yellow ochre
15 burnt umber
16 caput mortuum violet
17 sepia
18 indigo

Cobalt blue painted over palette colour

Cobalt blue painted under palette colour

▼ Swatch shows 60:40 mix of cobalt blue plus palette colour (on paper)

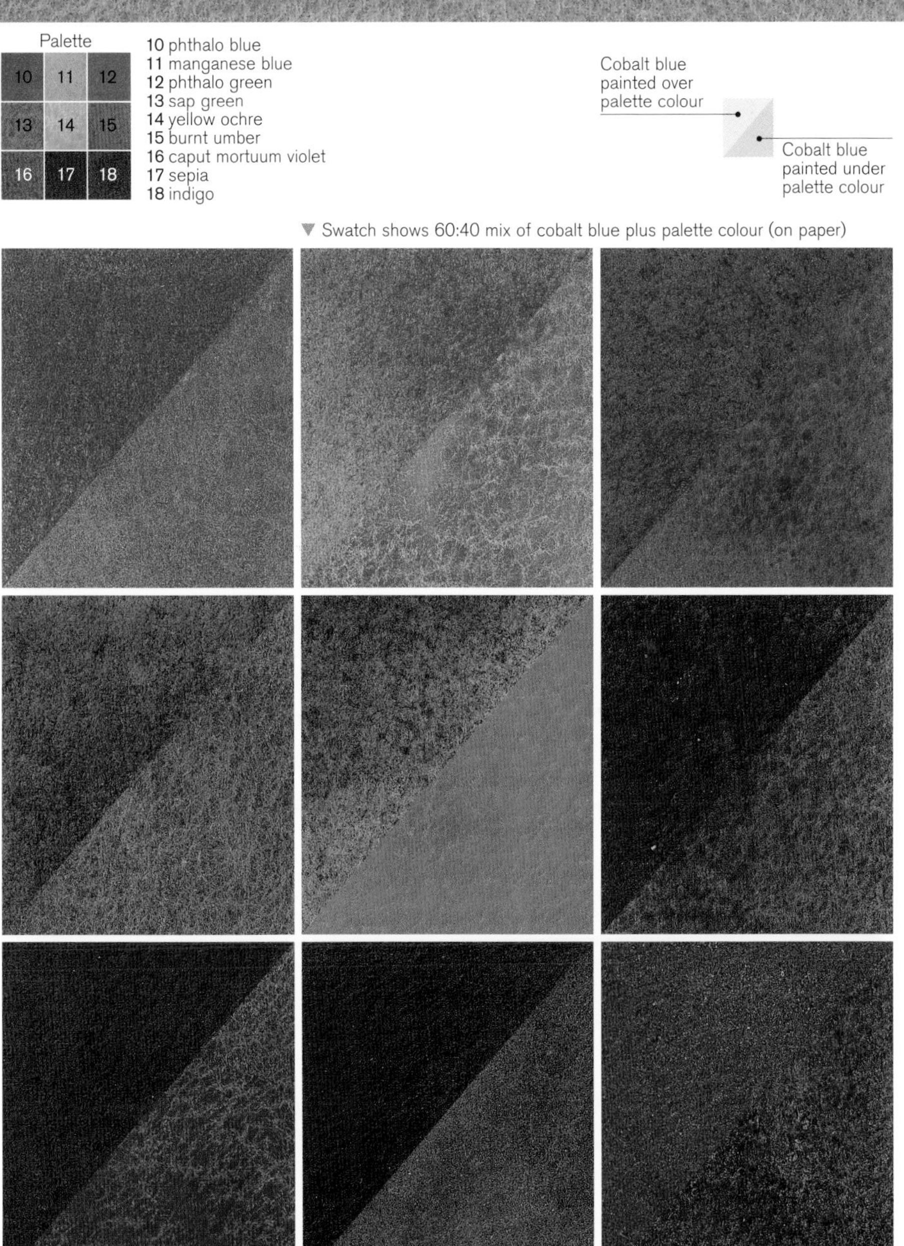

Phthalo Blue/1

Phthalocyanine (or more familiarly, phthalo) blue is transparent and staining. It is a mid-toned to almost dark blue and is available with either a green or red bias (the green bias is seen here). It mixes well and is an ideal blue for a limited transparent palette.

▼ Swatch shows 60:40 mix of phthalo blue plus palette colour (on mixing palette)

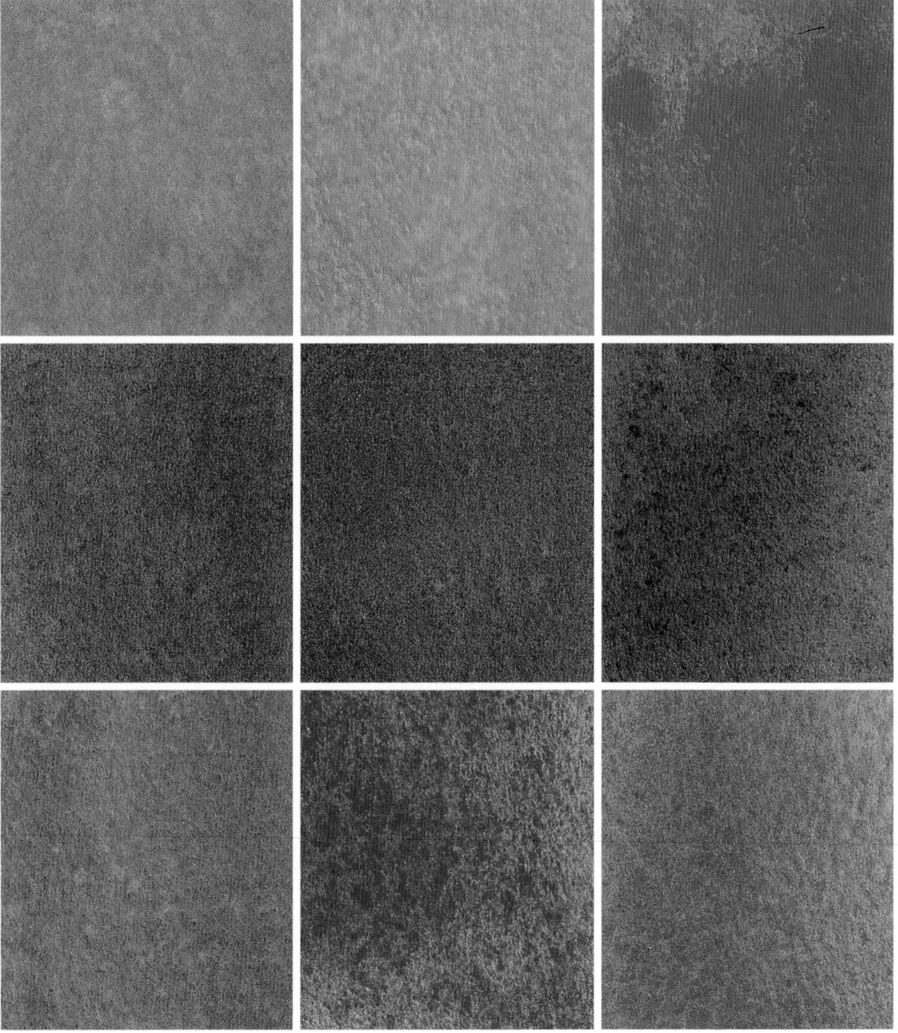

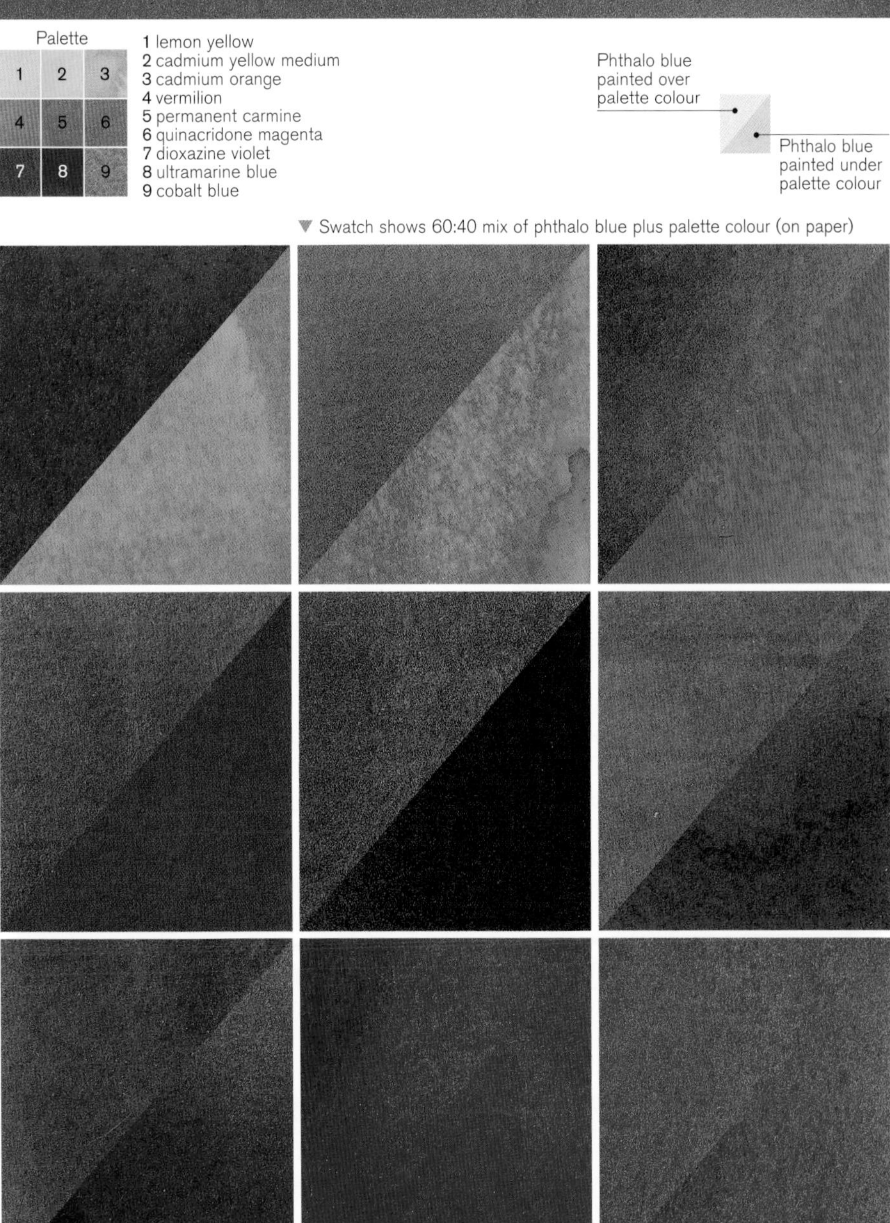

▼ Swatch shows 60:40 mix of phthalo blue plus palette colour (on paper)

Phthalo Blue/2

Transparency 4
Staining 2
Permanence 2

Granulation
as single colour 0
in mixes 1

Transparency

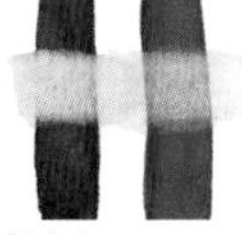
Staining

Granulation

▼ Swatch shows 60:40 mix of phthalo blue plus palette colour (on mixing palette)

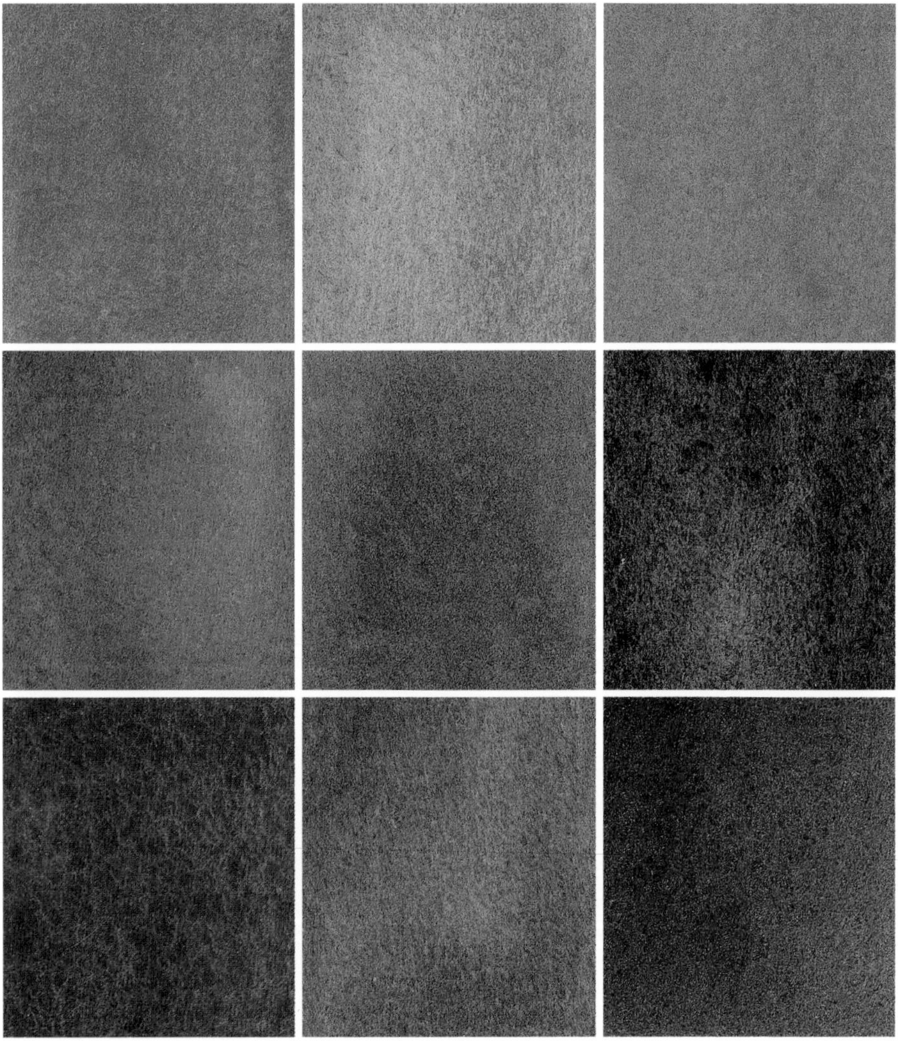

Palette

10 phthalo blue
11 manganese blue
12 phthalo green
13 sap green
14 yellow ochre
15 burnt umber
16 caput mortuum violet
17 sepia
18 indigo

Instead of overpainting the palette colour with itself in the mixes on paper, the upper triangle shows a single wash and the lower, a double wash.

Phthalo blue painted over palette colour

Phthalo blue painted under palette colour

▼ Swatch shows 60:40 mix of phthalo blue plus palette colour (on paper)

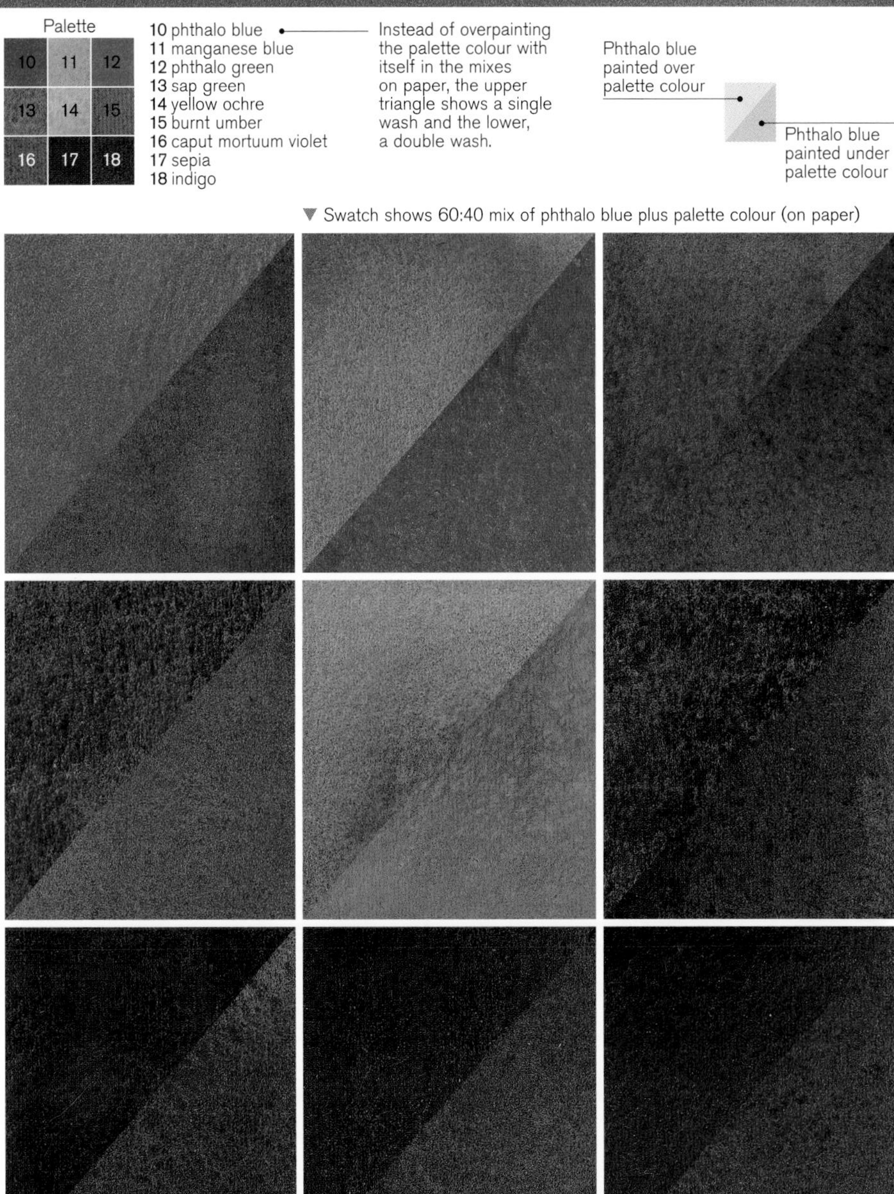

Cerulean Blue/1

The main characteristic of this early morning sky blue is its chalky granulation (it granulates more than cobalt blue, the other important sky colour pigment). This creates some magical three-dimensional mixes (see the mixes with yellow ochre on pages 134 and 135).

▼ Swatch shows 60:40 mix of cerulean blue plus palette colour (on mixing palette)

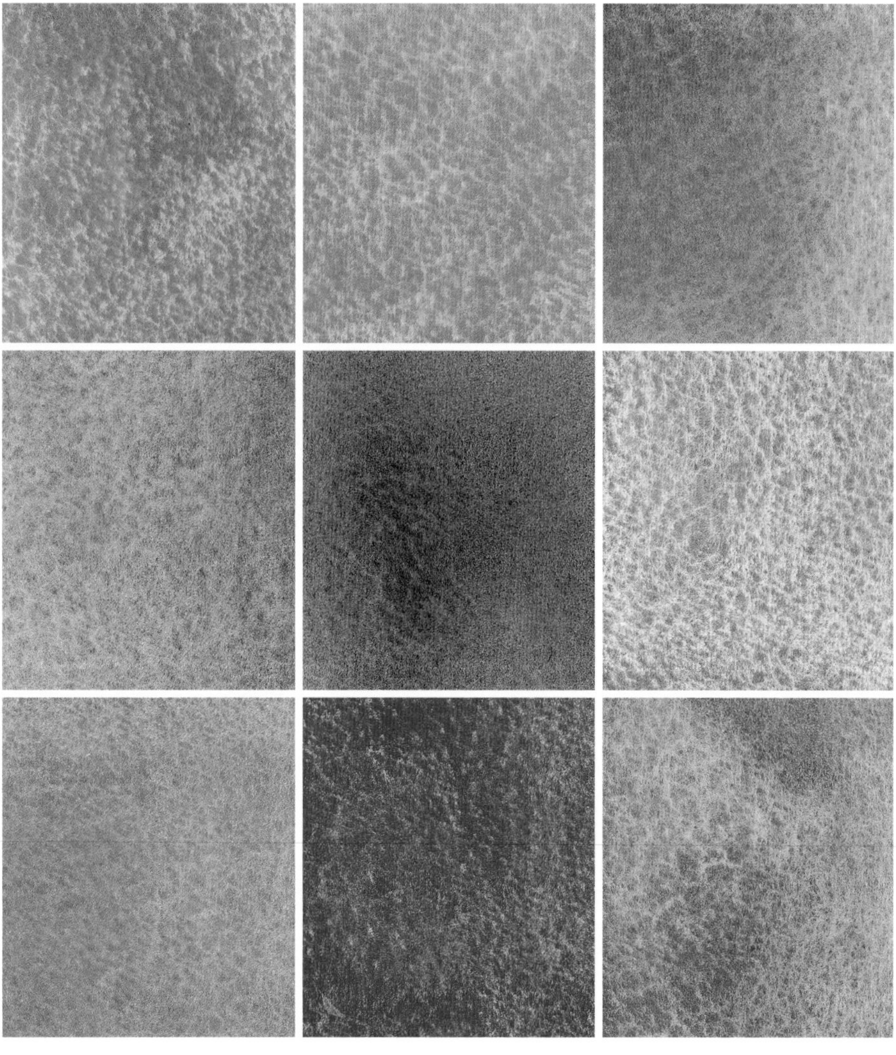

▼ Swatch shows 60:40 mix of cerulean blue plus palette colour (on paper)

Cerulean Blue/2

Transparency 3
Staining 1
Permanence 3

Granulation
as single colour 3
in mixes 3

Transparency

Staining

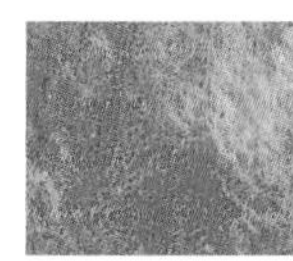
Granulation

▼ Swatch shows 60:40 mix of cerulean blue plus palette colour (on mixing palette)

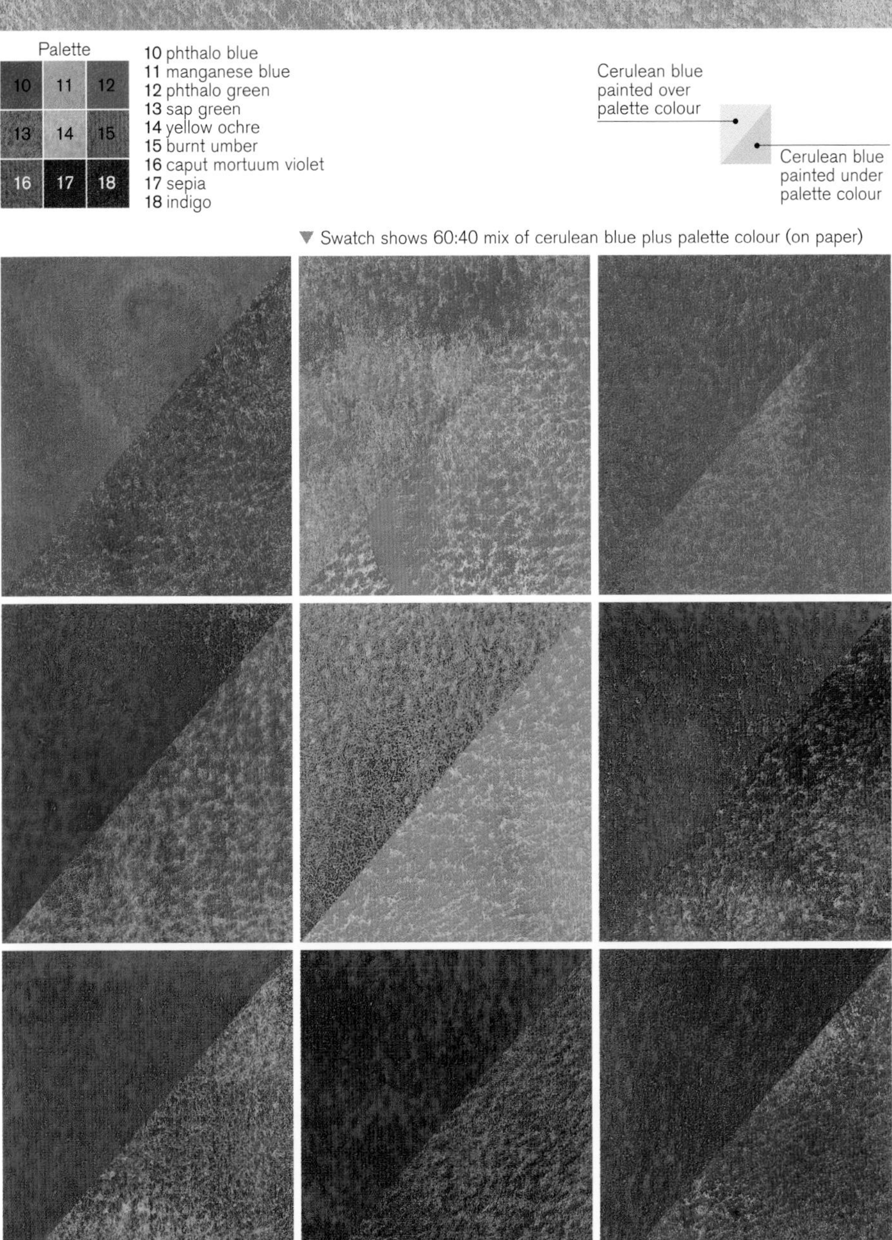

10 phthalo blue
11 manganese blue
12 phthalo green
13 sap green
14 yellow ochre
15 burnt umber
16 caput mortuum violet
17 sepia
18 indigo

▼ Swatch shows 60:40 mix of cerulean blue plus palette colour (on paper)

Manganese Blue/1

Manganese blue is brighter and greener than cerulean blue. The genuine pigment is very rare; most manufacturers produce a substitute (known as manganese blue hue) based on phthalo blue. It granulates to different degrees depending on the manufacturer.

▼ Swatch shows 60:40 mix of manganese blue plus palette colour (on mixing palette)

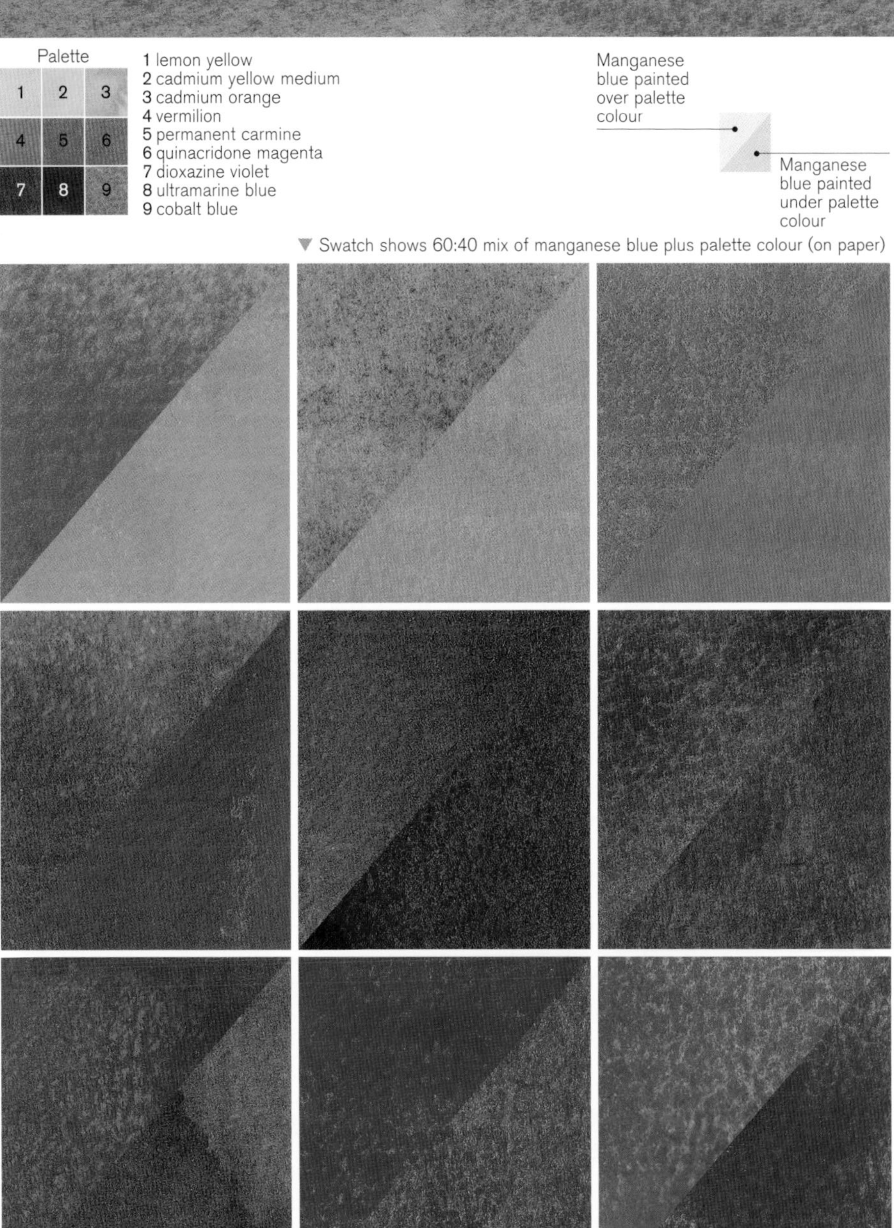

Palette

1	2	3
4	5	6
7	8	9

1 lemon yellow
2 cadmium yellow medium
3 cadmium orange
4 vermilion
5 permanent carmine
6 quinacridone magenta
7 dioxazine violet
8 ultramarine blue
9 cobalt blue

Manganese blue painted over palette colour

Manganese blue painted under palette colour

▼ Swatch shows 60:40 mix of manganese blue plus palette colour (on paper)

Manganese Blue/2

Transparency 2
Staining 1
Permanence 2

Granulation
as single colour 0/2
in mixes 3

Transparency

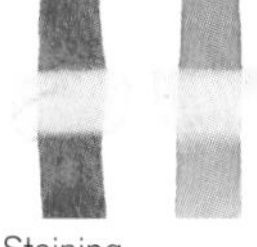
Staining

Granulation

▼ Swatch shows 60:40 mix of manganese blue plus palette colour (on mixing palette)

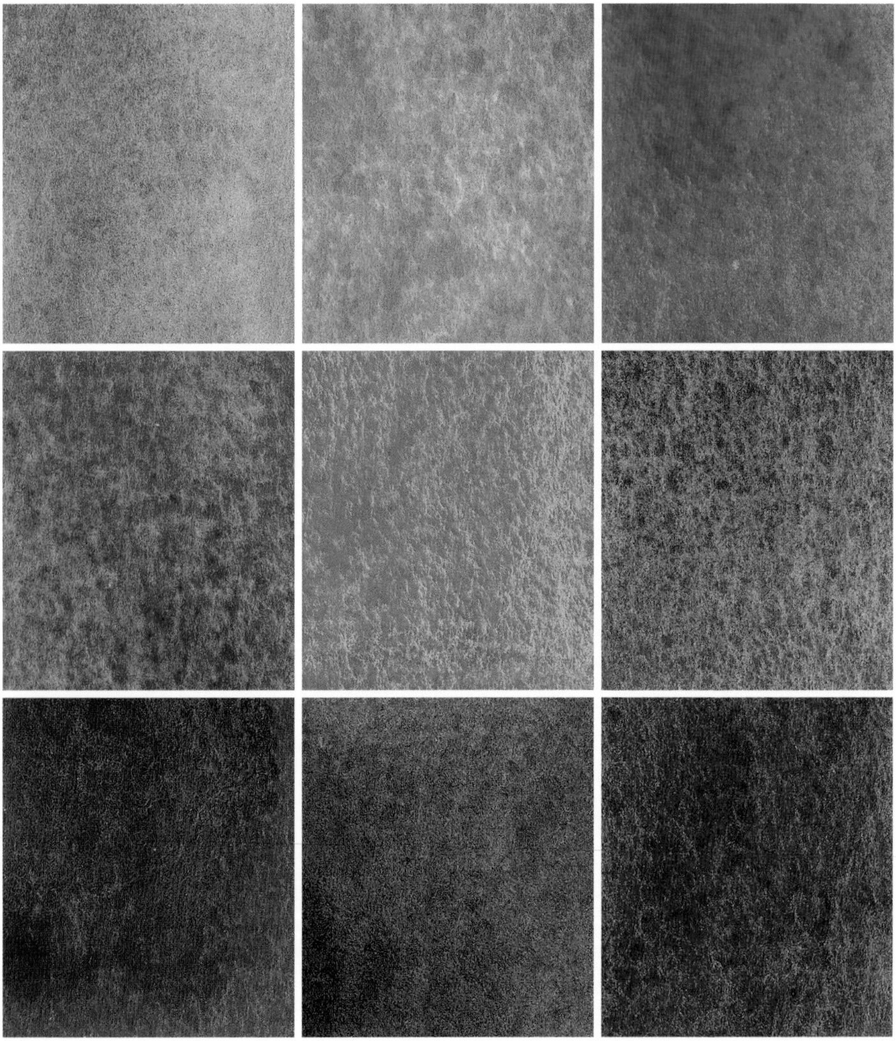

Palette

10 phthalo blue
11 manganese blue
12 phthalo green
13 sap green
14 yellow ochre
15 burnt umber
16 caput mortuum violet
17 sepia
18 indigo

Instead of overpainting the palette colour with itself in the mixes on paper, the upper triangle shows a single wash and the lower, a double wash.

Manganese blue painted over palette colour

Manganese blue painted under palette colour

▼ Swatch shows 60:40 mix of manganese blue plus palette colour (on paper)

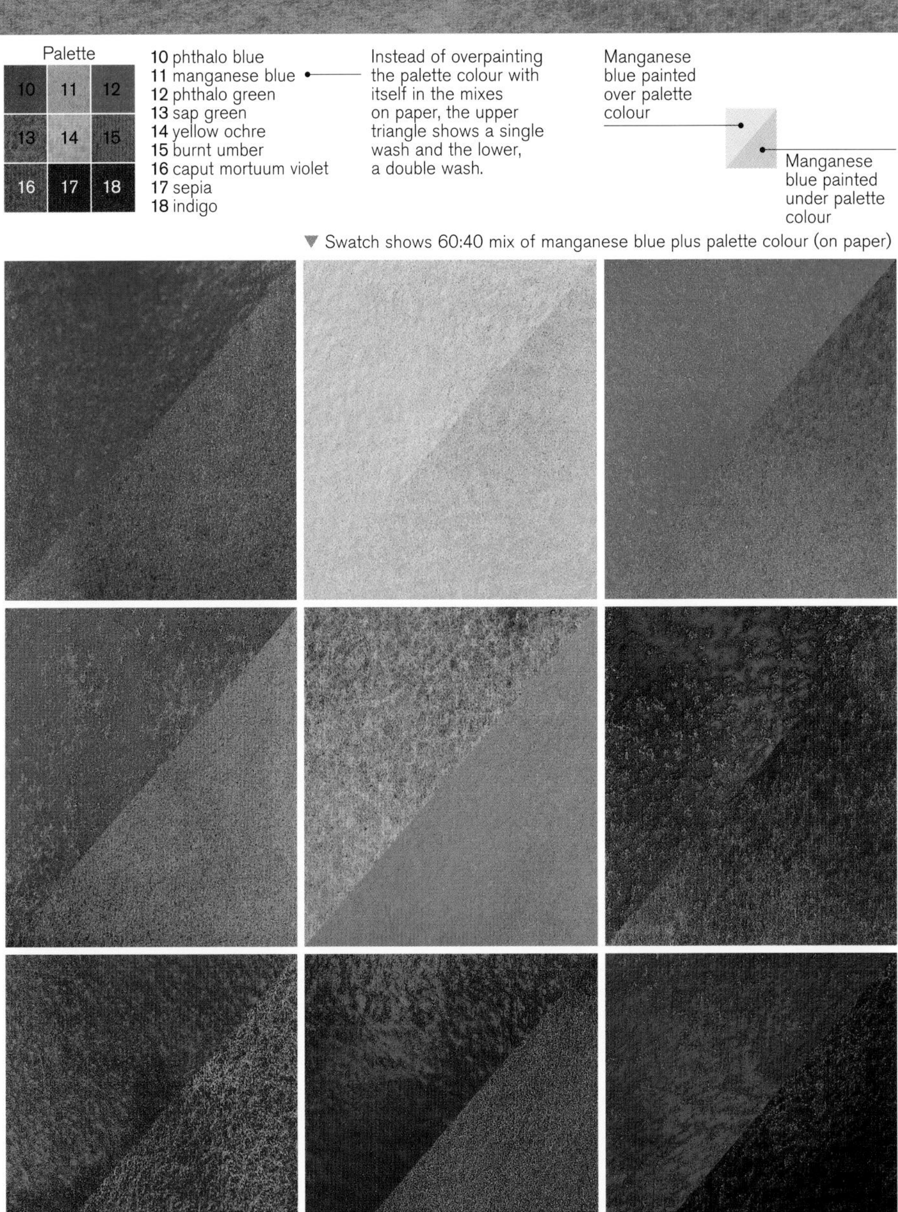

Cobalt Turquoise Light/1

This bright turquoise, lighter and more jewel-like than the slightly duller cobalt turquoise, is sometimes known as cobalt teal. Semi-opaque and granulating, it handles well in all washes and, when painted over burnt umber and caput mortuum violet, creates verdigris-like mixes.

▼ Swatch shows 60:40 mix of cobalt turquoise light plus palette colour (on mixing palette)

Palette

1	2	3
4	5	6
7	8	9

1 lemon yellow
2 cadmium yellow medium
3 cadmium orange
4 vermilion
5 permanent carmine
6 quinacridone magenta
7 dioxazine violet
8 ultramarine blue
9 cobalt blue

Cobalt turquoise light painted over palette colour

Cobalt turquoise light painted under palette colour

▼ Swatch shows 60:40 mix of cobalt turquoise light plus palette colour (on paper)

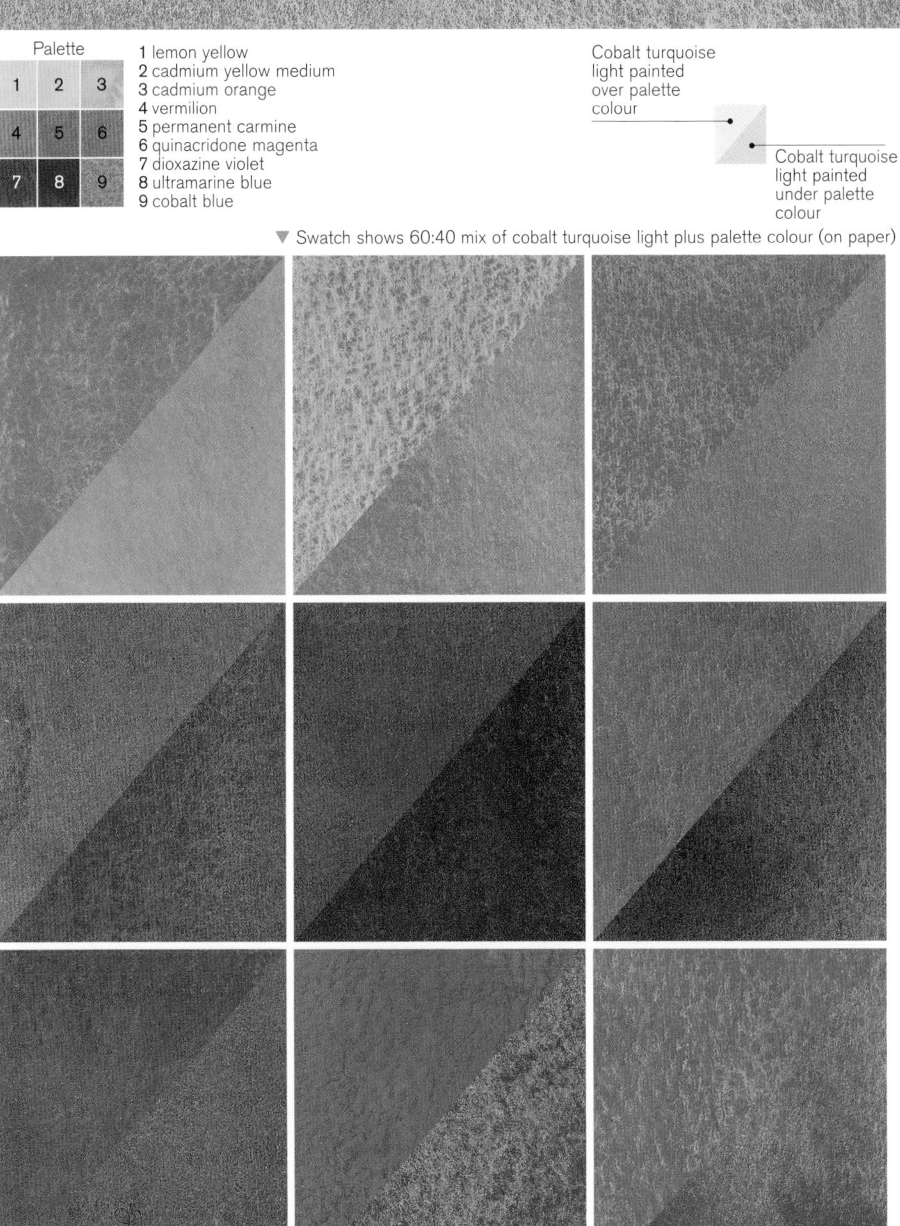

Cobalt Turquoise Light/2

Transparency 3
Staining 2
Permanence 3

Granulation
as single colour 3
in mixes 3

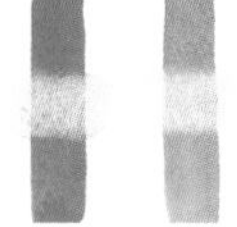

Transparency Staining Granulation

▼ Swatch shows 60:40 mix of cobalt turquoise light plus palette colour (on mixing palette)

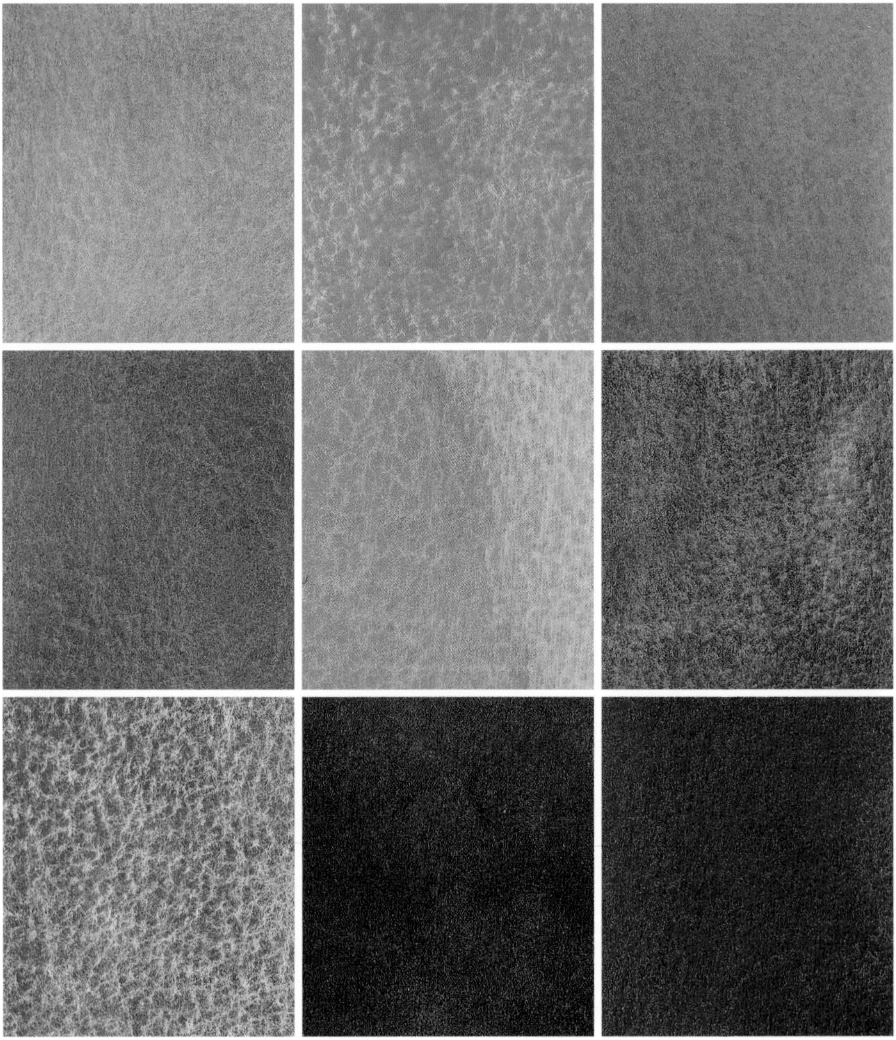

Palette

10	11	12
13	14	15
16	17	18

10 phthalo blue
11 manganese blue
12 phthalo green
13 sap green
14 yellow ochre
15 burnt umber
16 caput mortuum violet
17 sepia
18 indigo

Cobalt turquoise light painted over palette colour

Cobalt turquoise light painted under palette colour

▼ Swatch shows 60:40 mix of cobalt turquoise light plus palette colour (on paper)

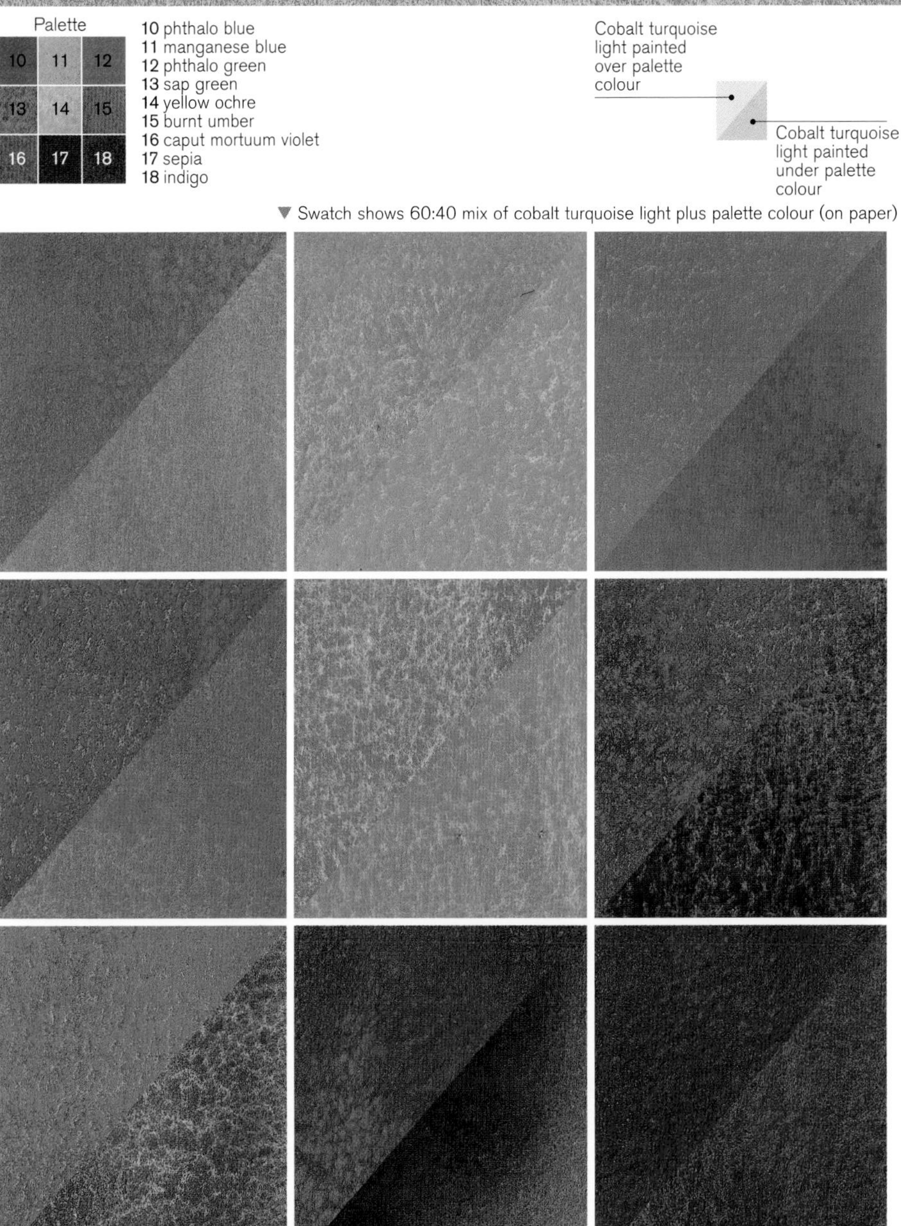

Cobalt Turquoise/1

More muted than the preceding colour, some mixes are greyer and slightly darker. As it has a darker tone, its granulation qualities are more obvious against lighter underwashes or the white of the support paper. It is semi-opaque and mixes well in most mixes.

▼ Swatch shows 60:40 mix of cobalt turquoise plus palette colour (on mixing palette)

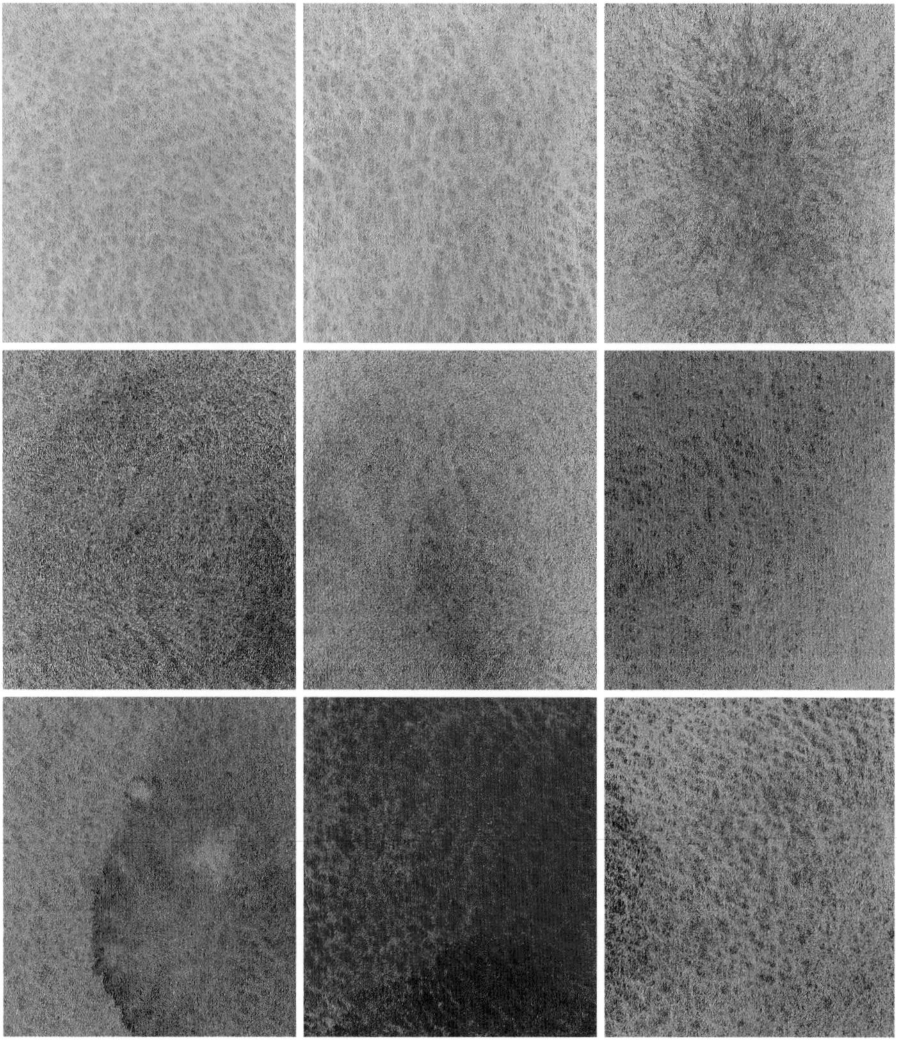

Palette

1 lemon yellow
2 cadmium yellow medium
3 cadmium orange
4 vermilion
5 permanent carmine
6 quinacridone magenta
7 dioxazine violet
8 ultramarine blue
9 cobalt blue

Cobalt turquoise painted over palette colour

Cobalt turquoise painted under palette colour

▼ Swatch shows 60:40 mix of cobalt turquoise plus palette colour (on paper)

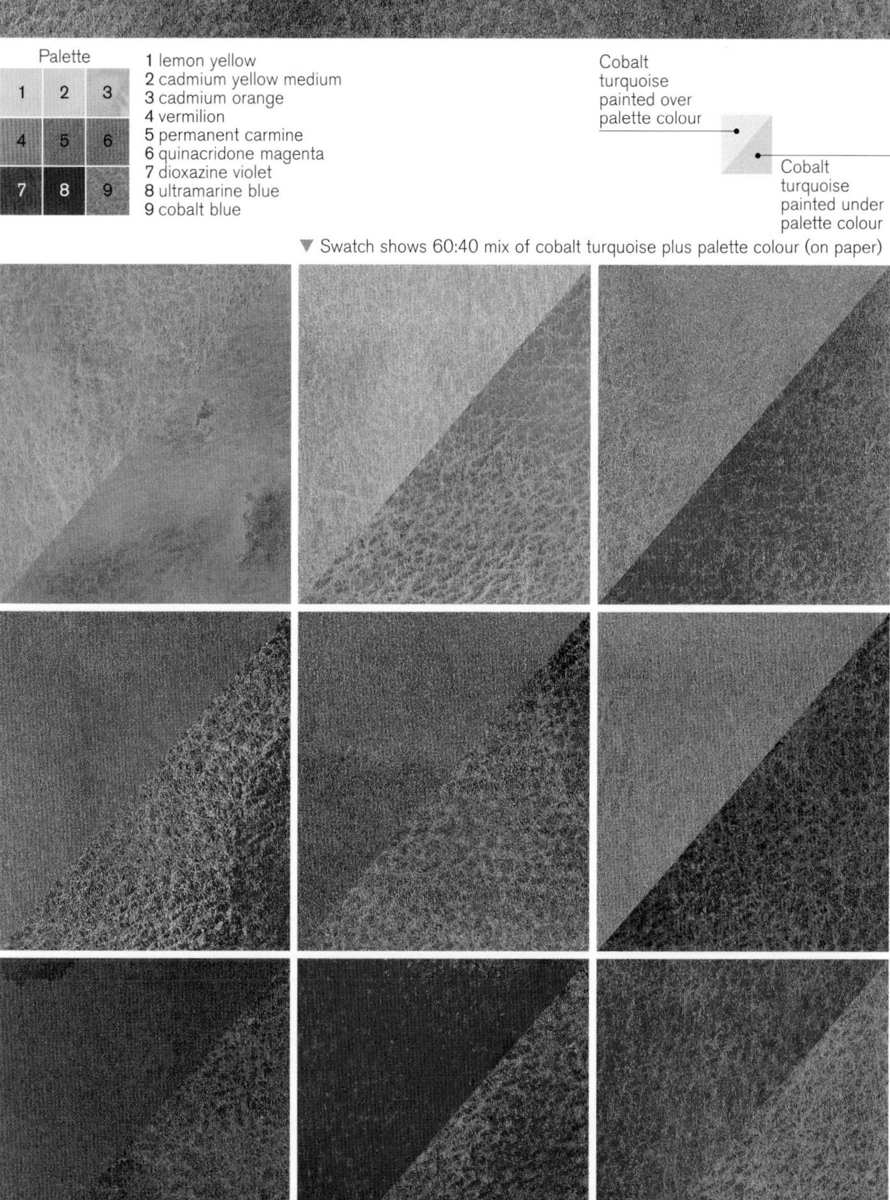

Cobalt Turquoise/2

Transparency 2
Staining 2
Permanence 3

Granulation
as single colour 2/3
in mixes 2

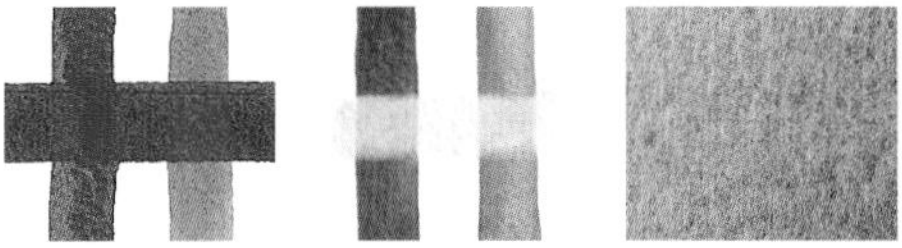

Transparency Staining Granulation

▼ Swatch shows 60:40 mix of cobalt turquoise plus palette colour (on mixing palette)

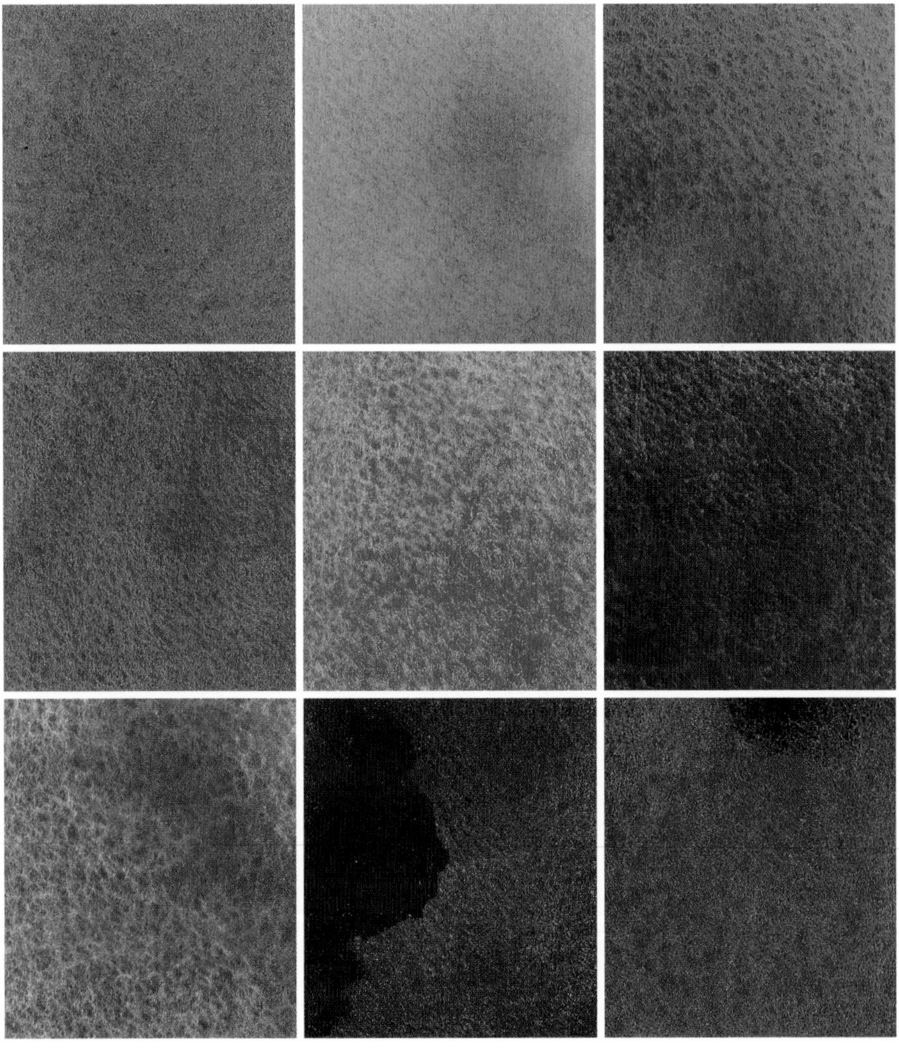

Palette

10	11	12
13	14	15
16	17	18

10 phthalo blue
11 manganese blue
12 phthalo green
13 sap green
14 yellow ochre
15 burnt umber
16 caput mortuum violet
17 sepia
18 indigo

Cobalt turquoise painted over palette colour

Cobalt turquoise painted under palette colour

▼ Swatch shows 60:40 mix of cobalt turquoise plus palette colour (on paper)

Phthalo Green/1

Phthalocyanine green is a strong, transparent, heavily staining, bluish green. It works well as the initial wash when working with glazed layers as it hardly moves when subsequent layers are added. As a single pigment it forms the basis of many manufactured mixed greens.

▼ Swatch shows 60:40 mix of phthalo green plus palette colour (on mixing palette)

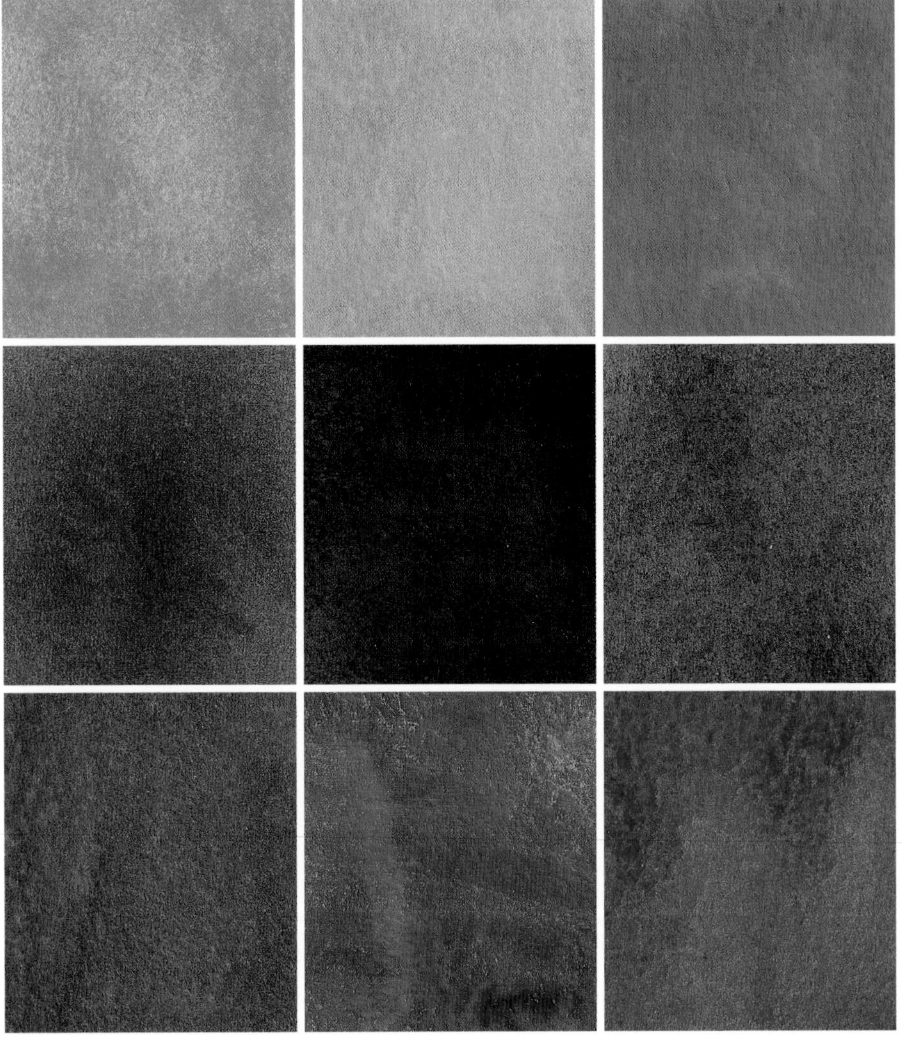

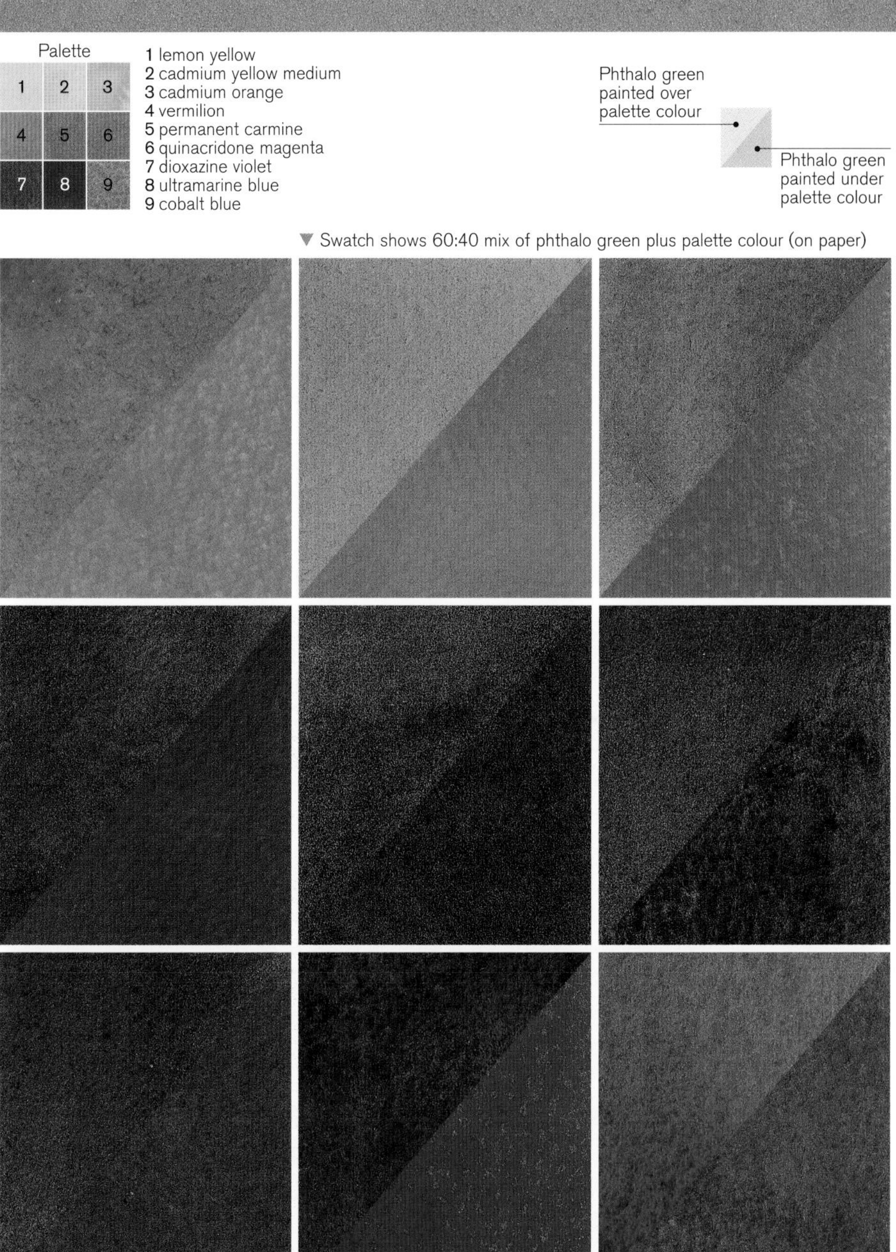

▼ Swatch shows 60:40 mix of phthalo green plus palette colour (on paper)

Phthalo Green/2

Transparency 4
Staining 3
Permanence 3

Granulation
as single colour 0
in mixes 0

Transparency

Staining

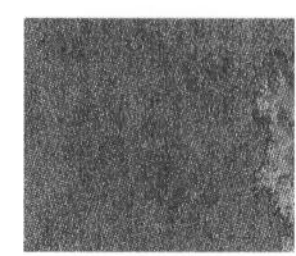

Granulation

▼ Swatch shows 60:40 mix of phthalo green plus palette colour (on mixing palette)

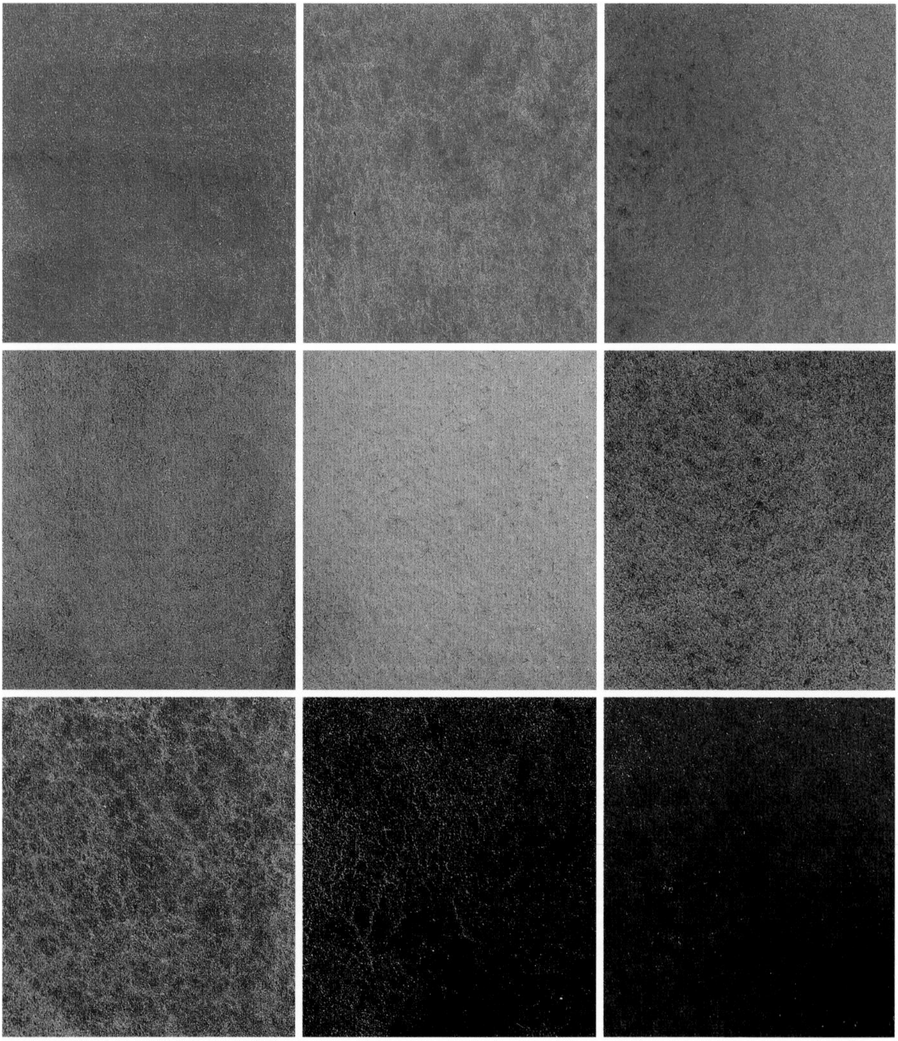

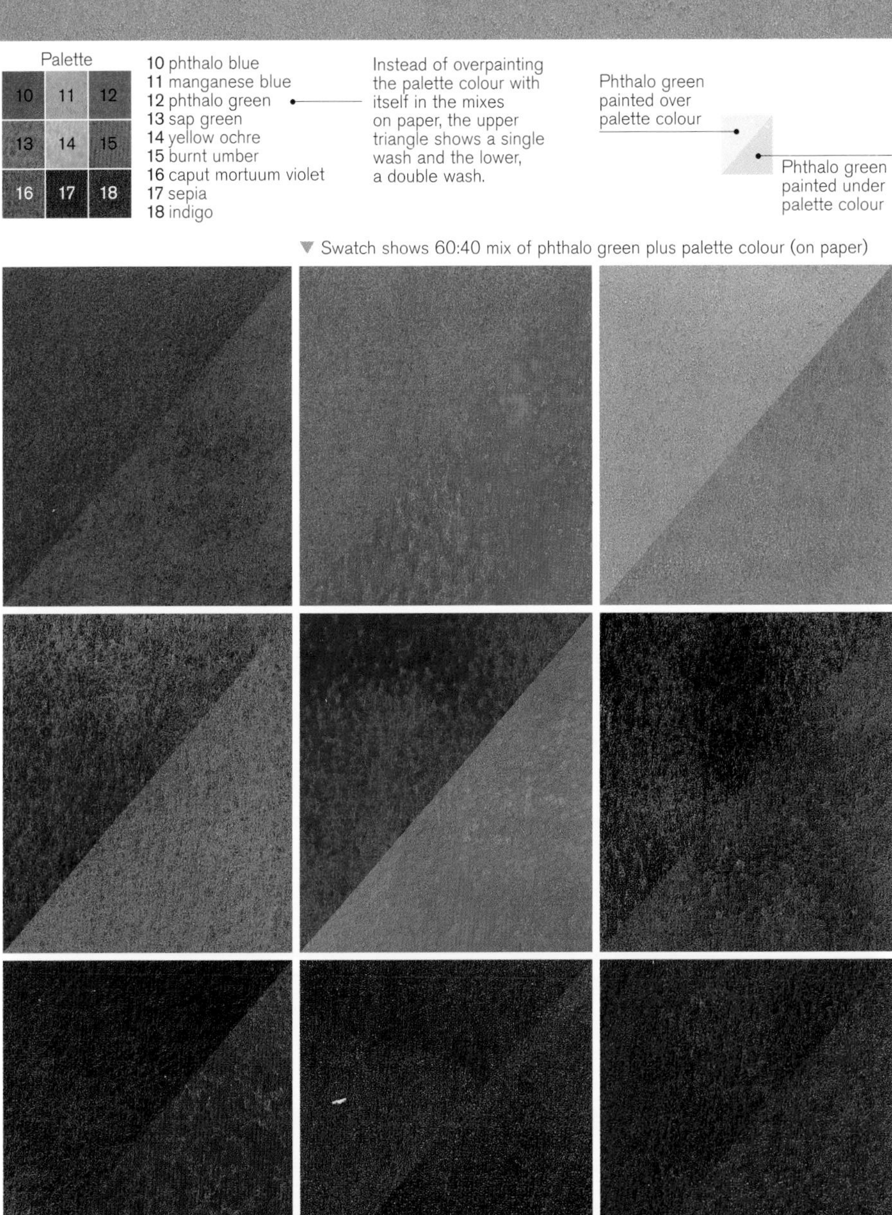

Instead of overpainting the palette colour with itself in the mixes on paper, the upper triangle shows a single wash and the lower, a double wash.

▼ Swatch shows 60:40 mix of phthalo green plus palette colour (on paper)

Viridian/1

This traditional cool green was very popular before the introduction of phthalo green. It is slightly duller and granulates readily. Its mixing ability varies according to manufacturer. When using viridian as an under- or overwash, keep it very dilute or prime first (see page 15).

▼ Swatch shows 60:40 mix of viridian plus palette colour (on mixing palette)

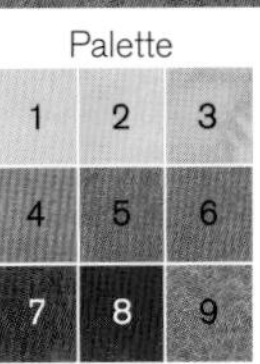

1 lemon yellow
2 cadmium yellow medium
3 cadmium orange
4 vermilion
5 permanent carmine
6 quinacridone magenta
7 dioxazine violet
8 ultramarine blue
9 cobalt blue

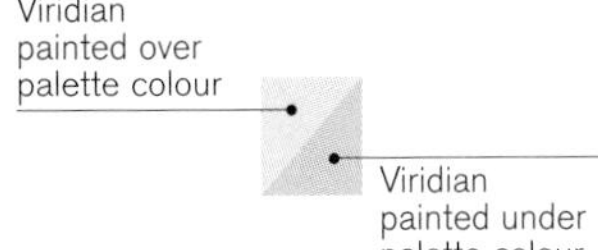

▼ Swatch shows 60:40 mix of viridian plus palette colour (on paper)

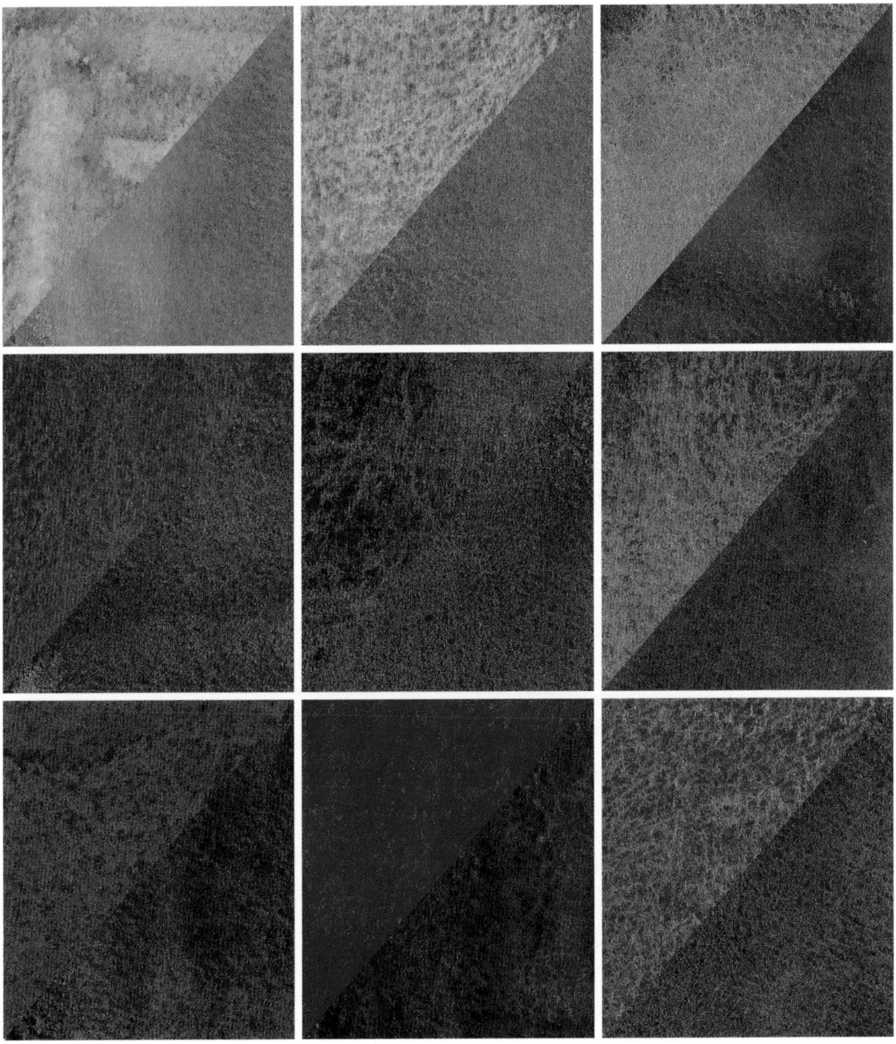

Viridian/2

Transparency 4
Staining 1
Permanence 2

Granulation
as single colour 0
in mixes 1

Transparency

Staining

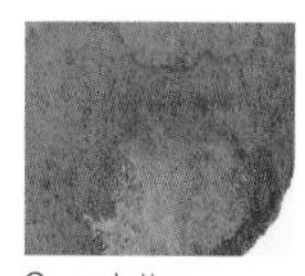
Granulation

▼ Swatch shows 60:40 mix of viridian plus palette colour (on mixing palette)

Palette

10	11	12
13	14	15
16	17	18

10 phthalo blue
11 manganese blue
12 phthalo green
13 sap green
14 yellow ochre
15 burnt umber
16 caput mortuum violet
17 sepia
18 indigo

Viridian painted over palette colour

Viridian painted under palette colour

▼ Swatch shows 60:40 mix of viridian plus palette colour (on paper)

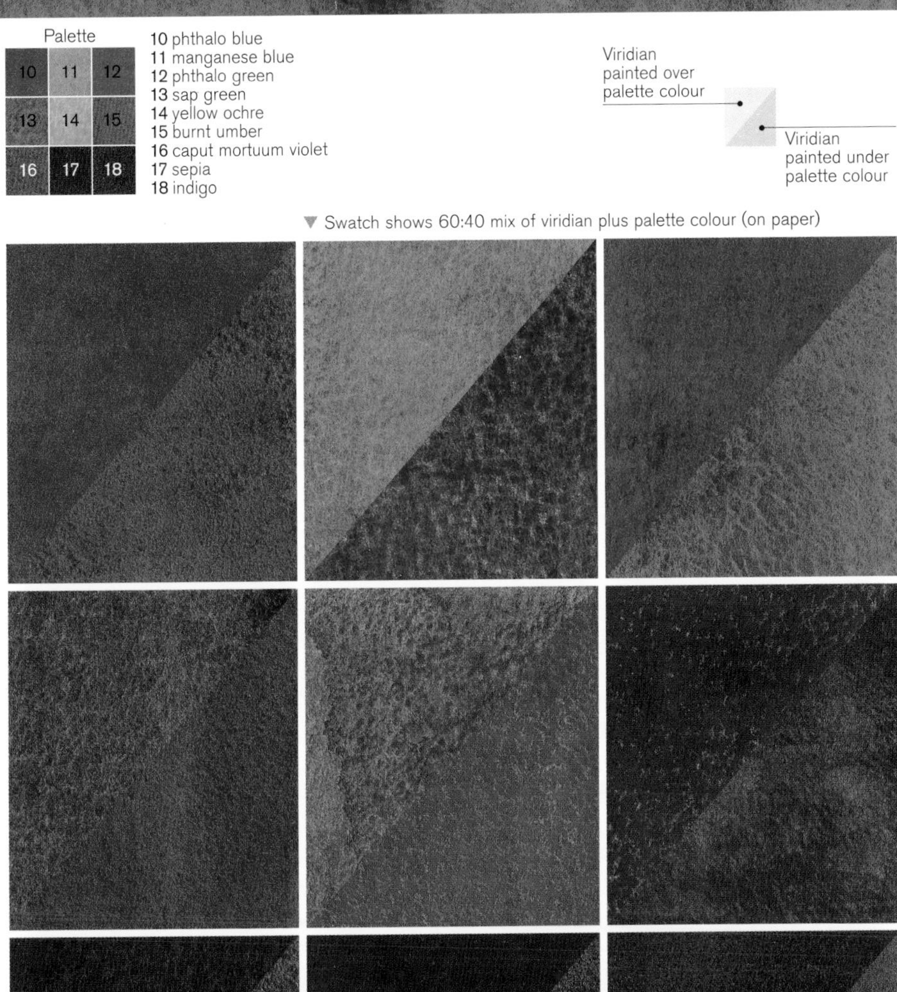

Terre Verte/1

This evocative name has been used for hundreds of years for a variety of green earth colours. It is available with either a yellow or blue hue (the latter is shown here). It is semi-transparent and granulates moderately. For flat washes, prime paper first as it can mottle slightly.

▼ Swatch shows 60:40 mix of terre verte plus palette colour (on mixing palette)

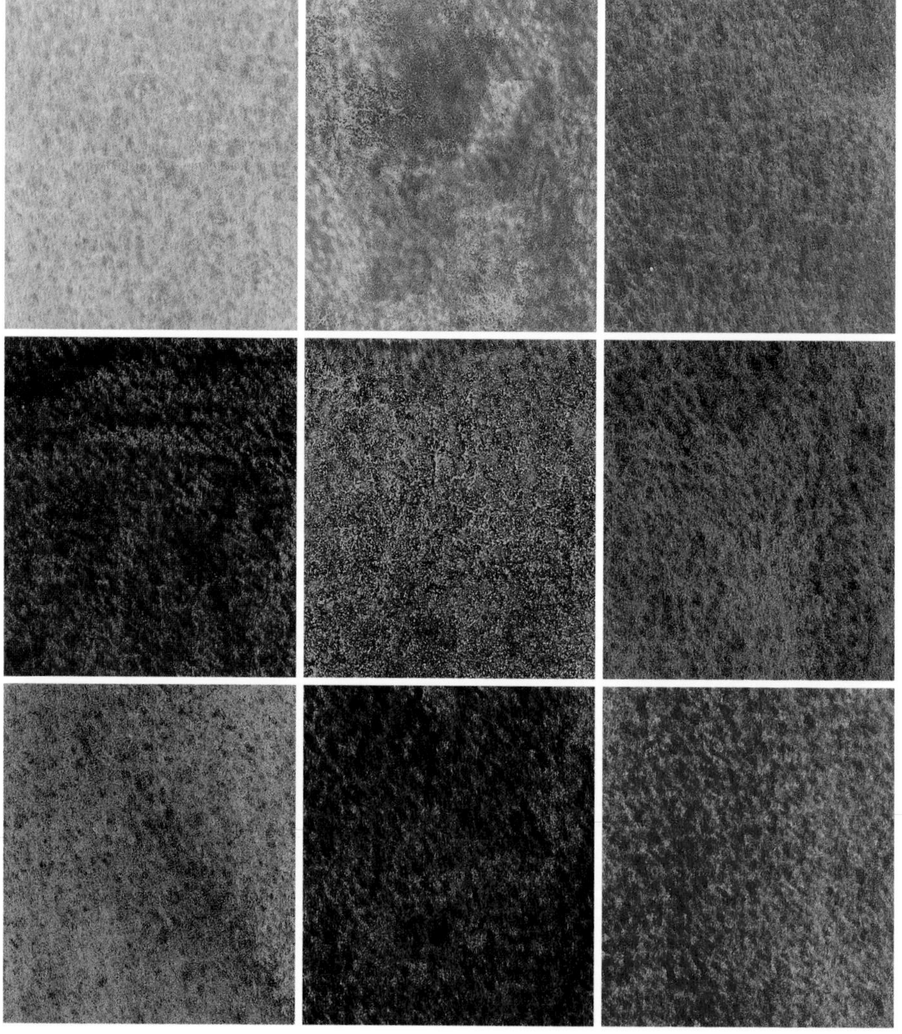

Palette

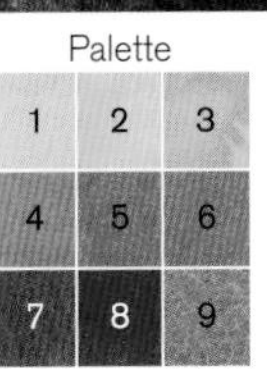

1 lemon yellow
2 cadmium yellow medium
3 cadmium orange
4 vermilion
5 permanent carmine
6 quinacridone magenta
7 dioxazine violet
8 ultramarine blue
9 cobalt blue

Terre verte painted over palette colour

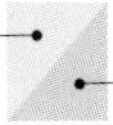

Terre verte painted under palette colour

▼ Swatch shows 60:40 mix of terre verte plus palette colour (on paper)

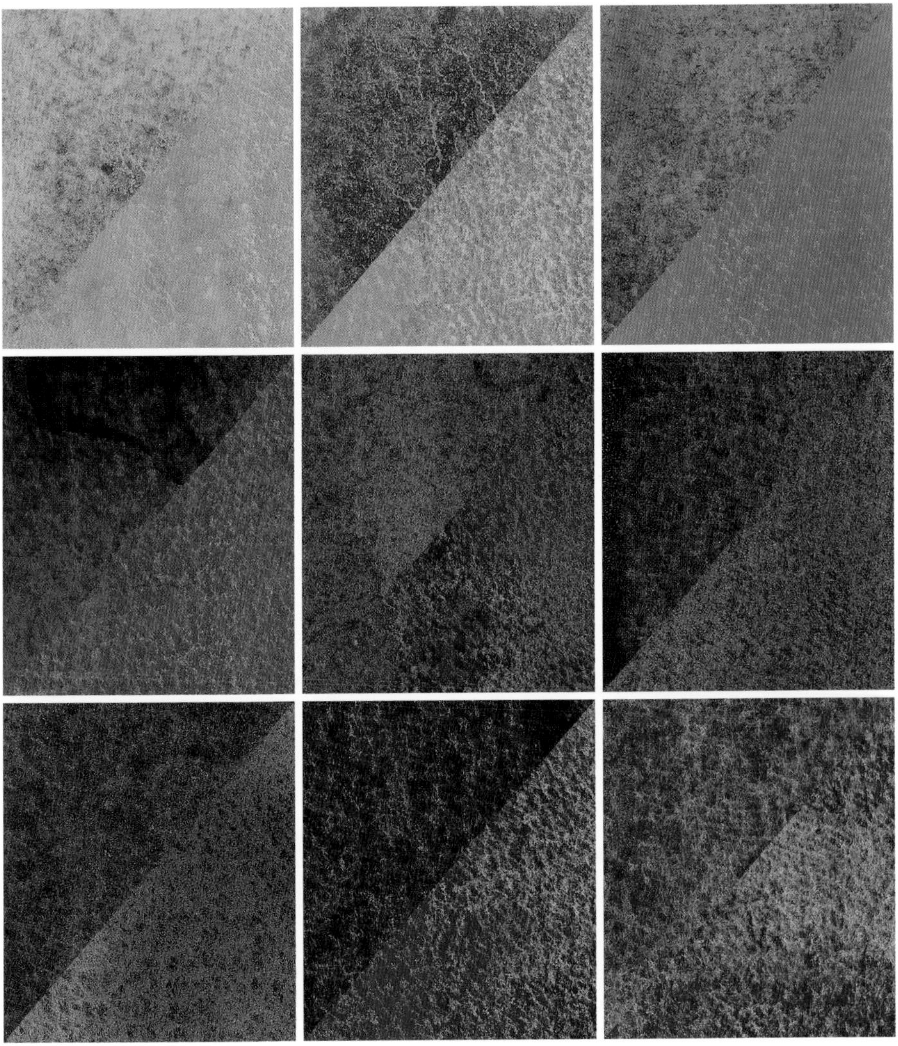

Terre Verte/2

Transparency 3
Staining 1
Permanence 3

Granulation
as single colour 1
in mixes 2

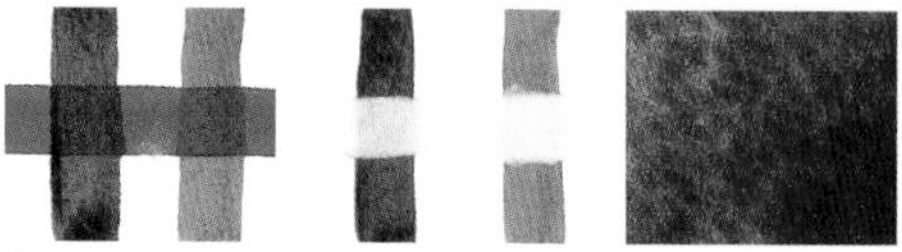

Transparency

Staining

Granulation

▼ Swatch shows 60:40 mix of terre verte plus palette colour (on mixing palette)

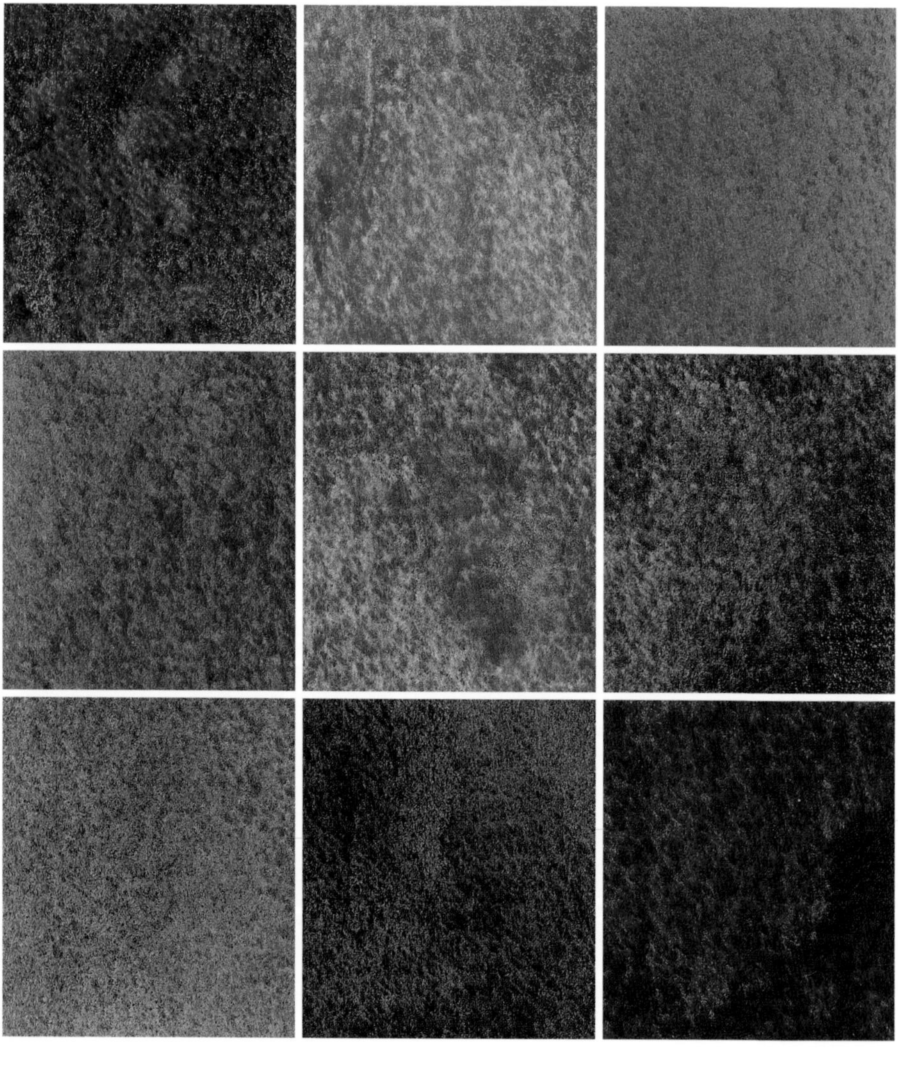

Palette

10	11	12
13	14	15
16	17	18

10 phthalo blue
11 manganese blue
12 phthalo green
13 sap green
14 yellow ochre
15 burnt umber
16 caput mortuum violet
17 sepia
18 indigo

Terre verte painted over palette colour

Terre verte painted under palette colour

▼ Swatch shows 60:40 mix of terre verte plus palette colour (on paper)

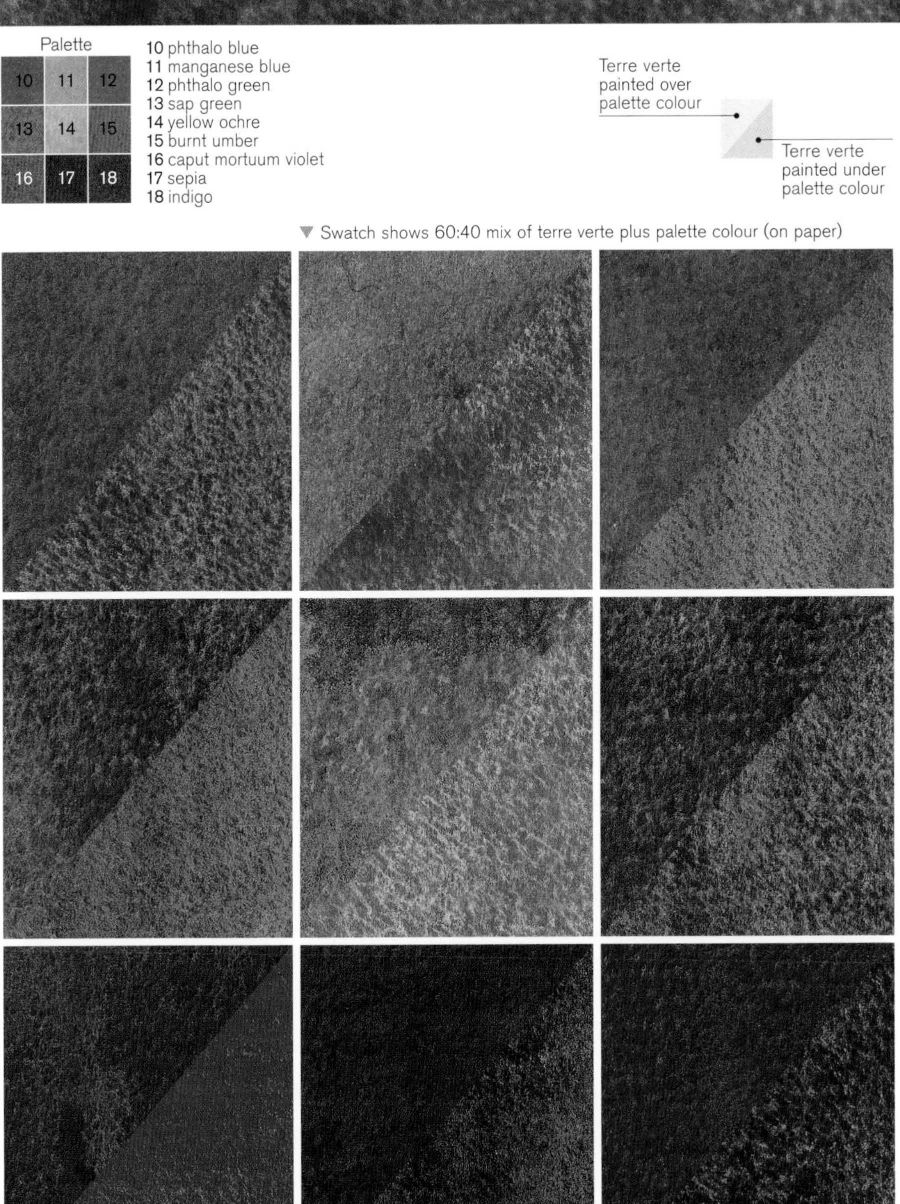

Hooker's Green Medium/1

A strong, semi-transparent green poised between blue and yellow; it can be "pushed" either way, making shadowy or sunlit greens. As a mid-green, it is similar to the range of permanent greens available. It mixes well and its naturalistic colour is perfect for a landscape palette.

▼ Swatch shows 60:40 mix of Hooker's green medium plus palette colour (on mixing palette)

Palette

1	2	3
4	5	6
7	8	9

1 lemon yellow
2 cadmium yellow medium
3 cadmium orange
4 vermilion
5 permanent carmine
6 quinacridone magenta
7 dioxazine violet
8 ultramarine blue
9 cobalt blue

Hooker's green medium painted over palette colour

Hooker's green medium painted under palette colour

▼ Swatch shows 60:40 mix of Hooker's green medium plus palette colour (on paper)

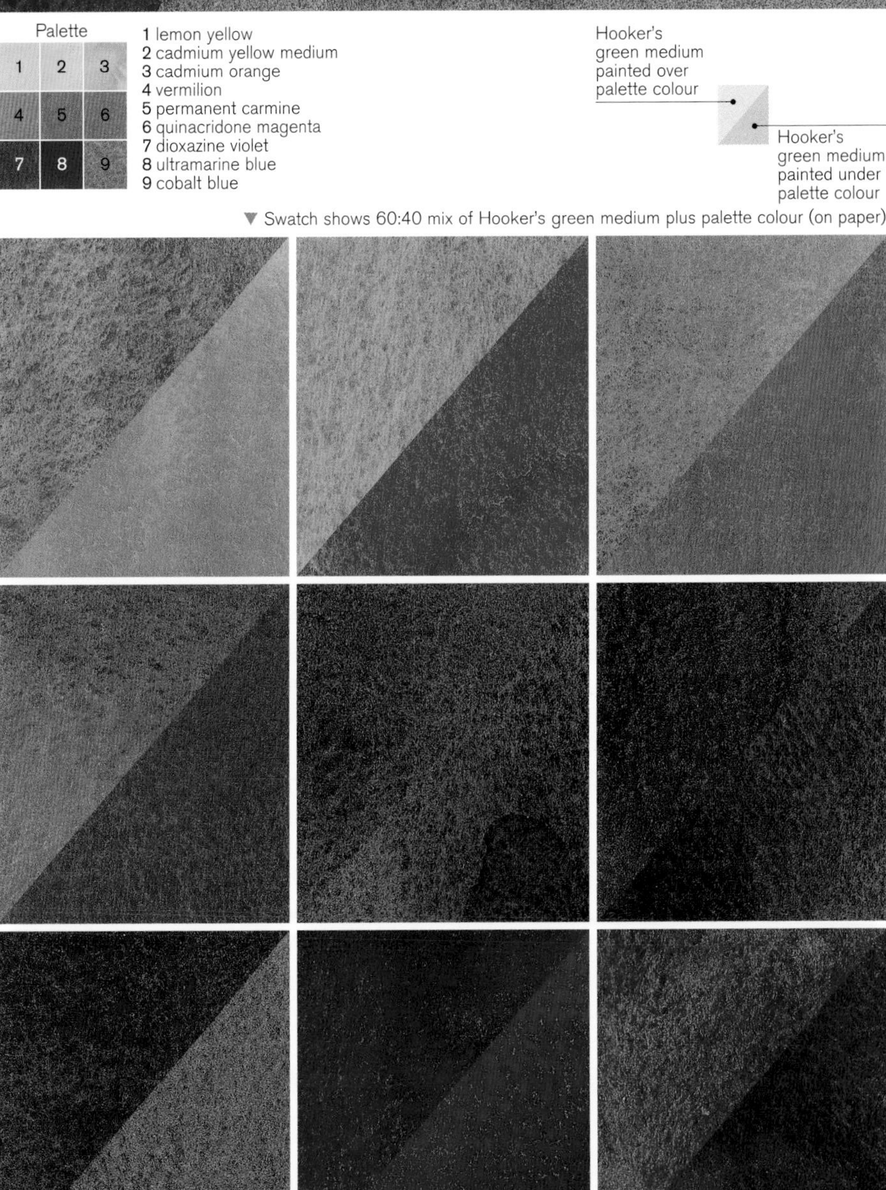

Hooker's Green Medium/2

Transparency 3
Staining 1
Permanence 2

Granulation
as single colour 0
in mixes 1

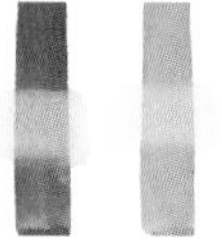

Transparency Staining  Granulation

▼ Swatch shows 60:40 mix of Hooker's green medium plus palette colour (on mixing palette)

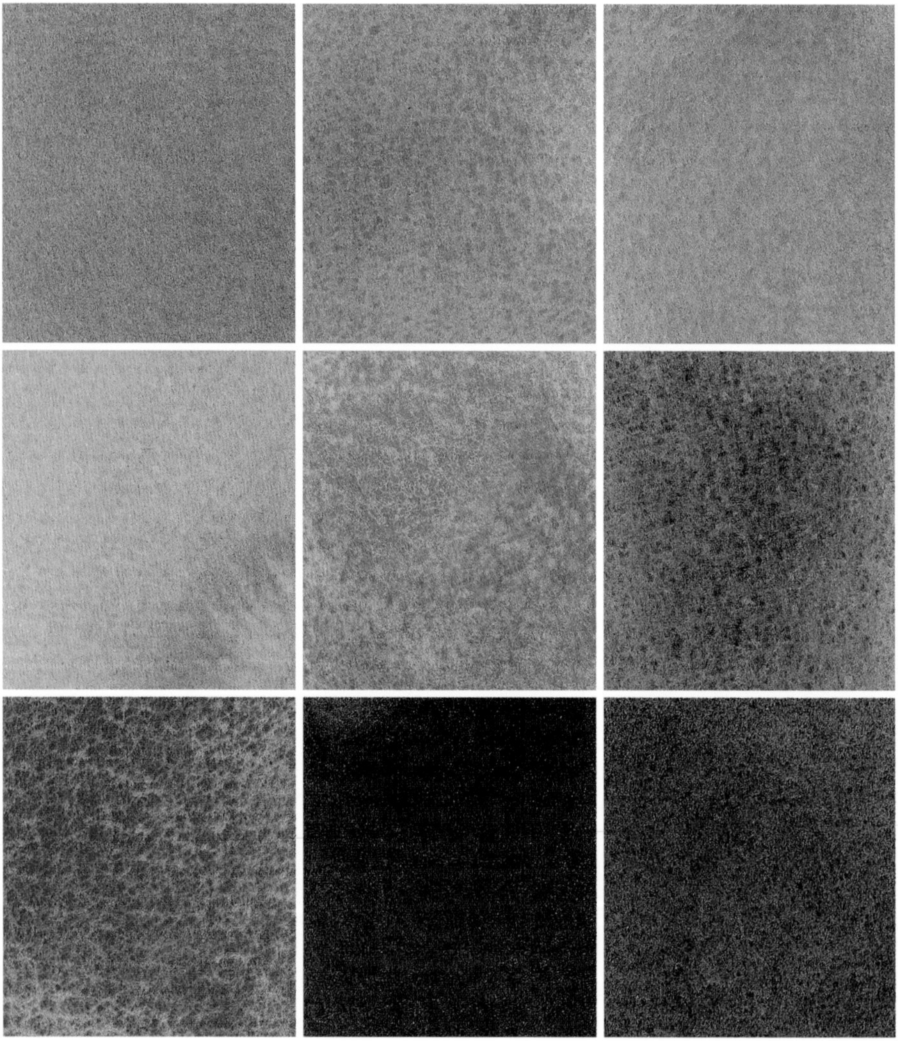

Palette

10	11	12
13	14	15
16	17	18

10 phthalo blue
11 manganese blue
12 phthalo green
13 sap green
14 yellow ochre
15 burnt umber
16 caput mortuum violet
17 sepia
18 indigo

Hooker's green medium painted over palette colour

Hooker's green medium painted under palette colour

▼ Swatch shows 60:40 mix of Hooker's green medium plus palette colour (on paper)

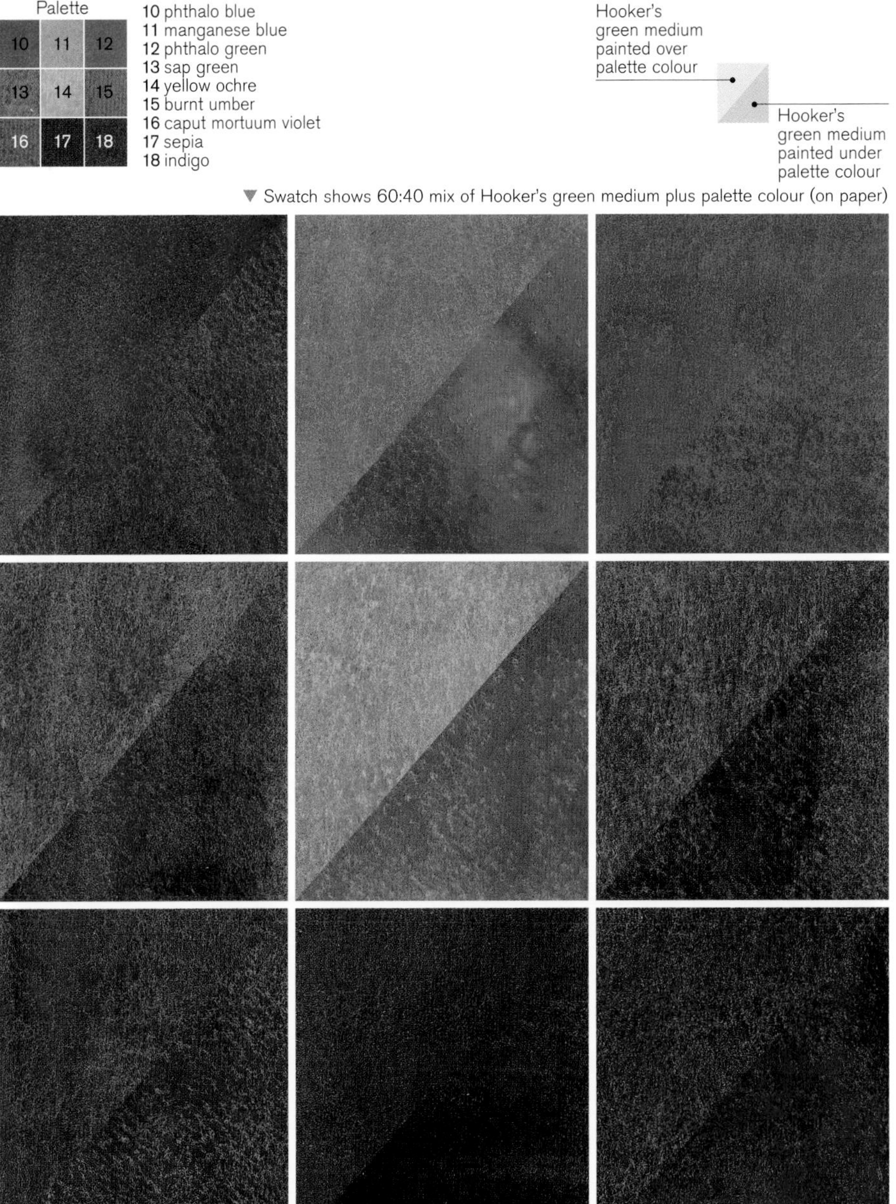

Phthalo Yellow-Green/1

This vivid green is visually placed between lemon yellow and a "true" green. Its sharp acid hue produces bright greens when mixed with blues, and subtle ochres when mixed with reds. Apply thinly as an inital wash as it tends to clump when re-wet with a second colour.

▼ Swatch shows 60:40 mix of phthalo yellow-green plus palette colour (on mixing palette)

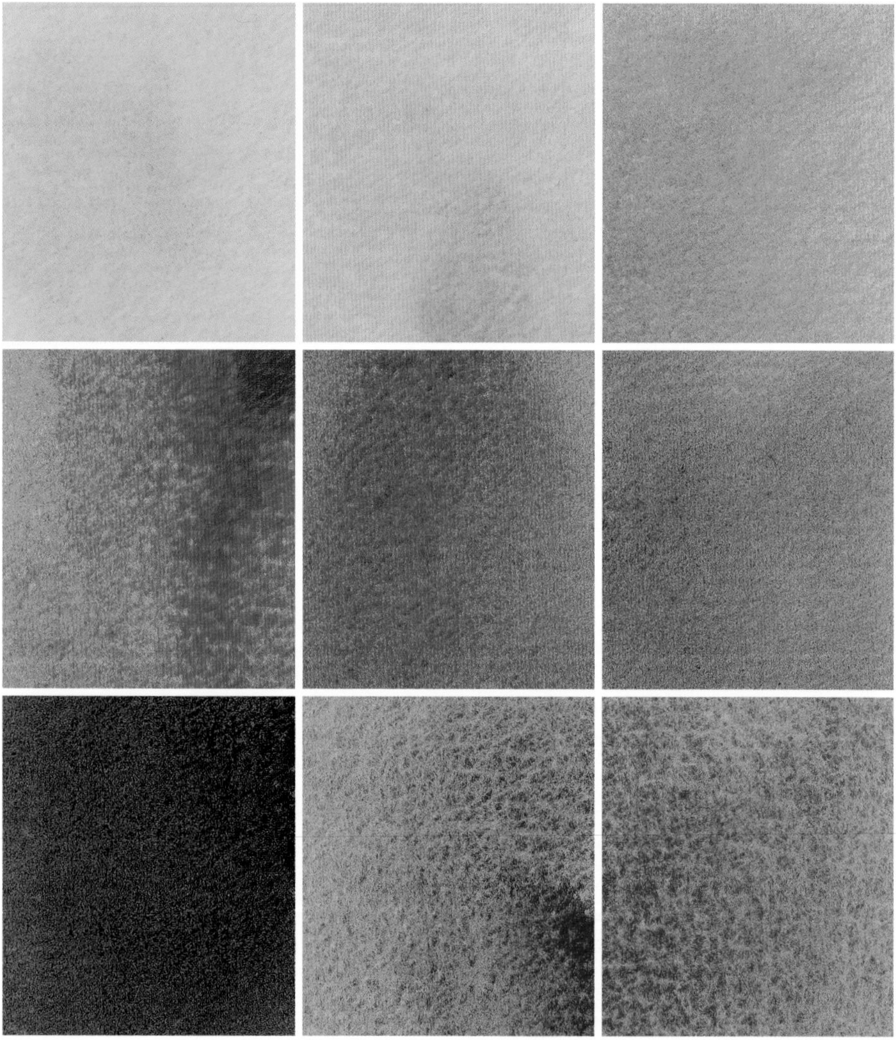

Palette

1	2	3
4	5	6
7	8	9

1 lemon yellow
2 cadmium yellow medium
3 cadmium orange
4 vermilion
5 permanent carmine
6 quinacridone magenta
7 dioxazine violet
8 ultramarine blue
9 cobalt blue

Phthalo yellow-green painted over palette colour

Phthalo yellow-green painted under palette colour

▼ Swatch shows 60:40 mix of phthalo yellow-green plus palette colour (on paper)

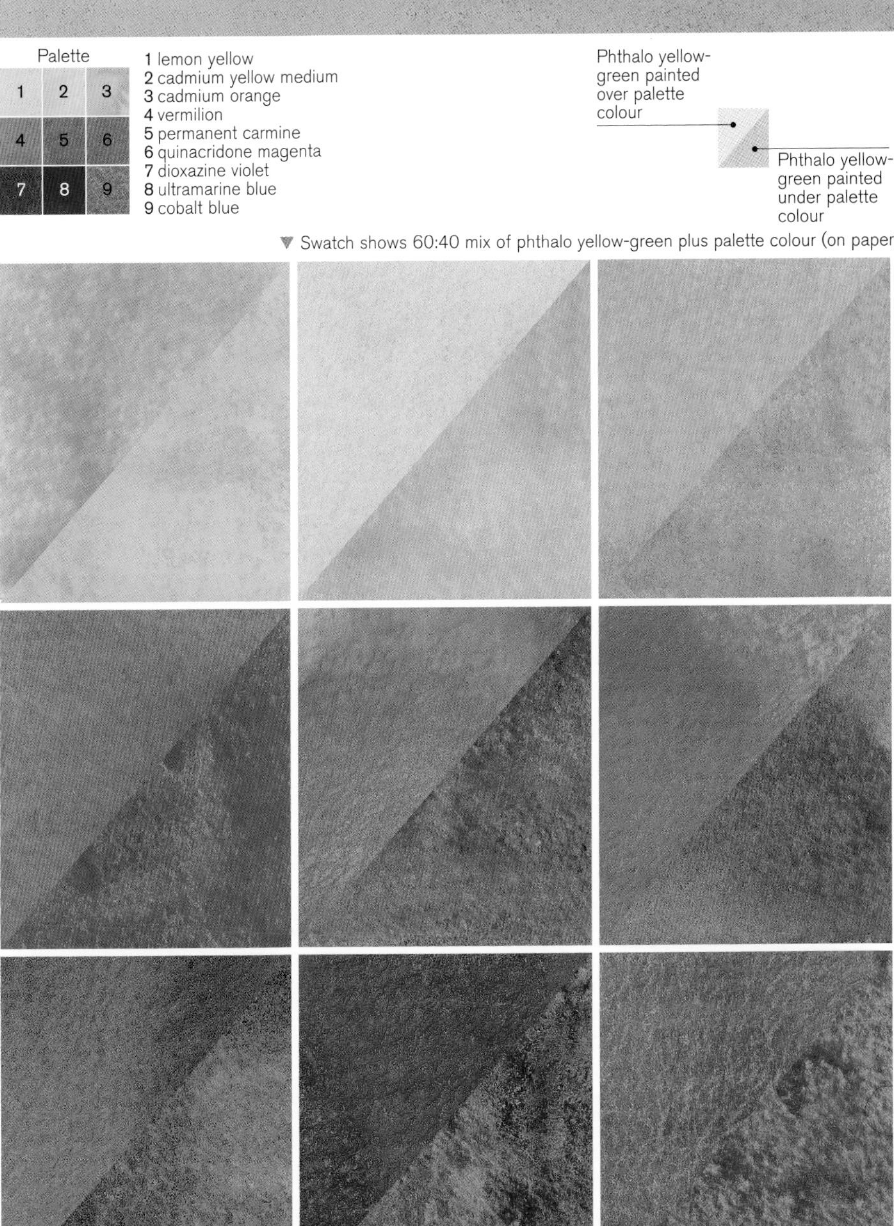

Phthalo Yellow-Green/2

Transparency 2/3
Staining 3
Permanence 2

Granulation
as single colour 0
in mixes 1

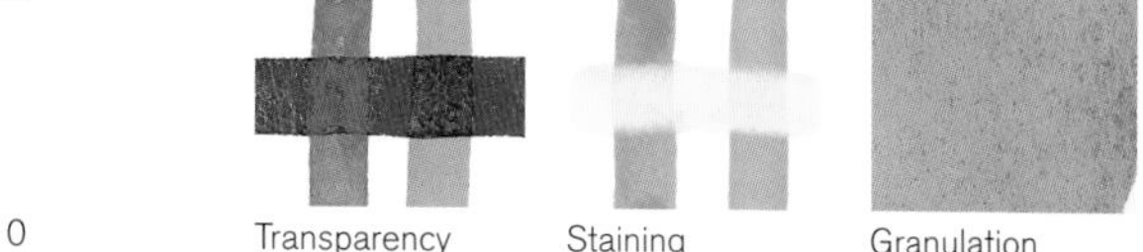

Transparency Staining Granulation

▼ Swatch shows 60:40 mix of phthalo yellow-green plus palette colour (on mixing palette)

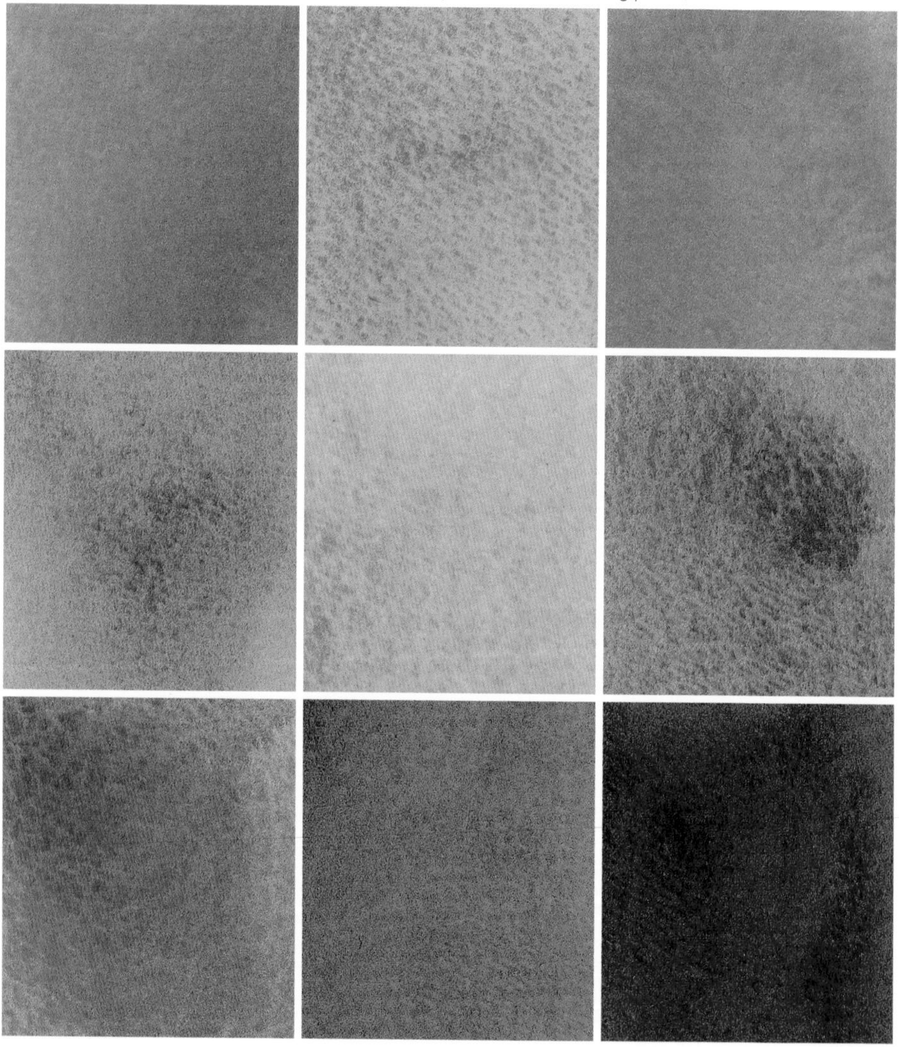

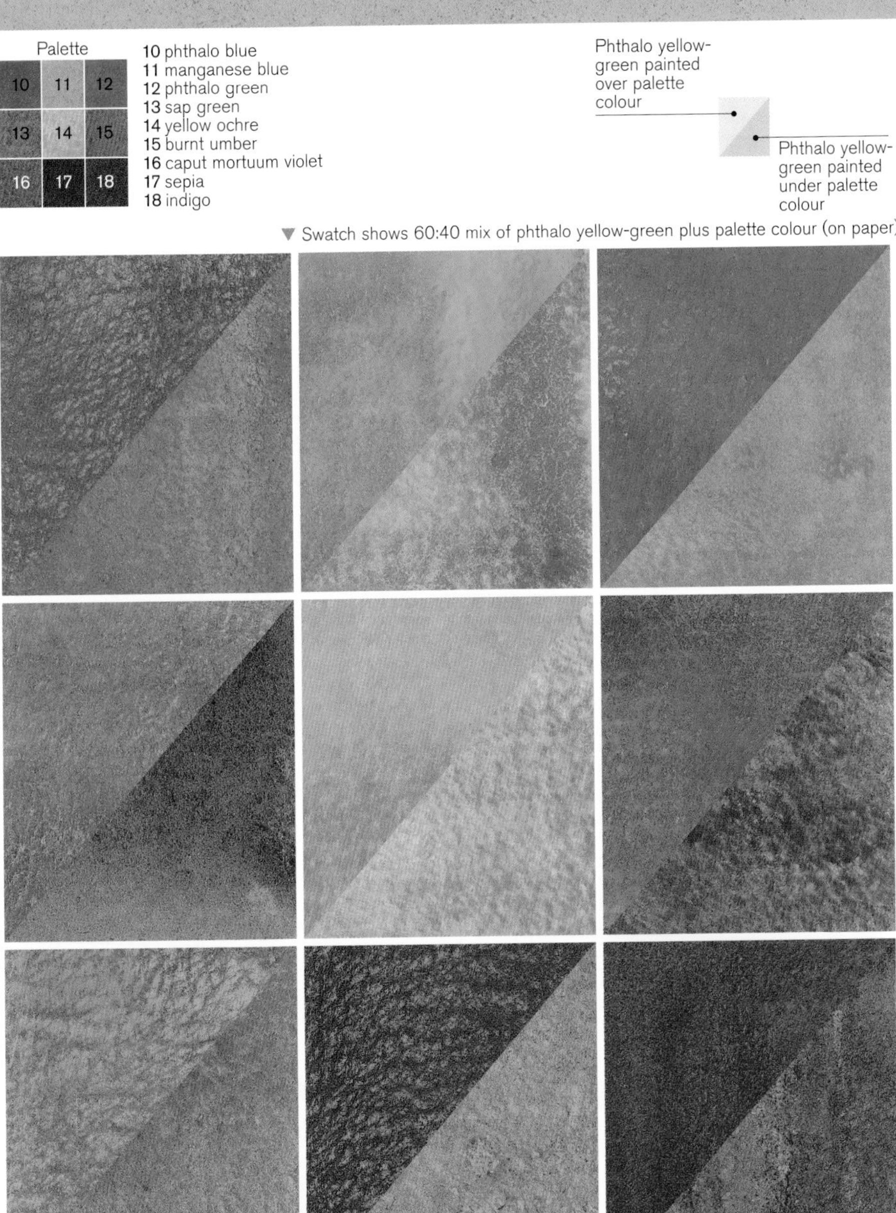

▼ Swatch shows 60:40 mix of phthalo yellow-green plus palette colour (on paper)

Sap Green/1

A sunny green, formed from a mix based on PG7 or PG 36 (see page 252), combined with yellow or orange. It is transparent, robust and mixes very well. It is useful in landscape palettes when mixed with other colours; use as a single colour with discretion as it is easily recognizable.

▼ Swatch shows 60:40 mix of sap green plus palette colour (on mixing palette)

Palette

1	2	3
4	5	6
7	8	9

1 lemon yellow
2 cadmium yellow medium
3 cadmium orange
4 vermilion
5 permanent carmine
6 quinacridone magenta
7 dioxazine violet
8 ultramarine blue
9 cobalt blue

Sap green painted over palette colour

Sap green painted under palette colour

▼ Swatch shows 60:40 mix of sap green plus palette colour (on paper)

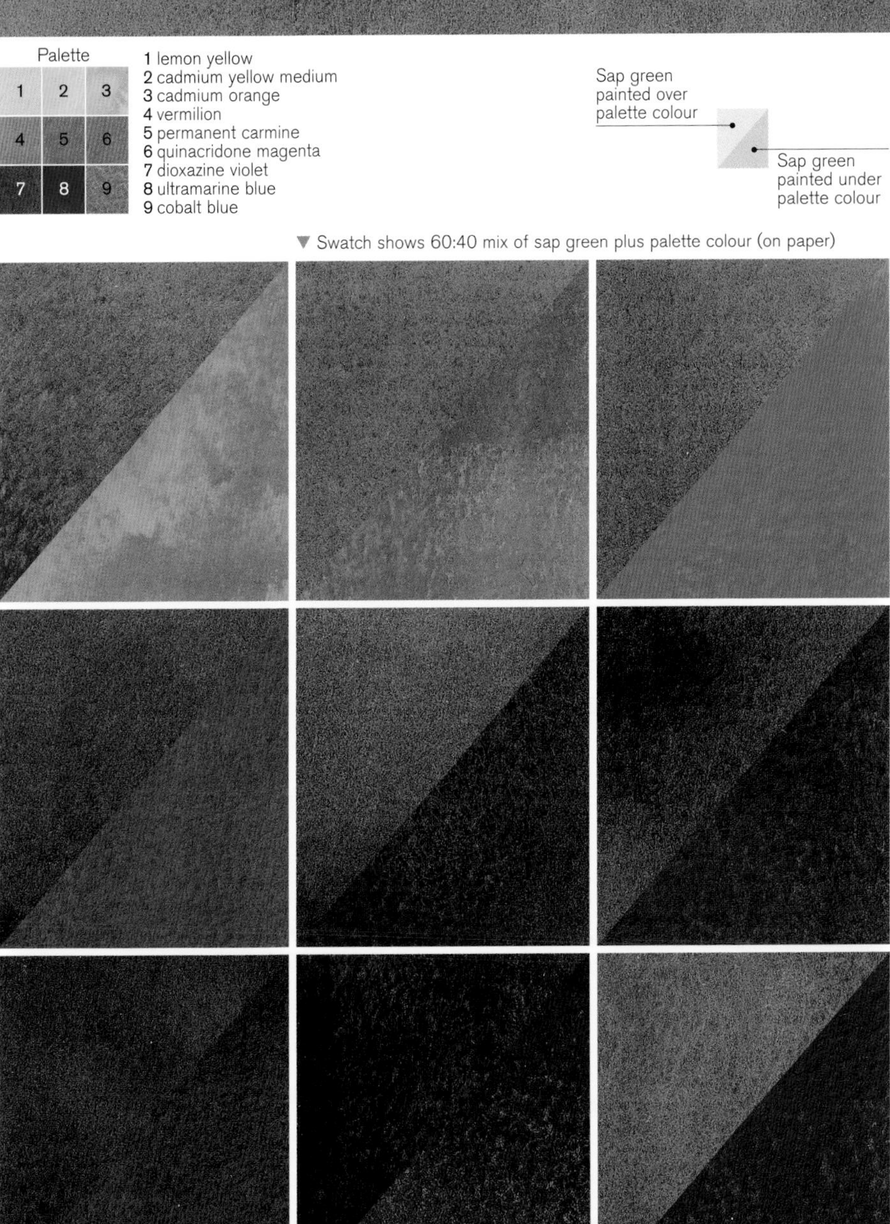

Sap Green/2

Transparency 3/4
Staining 2
Permanence 2

Granulation
as single colour 0
in mixes 1

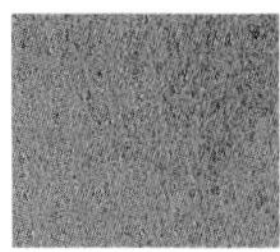

Transparency Staining Granulation

▼ Swatch shows 60:40 mix of sap green plus palette colour (on mixing palette)

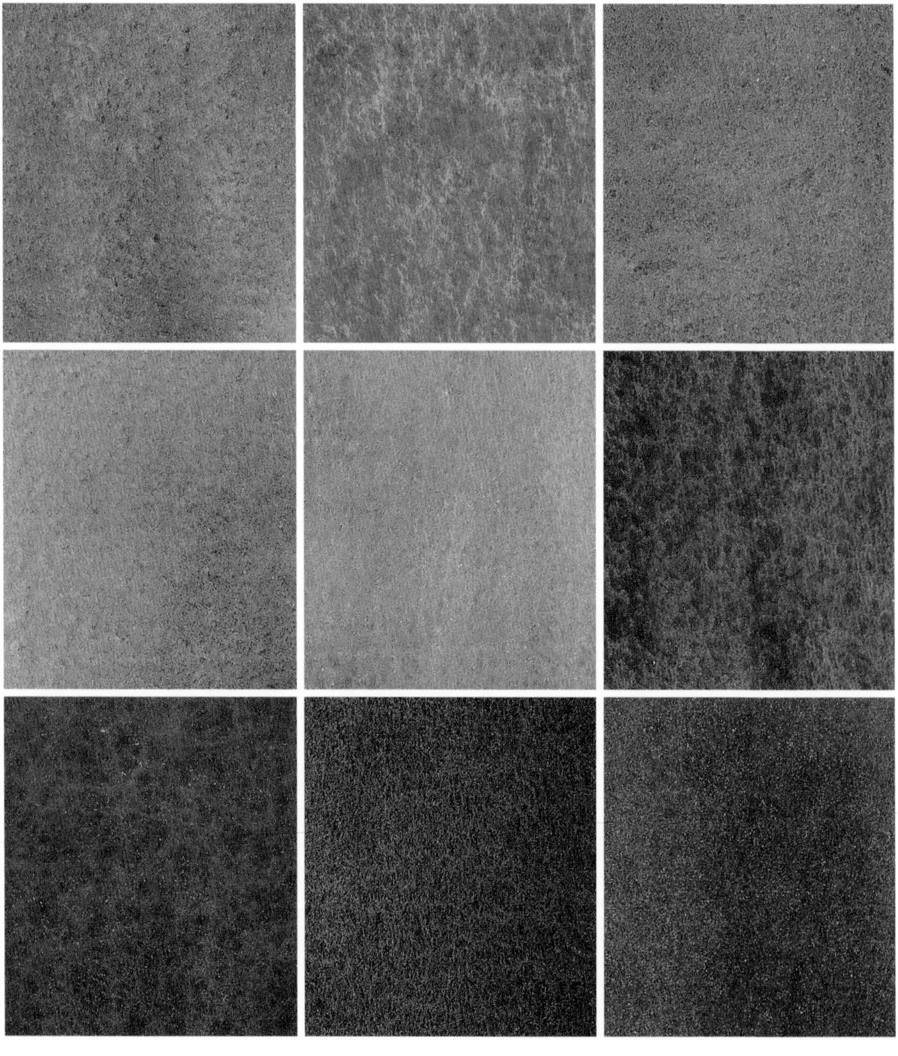

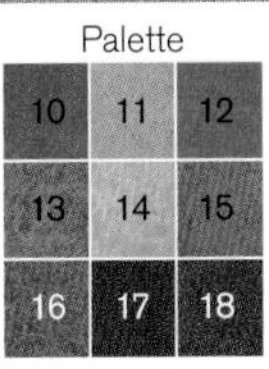

10 phthalo blue
11 manganese blue
12 phthalo green
13 sap green
14 yellow ochre
15 burnt umber
16 caput mortuum violet
17 sepia
18 indigo

Instead of overpainting the palette colour with itself in the mixes on paper, the upper triangle shows a single wash and the lower, a double wash.

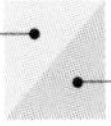

Sap green painted over palette colour

Sap green painted under palette colour

▼ Swatch shows 60:40 mix of sap green plus palette colour (on paper)

Green-Gold/1

Although not a well-known colour, this is an excellent addition to your palette. It softens most colours, yet retains a radiant glow. It will granulate when mixed with other granulating colours, but, as a single colour, granulation depends on the dilution (see panel above).

▼ Swatch shows 60:40 mix of green-gold plus palette colour (on mixing palette)

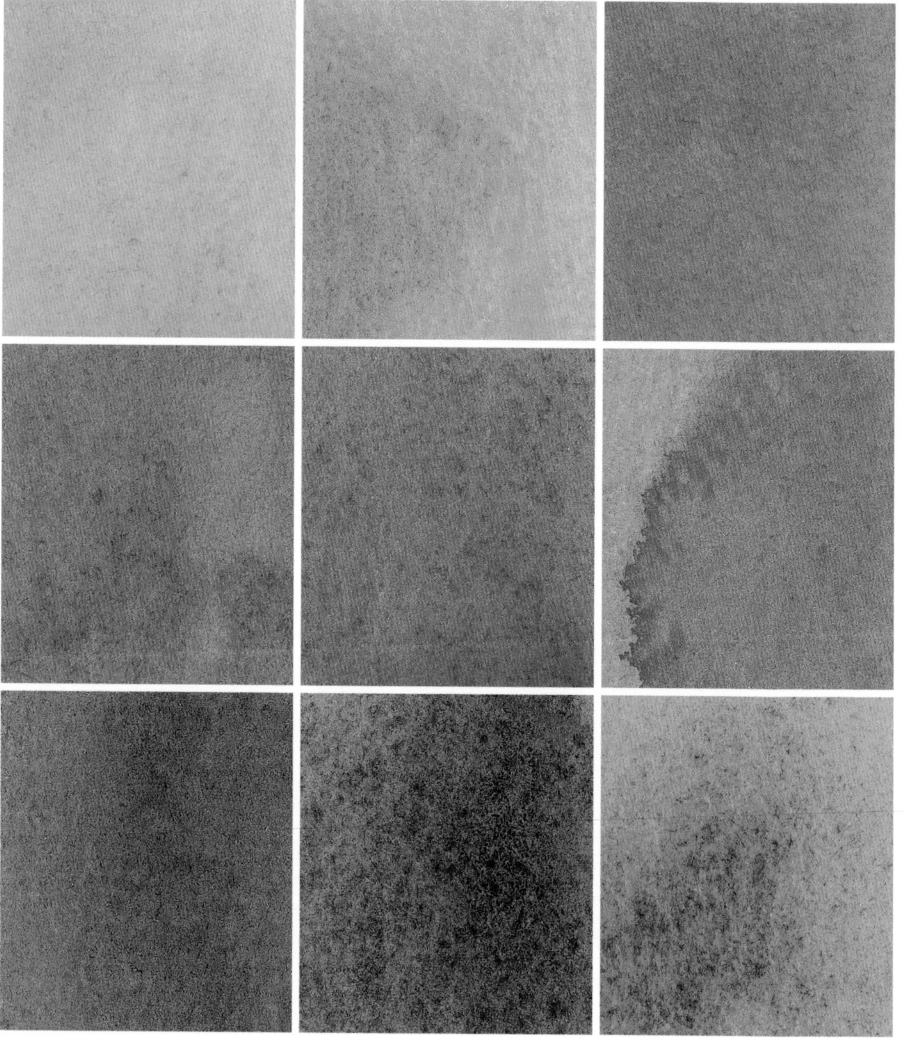

Palette

1	2	3
4	5	6
7	8	9

1 lemon yellow
2 cadmium yellow medium
3 cadmium orange
4 vermilion
5 permanent carmine
6 quinacridone magenta
7 dioxazine violet
8 ultramarine blue
9 cobalt blue

Green-gold painted over palette colour

Green-gold painted under palette colour

▼ Swatch shows 60:40 mix of green-gold plus palette colour (on paper)

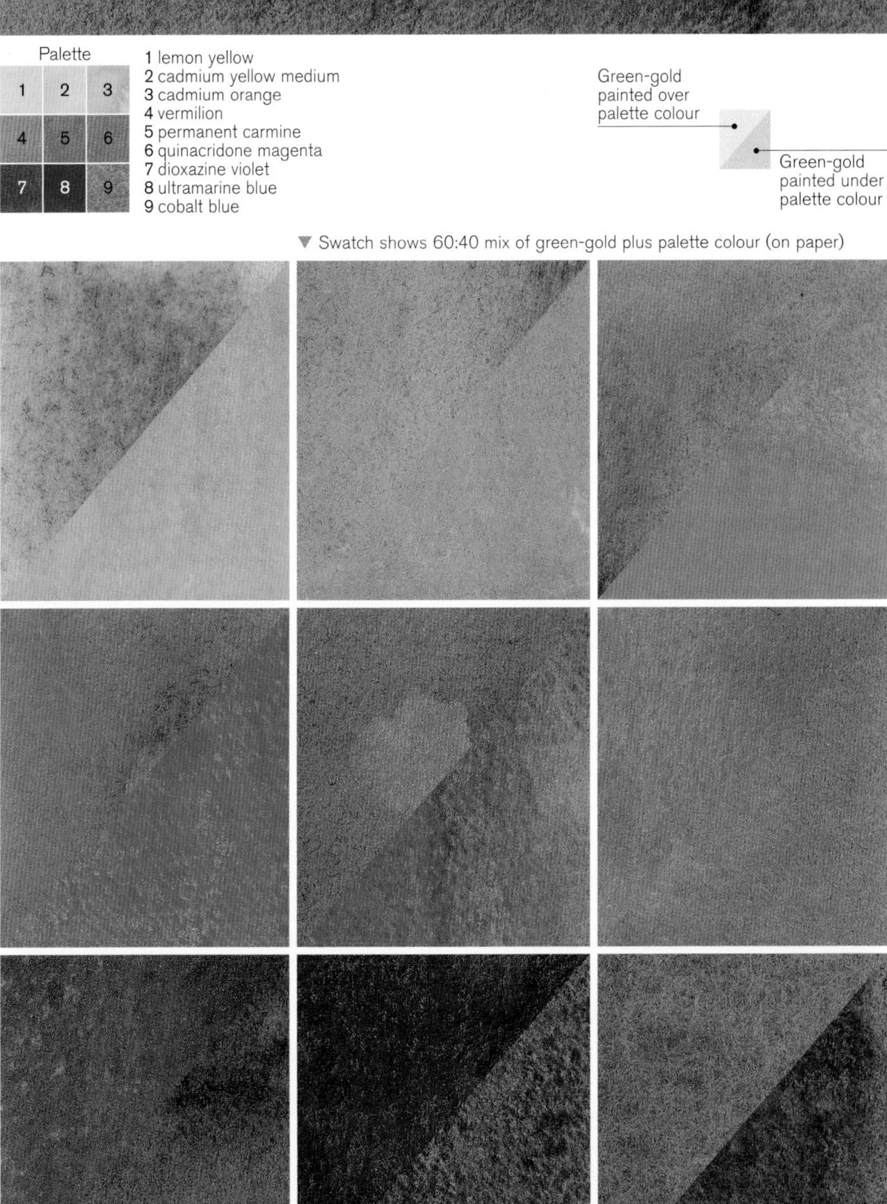

Green-Gold/2

Transparency 3/4
Staining 2
Permanence 2

Granulation
as single colour 0/2
in mixes 1

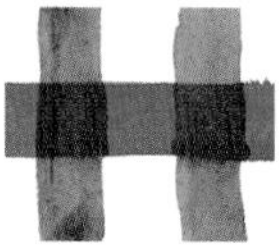

Transparency

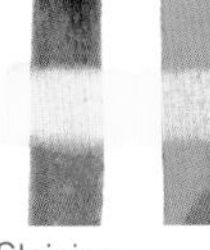
Staining

Granulation

▼ Swatch shows 60:40 mix of green-gold plus palette colour (on mixing palette)

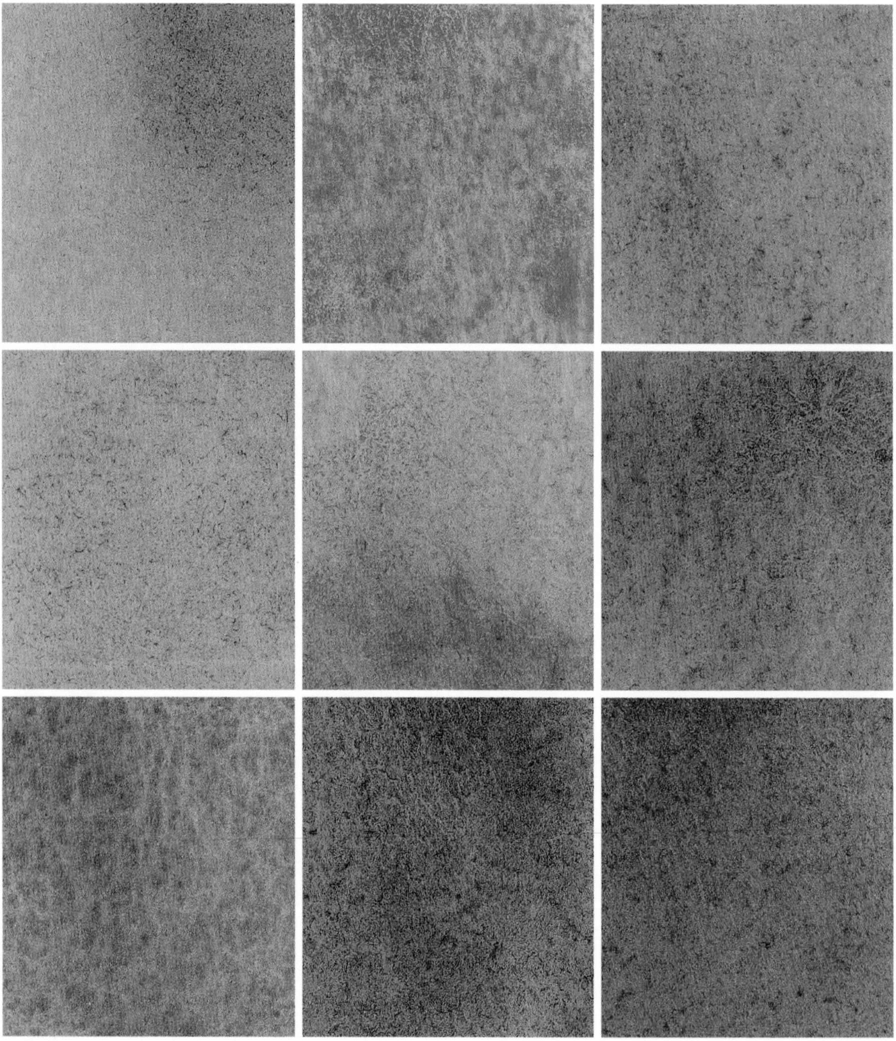

Palette

10	11	12
13	14	15
16	17	18

10 phthalo blue
11 manganese blue
12 phthalo green
13 sap green
14 yellow ochre
15 burnt umber
16 caput mortuum violet
17 sepia
18 indigo

Green-gold painted over palette colour

Green-gold painted under palette colour

▼ Swatch shows 60:40 mix of green-gold plus palette colour (on paper)

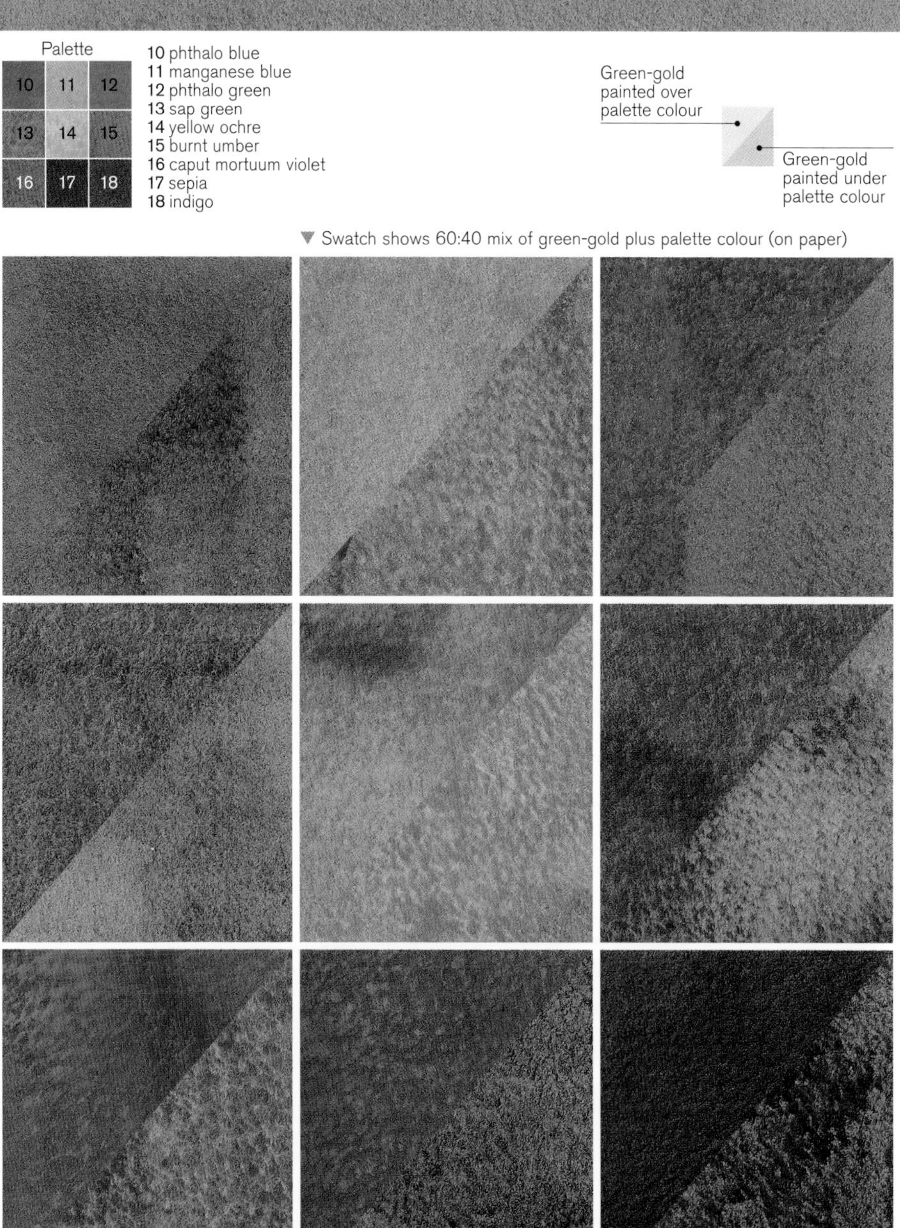

Titanium Buff/1

An opaque colour based on titanium white, titanium buff adds soft, warm, smoky layers to mixes. It works well in palette mixes or as the second layer in a mix on paper, but is more difficult to control as an initial wash because it moves around when a second layer is added.

▼ Swatch shows 60:40 mix of titanium buff plus palette colour (on mixing palette)

Palette

1 lemon yellow
2 cadmium yellow medium
3 cadmium orange
4 vermilion
5 permanent carmine
6 quinacridone magenta
7 dioxazine violet
8 ultramarine blue
9 cobalt blue

Titanium buff painted over palette colour

Titanium buff painted under palette colour

▼ Swatch shows 60:40 mix of titanium buff plus palette colour (on paper)

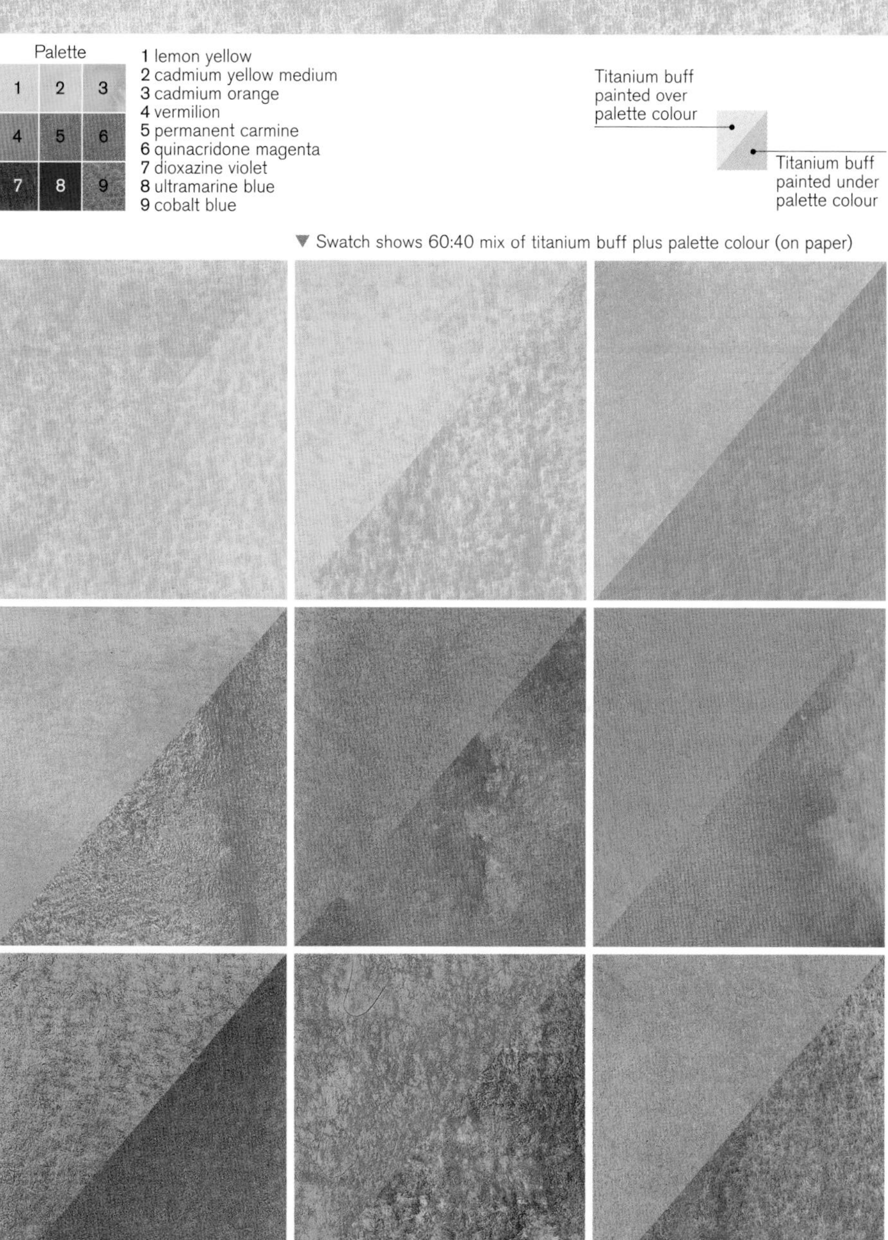

Titanium Buff/2

Transparency 1
Staining 0
Permanence 2

Granulation
as single colour 2
in mixes 1/2

Transparency

Staining

Granulation

▼ Swatch shows 60:40 mix of titanium buff plus palette colour (on mixing palette)

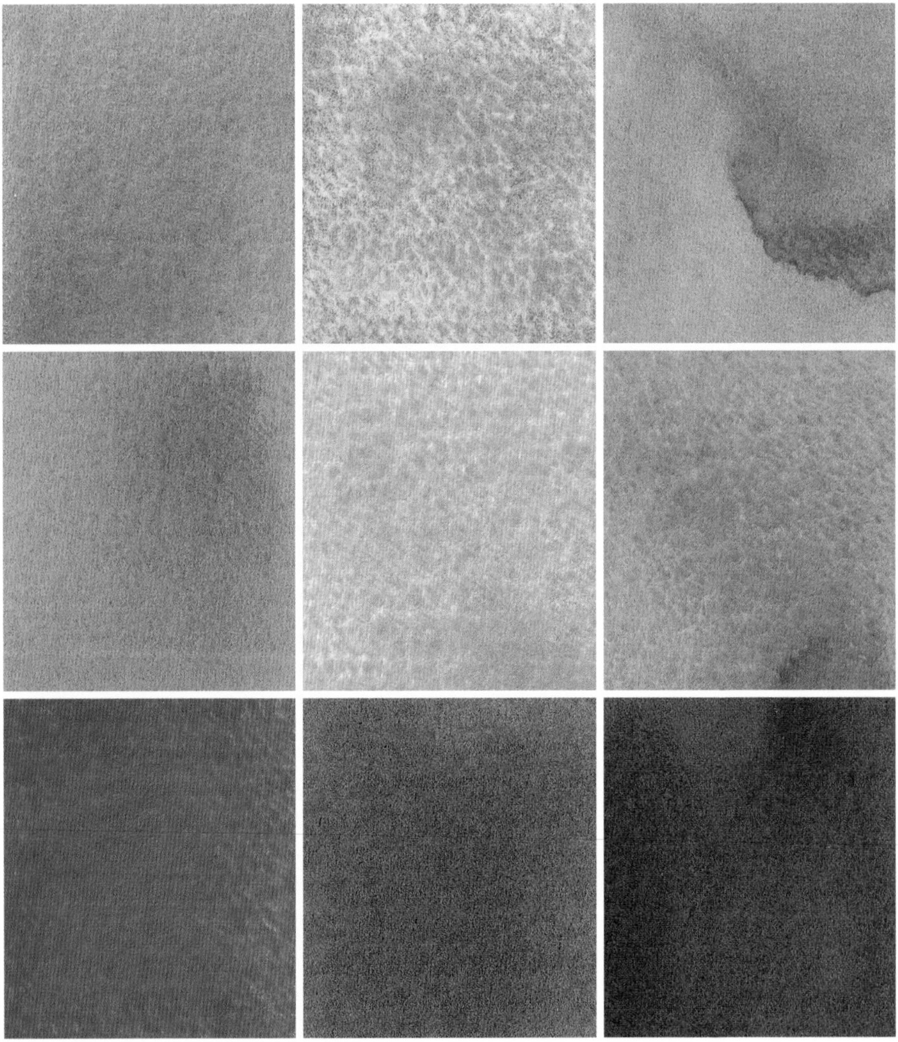

Palette

10	11	12
13	14	15
16	17	18

10 phthalo blue
11 manganese blue
12 phthalo green
13 sap green
14 yellow ochre
15 burnt umber
16 caput mortuum violet
17 sepia
18 indigo

Titanium buff painted over palette colour

Titanium buff painted under palette colour

▼ Swatch shows 60:40 mix of titanium buff plus palette colour (on paper)

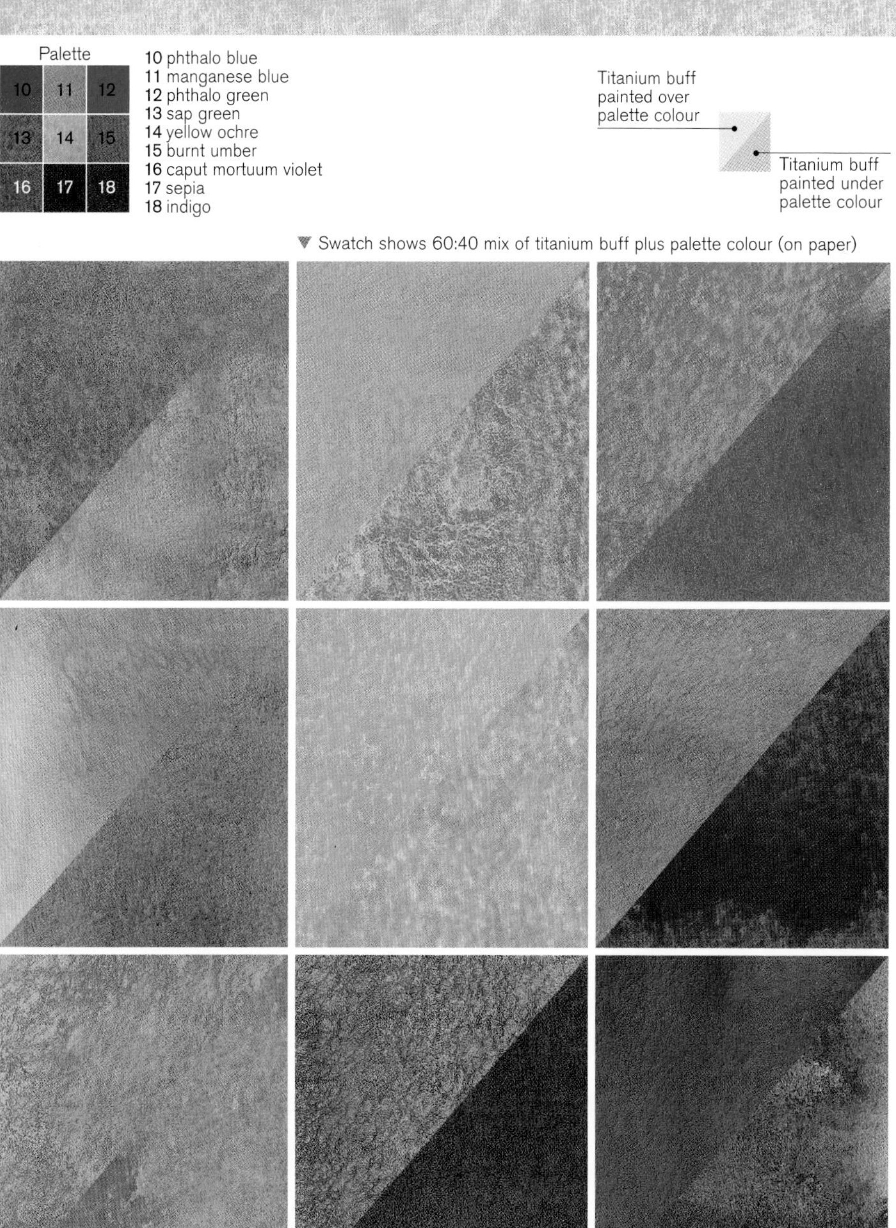

Raw Umber/1

This is an earth colour with a slight yellow/green bias and a transparent, rich character. It mixes well in all washes. Granulation varies between brands.

▼ Swatch shows 60:40 mix of raw umber plus palette colour (on mixing palette)

Palette

1 lemon yellow
2 cadmium yellow medium
3 cadmium orange
4 vermilion
5 permanent carmine
6 quinacridone magenta
7 dioxazine violet
8 ultramarine blue
9 cobalt blue

Raw umber painted over palette colour

Raw umber painted under palette colour

▼ Swatch shows 60:40 mix of raw umber plus palette colour (on paper)

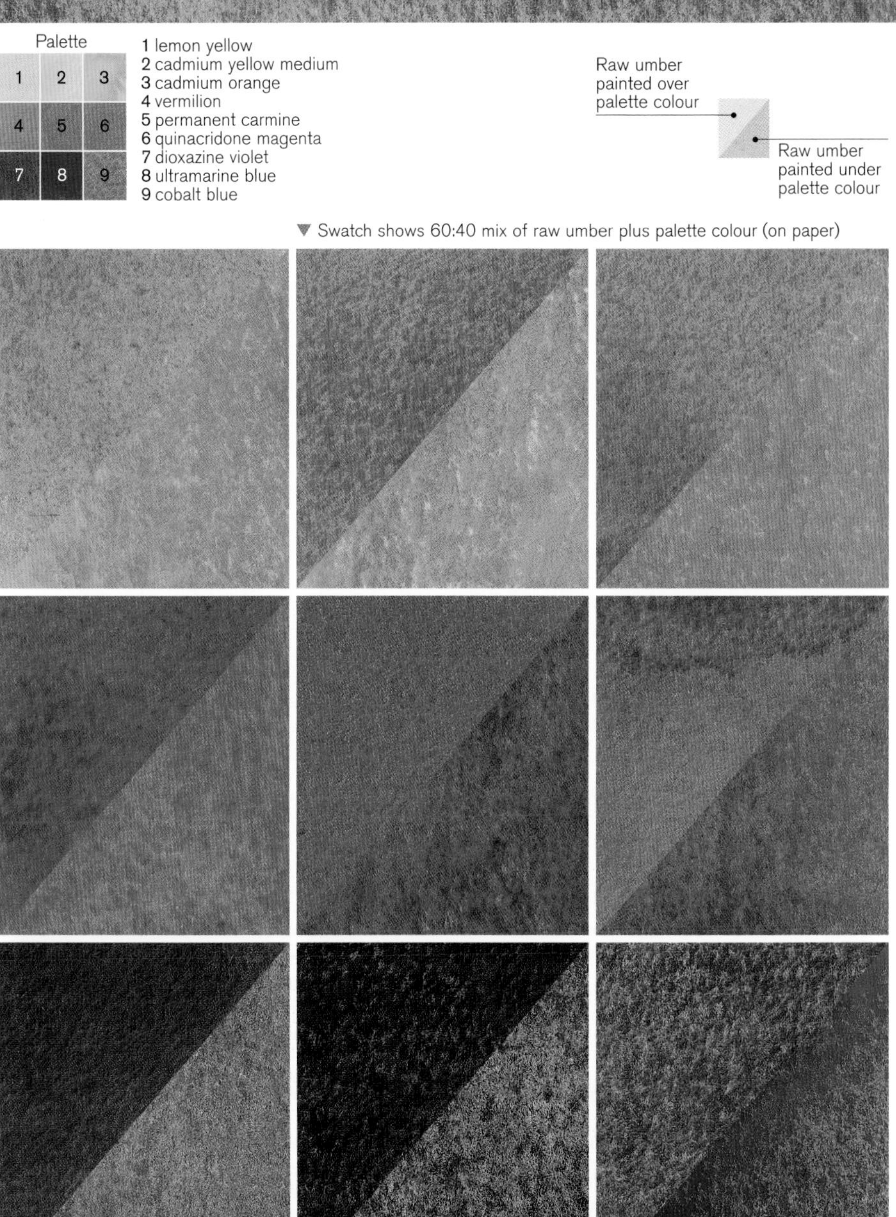

Raw Umber/2

Transparency 3/4
Staining 3
Permanence 3

Granulation
as single colour 0/1
in mixes 1

Transparency

Staining

Granulation

▼ Swatch shows 60:40 mix of raw umber plus palette colour (on mixing palette)

Palette

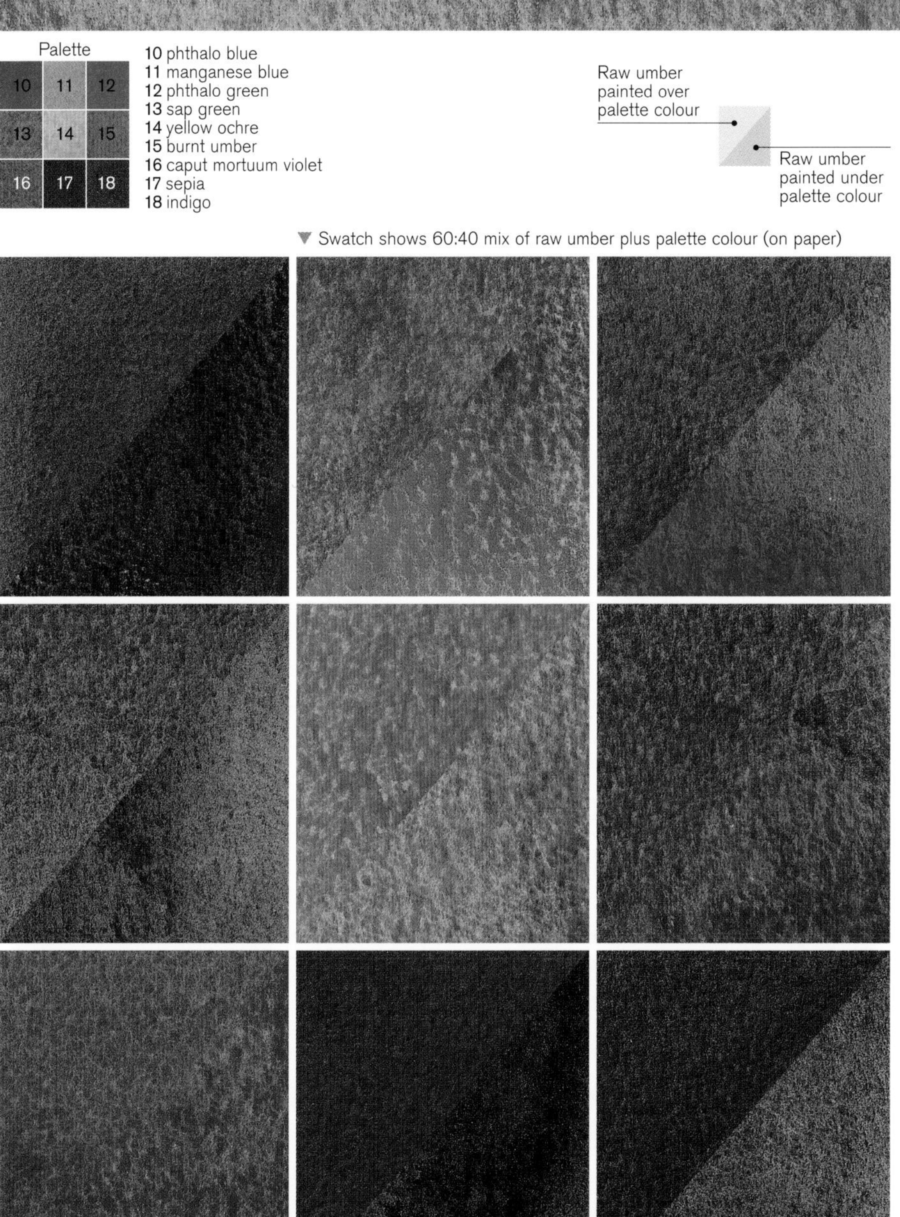

10 phthalo blue
11 manganese blue
12 phthalo green
13 sap green
14 yellow ochre
15 burnt umber
16 caput mortuum violet
17 sepia
18 indigo

Raw umber painted over palette colour

Raw umber painted under palette colour

▼ Swatch shows 60:40 mix of raw umber plus palette colour (on paper)

Yellow Ochre/1

This centuries-old earth pigment is semi-opaque and imparts a warm golden glow to mixes. Its opacity means that it dominates when applied as the second layer in a mix on paper. Mixed on a palette, it produces lovely matte colours (for example, see the mix with cobalt blue).

▼ Swatch shows 60:40 mix of yellow ochre plus palette colour (on mixing palette)

Palette

1	2	3
4	5	6
7	8	9

1 lemon yellow
2 cadmium yellow medium
3 cadmium orange
4 vermilion
5 permanent carmine
6 quinacridone magenta
7 dioxazine violet
8 ultramarine blue
9 cobalt blue

Yellow ochre painted over palette colour

Yellow ochre painted under palette colour

▼ Swatch shows 60:40 mix of yellow ochre plus palette colour (on paper)

Yellow Ochre/2

Transparency 2
Staining 1
Permanence 3

Granulation
as single colour 0/1
in mixes 1

Transparency

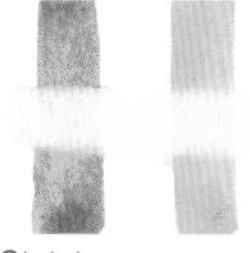
Staining

Granulation

▼ Swatch shows 60:40 mix of yellow ochre plus palette colour (on mixing palette)

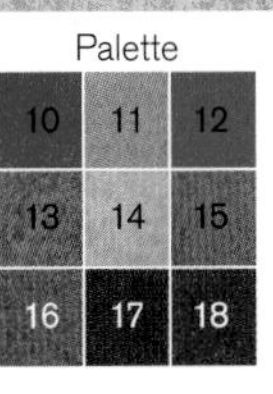

10 phthalo blue
11 manganese blue
12 phthalo green
13 sap green
14 yellow ochre
15 burnt umber
16 caput mortuum violet
17 sepia
18 indigo

Instead of overpainting the palette colour with itself in the mixes on paper, the upper triangle shows a single wash and the lower, a double wash.

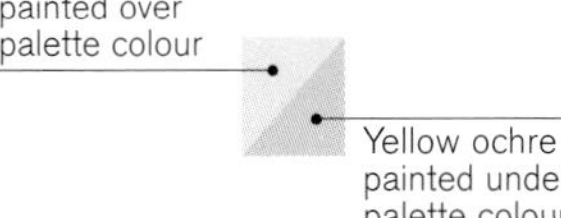

▼ Swatch shows 60:40 mix of yellow ochre plus palette colour (on paper)

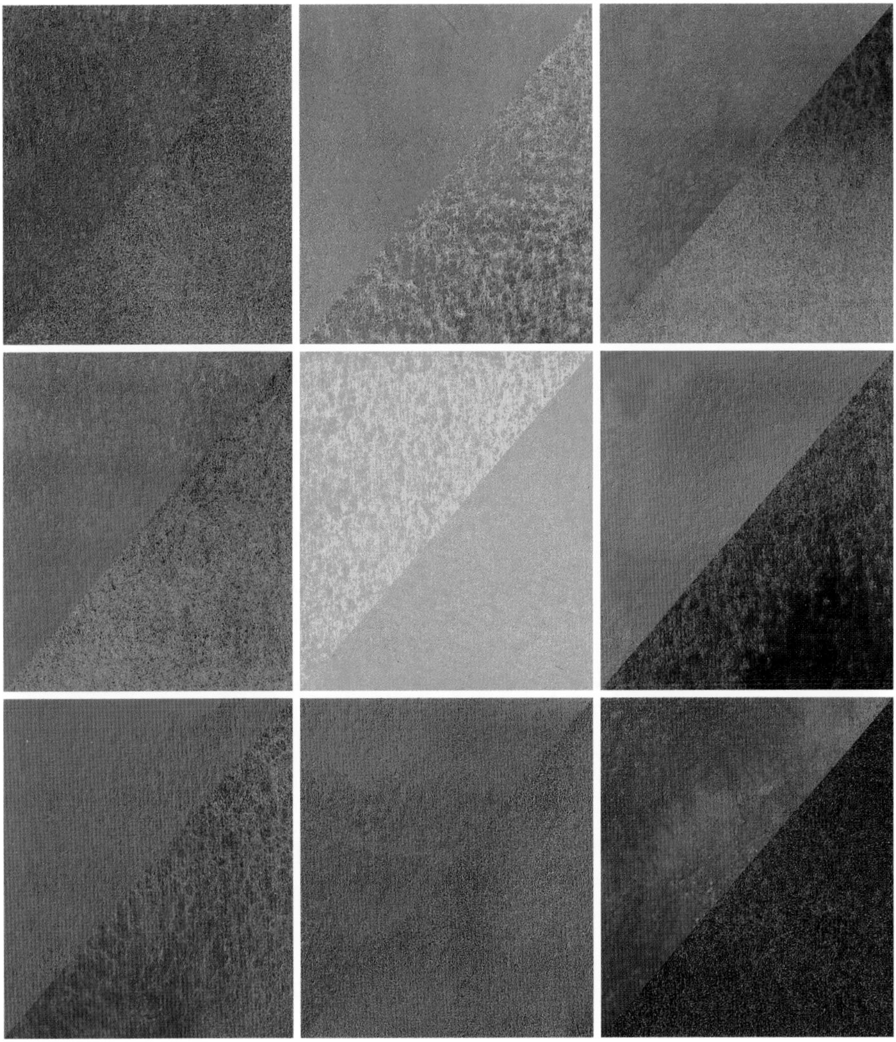

Quinacridone Gold/1

The pigment PO49 shown here is in limited supply; it is, however, still possible to purchase it or one of the new facsimile formulations. Its transparent gold hue becomes reddish-brown when it's applied as a very strong wash, and it mixes with blues and greens to make warm greens.

▼ Swatch shows 60:40 mix of quinacridone gold plus palette colour (on mixing palette)

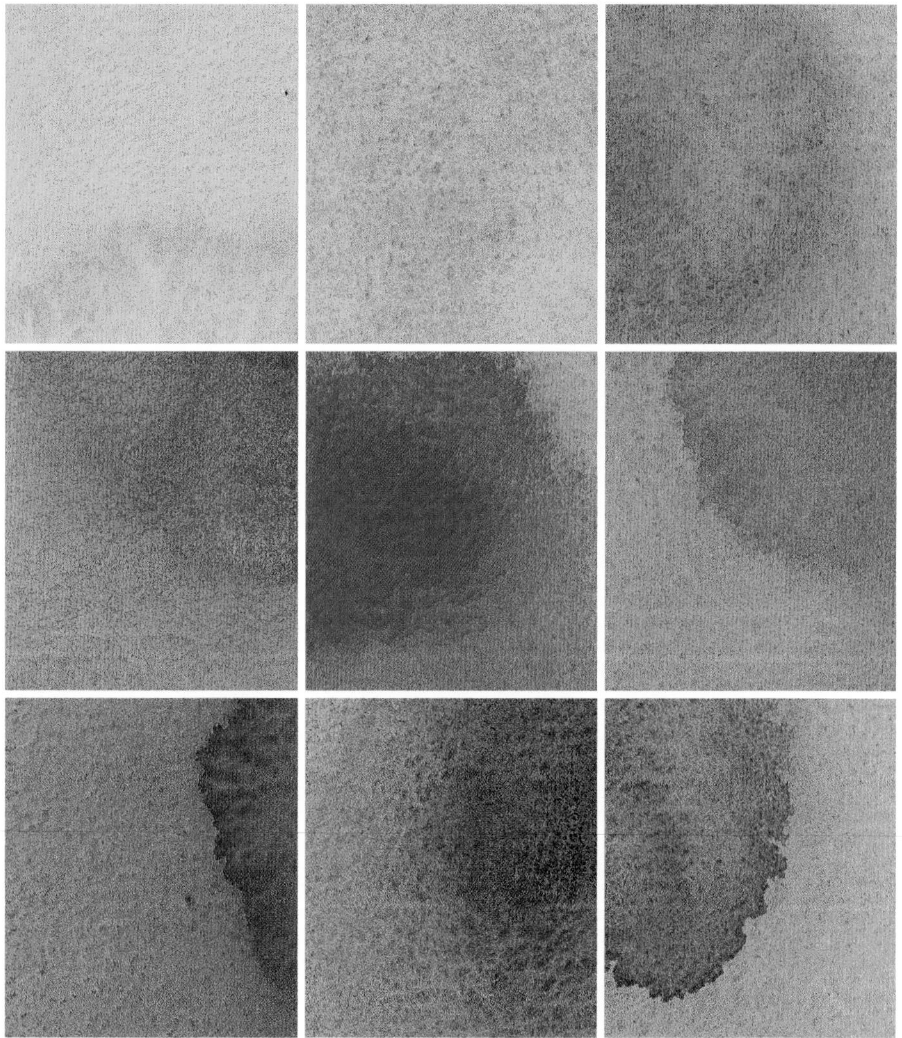

Palette

1	2	3
4	5	6
7	8	9

1 lemon yellow
2 cadmium yellow medium
3 cadmium orange
4 vermilion
5 permanent carmine
6 quinacridone magenta
7 dioxazine violet
8 ultramarine blue
9 cobalt blue

Quinacridone gold painted over palette colour

Quinacridone gold painted under palette colour

▼ Swatch shows 60:40 mix of quinacridone gold plus palette colour (on paper)

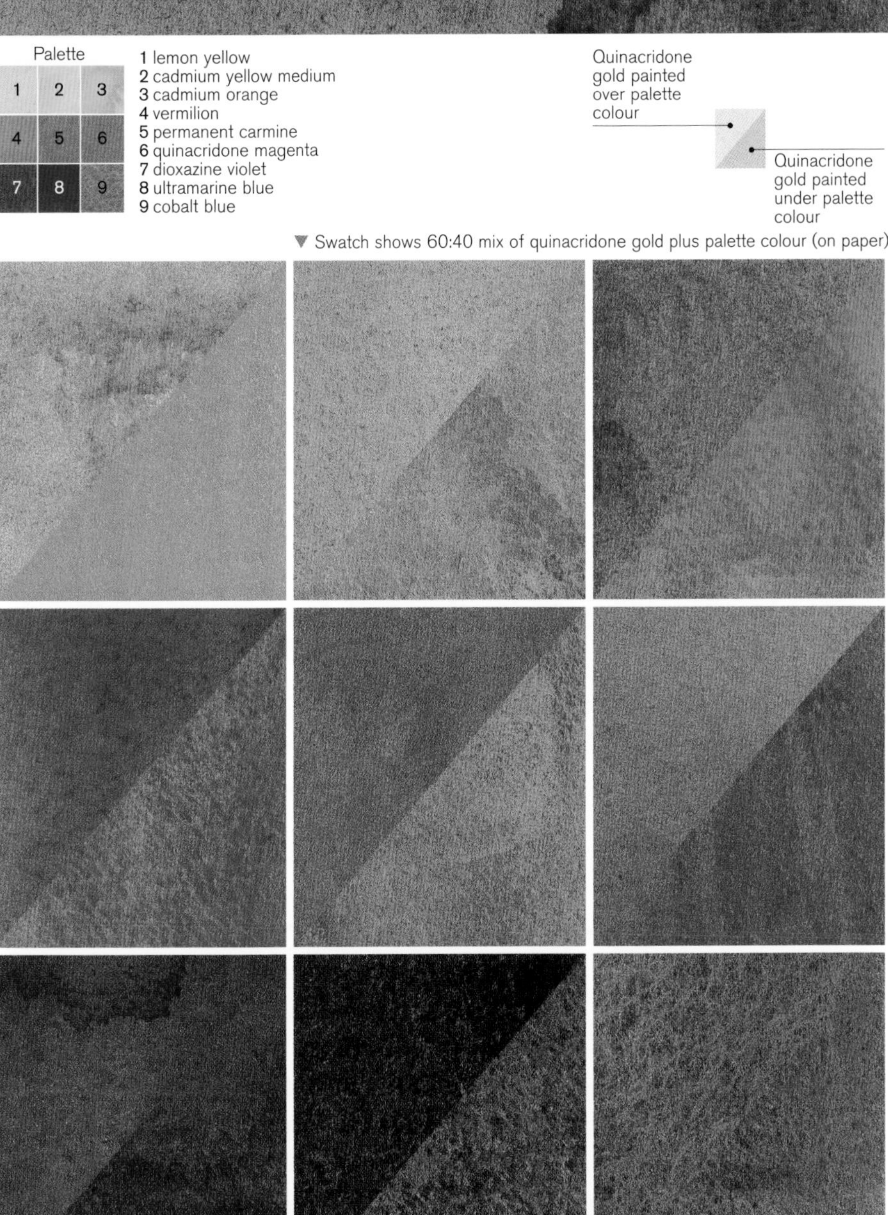

Quinacridone Gold/2

Transparency 4
Staining 1/2
Permanence 3

Granulation
as single colour 0
in mixes 0/1

Transparency Staining Granulation

▼ Swatch shows 60:40 mix of quinacridone gold plus palette colour (on mixing palette)

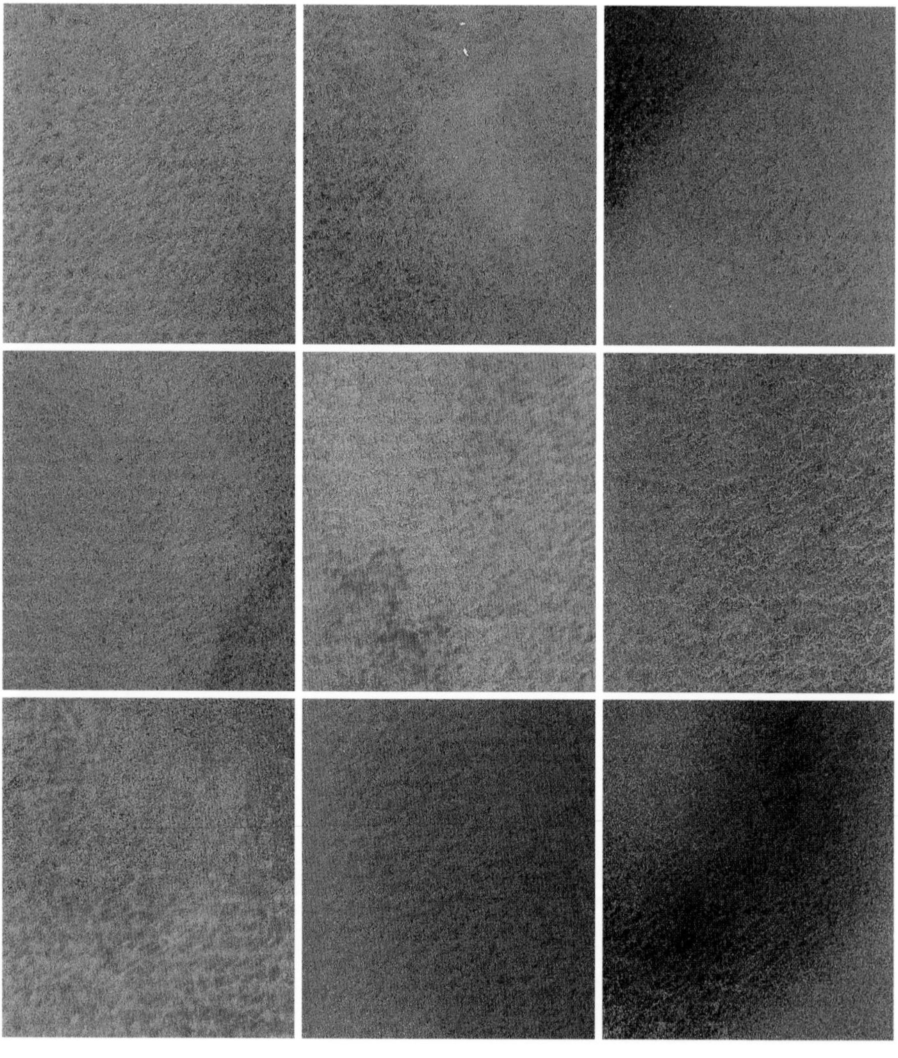

Palette

10 phthalo blue
11 manganese blue
12 phthalo green
13 sap green
14 yellow ochre
15 burnt umber
16 caput mortuum violet
17 sepia
18 indigo

Quinacridone gold painted over palette colour

Quinacridone gold painted under palette colour

▼ Swatch shows 60:40 mix of quinacridone gold plus palette colour (on paper)

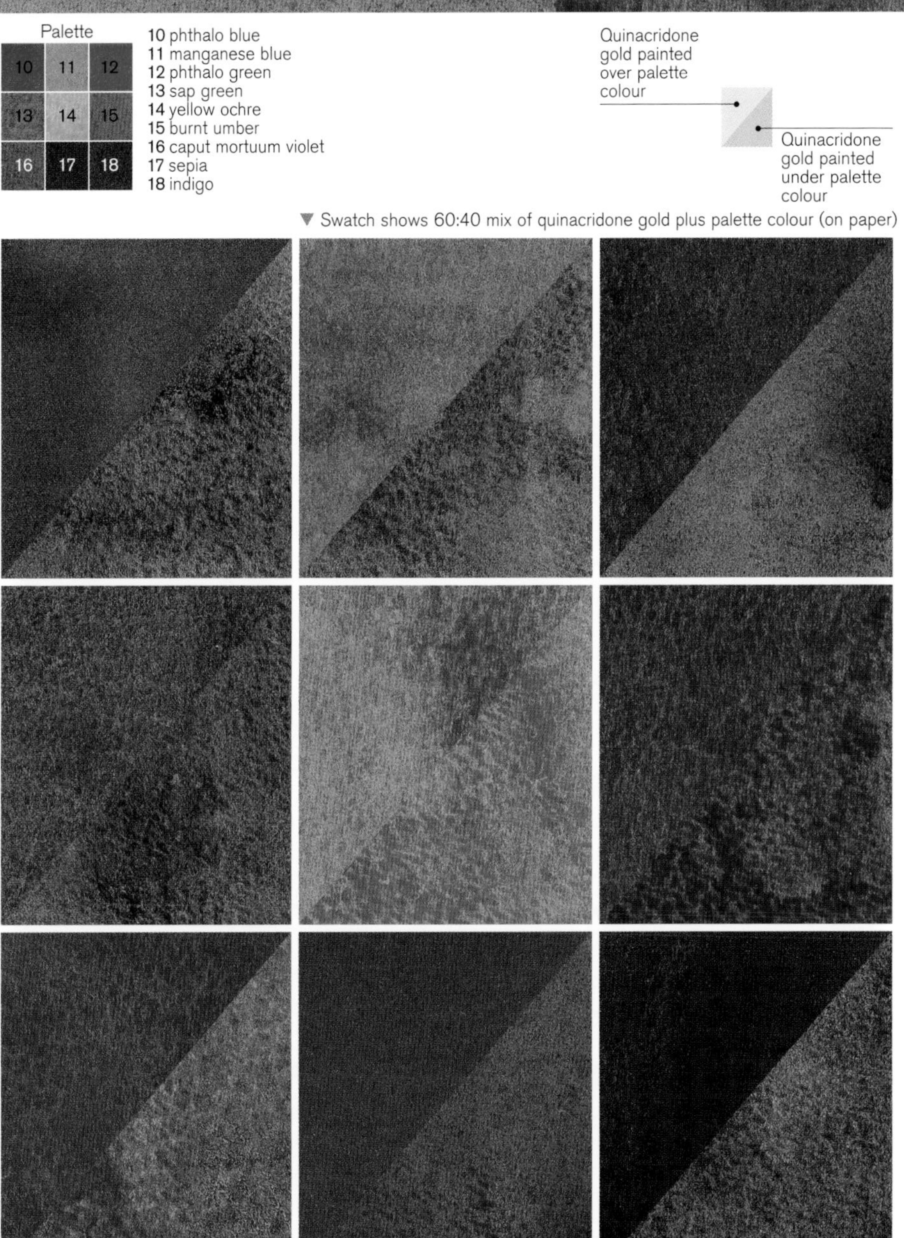

Raw Sienna/1

This colour may be used as an alternative to yellow ochre in a transparent palette. It is warmer in hue so tends to produce bronze/brown mixes, rather than warm greens (see page 184). It is also similar to quinacridone gold, but granulates more readily and is again slightly warmer.

▼ Swatch shows 60:40 mix of raw sienna plus palette colour (on mixing palette)

Palette

1 lemon yellow
2 cadmium yellow medium
3 cadmium orange
4 vermilion
5 permanent carmine
6 quinacridone magenta
7 dioxazine violet
8 ultramarine blue
9 cobalt blue

Raw sienna painted over palette colour

Raw sienna painted under palette colour

▼ Swatch shows 60:40 mix of raw sienna plus palette colour (on paper)

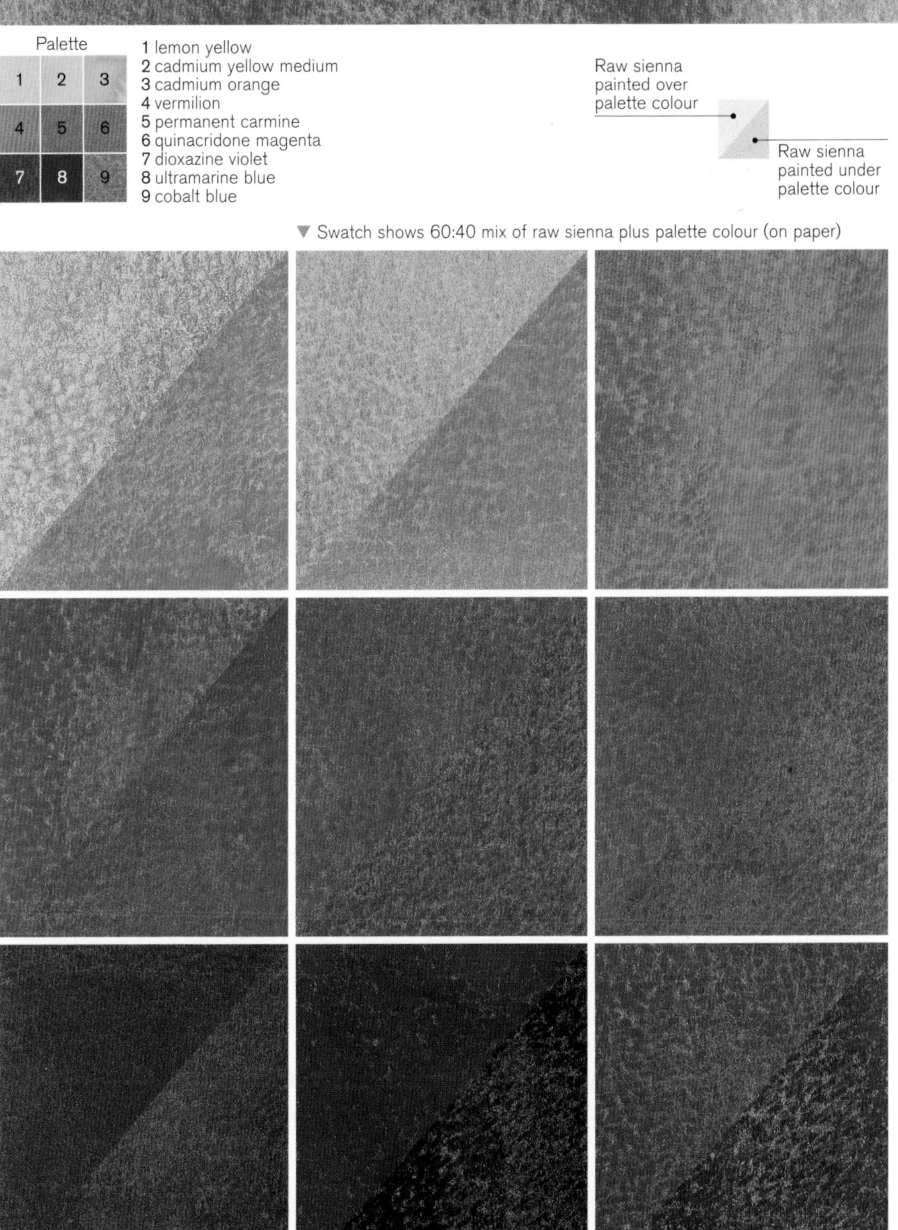

Raw Sienna/2

Transparency 2
Staining 1
Permanence 3

Granulation
as single colour 3
in mixes 2/3

Transparency Staining Granulation

▼ Swatch shows 60:40 mix of raw sienna plus palette colour (on mixing palette)

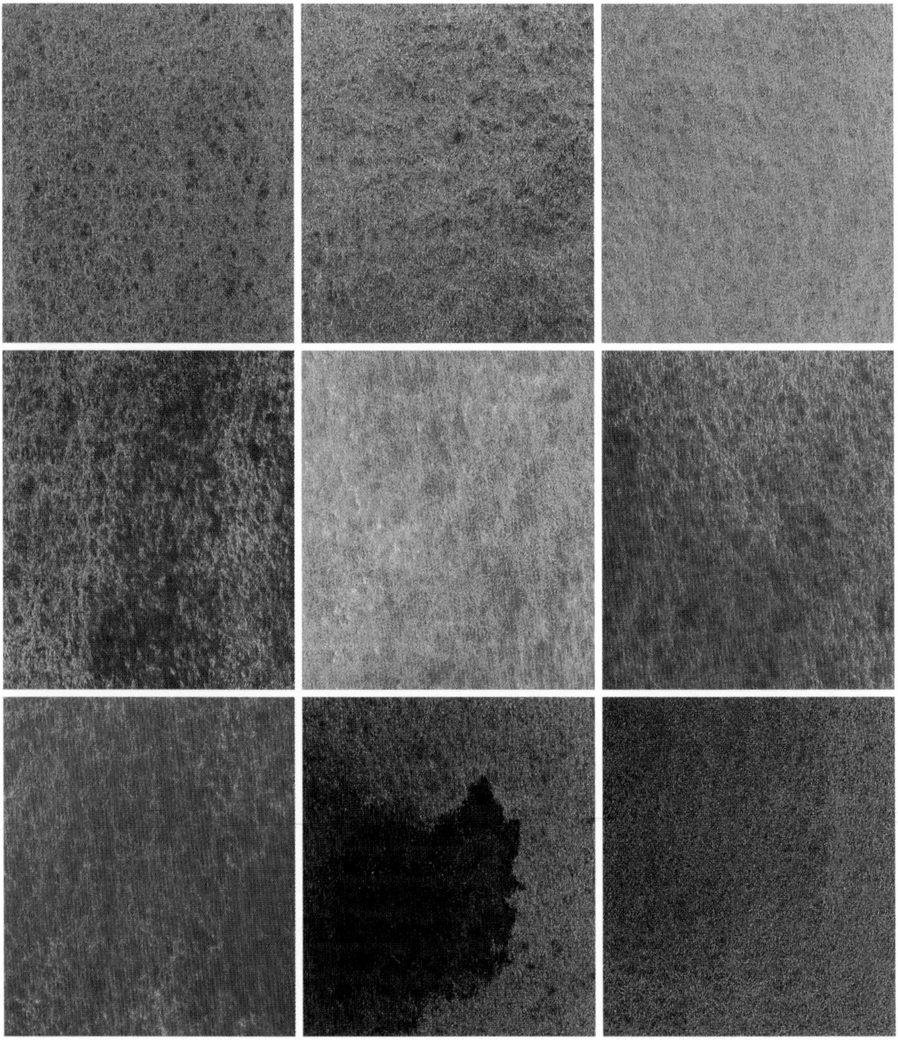

Palette

10	11	12
13	14	15
16	17	18

10 phthalo blue
11 manganese blue
12 phthalo green
13 sap green
14 yellow ochre
15 burnt umber
16 caput mortuum violet
17 sepia
18 indigo

Raw sienna painted over palette colour

Raw sienna painted under palette colour

▼ Swatch shows 60:40 mix of raw sienna plus palette colour (on paper)

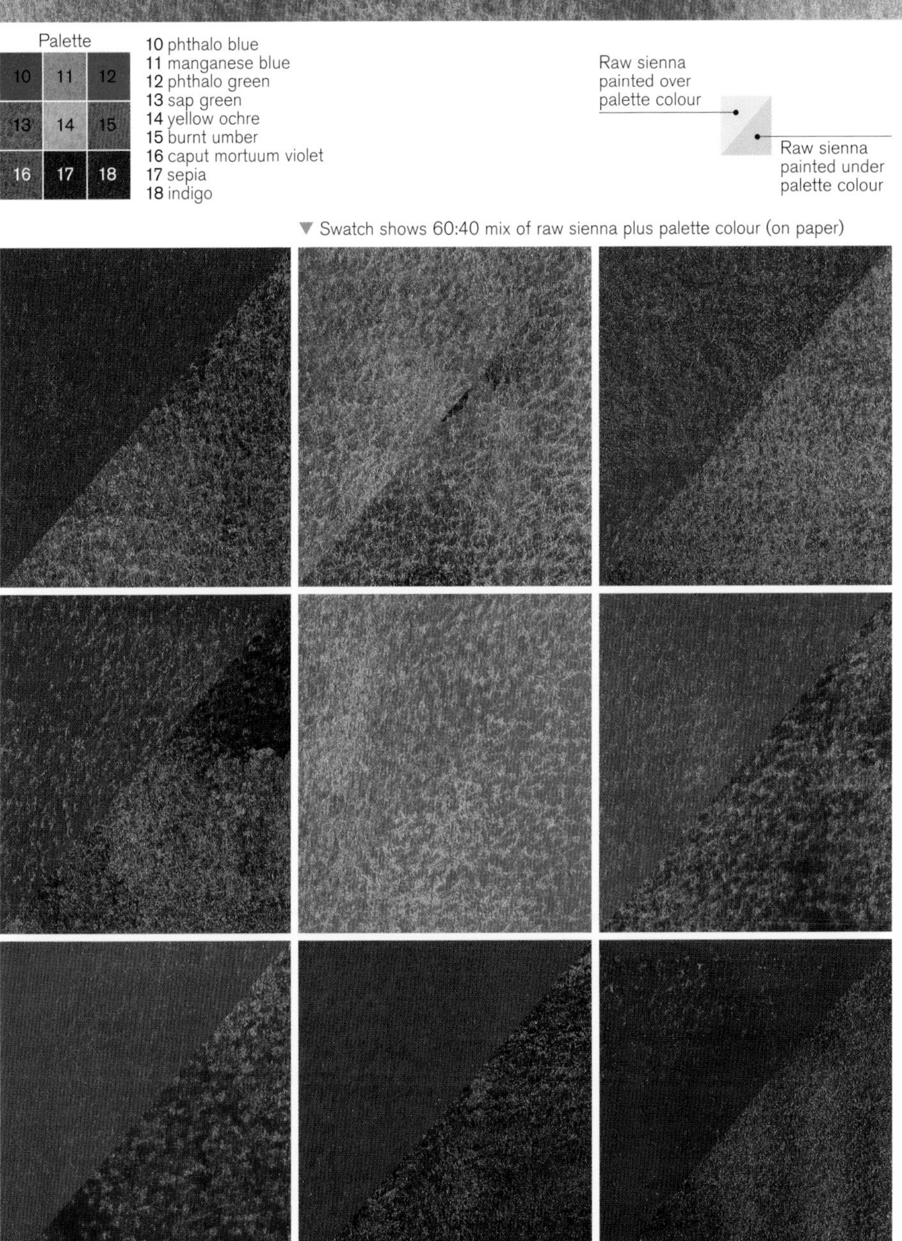

Transparent Red-Brown

This strong, transparent pigment is perfect if you do not want the opacity of Indian red or caput mortuum violet. It mixes with blues and greens to make some lovely neutrals and warm brown hues. It will dominate other colours so mix some samples before painting.

▼ Swatch shows 60:40 mix of transparent red-brown plus palette colour (on mixing palette)

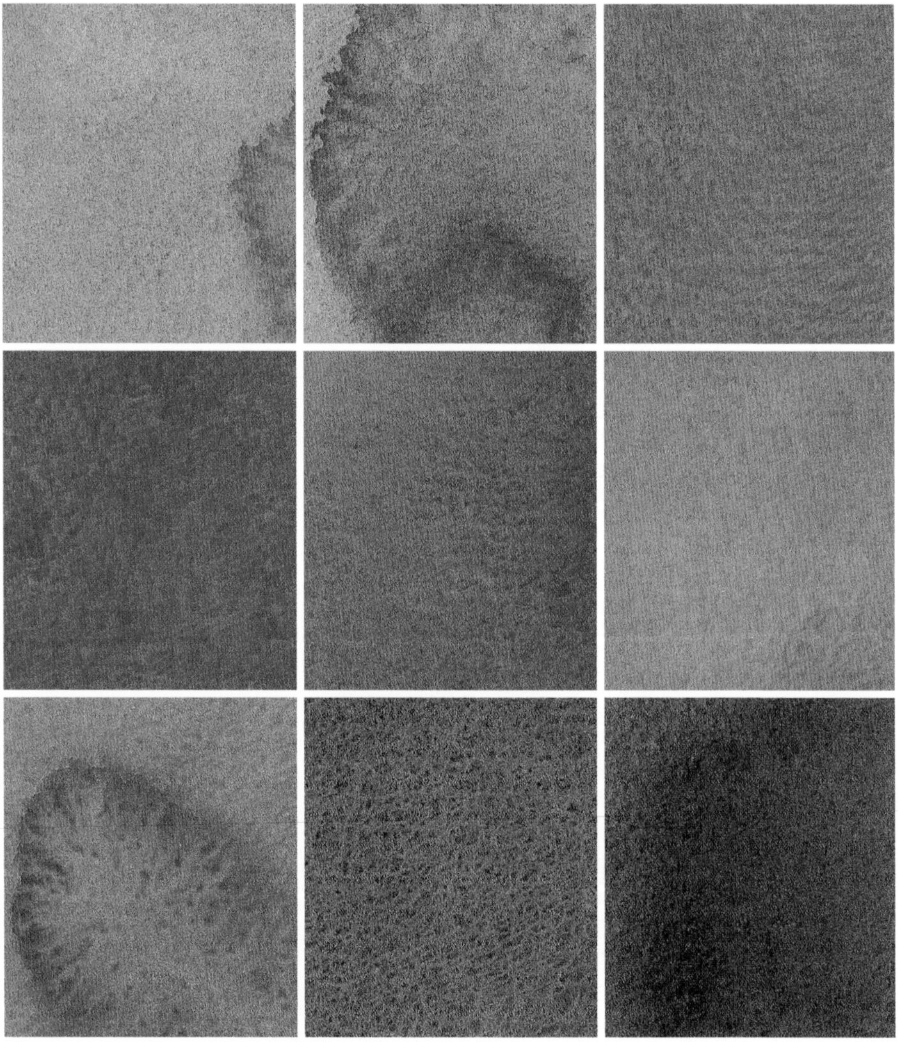

Palette

1 lemon yellow
2 cadmium yellow medium
3 cadmium orange
4 vermilion
5 permanent carmine
6 quinacridone magenta
7 dioxazine violet
8 ultramarine blue
9 cobalt blue

Transparent red-brown painted over palette colour

Transparent red-brown painted under palette colour

▼ Swatch shows 60:40 mix of transparent red-brown plus palette colour (on paper)

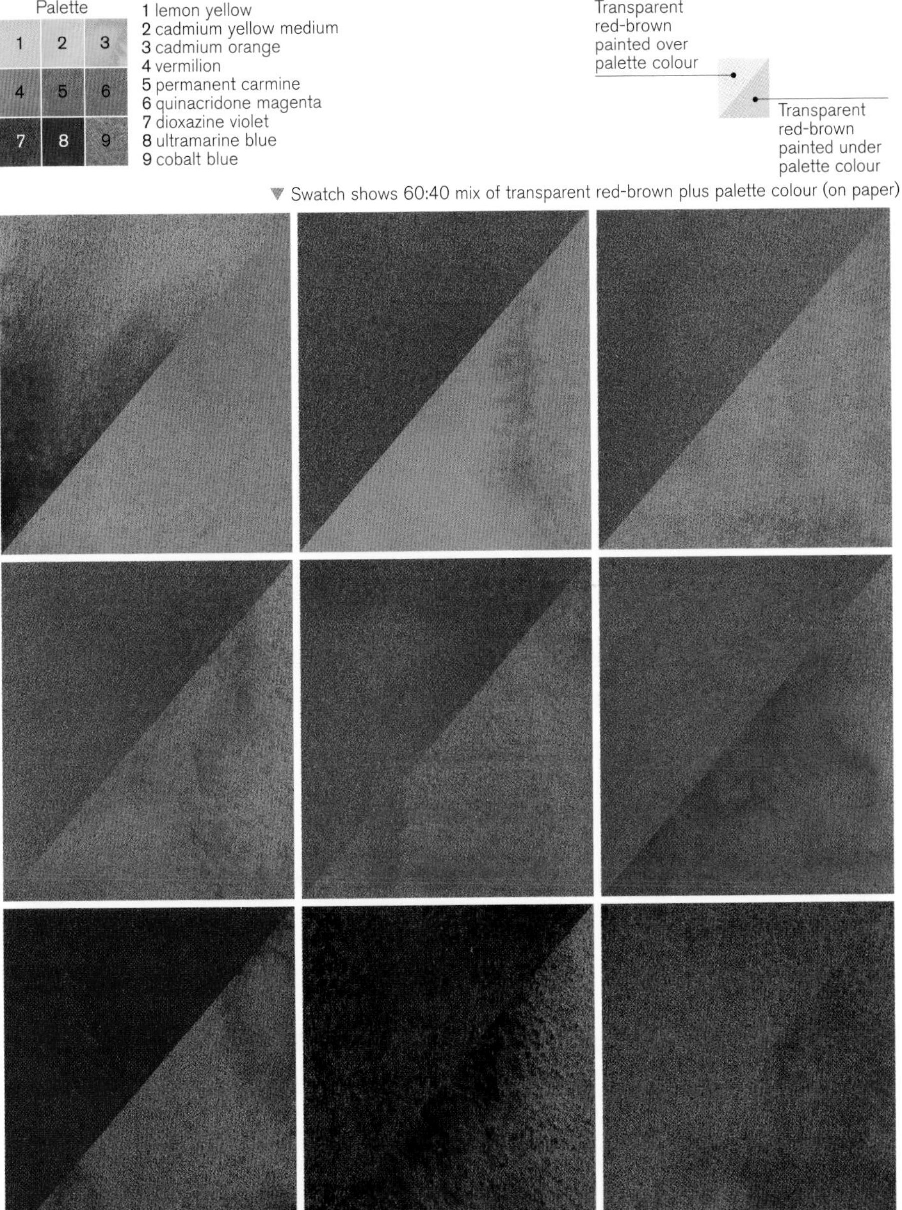

Transparent Red-Brown/2

Transparency 4
Staining 2
Permanence 3

Granulation
as single colour 1
in mixes 1

Transparency

Staining

Granulation

▼ Swatch shows 60:40 mix of transparent red-brown plus palette colour (on mixing palette)

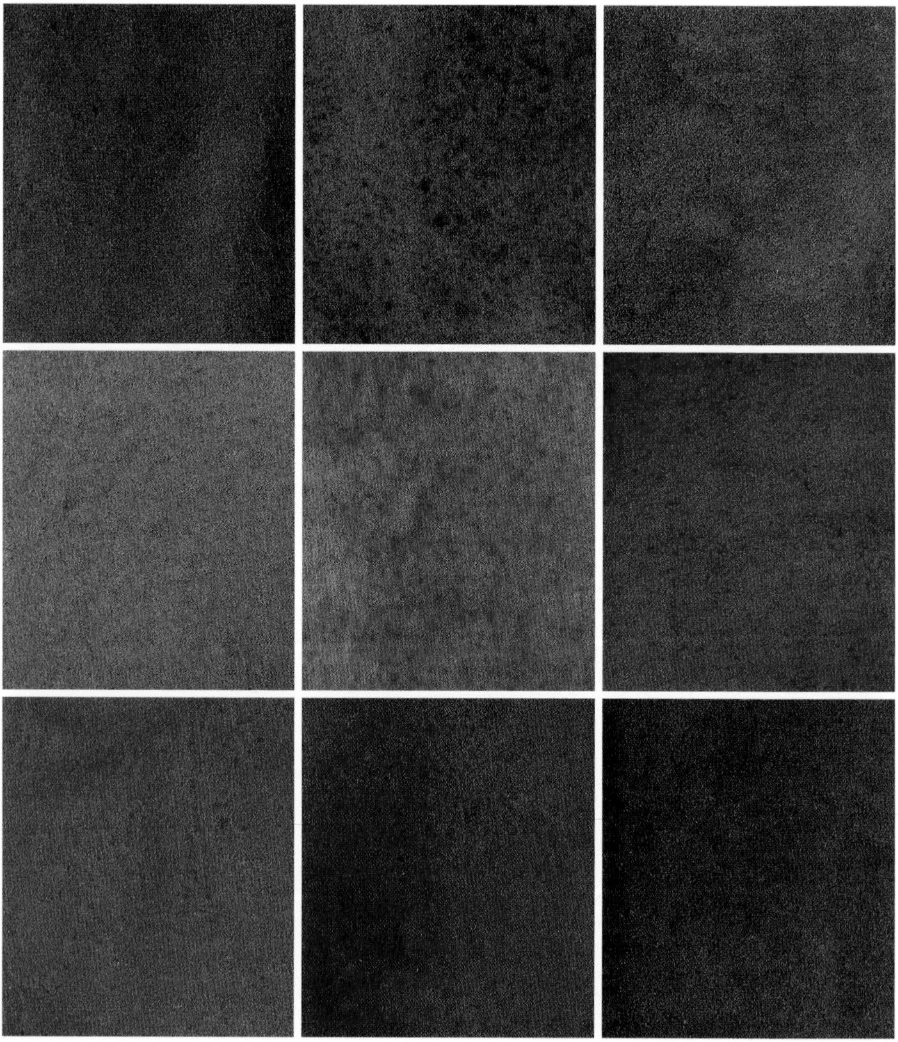

Palette

10	11	12
13	14	15
16	17	18

10 phthalo blue
11 manganese blue
12 phthalo green
13 sap green
14 yellow ochre
15 burnt umber
16 caput mortuum violet
17 sepia
18 indigo

Transparent red-brown painted over palette colour

Transparent red-brown painted under palette colour

▼ Swatch shows 60:40 mix of transparent red-brown plus palette colour (on paper)

Indian Red/1

An opaque, dull red with a touch of violet/grey, this pigment works well in palette mixes. Dilute it more than usual to increase transparency in an overglaze and to avoid muddy mixes in an underglaze. It creates a range of interesting neutrals when mixed with blue pigments.

▼ Swatch shows 60:40 mix of Indian red plus palette colour (on mixing palette)

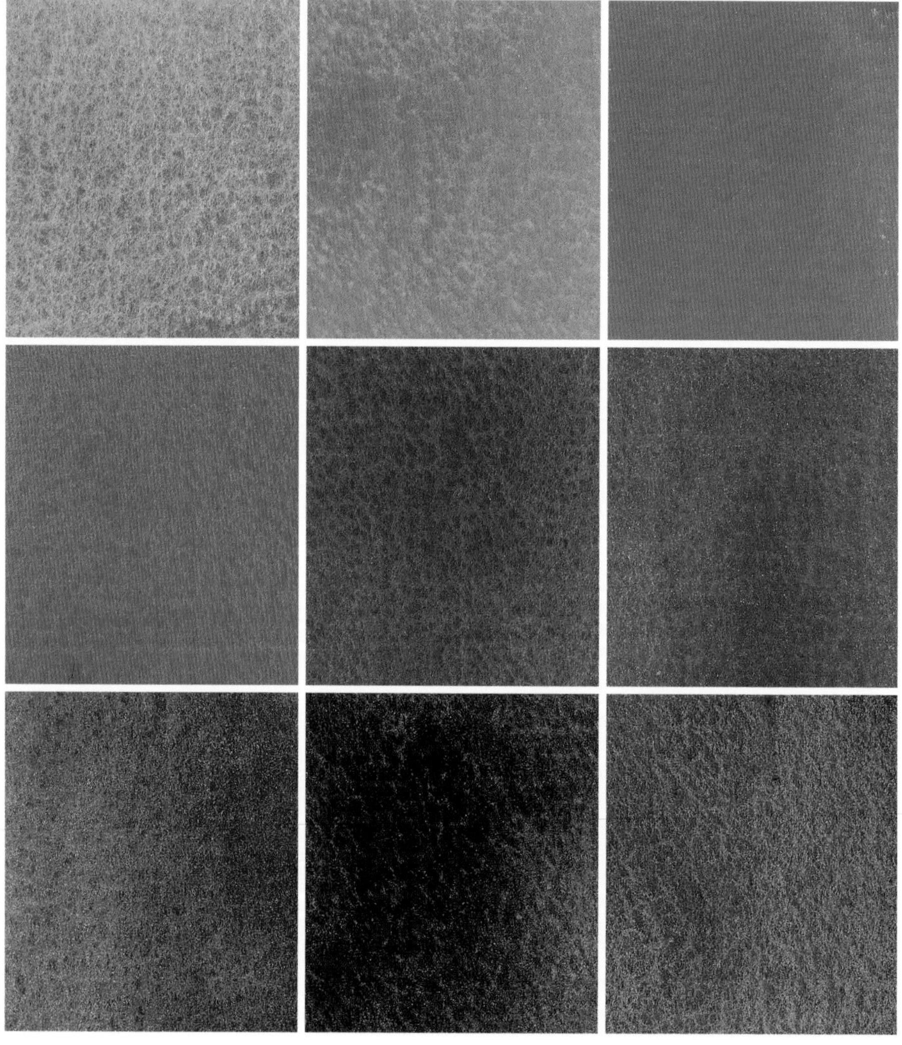

Palette

1	2	3
4	5	6
7	8	9

1 lemon yellow
2 cadmium yellow medium
3 cadmium orange
4 vermilion
5 permanent carmine
6 quinacridone magenta
7 dioxazine violet
8 ultramarine blue
9 cobalt blue

Indian red painted over palette colour

Indian red painted under palette colour

▼ Swatch shows 60:40 mix of Indian red plus palette colour (on paper)

Indian Red/2

Transparency 1
Staining 3
Permanence 3

Granulation
as single colour 0
in mixes 1

Transparency

Staining

Granulation

▼ Swatch shows 60:40 mix of Indian red plus palette colour (on mixing palette)

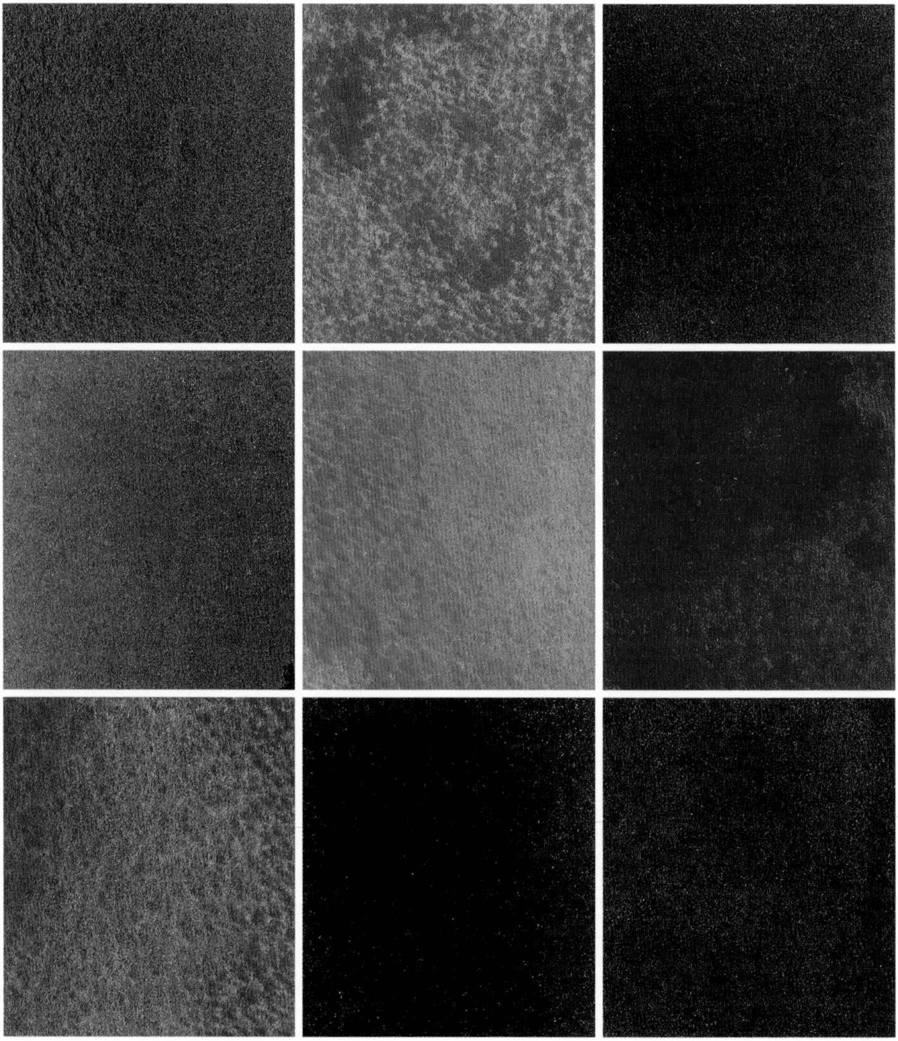

Palette

10	11	12
13	14	15
16	17	18

10 phthalo blue
11 manganese blue
12 phthalo green
13 sap green
14 yellow ochre
15 burnt umber
16 caput mortuum violet
17 sepia
18 indigo

Indian red painted over palette colour

Indian red painted under palette colour

▼ Swatch shows 60:40 mix of Indian red plus palette colour (on paper)

Potter's Pink/1

This muted pink/mauve earth colour was originally a ceramic colourant; some manufacturers have now introduced it as a watercolour pigment. In strong washes, it is opaque and rose-mauve; when diluted, it is transparent and a subtle clear pink. It has excellent granulation qualities.

▼ Swatch shows 60:40 mix of potter's pink plus palette colour (on mixing palette)

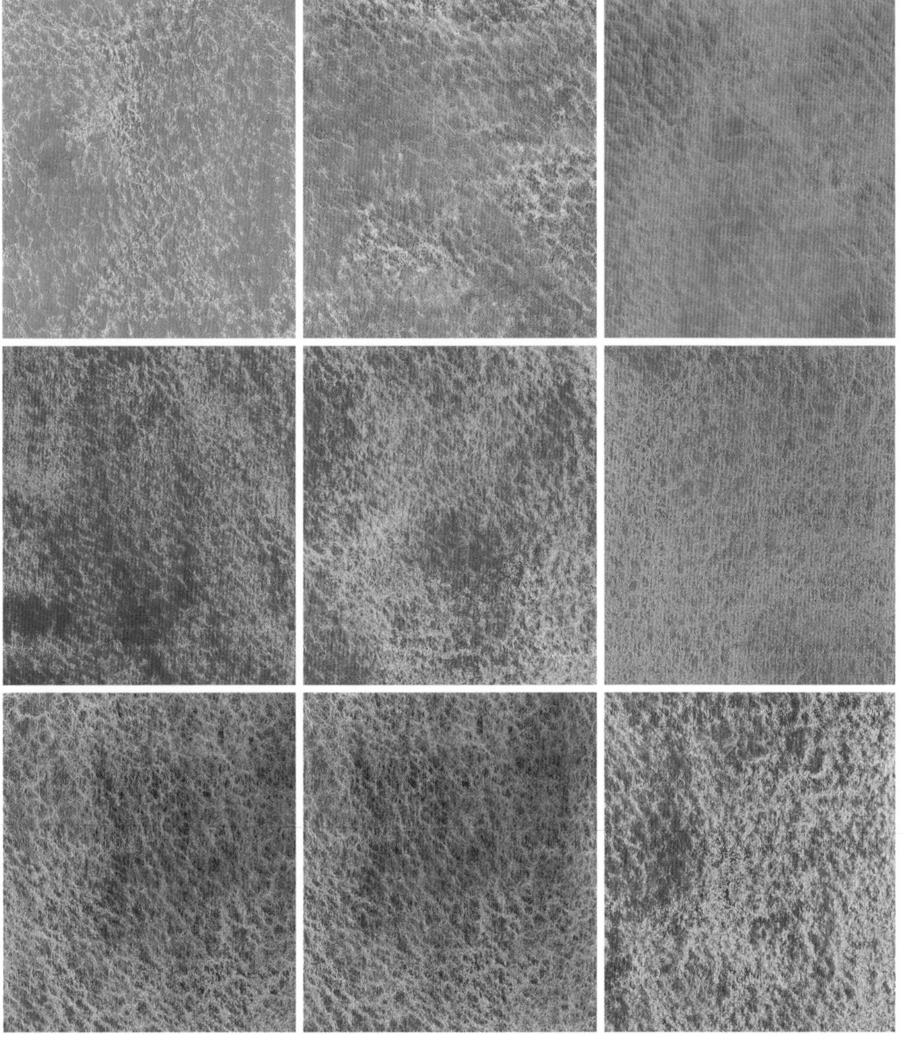

Palette

1	2	3
4	5	6
7	8	9

1 lemon yellow
2 cadmium yellow medium
3 cadmium orange
4 vermilion
5 permanent carmine
6 quinacridone magenta
7 dioxazine violet
8 ultramarine blue
9 cobalt blue

Potter's pink painted over palette colour

Potter's pink painted under palette colour

▼ Swatch shows 60:40 mix of potter's pink plus palette colour (on paper)

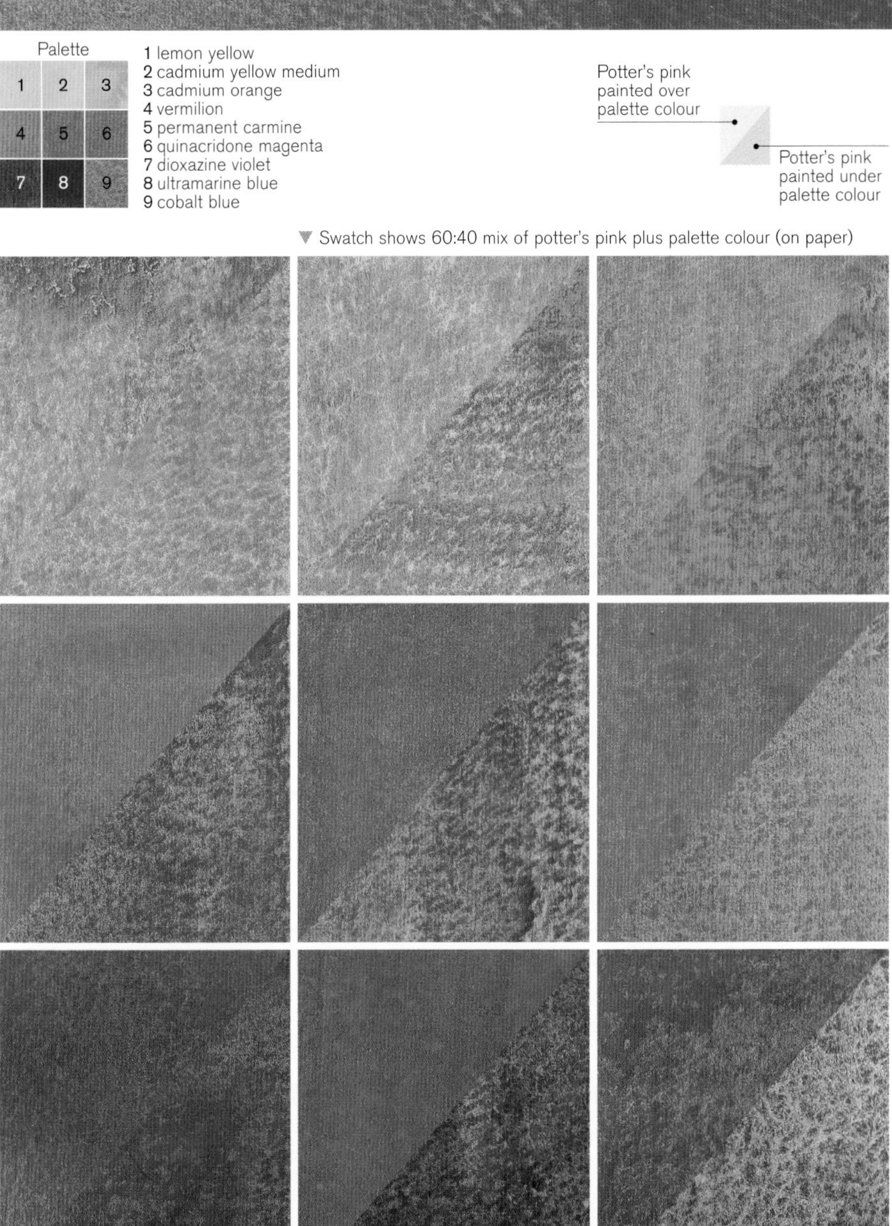

Potter's Pink/2

Transparency 1/4
Staining 0
Permanence 3

Granulation
as single colour 3
in mixes 3

Transparency

Staining

Granulation

▼ Swatch shows 60:40 mix of potter's pink plus palette colour (on mixing palette)

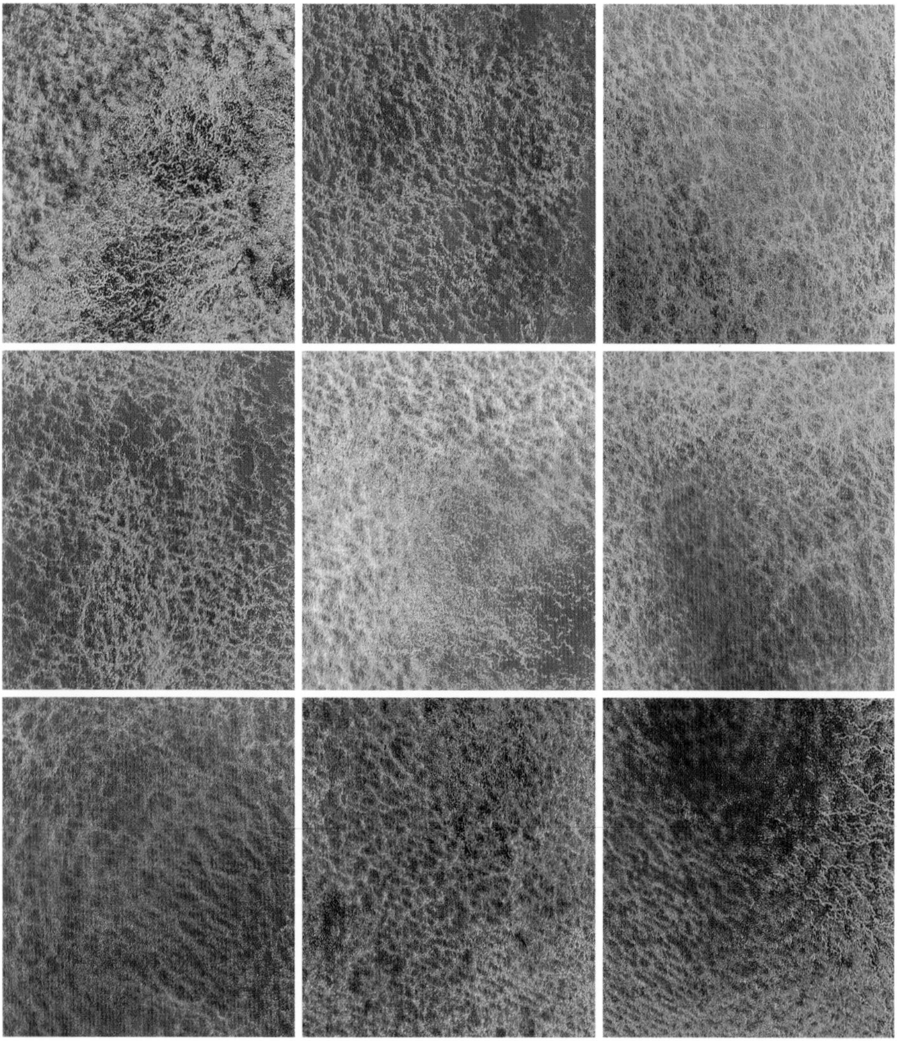

Palette

10	11	12
13	14	15
16	17	18

10 phthalo blue
11 manganese blue
12 phthalo green
13 sap green
14 yellow ochre
15 burnt umber
16 caput mortuum violet
17 sepia
18 indigo

Potter's pink painted over palette colour

Potter's pink painted under palette colour

▼ Swatch shows 60:40 mix of potter's pink plus palette colour (on paper)

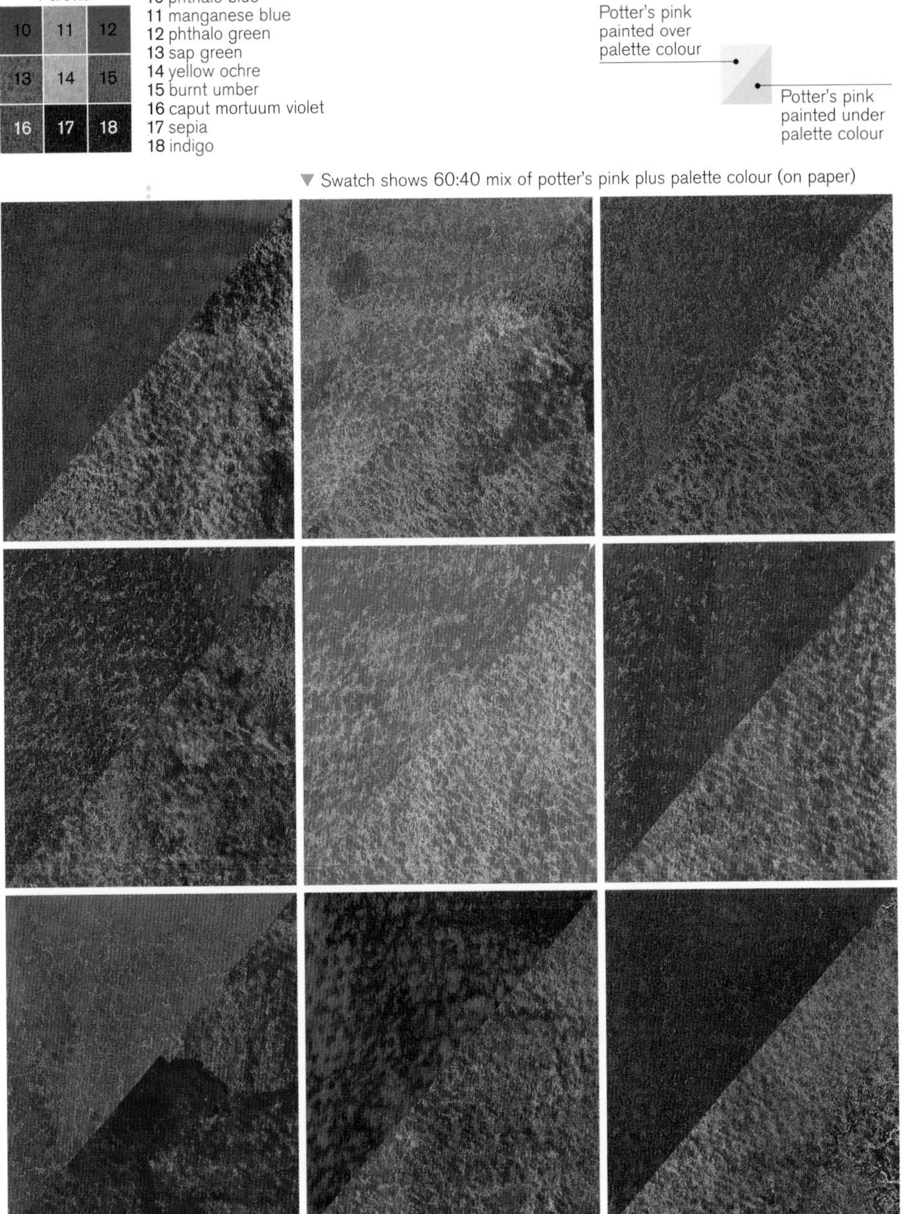

Caput Mortuum Violet/1

Sometimes known as Mars violet, this colour is based on the same PR101 pigment as Indian red (see page 252). It has a cooler hue with a touch of violet/grey. It is heavily staining and opaque, with a velvety matte finish. It works well in washes and will granulate in some mixes.

▼ Swatch shows 60:40 mix of caput mortuum violet plus palette colour (on mixing palette)

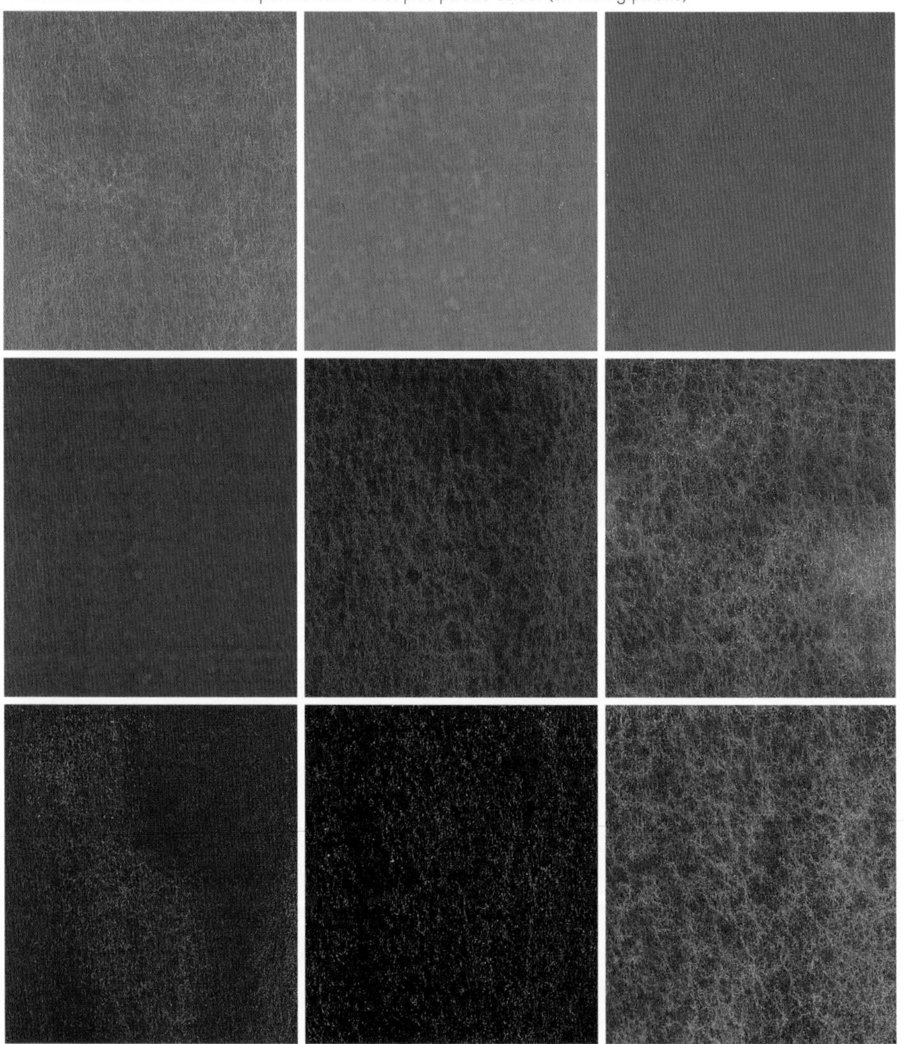

Palette

1 lemon yellow
2 cadmium yellow medium
3 cadmium orange
4 vermilion
5 permanent carmine
6 quinacridone magenta
7 dioxazine violet
8 ultramarine blue
9 cobalt blue

Caput mortuum violet painted over palette colour

Caput mortuum violet painted under palette colour

▼ Swatch shows 60:40 mix of caput mortuum violet plus palette colour (on paper)

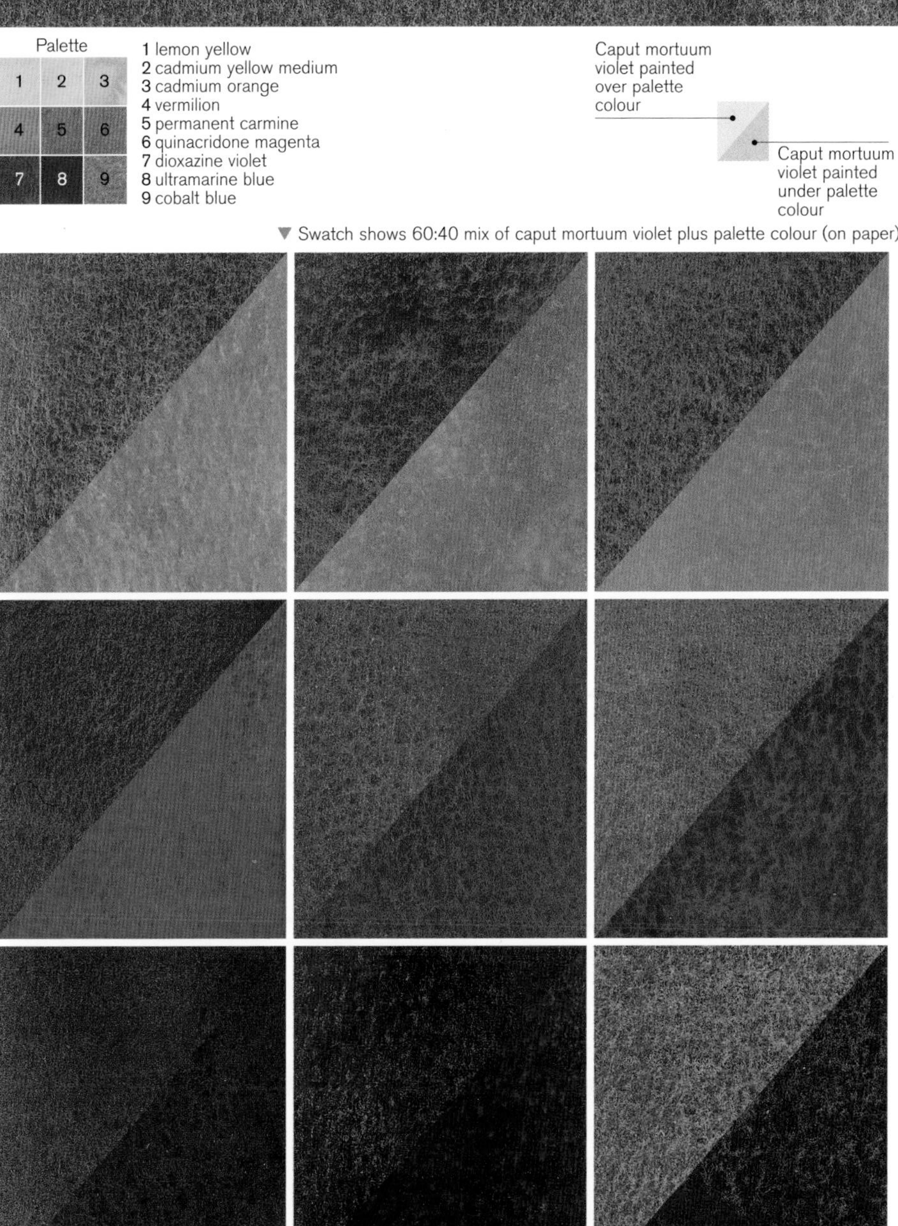

Caput Mortuum Violet/2

Transparency 1
Staining 3
Permanence 3

Granulation
as single colour 3
in mixes 2

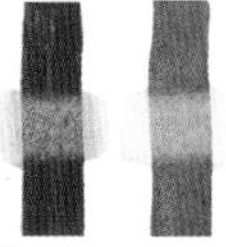

Transparency Staining Granulation

▼ Swatch shows 60:40 mix of caput mortuum violet plus palette colour (on mixing palette)

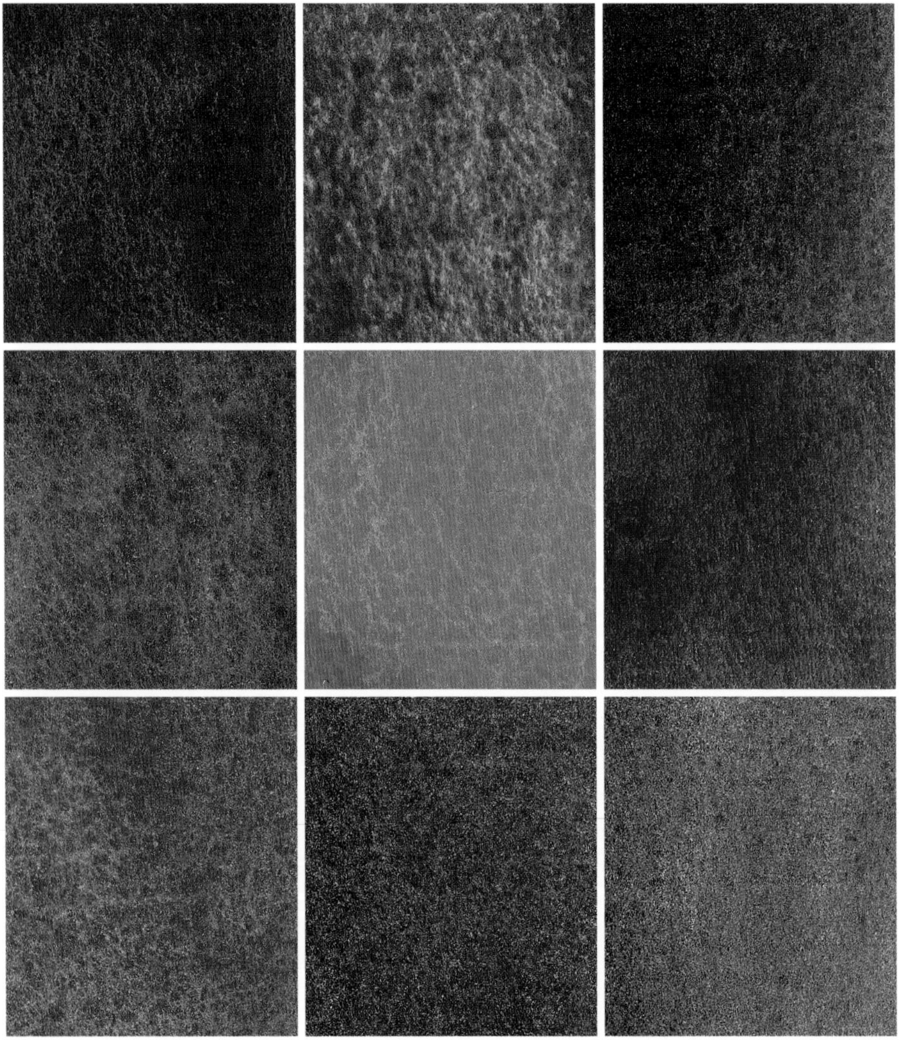

Palette

10	11	12
13	14	15
16	17	18

10 phthalo blue
11 manganese blue
12 phthalo green
13 sap green
14 yellow ochre
15 burnt umber
16 caput mortuum violet
17 sepia
18 indigo

Instead of overpainting the palette colour with itself in the mixes on paper, the upper triangle shows a single wash and the lower, a double wash.

Caput mortuum violet painted over palette colour

Caput mortuum violet painted under palette colour

▼ Swatch shows 60:40 mix of caput mortuum violet plus palette colour (on paper)

Purpurite Genuine/1

This subtle dark grey/lavender hue is a natural mineral pigment. It granulates in all mixes, creating warm, misty textures. It mixes well on a palette, but when using in glazed layers, keep the paint quite dilute to achieve a smooth wash.

▼ Swatch shows 60:40 mix of purpurite genuine plus palette colour (on mixing palette)

Palette

1	2	3
4	5	6
7	8	9

1 lemon yellow
2 cadmium yellow medium
3 cadmium orange
4 vermilion
5 permanent carmine
6 quinacridone magenta
7 dioxazine violet
8 ultramarine blue
9 cobalt blue

Purpurite genuine painted over palette colour

Purpurite genuine painted under palette colour

▼ Swatch shows 60:40 mix of purpurite genuine plus palette colour (on paper)

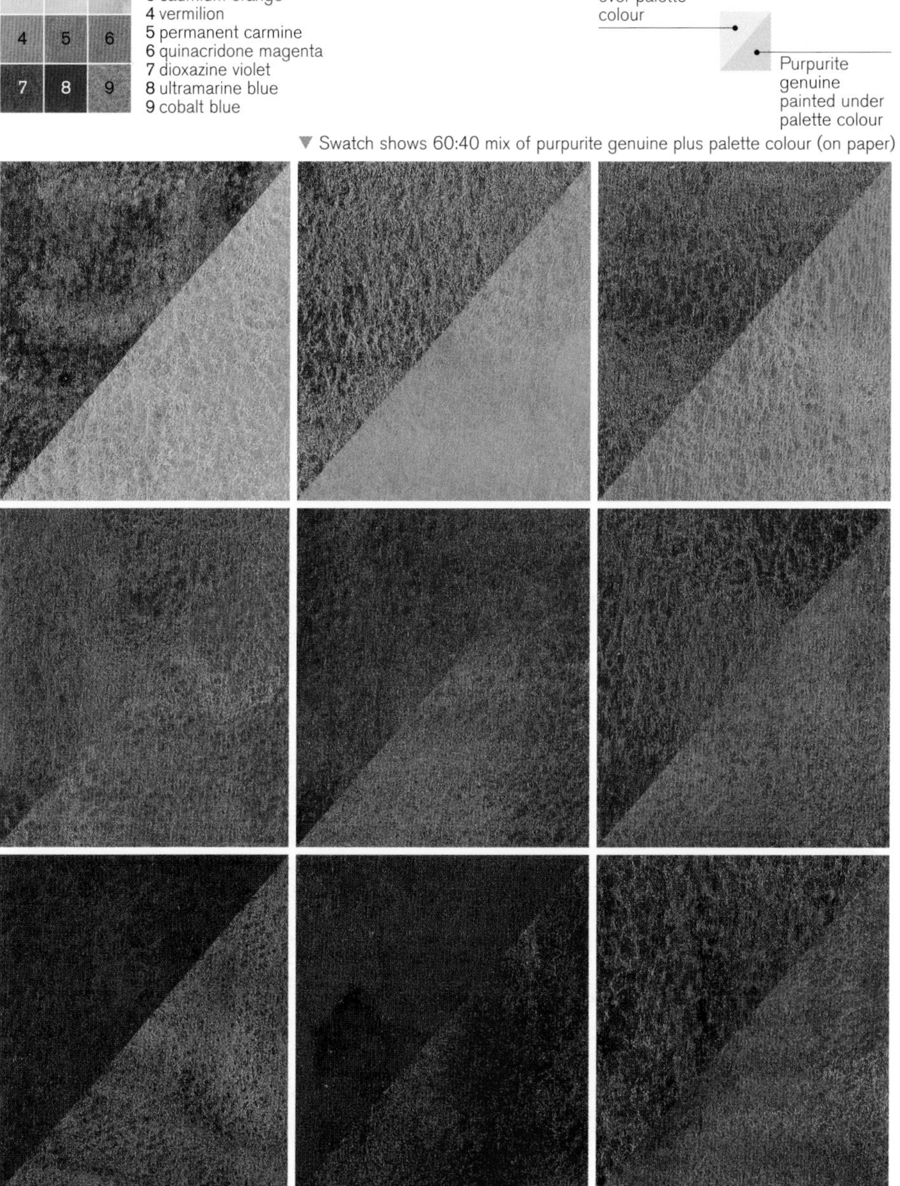

Purpurite Genuine/2

Transparency 2/3
Staining 1
Permanence 3

Granulation
as single colour 3
in mixes 3

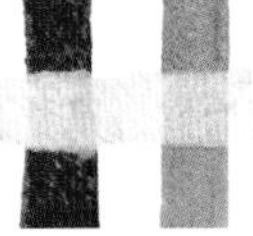

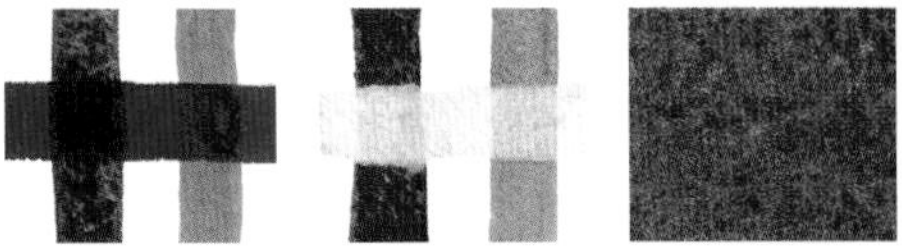

Transparency Staining Granulation

▼ Swatch shows 60:40 mix of purpurite genuine plus palette colour (on mixing palette)

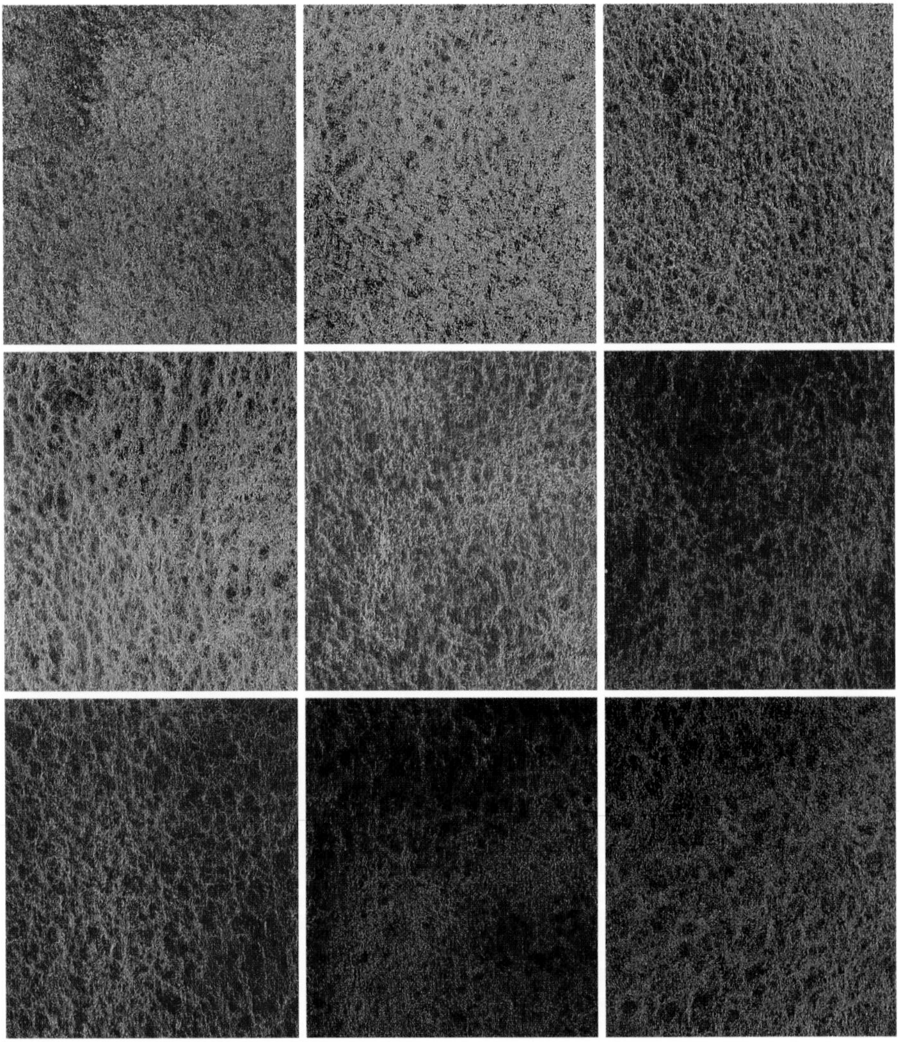

Palette

10	11	12
13	14	15
16	17	18

10 phthalo blue
11 manganese blue
12 phthalo green
13 sap green
14 yellow ochre
15 burnt umber
16 caput mortuum violet
17 sepia
18 indigo

Purpurite genuine painted over palette colour

Purpurite genuine painted under palette colour

▼ Swatch shows 60:40 mix of purpurite genuine plus palette colour (on paper)

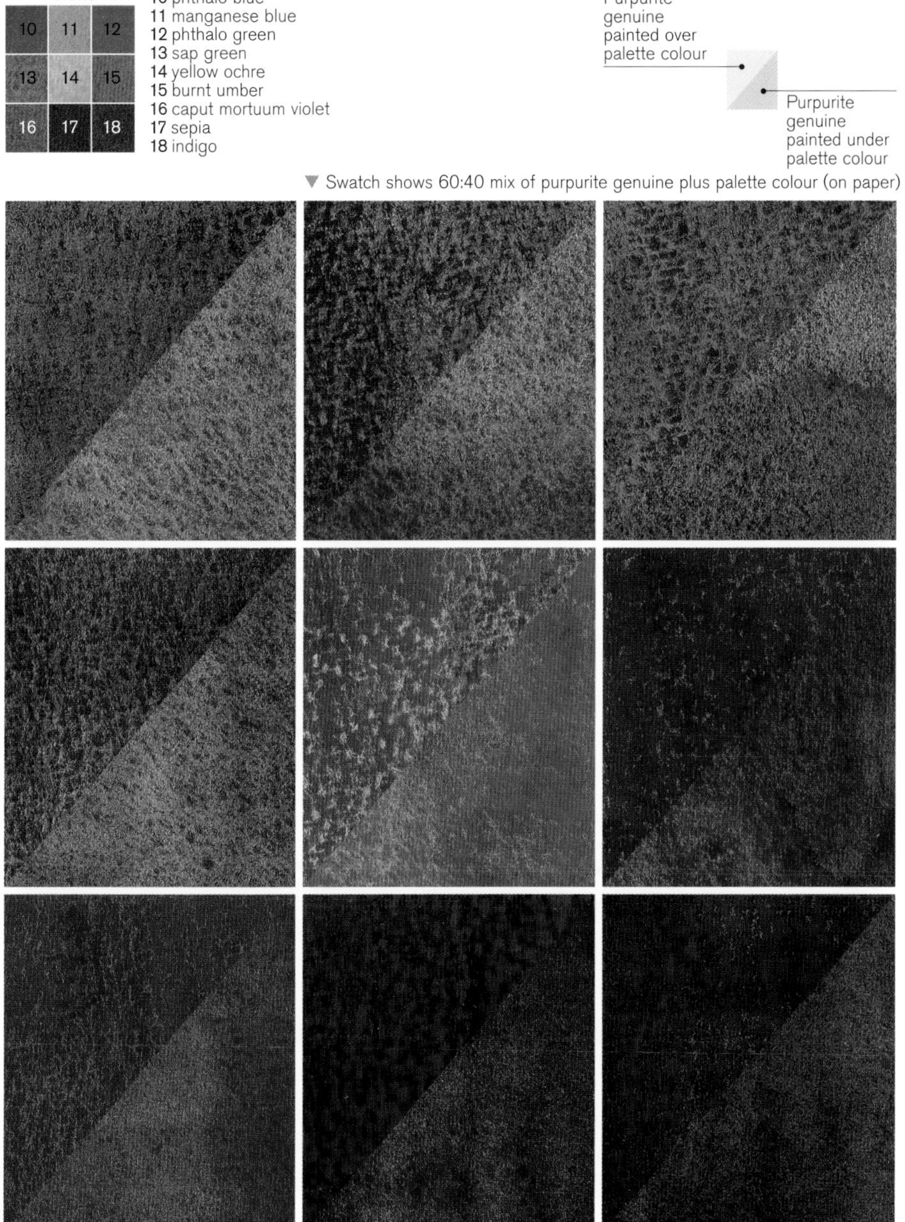

Burnt Umber/1

When raw umber pigment is calcinated or fired, a medium to deep brown colour with a touch of warm red results. This colour works well in all mixes, creating lovely shadow colours when mixed with cobalt or ultramarine blue. Glazed over oranges and reds, it produces glowing brown hues.

▼ Swatch shows 60:40 mix of burnt umber plus palette colour (on mixing palette)

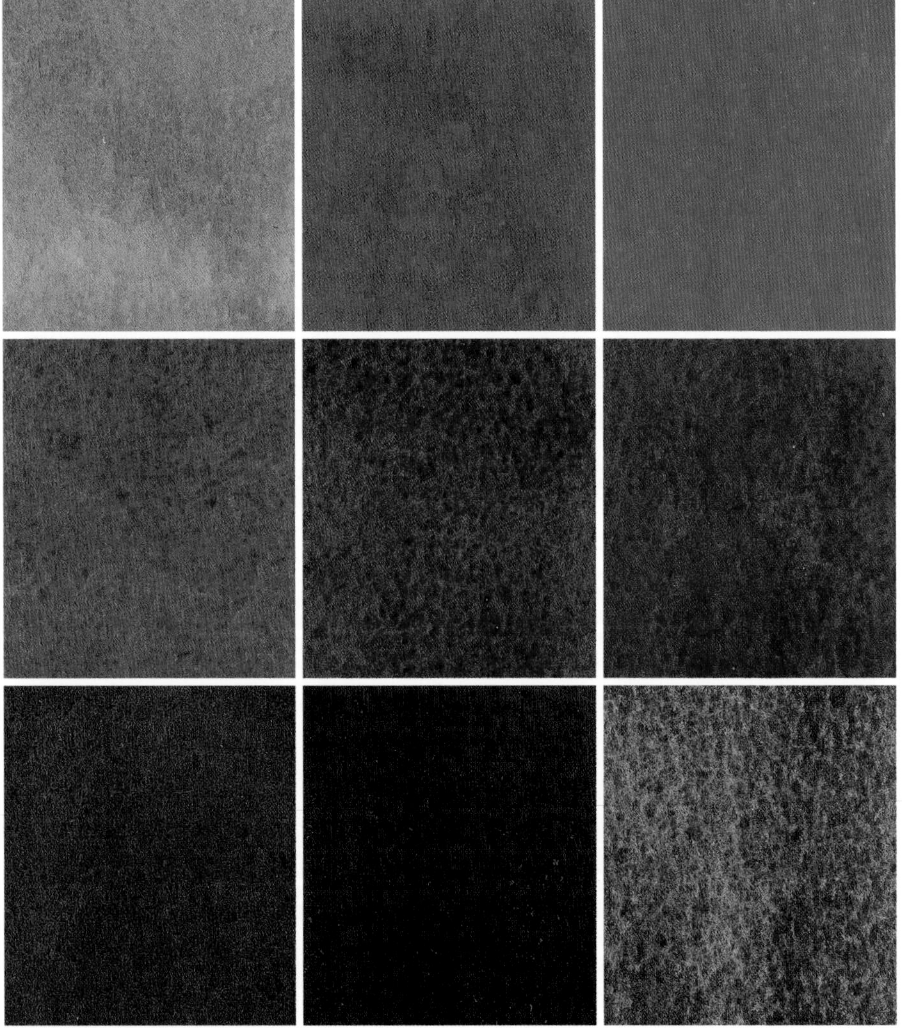

Palette

1	2	3
4	5	6
7	8	9

1 lemon yellow
2 cadmium yellow medium
3 cadmium orange
4 vermilion
5 permanent carmine
6 quinacridone magenta
7 dioxazine violet
8 ultramarine blue
9 cobalt blue

Burnt umber painted over palette colour

Burnt umber painted under palette colour

▼ Swatch shows 60:40 mix of burnt umber plus palette colour (on paper)

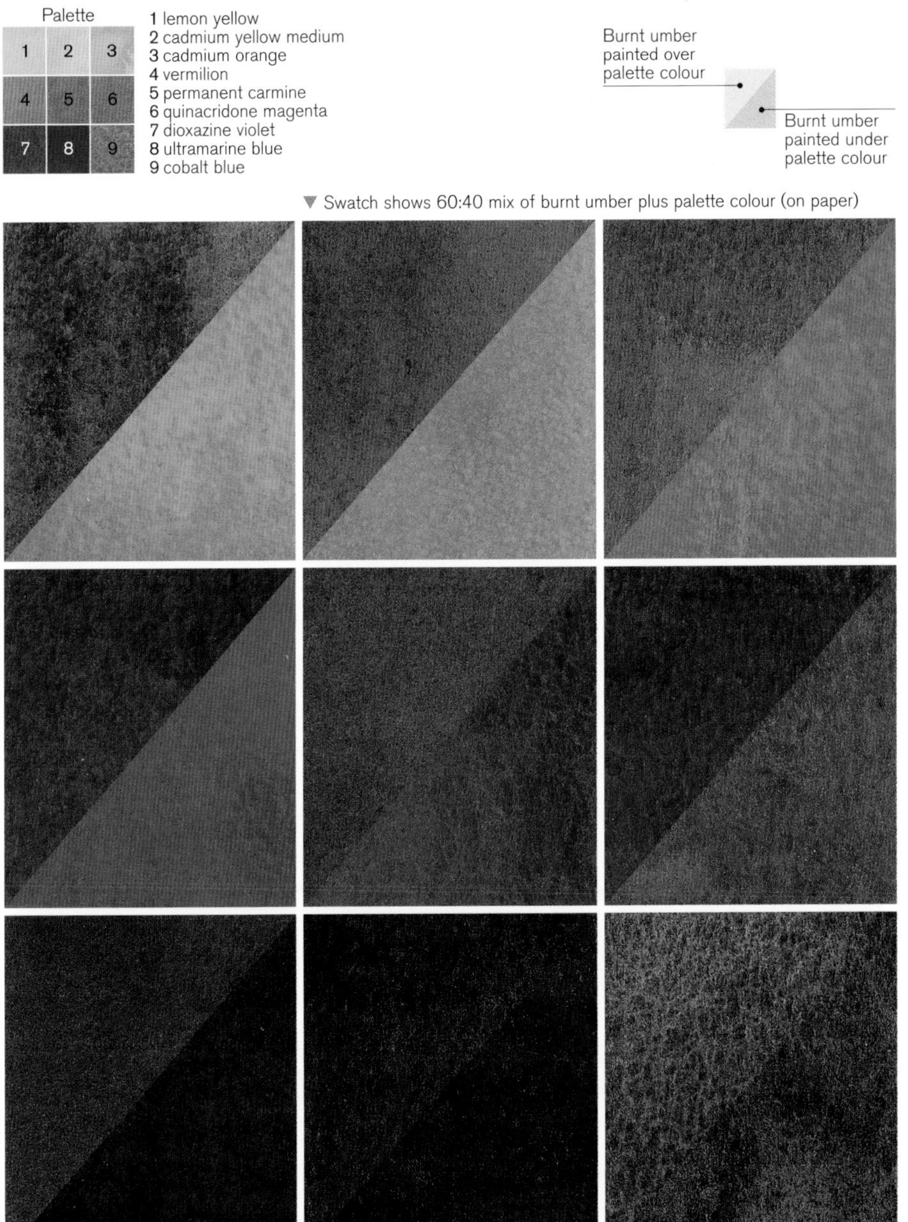

Burnt Umber/2

Transparency 3
Staining 3
Permanence 3

Granulation
as single colour 1
in mixes 1

Transparency

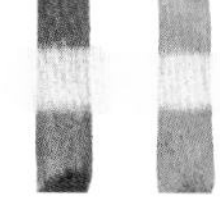

Staining

Granulation

▼ Swatch shows 60:40 mix of burnt umber plus palette colour (on mixing palette)

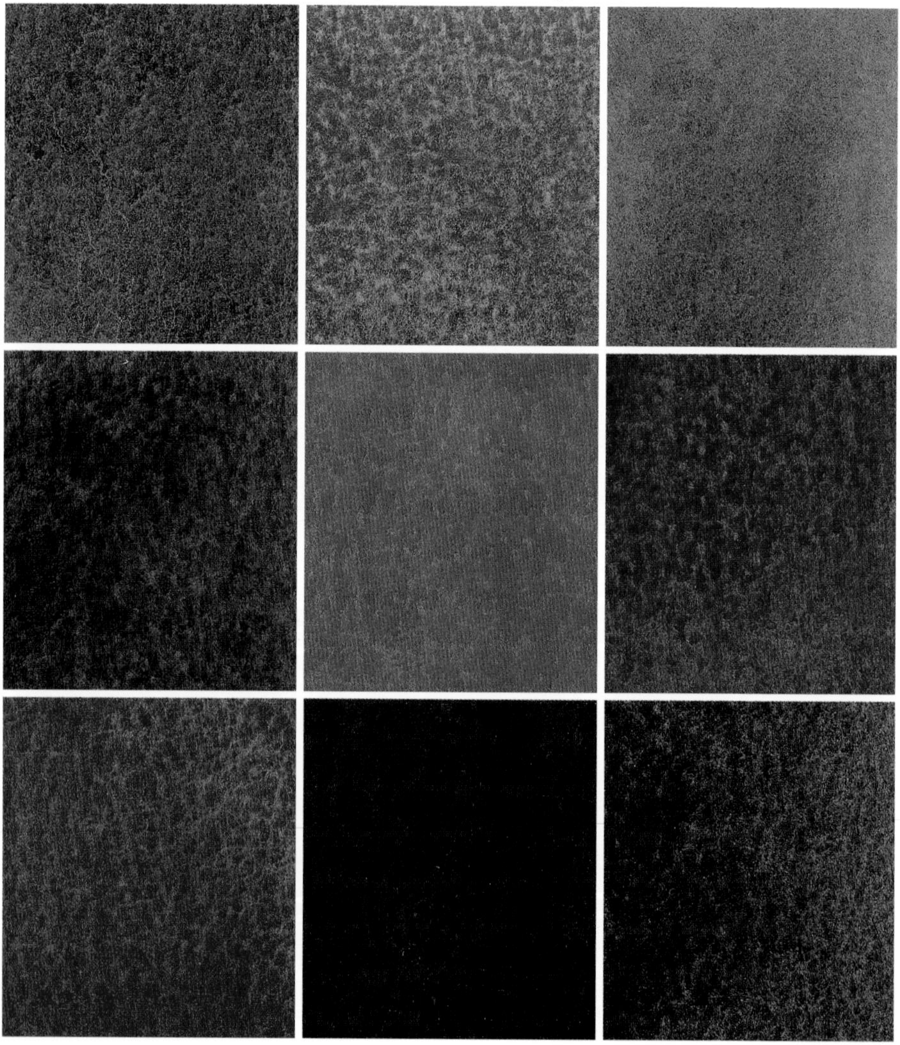

Palette

10	11	12
13	14	15
16	17	18

10 phthalo blue
11 manganese blue
12 phthalo green
13 sap green
14 yellow ochre
15 burnt umber
16 caput mortuum violet
17 sepia
18 indigo

Instead of overpainting the palette colour with itself in the mixes on paper, the upper triangle shows a single wash and the lower, a double wash.

Burnt umber painted over palette colour

Burnt umber painted under palette colour

▼ Swatch shows 60:40 mix of burnt umber plus palette colour (on paper)

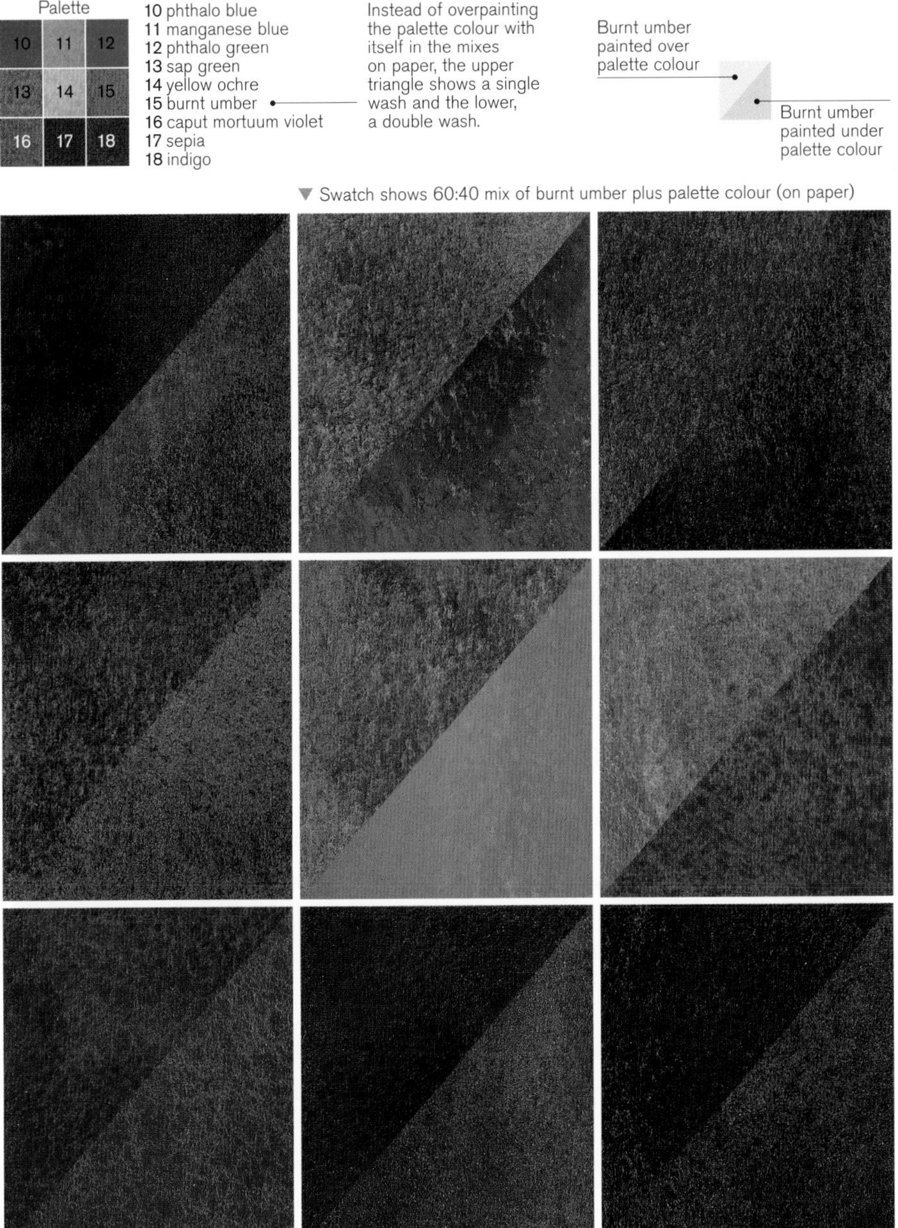

Sepia/1

This dark chocolate brown pigment appears as a well-balanced visual mix of red, blue and yellow. With the further addition of one of those colours, a richer variation will result. It usually creates flat washes, but occasionally granulates in mixes (see the mix with phthalo green).

▼ Swatch shows 60:40 mix of sepia plus palette colour (on mixing palette)

Palette

1	2	3
4	5	6
7	8	9

1 lemon yellow
2 cadmium yellow medium
3 cadmium orange
4 vermilion
5 permanent carmine
6 quinacridone magenta
7 dioxazine violet
8 ultramarine blue
9 cobalt blue

Sepia painted over palette colour

Sepia painted under palette colour

▼ Swatch shows 60:40 mix of sepia plus palette colour (on paper)

Sepia/2

Transparency 2/3
Staining 3
Permanence 3

Granulation
as single colour 0
in mixes 1

Transparency

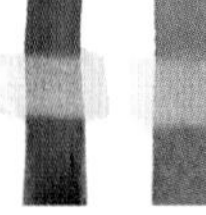
Staining

Granulation

▼ Swatch shows 60:40 mix of sepia plus palette colour (on mixing palette)

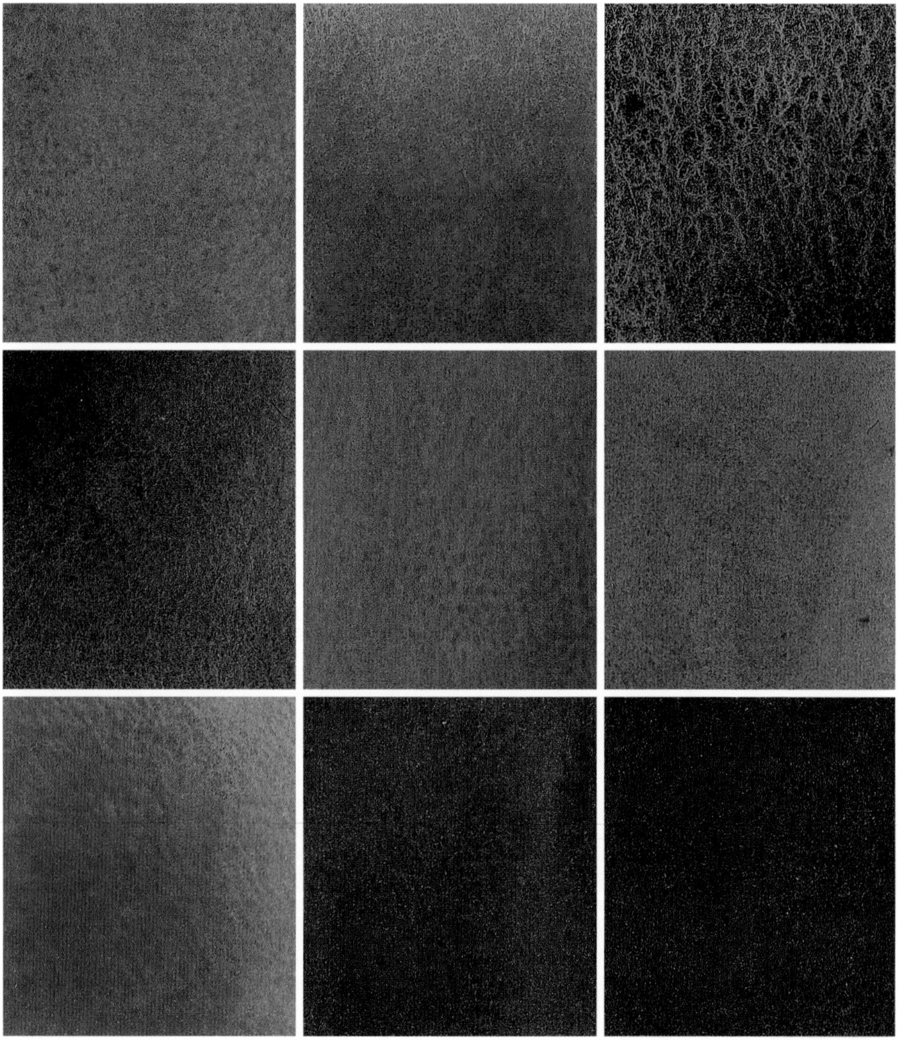

Palette

10	11	12
13	14	15
16	17	18

10 phthalo blue
11 manganese blue
12 phthalo green
13 sap green
14 yellow ochre
15 burnt umber
16 caput mortuum violet
17 sepia
18 indigo

Instead of overpainting the palette colour with itself in the mixes on paper, the upper triangle shows a single wash and the lower, a double wash.

Sepia painted over palette colour

Sepia painted under palette colour

▼ Swatch shows 60:40 mix of sepia plus palette colour (on paper)

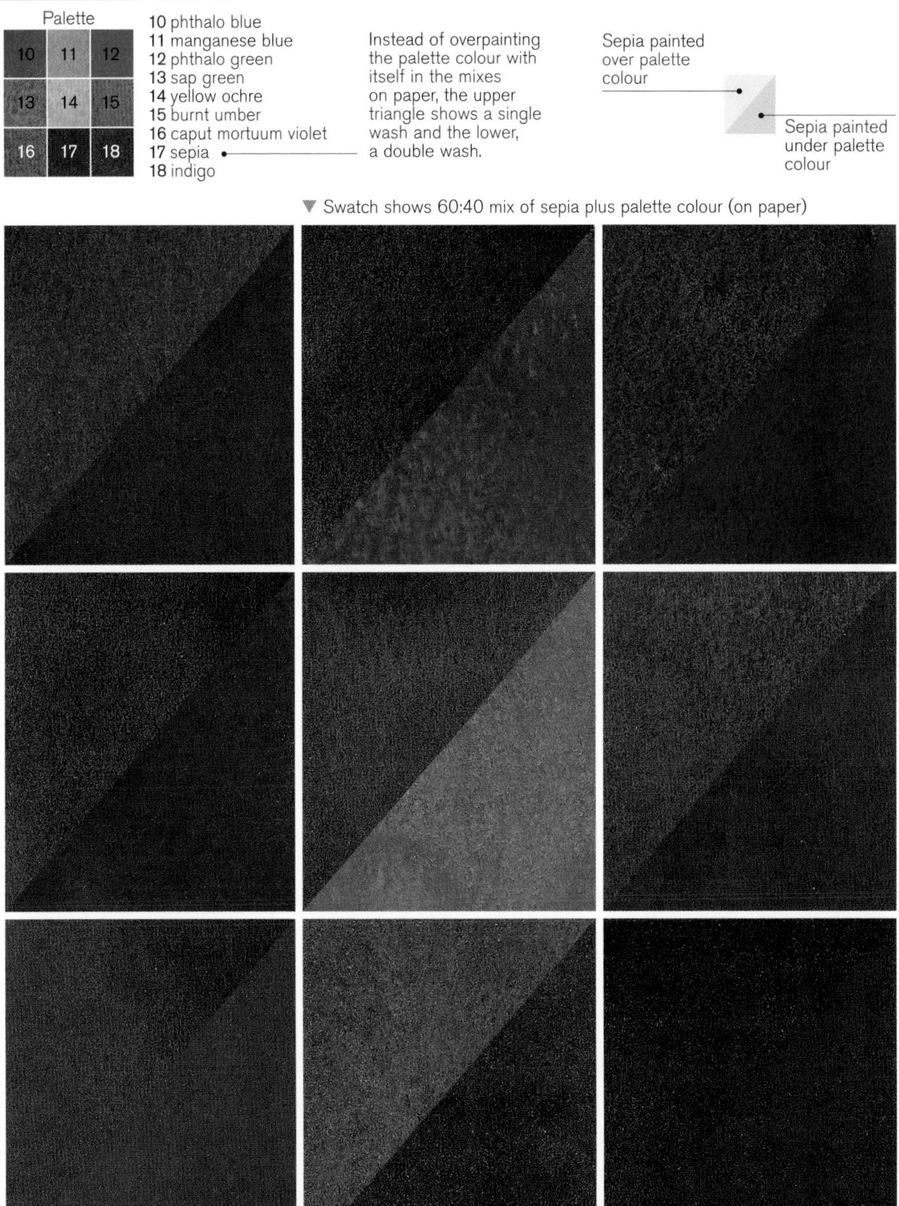

Indigo/1

This is an inky, semi-transparent, blue–black hue. As the original indigo pigment is fugitive, it is now produced from a mix of various blue pigments and lamp black. It mixes well in all washes, creating dark, mysterious shadow mixes with all the colours featured here.

▼ Swatch shows 60:40 mix of indigo plus palette colour (on mixing palette)

Palette

1	2	3
4	5	6
7	8	9

1 lemon yellow
2 cadmium yellow medium
3 cadmium orange
4 vermilion
5 permanent carmine
6 quinacridone magenta
7 dioxazine violet
8 ultramarine blue
9 cobalt blue

Indigo painted over palette colour

Indigo painted under palette colour

▼ Swatch shows 60:40 mix of indigo plus palette colour (on paper)

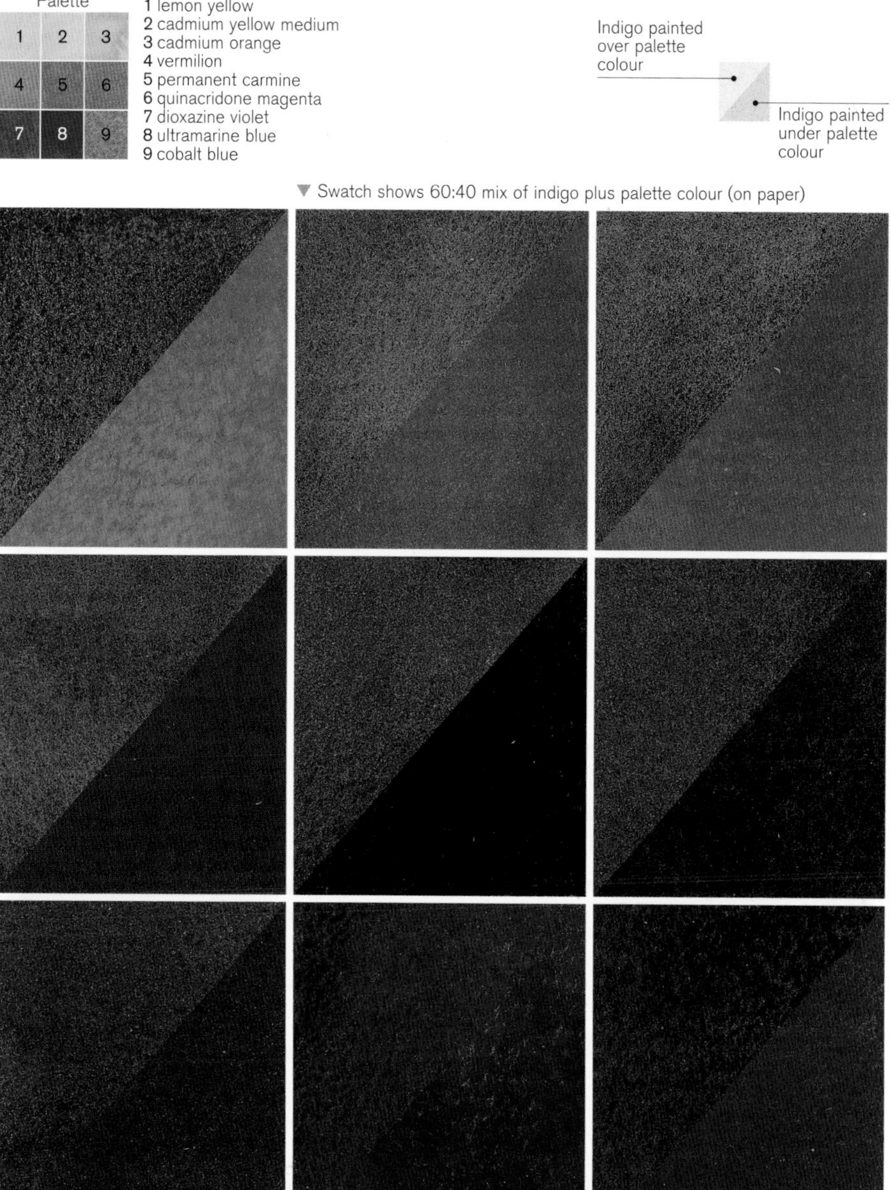

Indigo/2

Transparency 2
Staining 3
Permanence 2

Granulation
as single colour 0
in mixes 1

Transparency

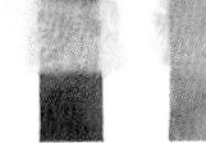
Staining

Granulation

▼ Swatch shows 60:40 mix of indigo plus palette colour (on mixing palette)

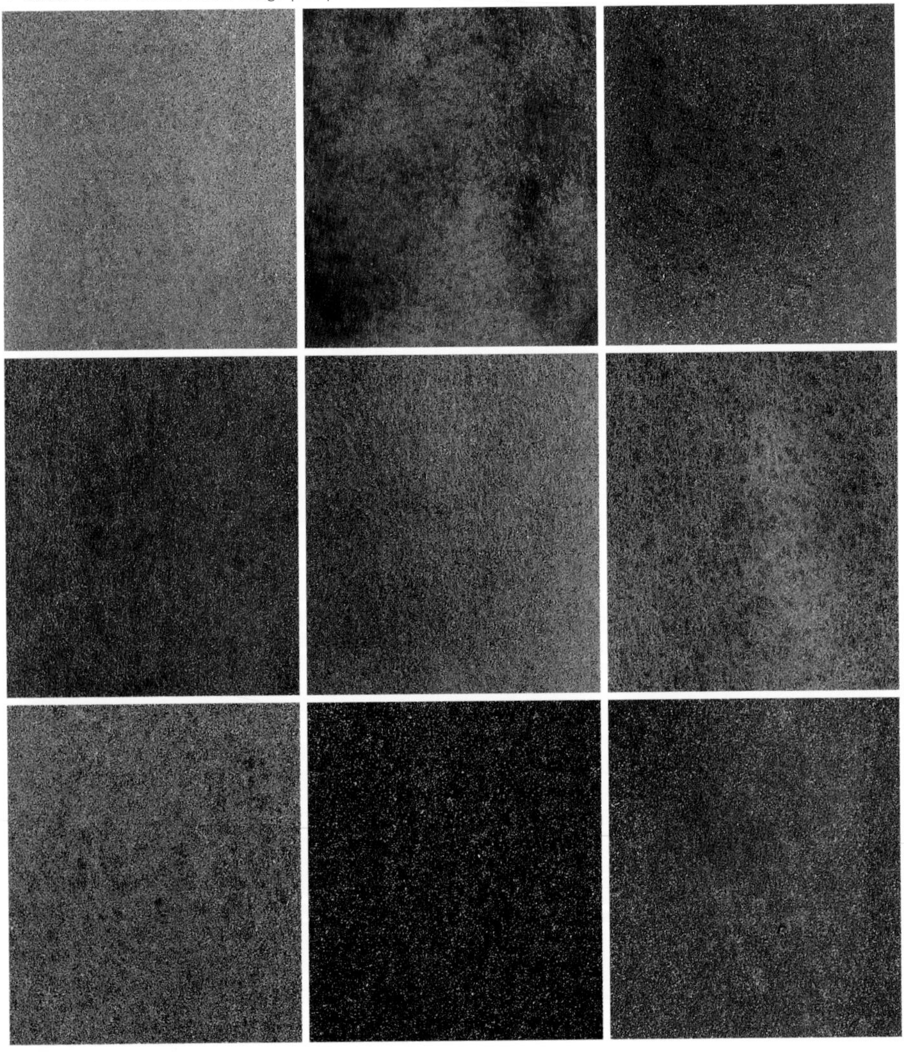

Palette

10	11	12
13	14	15
16	17	18

10 phthalo blue
11 manganese blue
12 phthalo green
13 sap green
14 yellow ochre
15 burnt umber
16 caput mortuum violet
17 sepia
18 indigo

Instead of overpainting the palette colour with itself in the mixes on paper, the upper triangle shows a single wash and the lower, a double wash.

Indigo painted over palette colour

Indigo painted under palette colour

▼ Swatch shows 60:40 mix of indigo plus palette colour (on paper)

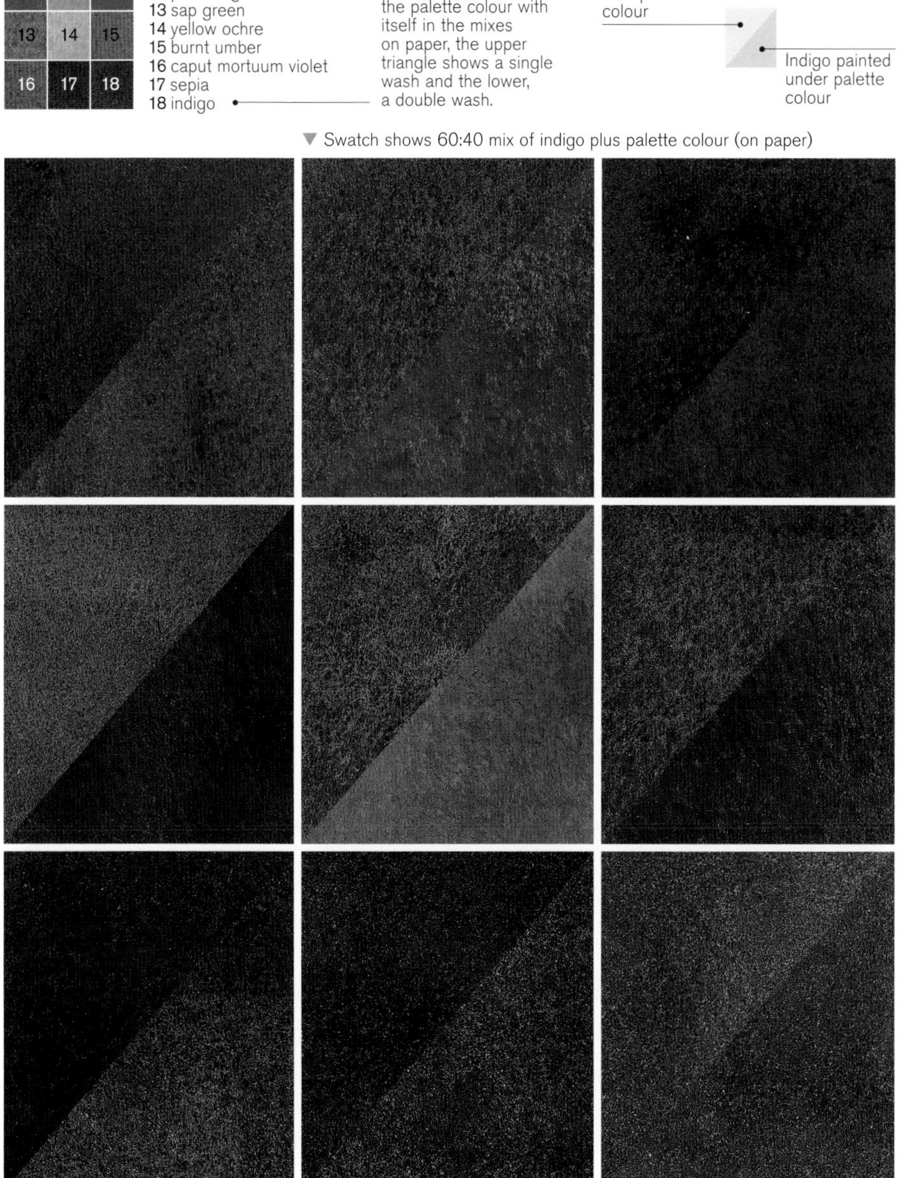

Perylene Green/1

This very dark green–black is reminiscent of the shadows seen in a coniferous forest; it is ideal for foliage. It generally mixes well and granulates slightly in palette mixes. It creates dark neutrals when mixed with violets or red–browns such as caput mortuum violet or Indian red.

▼ Swatch shows 60:40 mix of perylene green plus palette colour (on mixing palette)

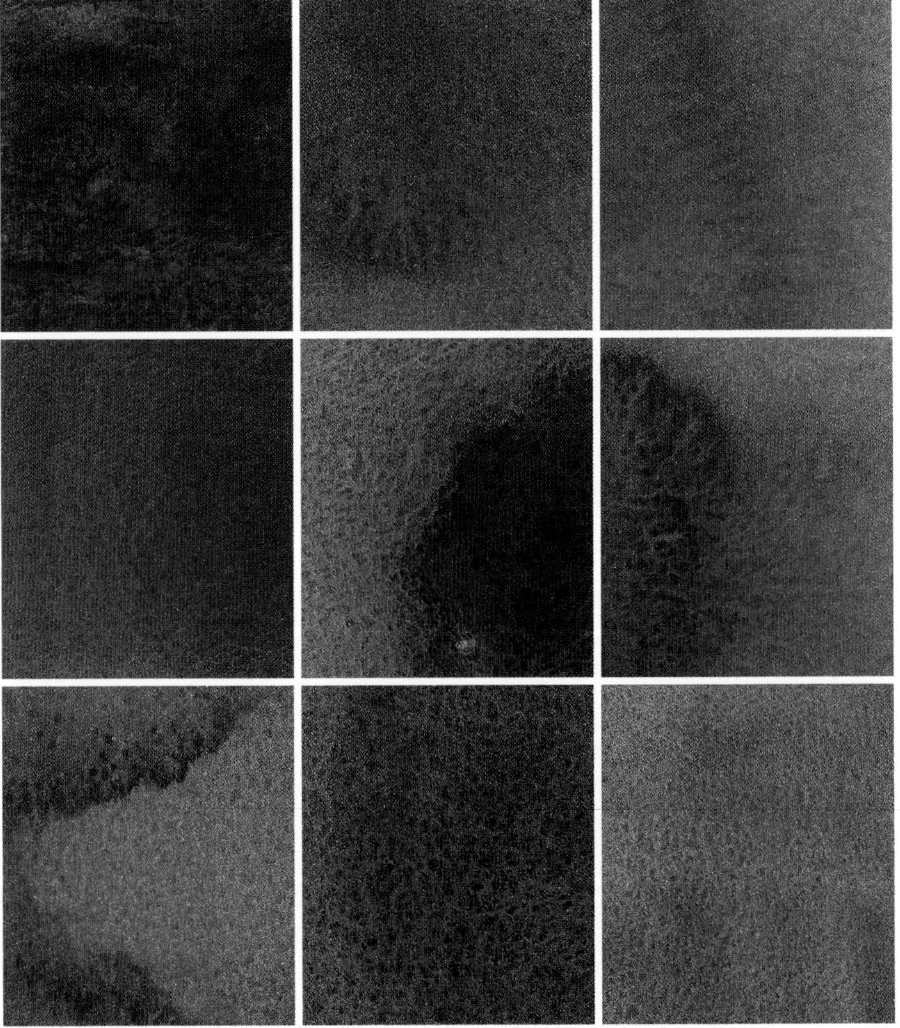

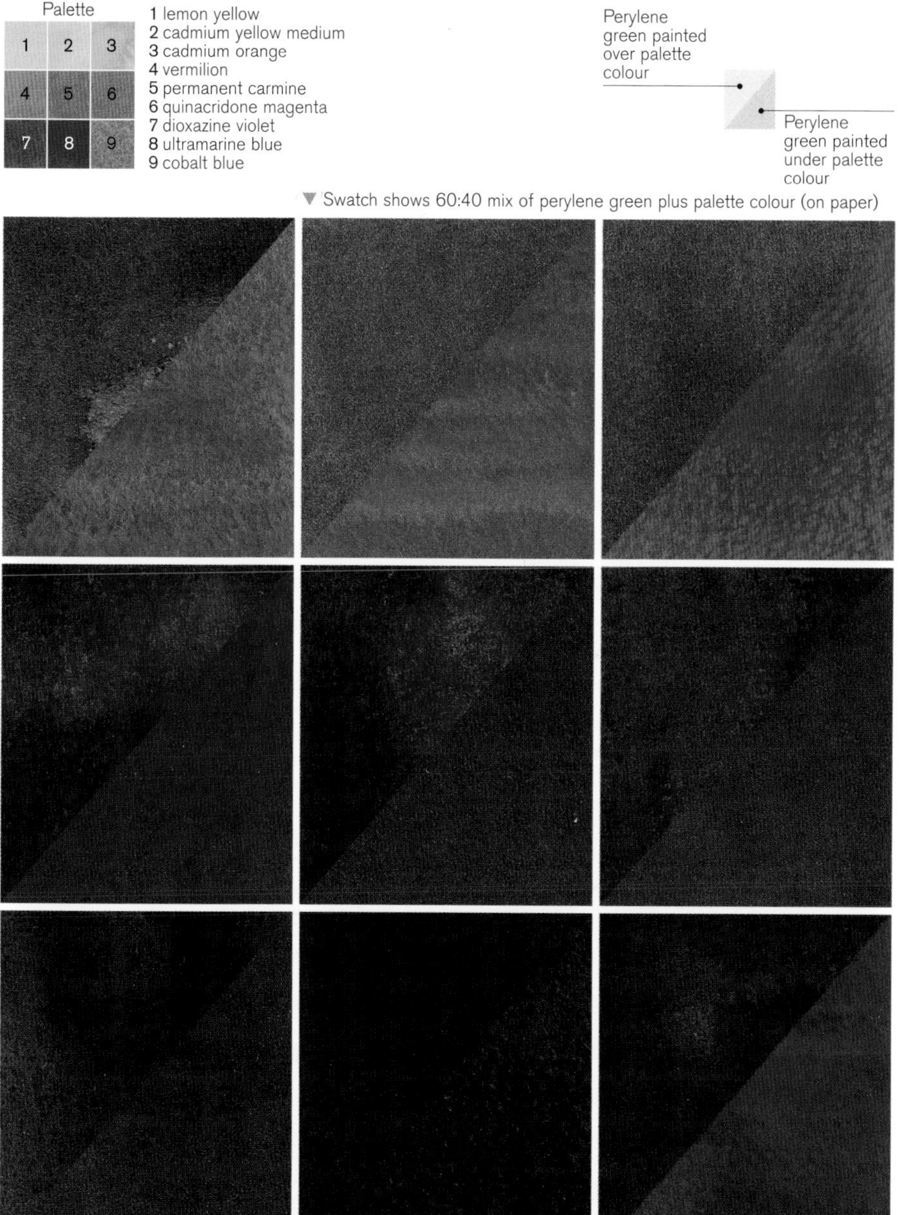

▼ Swatch shows 60:40 mix of perylene green plus palette colour (on paper)

Perylene Green/2

Transparency 2/3
Staining 3
Permanence 3

Granulation
as single colour 1
in mixes 1

Transparency

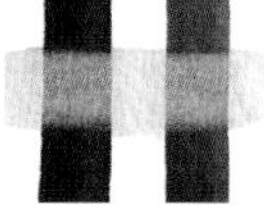
Staining

Granulation

▼ Swatch shows 60:40 mix of perylene green plus palette colour (on mixing palette)

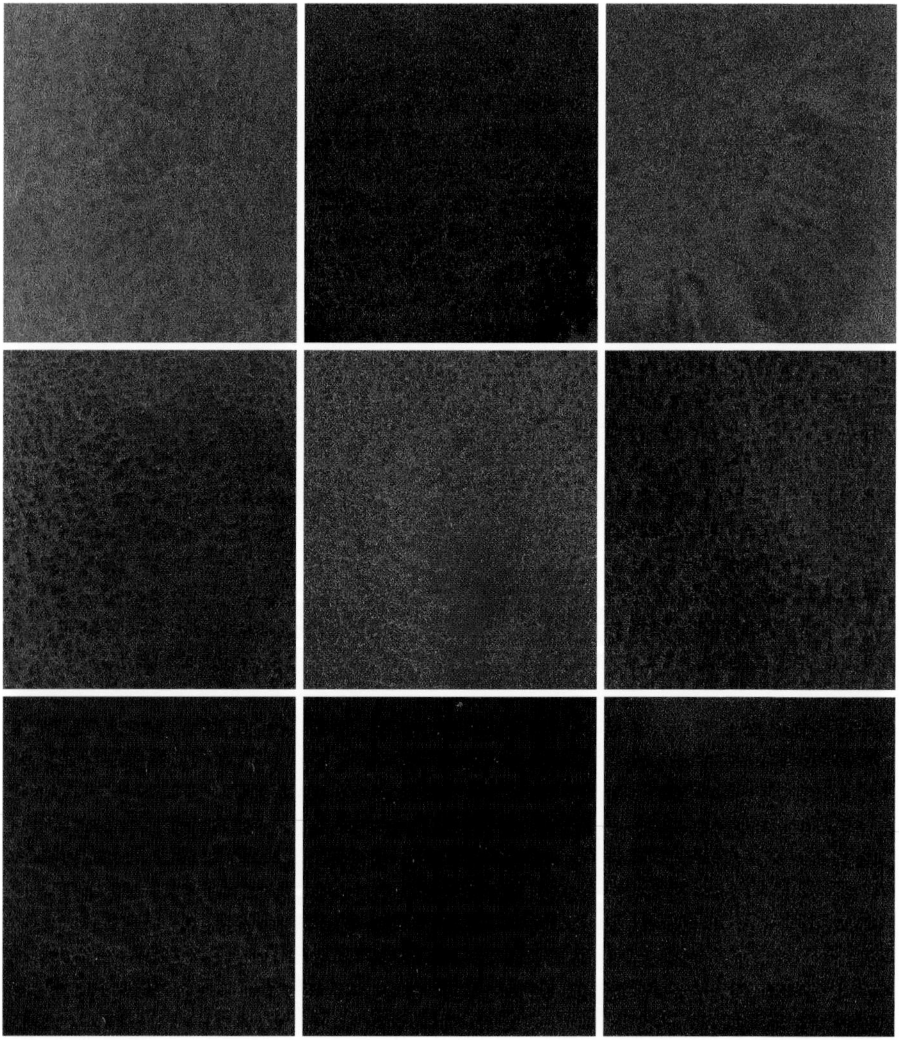

Palette

10	11	12
13	14	15
16	17	18

10 phthalo blue
11 manganese blue
12 phthalo green
13 sap green
14 yellow ochre
15 burnt umber
16 caput mortuum violet
17 sepia
18 indigo

Perylene green painted over palette colour

Perylene green painted under palette colour

▼ Swatch shows 60:40 mix of perylene green plus palette colour (on paper)

Davy's Grey/1

This pale, semi-opaque grey has a warm (almost yellow–green), chalky bias. It mixes well on a palette, creating soft colours. It can be difficult to apply as a glazed layer (either under or over another colour), so use it very dilute or prime first (see page 15).

▼ Swatch shows 60:40 mix of Davy's grey plus palette colour (on mixing palette)

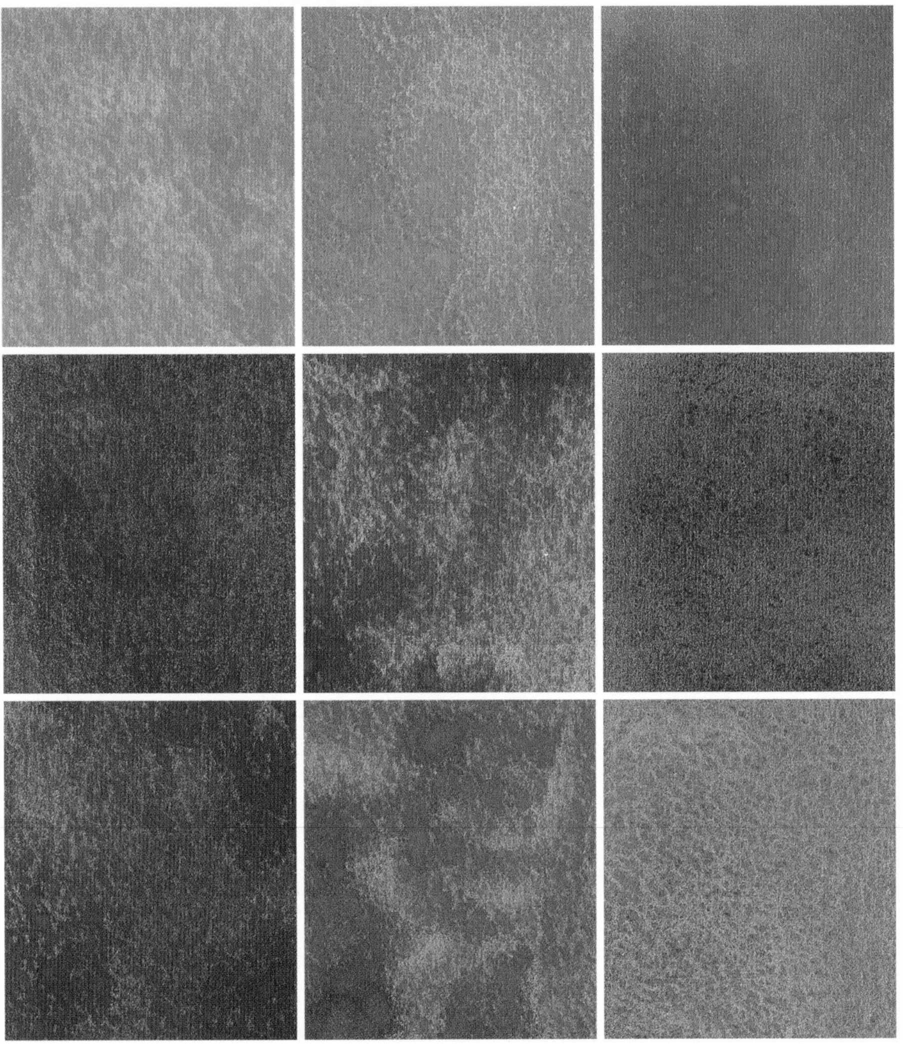

Palette

1	2	3
4	5	6
7	8	9

1 lemon yellow
2 cadmium yellow medium
3 cadmium orange
4 vermilion
5 carmine
6 quinacridone magenta
7 dioxazine violet
8 ultramarine blue
9 cobalt blue

Davy's grey painted over palette colour

Davy's grey painted under palette colour

▼ Swatch shows 60:40 mix of Davy's grey plus palette colour (on paper)

Davy's Grey/2

Transparency 1/2
Staining 1
Permanence 2

Granulation
as single colour 0
in mixes 1

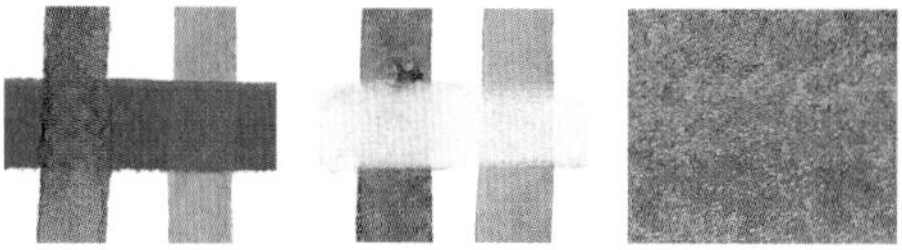

Transparency

Staining

Granulation

▼ Swatch shows 60:40 mix of Davy's grey plus palette colour (on mixing palette)

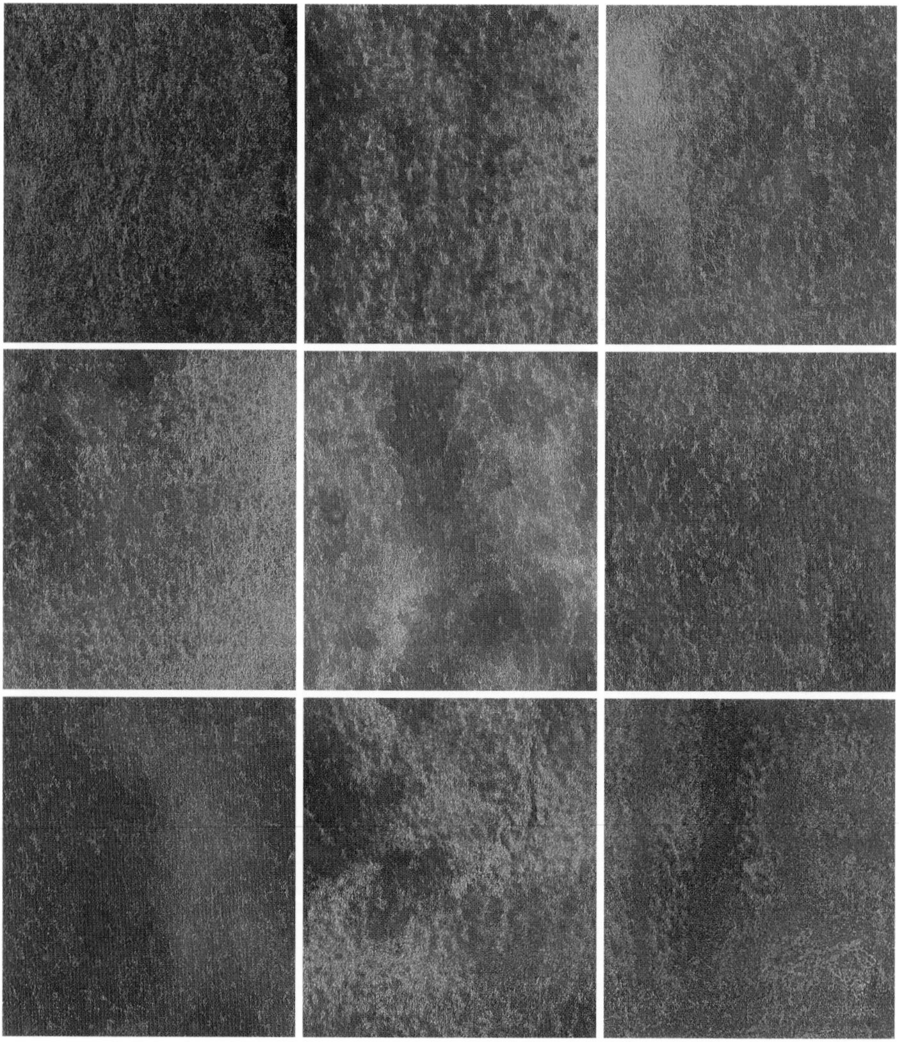

Palette

10	11	12
13	14	15
16	17	18

10 phthalo blue
11 manganese blue
12 phthalo green
13 sap green
14 yellow ochre
15 burnt umber
16 caput mortuum violet
17 sepia
18 indigo

Davy's grey painted over palette colour

Davy's grey painted under palette colour

▼ Swatch shows 60:40 mix of Davy's grey plus palette colour (on paper)

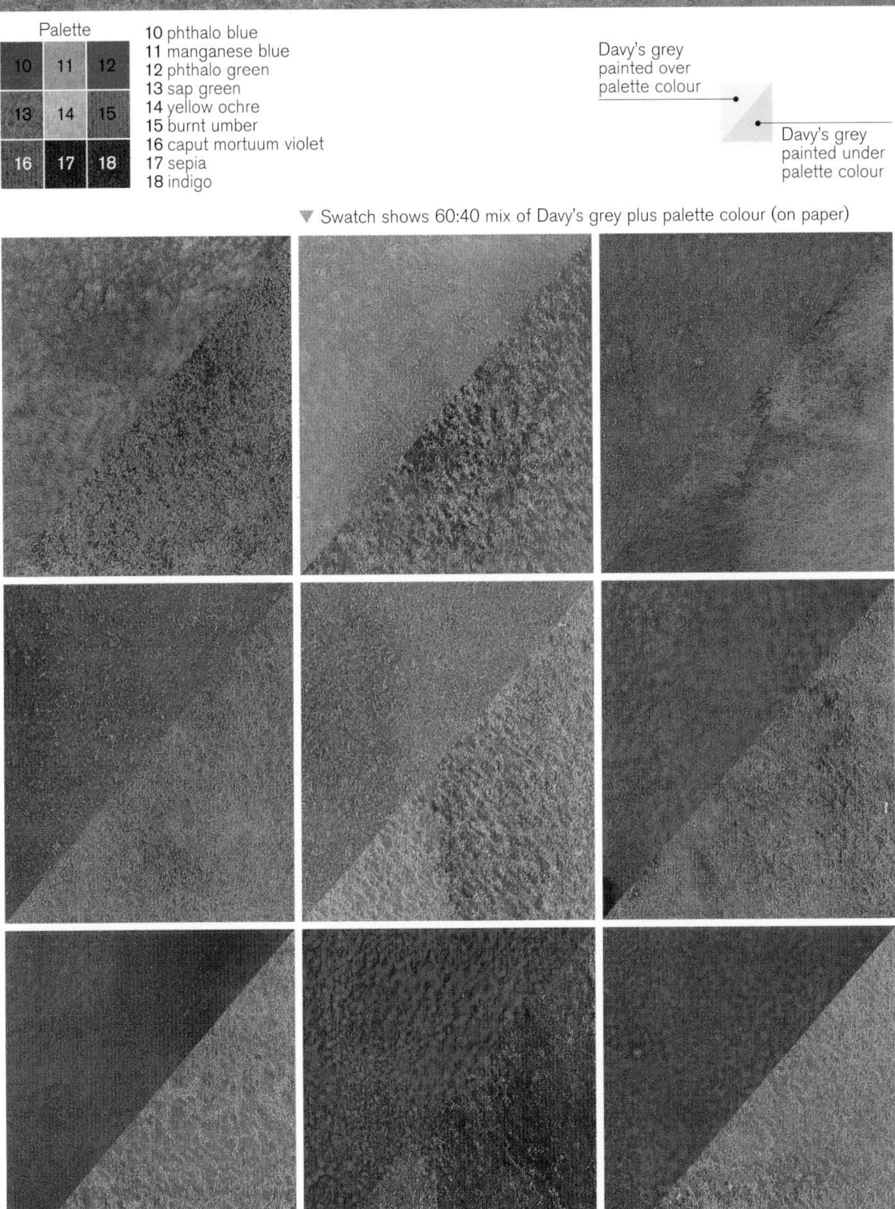

Ivory Black/1

More transparent than the standard lamp and carbon blacks, this pigment is better suited to colour mixing. When applying as an initial wash on paper, prevent muddy mixes by using thinly or priming the paper (see page 15) before adding the second colour. It granulates attractively.

▼ Swatch shows 60:40 mix of ivory black plus palette colour (on mixing palette)

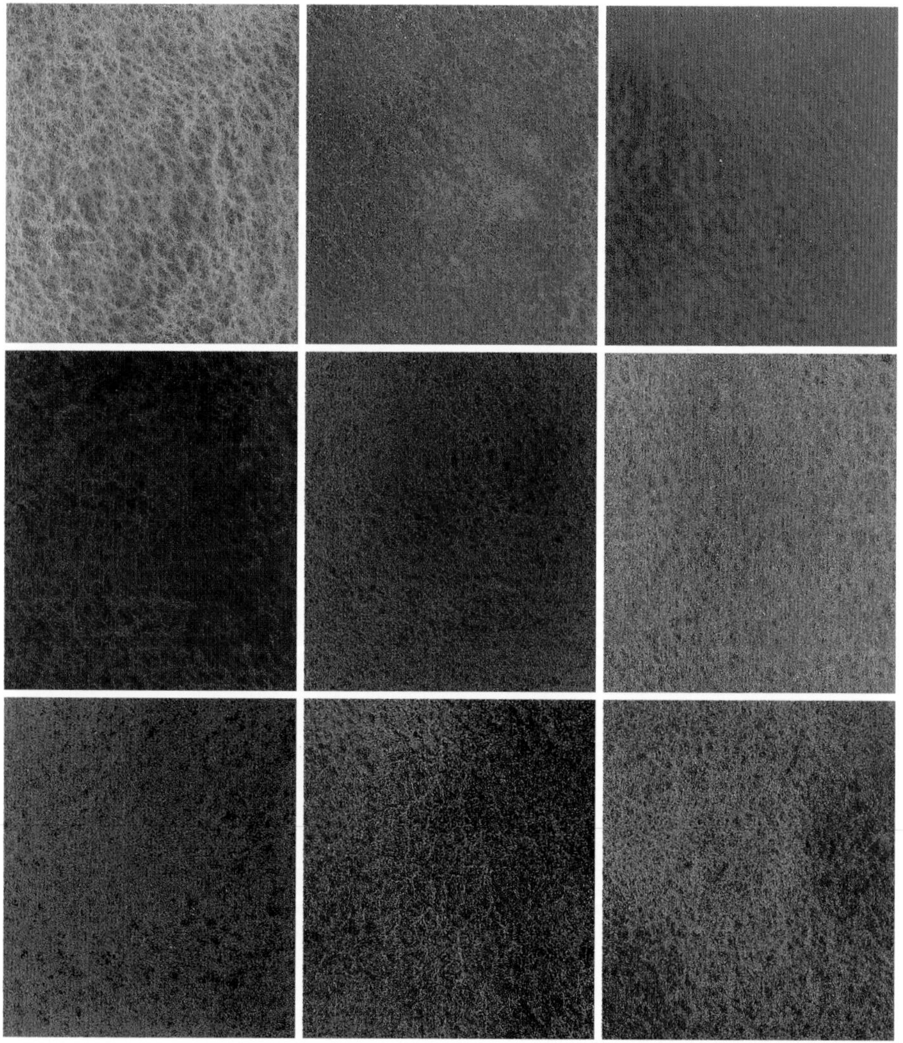

Palette

1	2	3
4	5	6
7	8	9

1 lemon yellow
2 cadmium yellow medium
3 cadmium orange
4 vermilion
5 permanent carmine
6 quinacridone magenta
7 dioxazine violet
8 ultramarine blue
9 cobalt blue

Ivory black painted over palette colour

Ivory black painted under palette colour

▼ Swatch shows 60:40 mix of ivory black plus palette colour (on paper)

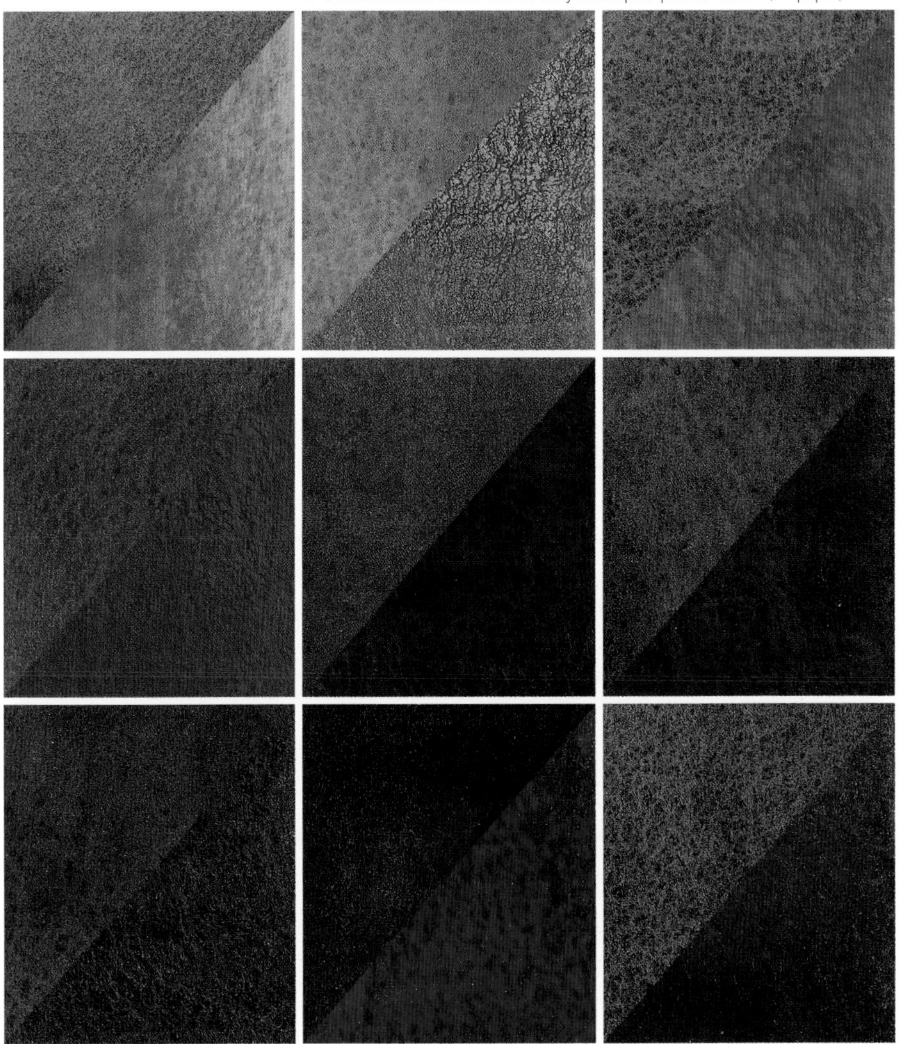

Ivory Black/2

Transparency 2
Staining 3
Permanence 3

Granulation
as single colour 2
in mixes 2

Transparency

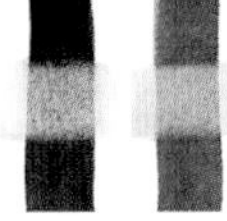
Staining

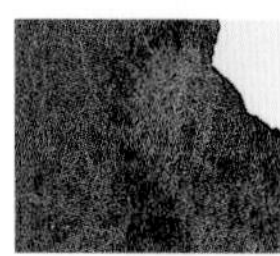
Granulation

▼ Swatch shows 60:40 mix of ivory black plus palette colour (on mixing palette)

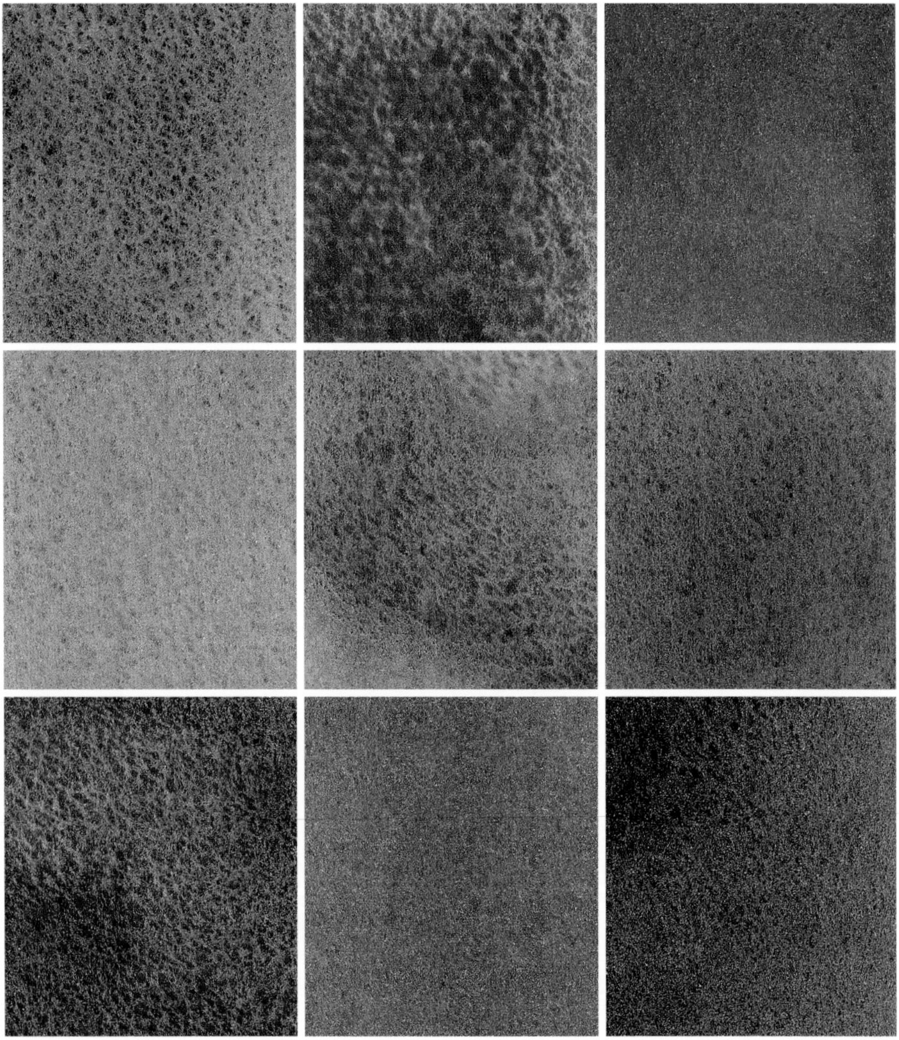

Palette

10	11	12
13	14	15
16	17	18

10 phthalo blue
11 manganese blue
12 phthalo green
13 sap green
14 yellow ochre
15 burnt umber
16 caput mortuum violet
17 sepia
18 indigo

Ivory black painted over palette colour

Ivory black painted under palette colour

▼ Swatch shows 60:40 mix of ivory black plus palette colour (on paper)

Chinese & Titanium White/1

Both of these whites are opaque; Chinese white is the more transparent. As the white of the paper is used to lighten washes or for highlights, these whites are usually mixed with colours to create body colour (see page 22).

Chinese white mixed with palette colour

Titanium white mixed with palette colour

▼ Swatch shows 60:40 mix of Chinese or titanium white plus palette colour (on mixing palette)

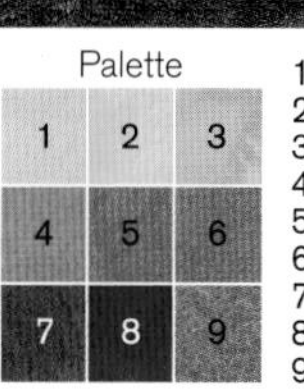

1 lemon yellow
2 cadmium yellow medium
3 cadmium orange
4 vermilion
5 permanent carmine
6 quinacridone magenta
7 dioxazine violet
8 ultramarine blue
9 cobalt blue

As it is not usual to paint white paint as an underlayer (i.e., straight onto the white of the paper), the panel above instead shows the difference between Chinese (left) and titanium white (right) when painted above neutral tint.

Chinese white painted **over** palette colour

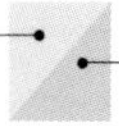

Titanium white painted **over** palette colour

▼ Swatch shows 60:40 mix of Chinese or titanium white plus palette colour (on paper)

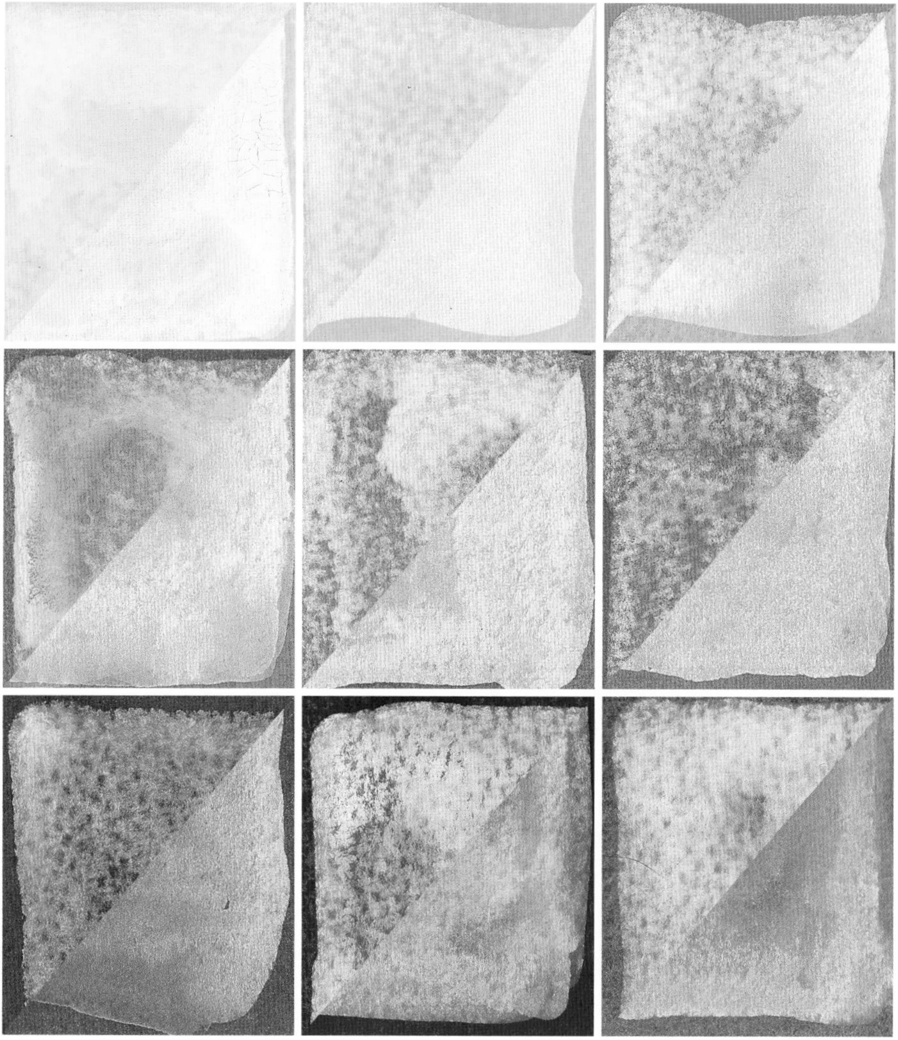

Chinese & Titanium White/2

Transparency 0/1
Staining 1
Permanence 3

Granulation
Chinese in mixes 1
Titanium in mixes 1

Chinese white
Titianium white
Transparency
Granulation

▼ Swatch shows 60:40 mix of Chinese or titanium white plus palette colour (on mixing palette)

Palette

10	11	12
13	14	15
16	17	18

10 phthalo blue
11 manganese blue
12 phthalo green
13 sap green
14 yellow ochre
15 burnt umber
16 caput mortuum violet
17 sepia
18 indigo

Colour mixes with the two whites are similar in tone and colour. The greater opacity of titanium white is balanced by the transparency of Chinese white, which allows the white of the paper to show through.

Chinese white painted **over** palette colour

Titanium white painted **over** palette colour

▼ Swatch shows 60:40 mix of Chinese or titanium white plus palette colour (on paper)

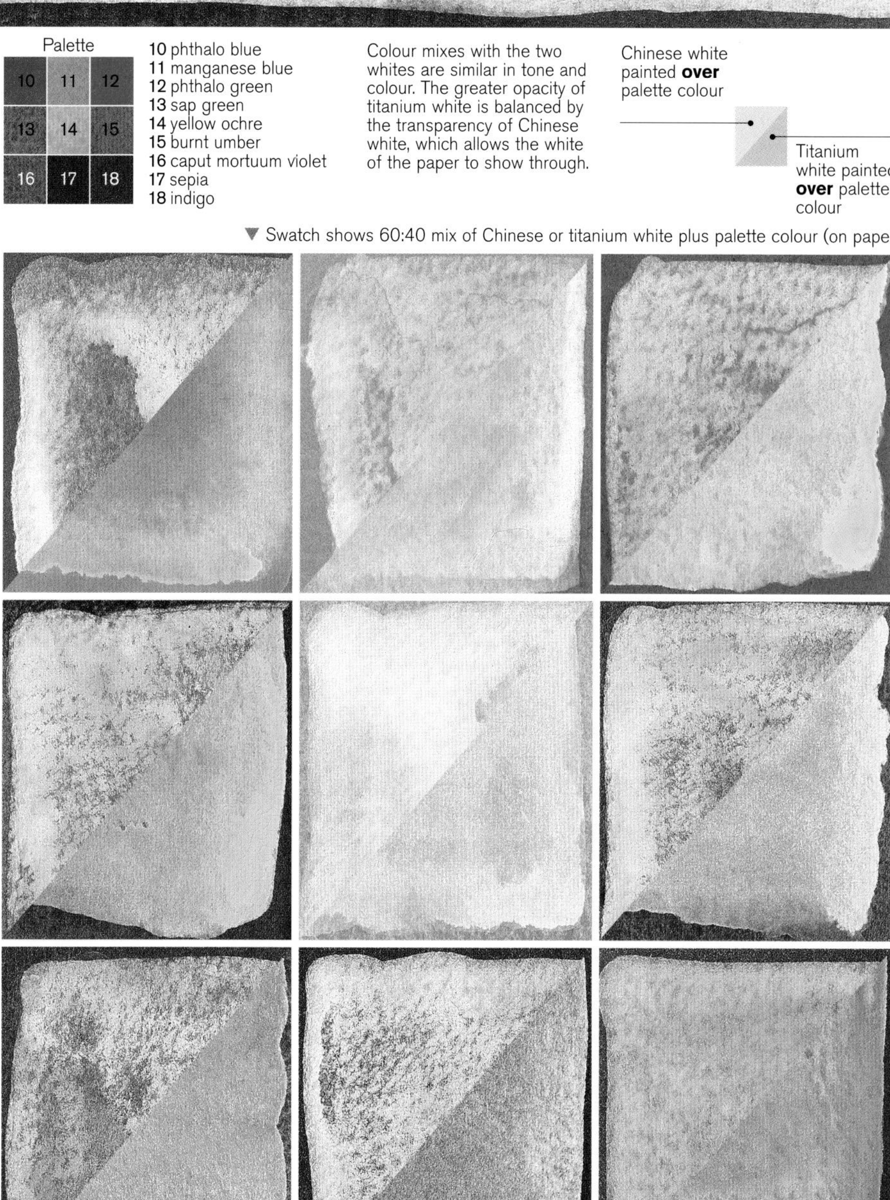

Transparent Mixes

Transparency is just one of the properties that make watercolour painting unique. This mixing chart features the more transparent pigments for those artists who like to work exclusively by building up layers or glazes. It is, of course, also possible to work with some of the more opaque pigments if they are heavily diluted with water and used as underlayers. Most of these colours also appear in the Colour Mixing Directory.

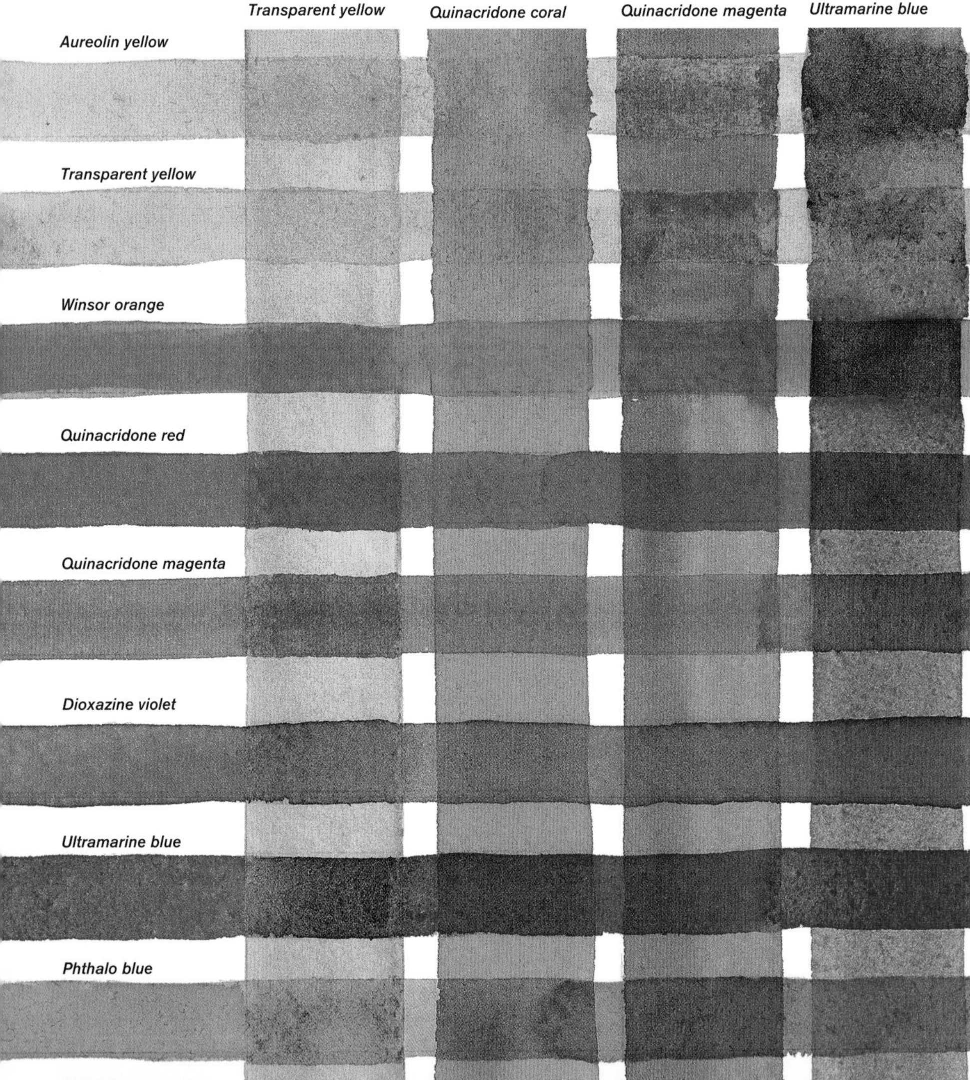

The nine colours on the top axis are painted beneath the vertical axis palette of 18 transparent colours. As all of these colours (on both the horizontal and vertical axes) are transparent and painted in equal strengths, whether they are painted above or beneath each other has little effect on the final result (see right).

Phthalo green under quinacridone magenta

Phthalo green over quinacridone magenta

Phthalo green under quinacridone gold

Phthalo green over quinacridone gold

Phthalo blue *Phthalo green* *Terre verte* *Raw umber* *Indanthrene blue*

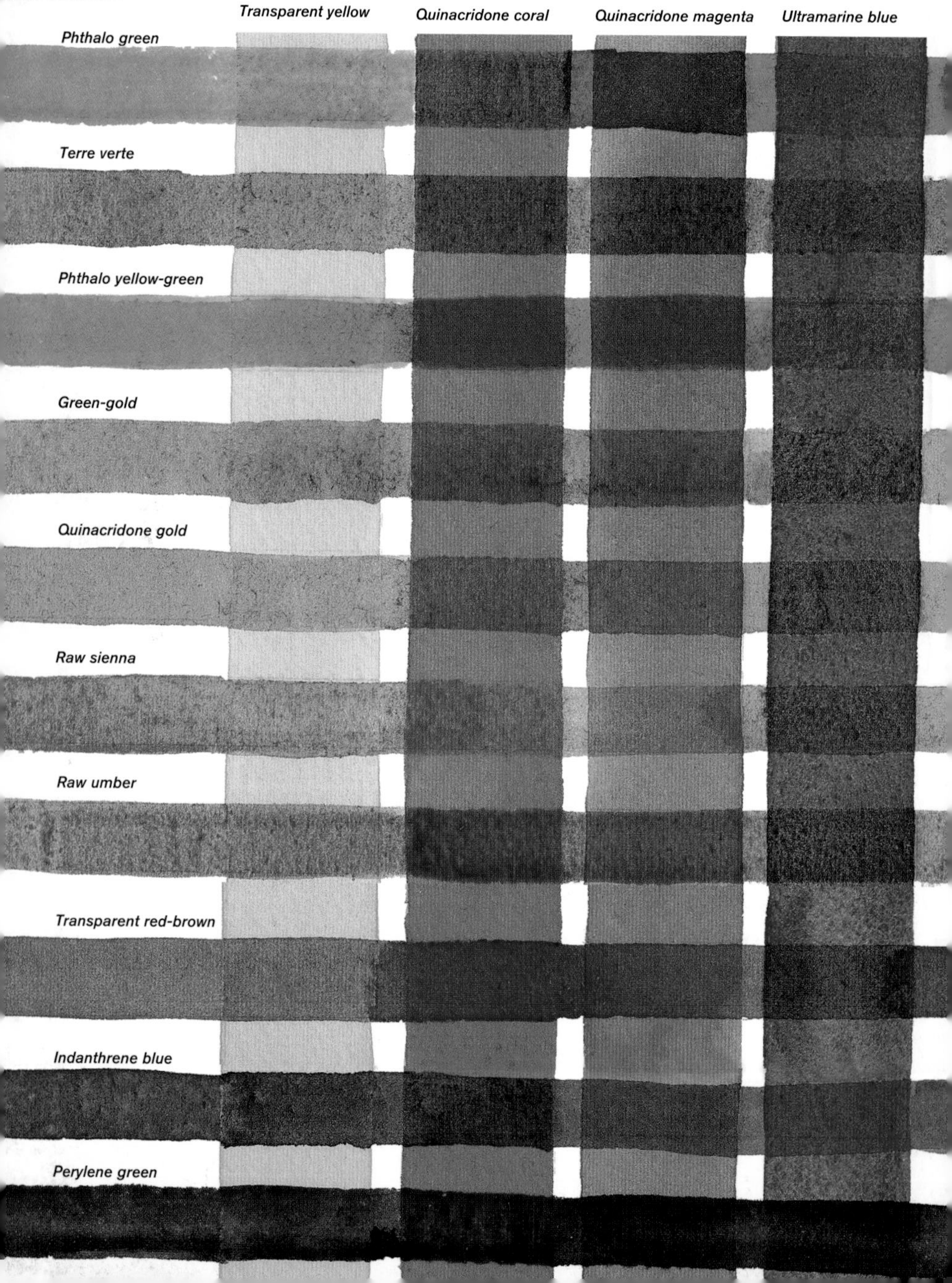

Transparent yellow | *Quinacridone coral* | *Quinacridone magenta* | *Ultramarine blue*

Phthalo green

Terre verte

Phthalo yellow-green

Green-gold

Quinacridone gold

Raw sienna

Raw umber

Transparent red-brown

Indanthrene blue

Perylene green

Phthalo blue
Phthalo green
Terre verte
Raw umber
Indanthrene blue

Mixing Greys

While mixing colours to achieve mossy greens or rich violet hues is exciting, it can be just as satisfying to create subtle greys with interesting nuances of colour or texture. We have seen how placing complementary colours next to each other intensifies both colours (pages 32–33), but complementary colours have another attribute: if mixed together, they create attractive greys or neutrals with depth and variation. It can be difficult to work out the exact complementary colour, but this is not necessary. Simply choose opposite colours from the colour wheel and experiment to find the mixes you like.

Characterful browns and greys can also be made by mixing the three primary colours together, as shown in the triangular mixes below. Take care that the mixes do not become muddy through overmixing (like the dull colour in your water pot after prolonged use).

Raw sienna

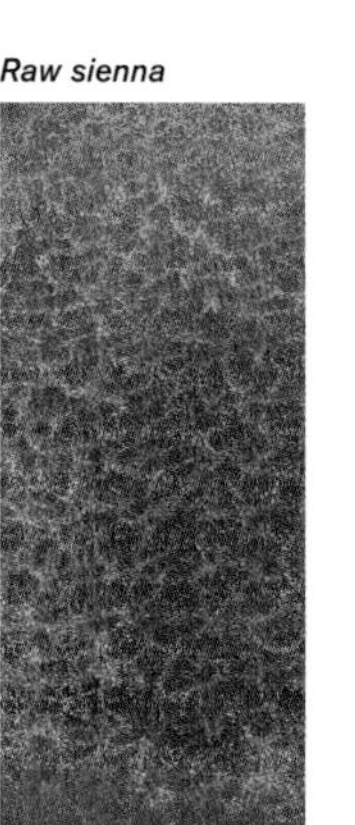

Cobalt blue

Cadmium red medium

Cobalt blue

Burnt sienna

Ultramarine blue

Quinacridone coral

Ultramarine blue

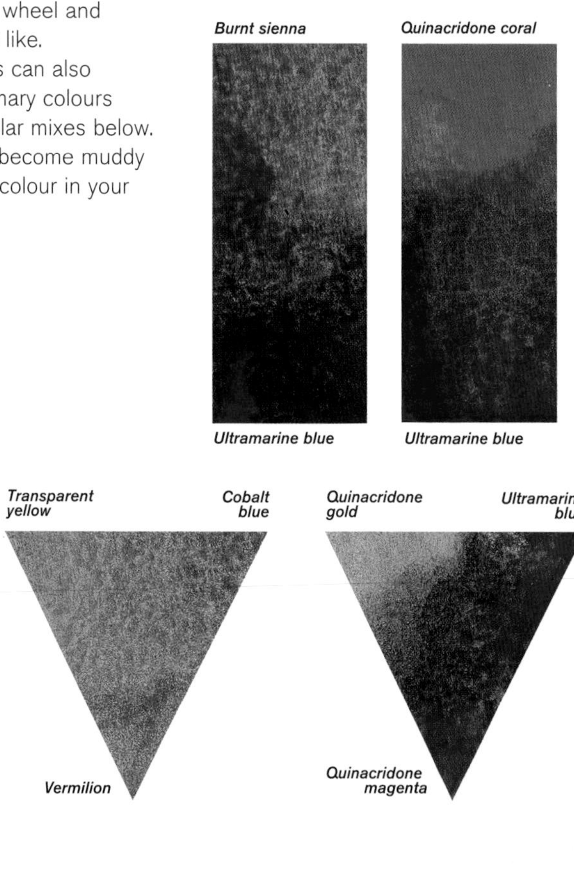

Transparent yellow — *Cobalt blue* — *Vermilion*

Quinacridone gold — *Ultramarine blue* — *Quinacridone magenta*

TIP: Mixing dynamic blacks

You can mix black with other colours as in the charts on pages 236–239. Deeper and richer blacks can be mixed as in the swatches below.

Burnt umber and indanthrene blue

Transparent red-brown, phthalo green and dioxazine violet

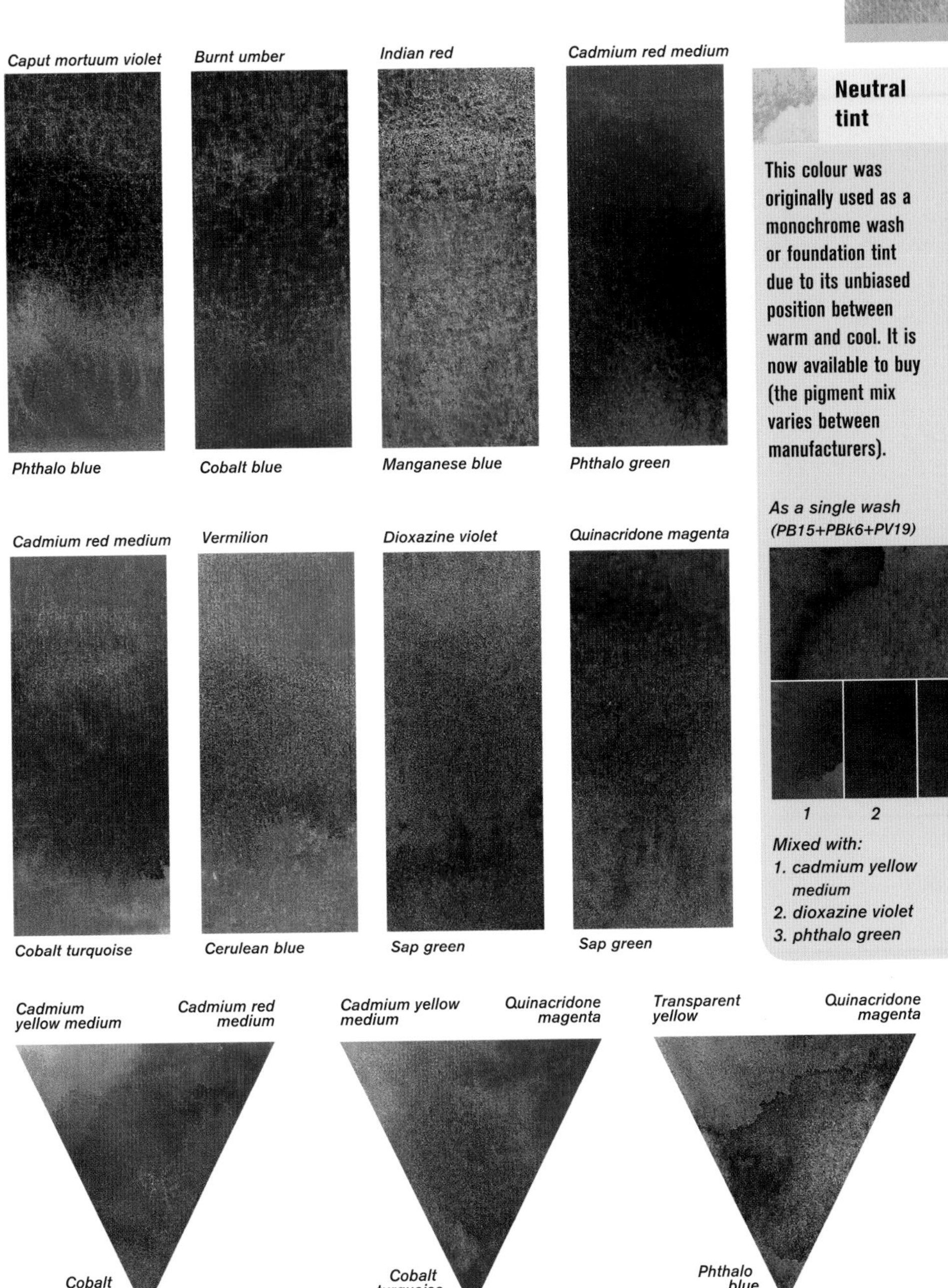

Neutral tint

This colour was originally used as a monochrome wash or foundation tint due to its unbiased position between warm and cool. It is now available to buy (the pigment mix varies between manufacturers).

As a single wash (PB15+PBk6+PV19)

Mixed with:

1. *cadmium yellow medium*
2. *dioxazine violet*
3. *phthalo green*

Comparison Charts

An enormous range of colours is available; the 50 colours featured on the preceding pages are a useful selection. Most artists work with a basic palette of 12–18 colours, adding extra ones as required, although some artists work with as few as three colours.

Paint manufacturers are constantly refining their products to improve lightfastness, workability and non-toxicity (NB be careful not to inhale paint when spraying, and never put a paint brush in your mouth to refine its point). New colours with increased granulation or transparency have been developed, along with luminescent paints and a range made with authentic mineral pigments (PrimaTek). Visit the manufacturers' websites to see what's new; some companies provide the C.I. names for each colour so that you can accurately compare colours in the virtual world.

Pigment key

PY = pigment yellow
PO = pigment orange
PR = pigment red
PV = pigment violet
PB = pigment blue
PG = pigment green
PBr = pigment brown
PBl = pigment black
PW = pigment white

For example, PB28 = cobalt blue

Colour index (C.I.) name

The C.I. name is the international standard code for each pigment. Although daunting at first, it is an excellent way to discover exactly which pigment you are using (a little like knowing the nutritional value of the food you eat). Pigments are manufactured for all types of industry, principally automotive and plastic, so the colours of the art world are governed by what is fashionable for Ford or DuPont.

The C.I. name tells you whether a colour has been made from a single pigment or mixed from more than one. It is generally considered better if a colour is made from a single pigment; the more pigments used, the duller the colour. (This is even more important when you consider that most artists do not use colours straight from the tube and that further mixing takes place on a palette or on paper.) However, modern manufacturing processes now allow for mixed-pigment colours that retain brightness (the range of bright proprietary greens available proves this).

The C.I. name also helps to clarify the situation when more than one manufacturer has used the same name for a colour, even though each manufacturer actually produces it from different pigments. Conversely colours made from the same pigment may be given different names by separate manufacturers.

You may also see another number called the C.I. number, which similarly identifies each pigment using a 5-digit number. Of the two systems, the C.I. name is more user-friendly and more prevalent.

A single pigment.

Three C.I. names denote three pigments.

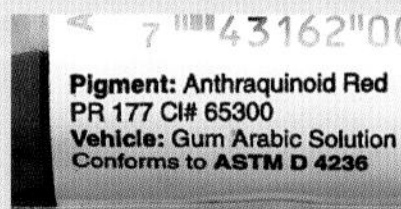

The pigment name, its C.I. name and C.I. number and the binder used.

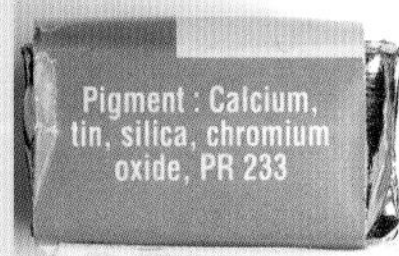

C.I. information can be found on the wrappers of pans.

At-a-glance comparison chart

This chart has been organized into colour groups to show some of the selection for sale. The colours run from cool to warm across each page and represent most of the generic names you will see.

Use the chart to avoid buying colours that are too close to each other or, conversely, use it to choose similar colours to experiment with for different properties.

Most manufacturers produce some pigments with their own name as part of the colour name, for example, Winsor yellow, Sennelier red and Grumbacher vermilion. These have not been included; to reference them, check the C.I. name on the tube against the C.I. names on the lower part of this chart.

The C.I. names are grouped into colour families, roughly correlating to the generic pigment names above; the pigment names may appear on the label with any of the C.I. names of that colour family.

PY3 PY40 PY53 PY97

PY150 PY154 PY175 PY184

PY35 PY65

PY37 PY153 PO20 PO43 PO62 PO73

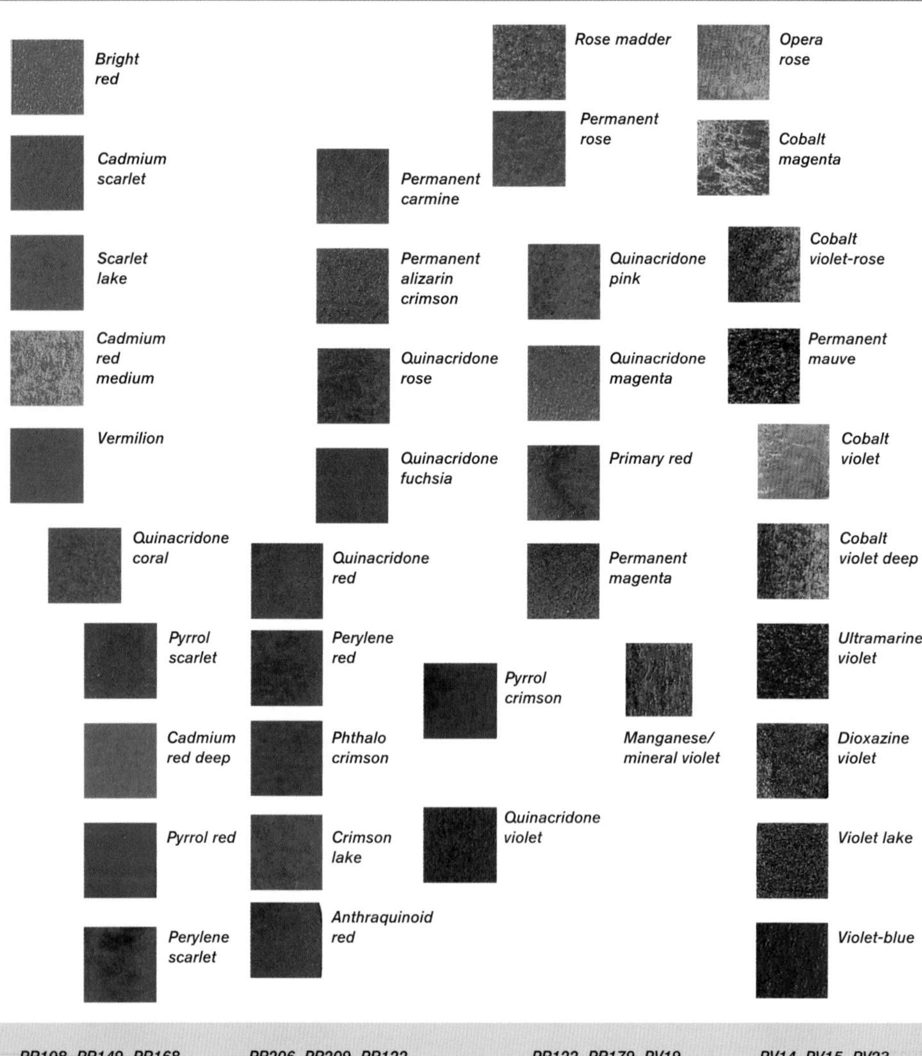

PR108 PR149 PR168 PR178 PR242 PR254 PR255

PR206 PR209 PR122 PR176 PR202 PR264

PR122 PR179 PV19

PV14 PV15 PV23 PV49

What does the word "hue" in a pigment name indicate?

The word "hue" is used in two ways. First, it describes a colour (i.e. red or blue). Second, manufacturers use it as part of the pigment name when the colour does not contain the original compound. This is not necessarily a disadvantage – the new formulation may be more permanent or less toxic, or it may be cheaper and

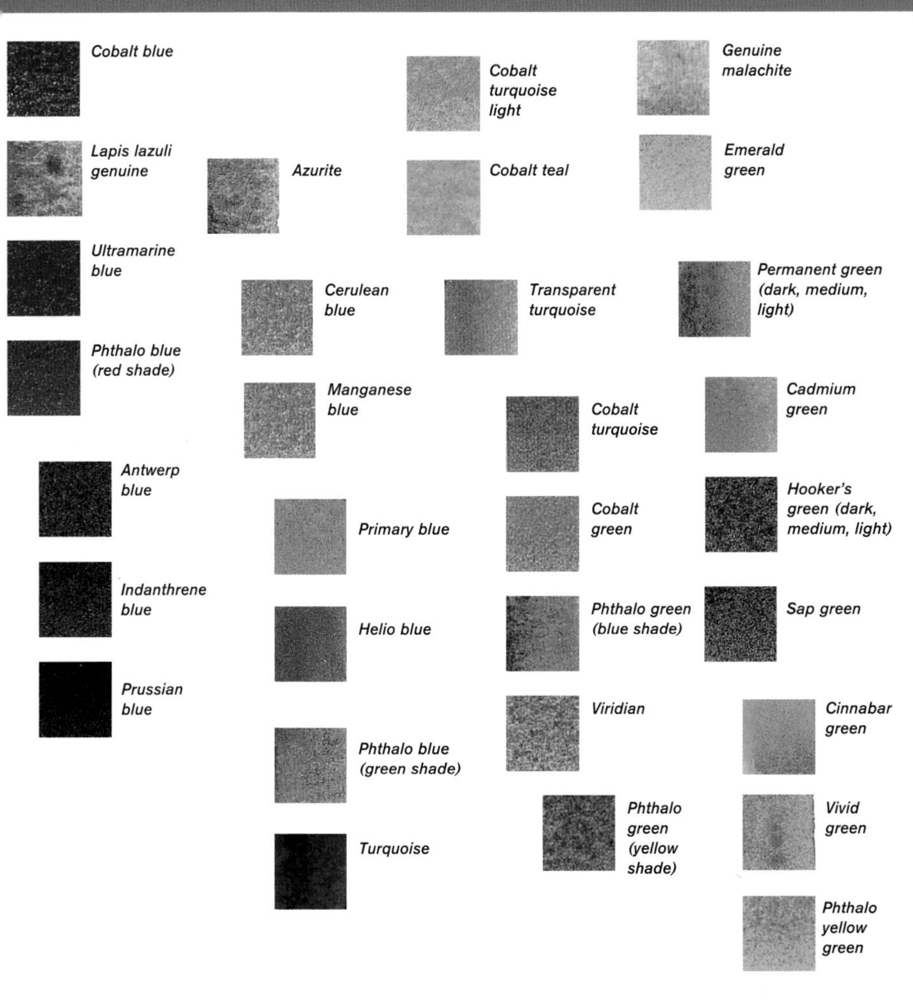

PB27 PB28 PB29 PB60

PB15 PB33 PB35 PB36

PG7 PG18 PG19 PG50

PG7 PG36

therefore more accessible to schools and students. You may find that "hue" is added to the pigment names of several of the colours featured in the directory, namely manganese blue, Naples yellow, Indian yellow and Davy's grey.

Note: Many of the greens available are mixes of pigments formulated to match old paint colours or to create new brighter ones.

Oxide of chromium

Terre verte

Verona green earth

Green earth

Green umber

Olive green

Green-gold

Yellow ochre

Raw sienna

Quinacridone gold

Gold ochre

Raw umber

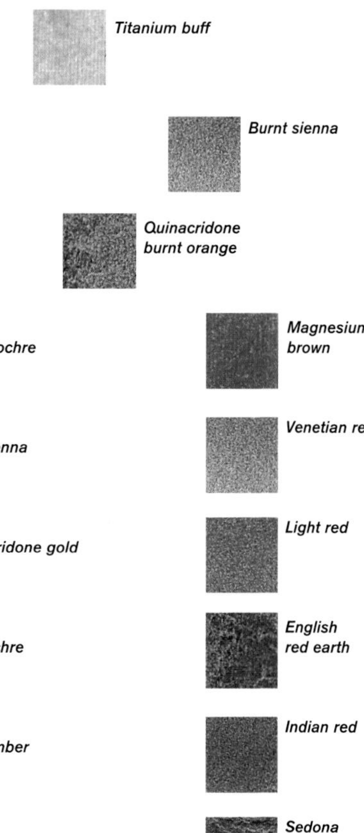

Titanium buff

Burnt sienna

Quinacridone burnt orange

Magnesium brown

Venetian red

Light red

English red earth

Indian red

Sedona genuine

PG17 PG23 PG26

PY42 PY43 PO43 PO49 PO62 PY129 PBr7

PR101

PR101 (Synthetic red oxide is the basis for a wide range of colours: Venetian red, English red, some burnt siennas, Indian red, transparent red oxide and other proprietary names.)

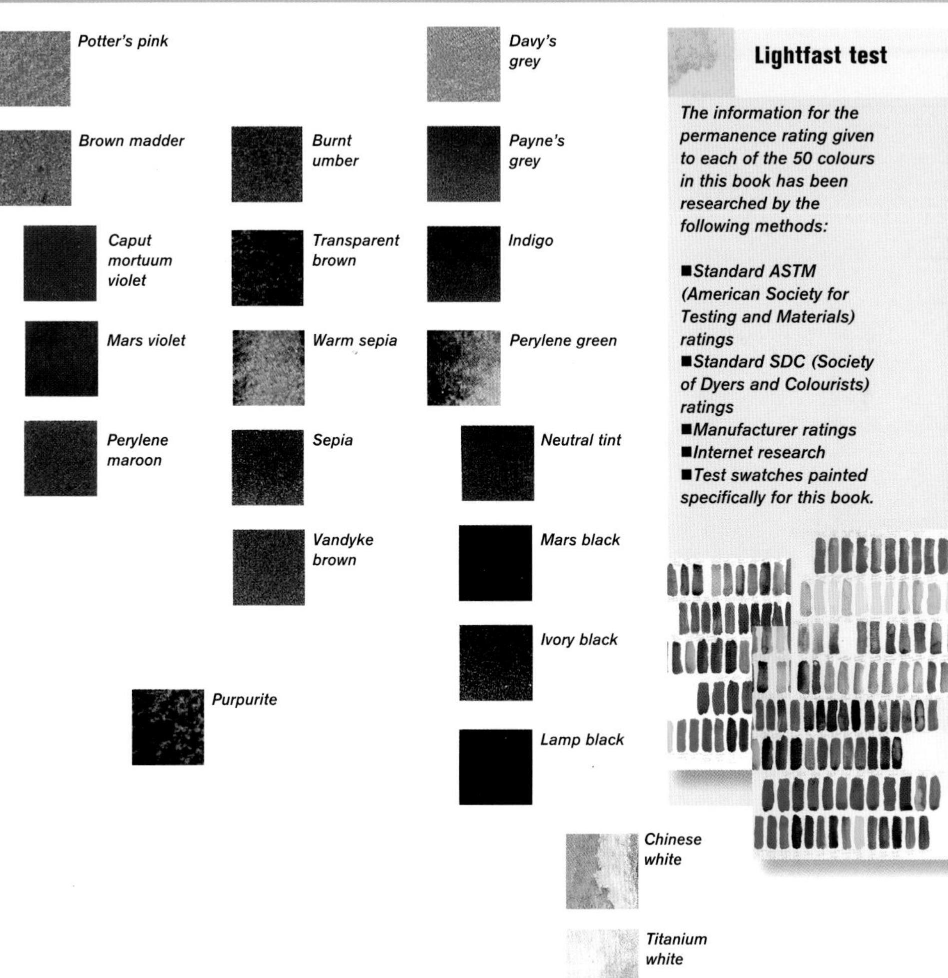

Lightfast test

The information for the permanence rating given to each of the 50 colours in this book has been researched by the following methods:

- *Standard ASTM (American Society for Testing and Materials) ratings*
- *Standard SDC (Society of Dyers and Colourists) ratings*
- *Manufacturer ratings*
- *Internet research*
- *Test swatches painted specifically for this book.*

PBr7 generally combined with a black, red or violet pigment.

PBk6 PBk7 PBk9 PBk31

Note: Several dark colours are a mix of lamp black PBk6 and one (or more) other pigment(s). For example, indigo is usually a mix of PBk6 and a blue pigment.

PW4 PW6

Index

Page numbers in italics refer to captions.

SUPPLIERS

Daler-Rowney Ltd
Peacock Lane
Southern Industrial Estate
Bracknell
Berkshire RG12 8ST
United Kingdom
Customer service line:
+44 (0)1344 461010
Web: www.daler-rowney.com

Daniel Smith Artists' Materials
PO Box 84268
Seattle
WA 98124-5568
USA
Web: www.danielsmith.com
USA & Canada
Tel: 800-426-6740
Fax: 800-238-4065
International Orders
Tel: +1 206-223-9599
Fax: +1 206-224-0404

Grumbacher
c/o Sanford L.P.
2707 Butterfield Road
Oak Brook
IL 60523
USA
Tel: +1 630 481 2000
Web: www.grumbacherart.com

Lukas Artists Colours and Canvas Factory
Dr. Fr. Schoenfeld GmbH
Harffstrasse 40
D-40591 Düsseldorf
Germany
Tel: +49 211 7813 0
Web: www.lukas-online.com

Bockingford watercolour paper *supplied by:*
R. K. Burt & Co. Ltd.
Wholesale paper distributors since 1892.
Web: www.rkburt.co.uk

Sennelier
Max Sauer S.A.
Z.I. 2, rue Lamarck – BP 204
22002 St-Brieuc Cedex
France
Tel: +33 02 96 68 20 00
Web: www.sennelier.fr

Winsor and Newton
Whitefriars Avenue
Wealdstone
Harrow HA3 5RH
United Kingdom
Tel: +44 (0)20 8427 4343
Web: www.winsornewton.com